Among Friends

A DAILY DEVOTIONAL FOR WOMEN BY WOMEN

ROSE OTIS, Editor

REVIEW AND HERALD® PUBLISHING ASSOCIATION
HAGERSTOWN, MD 21740

Bible texts credited to Amplified are from *The Amplified Bible.* Copyright © 1965 by Zondervan Publishing House. Used by permission.

Bible texts credited to Jerusalem are from *The Jerusalem Bible,* copyright © 1966 by Darton, Longman & Todd, Ltd., and Doubleday & Company, Inc. Used by permission of the publisher.

Bible texts credited to Moffatt are from: *The Bible: A New Translation,* by James Moffatt. Copyright by James Moffatt 1954. Used by permission of Harper & Row, Publishers, Incorporated.

Scripture quotations marked NASB are from the *New American Standard Bible,* © The Lockman Foundation 1960, 1962, 1963, 1968, 1971, 1972, 1973, 1975, 1977.

Texts credited to NEB are from *The New English Bible.* © The Delegates of the Oxford University Press and the Syndics of the Cambridge University Press 1961, 1970. Reprinted by permission.

Texts credited to NIV are from the *Holy Bible, New International Version.* Copyright © 1973, 1978, 1984, International Bible Society. Used by permission of Zondervan Bible Publishers.

Texts credited to NKJV are from the New King James Version. Copyright © 1979, 1980, 1982, Thomas Nelson, Inc., Publishers.

Bible Texts credited to NRSV are from the New Revised Standard Version of the Bible, copyright © 1989 by the Division of Christian Education of the National Council of the Churches of Christ in the U.S.A. Used by permission.

Bible texts credited to RSV are from the Revised Standard Version of the Bible, copyright © 1946, 1952, 1971, by the Division of Christian Education of the National Council of the Churches of Christ in the U.S.A. Used by permission.

Bible texts credited to TEV are from the *Good News Bible*—Old Testament: Copyright © American Bible Society 1966, 1971, 1976.

Verses marked TLB are taken from *The Living Bible,* copyright © 1971 by Tyndale House Publishers, Wheaton, Ill. Used by permission.

Manuscript editors: James Cavil, Laurie Gust, Shirley Welch
Coordinating editor: Gerald Wheeler
Designer: Bill Kirstein
Cover designer: Helcio Deslandes
Cover cloth: Marcus Brothers Textiles, Inc.
Typeset: 10/11 Sabon

PRINTED IN U.S.A.

97 96 95 94 93 92   10 9 8 7 6 5 4 3 2 1

R&H Cataloging Service
Among friends. Rose Otis, editor.

   1. Devotional calendars—Seventh-day Adventists.
2. Devotional calendars—women. 3. Women—religious
life. 4. Devotional literature—Seventh-day Adventists.
I. Otis, Rose, ed.
              242.643

ISBN 0-8280-0692-X

Introduction

One of the early priorities of the newly established General Conference Office of Women's Ministries was to spearhead the development of a devotional book written "by women for women." The 30 members of our Women's Ministries World Advisory viewed this project as one way to affirm women. God gifted women with the ability to nurture others, but even the nurturers need nurturing—and this book is in response to this need.

Among Friends benefits women in two ways. First by providing spiritual food, and second by granting scholarships through the General Conference Women's Ministries Scholarship Fund that will receive 100 percent of the royalties.

When we began this project in the spring of 1991, we wrote to more than 100 experienced and novice writers inviting them to contribute to this first-of-its-kind devotional. We were looking for personal experiences that demonstrated our loving heavenly Father's concern and unconditional love for His "End-time Daughters."

Plans for this special devotional spread by word of mouth, and before the final deadline more than 170 women responded, and our dream became a reality. First-ladies, laywomen, women in ministry, and others have opened their hearts to share personal spiritual insights with you the reader.

As you turn to *Among Friends* to begin each morning, may you be nurtured and filled with the reality that you are a part of a wonderful sisterhood because we have all been adopted by the same heavenly Father.

Rose Otis, Director
Office of Women's Ministries

Acknowledgments

This book, the blooming of a wistful thought, would not have been possible without the tireless work of many. Foremost, of course, are the nearly 200 women who contributed readings. Then there are Patty Davis and Celia Cruz, who spent months keying in and organizing devotionals. Celia Cruz also wrote the biographical sketches. Annabelle Kendall, Ella Rydzewski, Lyndelle Chiomenti, Irene Gilbert, Martha Lund, and Evelyn Kuhn helped proofread the devotionals. And last but not least, Arlene Taylor, who encouraged and assisted in countless ways.

Rose Otis

Biographies

The following information will give you insights into the lives of the many gifted women who made this devotional book possible and will tell you where you can find their contributions.

◇ ◇ ◇

Nora Agboka lives with her husband in West Africa, where she teaches. They have three daughters. She is actively involved in her church's welfare work, and is an assistant Sabbath school superintendent and school board member. **May 9.**

Jane Allen, a communication director, lives on a lakefront in Florida. She enjoys bird-watching, interior design, quilting, and writing, and has been published in several church magazines over the past 20 years. She has also coauthored a book, *Single Servings.* This devotional first appeared in the *Adventist Review,* June 1, 1989. **July 27.**

Nettie Anderson is an administrative assistant and editor, and lectures concerning effective family relations. She is a minister's wife, has three daughters and enjoys jogging, sewing, crafts, and reading. **Oct. 3.**

Mabel Owusu-Antwi comes from Ghana, West Africa. She recently graduated with a B.A. in English literature from Andrews University, where her husband is a seminarian studying for his Ph.D. in Old Testament theology. **Aug. 14.**

Vertibelle Awoniyi is from Jamaica and writes from the Adventist Seminary of West Africa in Nigeria, where she is a nurse and head of the Human Sciences Department, and a minister's wife. She is an honorary chief of the Ilishan community for her contribution as a nurse. **May 14.**

Audrey Balderstone and her husband own and operate a garden landscaping company in England. She is active in her church and community in organizing flower festivals and fund-raising projects; she also conducts a bimonthly home fellowship group meeting and has two sons. She is president of the Adventist Business and Professionals Association (British ASI) and is the SDA representative on the Women's World Day of Prayer Committee. **Jan. 30, Sept. 26, Oct. 7.**

Michele Beach is the chairperson of the English Department at Takoma Academy in Takoma Park, Maryland, and also teaches French and journalism. She enjoys traveling around the world, ethnic entertainment, gourmet cuisine, medieval art and literature, tennis, skiing, and photography. **July 26, Dec. 10.**

Judi Wild Becker is the owner/manager of a wholesale food distribution company in California and is a widow. She is a member of the Norman Steels chorale at Pacific Union College and the Napa Valley women's ensemble. Her other interests are photography, videotaping, travel, poetry, and writing. **May 8.**

Heidi Otis Bowen is an emergency room nurse at an Adventist hospital outside of Washington, D.C. Heidi is working toward a master's degree in nursing and enjoys cross-stitch and water sports, when she isn't absorbed with her two children, Ryan and Heather. She's the daughter of Harold and Rose Otis. **Jan. 8.**

Carol Bradfield was born to missionary parents in Africa. She and her husband have spent 40 years in mission service in Africa, and their three married sons are also in mission service. She is an accountant and is the local church treasurer. Her hobbies include knitting, crocheting, and stamp collecting. **Aug. 31.**

Ellen Bresee, the cofounder of Shepherdess International, has served with her husband in pastoral and evangelistic team ministry for many years and has taught elementary school. She is the mother of three sons and one daughter, is a published writer, marriage counselor, and speaker, and trains division Shepherdess International leaders. **Mar. 30, May 10, June 11, Nov. 2, Nov. 23.**

Hazel Burns and her husband live in Kettering, Ohio, and have two grown children. She began a women's ministries program in her local church 10 years ago and is still actively involved in it. She is a homemaker, church and neighborhood Bible study leader, lecturer, and seminar instructor. Her interests include baking, quilting, painting, hiking, skiing, and family outings. **May 1, May 20.**

Nellie Carter and her husband live in Maryland, where she is a church pastor. Previously she was a Bible worker in Indiana. **Nov. 15.**

Virginia Cason is a homemaker and public speaker. She and her husband live in California and have four grown children. She has written programs and lessons for Vacation Bible School and Sabbath school, as well as songbooks for children. She teaches voice and is a radio DJ, a ham radio operator, and a private pilot. Virginia is the daughter of H.M.S. Richards, Sr. **June 21, July 8.**

L. Cassels was a UPI religion writer when this article appeared in the Palo Alto *Times,* Palo Alto, California, December 17, 1970. **Dec. 25.**

Premila M. Cherian was the director of the Home Sciences Department at Spicer Memorial College for 25 years prior to her retirement. She and her husband have three children. She enjoys writing, cooking, reading, and spending time with her grandchildren. **Sept. 29, Oct. 16.**

Lyndelle Chiomenti is the editor of the easy English version of the adult Sabbath school quarterly. She is married and enjoys writing, reading, crocheting, antiques, history, water gardening, and biblical studies. **Jan. 31, Feb. 18, Mar. 10, June 3, June 7.**

Birol C. Christo lives with her husband in India. She is a retired teacher, the mother of five grown children, the Shepherdess International coordinator for the Southern Asia Division, and spends all her spare time sewing and making craft items to sell as fund-raisers to help orphans. **Jan. 13, July 10, Dec. 8.**

Ginger Mostert Church is a marketing representative for the Review and Herald Publishing Association. She teaches seminars on possibility thinking, and has had articles published in several church magazines as well as in local newspapers. She enjoys traveling, cross-stitch, reading, and writing. She and her husband have two grown sons. **July 22, Nov. 13, Nov. 14, Nov. 25.**

Carel Sanders Clay, her husband, and three children live in California. She is a registered nurse, Sabbath school teacher, and newsletter editor/reporter. She enjoys quilting, sewing, gardening, writing, and public speaking. **May 18, May 19, Nov. 12, Dec. 9, Dec. 21.**

Joan Coggin is a cardiologist, special assistant to the president for international affairs, and associate dean for international programs at Loma Linda University. She has written many articles for medical publications. She is a deaconess and Sabbath school superintendent, and loves to travel and meet people. **June 24.**

Carole Spalding Colburn is an administrative assistant at the General Conference of SDA. Prior to her move to Maryland, she lived in the Far East, where she and her husband served as missionaries for most of their adult life. She has been involved in all levels of children's Sabbath school and enjoys crafts, reading, and jogging. **July 15.**

Cynthia R. Coston is a homemaker, pastor's wife, and mother of two very young boys. She lives in Virginia and is a pianist, harpist, and vocalist. She is very involved in children's ministry at her church. **Oct. 19, Oct. 29.**

Judy Coulston has a Ph.D. in nutrition and is an international speaker, TV host, and producer, and is on a retainer as the nutritional consultant with the Los Angeles Rams. She is actively involved in church as a Sabbath school superintendent, chorister, health ministries director, and member of an SDA women's evening fellowship group. **Mar. 22, July 2.**

Judith Stetson Crabb was a single parent of two boys for 16 years and has recently remarried. She and her husband have four children and make their home in California, where she is an assistant chaplain at St. Helena Hospital. She has been actively involved in earliteen and adult Sabbath school, Ingathering, and literature evangelism. **Aug. 25.**

Olive Crouch is a homemaker and mother of four children, and will soon be a grandmother. She helps her husband with Pathfinders and is a Sabbath school leader and assistant treasurer of her local church. Her hobbies include reading and quilting. **Aug. 7.**

Celia Cruz is the administrative secretary in the Office of Women's Ministries at the General Conference, a pastor's wife, and mother of five children. She teaches junior/earliteen Sabbath school, presents seminars on various topics, is a published writer, and raises weimaraners. Her interests include children and youth, dogs, needlework, clothing construction, reading, writing, and ceramics. **Apr. 3, Apr. 13, Nov. 20.**

Phyllis Dalgleish, a receptionist, is the mother of three grown daughters, a widow, and a writer of children's stories. Her first book, *Hattie Hippo,* will be published this year. She has worked in many of the Sabbath school departments in her church and enjoys crocheting, knitting, calligraphy, cooking, and writing. **Apr. 8.**

Sandy Dancek has been a literature evangelist for 23 years, is the mother of four grown children, a grandmother, and a published writer. She and her husband make their home in West Virginia. Her interests are piano, organ, and flower arranging. **Oct. 9.**

Wanda Davis is the manager of the Department of Pastoral Care at a regional hospital, Sabbath school leader, women's ministries coordinator, and church elder. She and her husband and three children live in West Virginia. **Jan. 9, Nov. 7.**

Evelyn Delafield was a hospital chaplain until her retirement several years ago. She is the author of a book, *The Love Prescription,* enjoys her flower garden and sharing flowers with the sick and shut-ins, and assists her husband in establishing service and fellowship clubs for the retired denominational workers of North America. She has two children and five grandchildren. **Jan. 20, Apr. 27, Sept. 17.**

Sandra Doran lives in Rhode Island with her pastor husband and two children. She is the administrator of a Montessori school, enjoys preaching and presenting seminars, has authored several books, the latest of which is *Every Time I Say Grace, We Fight* ("Practical Help for Marriages Divided by Religion but United by Love"), and has written extensively for religious magazines. These devotionals first appeared in the *Adventist Review,* Feb. 7, 1991; Feb. 11, 1988. **May 16, Aug. 22.**

Lily Dowuona is an administrative secretary for the Central African Union in Cameroon. She and her husband are from Ghana. **Sept. 24.**

Yvonne Minchin Dysinger is the author of *Adventist Tentmakers— Opening Doors Where Others Cannot* and has written for various publications. She is the mother of four children, a nurse (M.P.H.), and is currently the administrative assistant in the Center for International Relations of the General Conference. She and her physician husband have been missionaries in Cambodia, Tanzania, Singapore, and Pakistan. She enjoys sewing, travel, knitting, and hiking and backpacking (she climbed Mount Kilimanjaro in 1978). **Sept. 9.**

Doris E. Everett, a retired widow and the mother of five children, is the women's ministries coordinator for her church, hosts a weekly prayer group, tells children's stories, and has a nursing home ministry. Her interests are bird-watching, piano, reading, and writing. **Mar. 19, Apr. 7.**

Jocelyn Fay has written extensively for several union publications and the *Adventist Review.* She is the public relations director for Atlantic Union College (on leave from Southeastern California Conference, where she serves as communication director), and enjoys gardening, sightseeing, and antiquing. She lives with an Angora cat named Maudy. **Jan. 11, July 31.**

Lois Fitchen writes from McMinnville, Oregon. Her devotional first appeared in the *Adventist Review,* Apr. 28, 1988. **June 17.**

Karen Flowers, an associate director for the General Conference Department of Church Ministries, is a member and certified family life educator of the National Council on Family Relations. She has coauthored several books and resource manuals and written numerous articles for various publications. She and her husband have two teenage sons. Her hobbies are reading, writing, and needlework. **July 24, Nov. 30.**

Anita Folkenberg is a registered nurse and lives with her husband in the

Washington, D.C., area, where he is the president of the General Conference of Seventh-day Adventists. They spent 19 years as missionaries in the Inter-American Division, where they raised their two children, who are now married. Her special interests are shelling, reading, cross-stitch, walking, history, and traveling with her husband and supporting his ministry. **Sept. 14.**

Gillian Ford is a full-time PMS/menopause educator and has authored a handbook and various brochures on the subject. She has also written children's stories for a Christian magazine for the past nine years and works part-time as a graphic artist. She is married to a minister, has three stepchildren, and is in the process of writing a book. **Sept. 3.**

Joyce Fortner lives with her husband and six children in Louisiana, where he is a minister and she is a principal and school teacher. She is a member of the NAD Children's Ministries Advisory and the local chapter of the Women's Commission and is a published writer. She has been miraculously healed of cancer and enjoys her children, sports, reading, sewing, cooking, and baking. **May 29.**

Cherryl A. Galley is presently working on a Ph.D. in counseling psychology. Her special interests are singing, piano, swimming, skating, sewing, photography, horseback riding, and writing. **Oct. 21.**

Gillian Geraty and her husband make their home in Massachusetts, where she is a title examiner for real estate attorneys. She is the daughter of missionaries to the Middle East, where she spent much of her childhood. She enjoys reading, architecture, and music. **Feb. 26.**

Evelyn Glass is a homemaker, mother, and farmer. She is the women's ministries director for the Mid-American Union, church clerk, junior-earliteen leader, Maplewood Academy development director, and a member of the Minnesota K-12 board. She has written articles for local and state newspapers and Christian publications. She enjoys folk painting, sewing, knitting, refinishing furniture, reading, speaking, and community programs and committees. **Feb. 8, Mar. 23, Nov. 29, Dec. 20.**

Sue Gleason is a registered nurse and pastor's wife. She and her husband and two children recently moved to Virginia. She teaches youth Sabbath school, is on the church social committee, and is a counseling partner with her husband. She enjoys quilting, needlework, crafts, and shopping. This devotional first appeared in the Southern New England Conference's *Shepherdess Newsletter,* April 1986. **Aug. 15.**

Carla Gober, a clinical nurse specialist in spiritual care, was listed in *Who's Who in American Nursing,* 1990/1991. Several of her articles have been published in professional journals, and she has coauthored a devotional book for nurses. She conducts grief recovery classes, teaches, and presents sermons and seminars on various topics. Her hobbies include writing, flowers, mountain biking, and people. **Jan. 18, Sept. 13.**

Ada Gonzalez de Garcia is the director of counseling and guidance at the University of Montemorelos in Mexico. She and her husband have two sons and have coauthored a book about marriage. Her hobbies include music (she also teaches piano), sewing, knitting, and traveling. **June 1.**

Ramona Perez-Greek is the assistant director of women's ministries for the

North American Division. She has a Ph.D. in nursing, has been a university professor, is the first lady of the Gulf States Conference, a mother, and a writer. May 2.

Lourdes E. Morales Gudmundsson teaches Spanish language and literature at a university, is involved in her local church choir and as the personal ministries director, and leads a weekly Bible study group. She has written for various Spanish and English publications, has two books that are to be released this year, and is working with her husband to develop a Spanish television ministry that is scheduled to be aired this year. Mar. 1.

Heather Guttschuss is a registered nurse living in California. She spent several years as a missionary in Africa and has three books published by Pacific Press Publishing Association. She enjoys skiing and swimming. Jan. 12.

Patricia A. Habada has a doctorate in education curriculum and supervision and is a curriculum specialist for the General Conference Church Ministries Department. She is married and has three daughters, has authored and edited countless instructional manuals, and has written numerous articles for denominational journals. Her hobbies include writing, boating, walking, music, and reading. Apr. 25, Sept. 10.

Viviane Haenni is a pastor in Switzerland on leave of absence while she completes her doctoral degree at Andrews University. She has written for numerous publications and currently is completing a book. Some of her special interests are jogging, skiing, writing, painting, and traveling. Aug. 26, Oct. 14.

Madlyn Lewis Hamblin, the co-owner of the Hamblin Company, is the mother of two children, enjoys organizing and conducting outreach seminars for her community, and is the publicity director for the Michigan Women's Commission, a local church elder, and Sabbath school superintendent. She has written more than 200 articles for newspapers and magazines, and a book, *Promise in the Cornfield*. Her interests are interior design, reading, and people. July 19.

Adjiko Hansen shares a traumatic personal experience with our readers from her home in Accra, Ghana, in the Africa-Indian Ocean Division. Jan. 15.

Lea Hardy, a retired teacher, stays busy writing plays and skits for her local church and a weekly radio program, developing a creative writing program for schools, and promoting women's ministries. She is also a published writer. Feb. 11, May 30, Sept. 12.

Beatrice Harris and her husband celebrated their fiftieth wedding anniversary in June 1992. She has two grown children, is a retired Bible instructor, a local church elder, and an associate personal ministries leader, and has written articles for several religious magazines. This devotional first appeared in the *Adventist Review*, May 31, 1990. July 23.

Chessie Harris, the founder of Harris Home for Children/Harris Family Foundation, was voted the International Woman of the Year in 1990. She has also been the recipient of awards from United Way of America, *Women's Day*, and President George Bush, and the governor of the state of Alabama proclaimed July 6, 1989, as "Chessie Harris Day." She is a published writer, local church elder, and earliteen Sabbath school teacher. The book *Promise in the Cornfield* is her life story. Mar. 16.

Deborah M. Harris has a Ph.D. in special education, is a university professor in Florida, mother of two children, and public speaker. Her interests include swimming, children, and public speaking. **Jan. 3, Mar. 12.**

Peggy Harris is the president of the Association of Adventist Women, an insurance agent, local church elder, and grandmother. She is a published writer and enjoys presenting seminars. Her interests include hospitality ministries, piano, organ, and her granddaughters. **Mar. 21.**

Jeanne Hartwell, an associate in pastoral care, lives with her husband and two children in South Carolina. She teaches an adult Sabbath school class and has written articles for Christian magazines. Her hobbies include music, cross-stitch, reading, sewing, compiling family albums, and collecting soup recipes. **July 13.**

Susanne Hatzinger is a homemaker and mother in Austria. She presents seminars on nutrition and weight reduction and is a deaconess. Her interests are gardening, music, traveling, and ministry for elderly people and children. **Apr. 19.**

Raquel Haylock is secretary in the General Conference Church Ministries Department. She, her husband, and three children spent many years as missionaries in the Inter-American Division. She has written articles about children for religious publications and has worked in children's Sabbath school departments. Her hobbies are reading, flowers, and helping people. **Sept. 8.**

Edna Heise is a homemaker and seminar presenter in Australia. She and her pastor husband have three grown children. She has coauthored a book, *In Letters of Gold,* and written many articles for religious publications. Pencil and pastel drawing, gardening, and fund-raising are among her special interests. **May 21.**

Carolyn T. Hinson teaches elementary school, is a conference women's ministries director, teaches Sabbath school, is a counselor, and is involved with personal ministries in her local church. She is married to a minister and has three adult children. Her special interest is working with children ages 2 to 8. **Nov. 4, Dec. 5.**

Kyna Hinson is a journalist and an assistant college professor. She is involved in women's ministries in her local church and conference, and works with teenagers. She has written many articles for several religious magazines, and enjoys embroidery, reading, and baking. **May 26, July 20, Oct. 30.**

Nancy Hoag is a free-lance writer who left the classroom to write full-time. She's written a cookbook and a book of short stories while following her Forest Service husband from Montana to Washington, D.C. **Jan. 29.**

Fannie L. Houck is a free-lance writer living in Washington State. She and her husband have three grown children. She is a local church elder and women's ministries leader, and holds several other church offices as well. She is a published writer of five books and hundreds of articles, poems, and puzzles. **Jan. 22, Jan. 24, Feb. 1, Apr. 5, May 11, Aug. 12, Sept. 23.**

Mary Johnson's devotionals first appeared in *Bouquets,* vol. 1, nos. 1, 2, 1990; vol. 2, nos. 1, 3, 4, 1991. **Oct. 18, Oct. 24, Dec. 12, Dec. 17, Dec. 26.**

Sandy Johnson, an editorial assistant for *Primary Treasure* and *Our Little*

Friend, has written many articles in Christian publications. She has worked in the children's departments in her local church and enjoys reading, writing, cooking, baking, decorating, and traveling. **Aug. 3, Oct. 20.**

Madeline S. Johnston is a free-lance writer, part-time secretary, advice columnist for *Guide,* and mother of four grown children. She has served overseas as a missionary, and written several books and numerous articles. Writing, knitting, genealogy, photography, and birding are among her special interests. She and her husband make their home in Berrien Springs, Michigan. **Jan. 4-7, July 16-18, Aug. 19, Sept. 11, Oct. 5.**

Jeanne Jordan, a retired teacher, lives in Michigan with her husband. They have been married for 44 years, served as missionaries for 12 years, and have two grown children. She has authored three books and countless articles in church magazines, and enjoys reading, traveling, and words. **Mar. 4, Sept. 28, Oct. 4, Oct. 13.**

Sophie Kaiser, a retired widow, has been active in children's Sabbath school, Pathfinders, women's support groups, and cooking schools. She enjoys gardening, cooking, baking, reading, singing, traveling, and young people. **July 12.**

Janet Kangas, Ph.D., is the editor of *Mission.* She has written many articles for church magazines and has coauthored two books: *Daughter of Sonlight* and *The World of the Adventist Teenager.* Her hobbies are postcards, travel, and swimming. **Jan. 2, Feb. 4, Feb. 17, Feb. 22, Mar. 11, Mar. 29, Apr. 18, Apr. 26, Aug. 29, Sept. 4, Sept. 20, Oct. 6, Dec. 24.**

Louise Hannah Kohr lives in Washington State, where she has spent the past five years caring for her husband, who has suffered a major stroke. They have four grown children. She has been a storyteller for more than 60 years and has written four children's books and two adult books. Her interests are children, books, and flowers. **Feb. 16, June 30.**

Karen Kotoske is a dental hygienist and the director of the Amistad Foundation. She and her husband and two cats make their home in California. She enjoys reading, photography, gardening, and linking people up with other people or organizations for mission projects. **Dec. 14.**

Andrea Kristensen, a single parent of one teenager, is the editor of *Junior* and *Teen* Sabbath school lesson quarterlies and *Junior/Teen Program Helps.* She lives in Maryland and enjoys biking, rafting, reading, writing, and cooking. **July 4.**

Constance M. Laryea, a teacher, is the national head for preschool education in Ghana. She has had many articles and manuscripts published on early childhood education, and enjoys reading, cooking, flower gardening, dress design and construction, singing, and writing. **May 22.**

Lorna Lawrence is a school principal and teacher, composer, and concert soloist living in California. She is currently enrolled in a Ph.D. program in crisis counseling and is a published writer. Her special interests include counseling, traveling, marketing, and composing and arranging music for guitar, keyboard, and vocal arrangements. **Feb. 25, May 5, May 7.**

Gina Lee, an accountant, is a published writer of more than 300 stories, and has contributed to two books. She makes her home in California with two dogs and four cats and is actively involved in animal protection, environmental protection, vegetarianism, and collecting books. This devotional first appeared in the *Adventist Review,* Nov. 29, 1990. **July 25.**

Tania Lehmann and her husband live in France, where her husband is a college professor and she is a librarian. They have three grown children. Tania spent 12 years as a missionary's child and later spent seven years in mission service with her husband. **May 28, Sept. 22.**

Gerita Liebelt writes from Worland, Wyoming. She is a registered nurse, minister's wife, and currently a homemaker. She has written a book, *From Dilemma to Delight* ("Creative Ideas for Happy Sabbaths"), and is a youth and VBS leader in her local church. Her devotionals first appeared in *The Heart of the Home,* vol. 6, nos. 2, 4-6. **Mar. 6, Mar. 26, Dec. 2.**

Karen D. Lifshay writes from Angwin, California. This devotional first appeared in the *Adventist Review,* Apr. 13, 1989. **Aug. 8.**

Joyce Hanscom Lorntz and her husband are both pastoring in North Carolina and have three children. She is a nationally certified counselor, a published writer, is involved in women's ministries, speaks to women's groups, and enjoys flower gardens. **Apr. 23.**

Aileen Ludington is a board-certified physician with 25 years of practice experience. She spent seven years as medical adviser for the *Westbrook Hospital* television series and is presently the medical director of the Lifestyle Medicine Institute in Loma Linda. She is married and has six grown children. **July 9, Sept. 15, Oct. 11, Nov. 11.**

Elizabeth Mabena is a registered nurse, a mission president's wife, and the mother of six children (two sets of twins!). She lives in South Africa, has written many articles for Shepherdess International, and enjoys knitting, sewing, gardening, reading, writing, and soul winning. **Aug. 30.**

Pat Madsen, a homemaker living in California, is a published writer of poems, songs, and stories. She has served as Sabbath school superintendant and is involved in a Bible study group. Her hobbies include walking, music, writing, gardening, traveling, and the study of herbs. **Mar. 31, Apr. 2.**

Anita Marshall lives with her husband in England, where she is a writer and computer typesetter for Stanborough Press. She is actively involved in Vacation Bible School, has written a manual on VBS, has had many articles published in magazines, and has written two books for teenagers. **Jan. 17, Feb. 28, May 17, June 8, Aug. 6, Aug. 23, Oct. 2, Nov. 3.**

Lynne Marie Martin is a pseudonym. **Dec. 28.**

Eunice M. Mason, a senior accountant from England, lives with her husband and three children at Maluti Adventist Hospital in Lesotho. She also teaches Bible, cooking, and knitting. Her hobbies are knitting, sewing, and computer. **Apr. 15.**

Selma Chaij Mastrapa is a psychologist who lives in Maryland. She is a church elder, Sabbath school teacher, and chair of the Women of the Year Committee. She enjoys the study of different cultures, music, reading, walking, and traveling. **Nov. 5.**

Betsy Matthews is the assistant treasurer for the Pacific Union Conference. She and her husband, Dan Matthews, host of *Christian Lifestyle Magazine*, live in California and have three grown children. She enjoys music, sewing, flower gardening, reading, and traveling. **Apr. 9, Oct. 31.**

P. Deirdre Maxwell, an administrative assistant at St. Helena Hospital in California, has been a leader and teacher in all the Sabbath school departments in the local church and has served as a local church elder. She has written articles for church magazines and is currently editing her father's *Uncle Arthur's Bedtime Stories* to bring them up-to-date for republication. **Aug. 4, Nov. 6.**

Wilma McClarty is an English and speech professor at Southern College, a wife, and a mother of two. She is a public speaker and writer who has received many honors and awards, one of the most recent being the Sears-Roebuck Teaching Excellence and Campus Leadership Award for 1991. **Jan. 14, Jan. 16, Jan. 28, Mar. 5, Mar. 13, Mar. 20, Mar. 25, Apr. 12, Apr. 30, Aug. 27, Sept. 27.**

Gloria C. McLaren, a hospice chaplain and nurse, was born in Jamaica. She is a wife and mother of five children and enjoys writing, sewing, crochet, and singing, and is a group facilitator on grieving. **July 30, Aug. 28.**

Tokio Megashie is from Japan. Her devotional originally appeared in the *Texico Team Mates,* a newsletter for pastor's wives, in February 1988. **June 10.**

Myrna Melling is the administrator of the Preventive Medicine Research Institute in California. By the time she was 20 she was divorced with three small children, and soon became a Seventh-day Adventist. She recently completed her B.A. in business administration. Her special interests include music, personal growth, travel, reading, and cooking. **Jan. 26, Apr. 16, July 3.**

Lorabel Midkiff writes from Chattanooga, Tennessee. This devotional first appeared in the *Adventist Review,* Apr. 11, 1991. **Sept. 7**

Marian Miller, a victim of throat cancer, has been an inspiration to all who know her and have been inspired by her trust in God and her deep appreciation of each new day. Marian and her husband, Cyril Miller, have dedicated their lives to serve others. Marian writes from her home in Burleson, Texas. **Nov. 24, Dec. 11.**

Bonnie Moyers, a mother of two grown children, went back to school at age 45 and is working toward a bachelor's degree in journalism and English. She has written numerous articles for many religious magazines and enjoys reading, writing, physical fitness, sewing, cooking, drawing, painting, piano, organ, and singing. This devotional first appeared in the *Adventist Review,* May 11, 1989. **July 28.**

Ruth Murrill is a housewife living in Maryland. She and her husband, Bill, spent 15 years as missionaries in Burma, where her two sons were born. She has held many church offices through the years. Ruth is a sister of a former General Conference president, Neal C. Wilson. **Feb. 14.**

Joan M. Neall was born in Australia, lived in England, and now makes her home in Dayton, Tennessee, where she is a registered nurse. She and her husband have four grown children. She is the women's ministries leader at her local church. She enjoys nature, sewing, journalism, and her grandchildren. Dec. 13.

Renate Noack is a housewife and mother in Germany. She has been actively involved in youth and women's ministries for the past 25 years. She is the women's ministries director for the South German Union and has written many articles and coauthored several books with her husband. Nov. 8-10.

Myrna Suele Nortey is a lab instructor and college student majoring in biology who lives in Alabama. She is involved in community outreach projects and enjoys children, tennis, reading, family, cooking, counseling, and languages. Sept. 21.

Thelma Nortey is a medical laboratory technologist and homemaker born in Ghana. She is currently living in Côte d'Ivoire, where her husband is the president of the Africa-Indian Ocean Division. She and her husband have one grown son. Her special interests include reading, gardening, counseling, and giving Bible studies. Feb. 24.

Constance C. Nwosu, a Nigerian, is the dean of women and chairperson of the Language and Communication Department at the Adventist Seminary of West Africa and is actively involved in the local church. She contributed a dozen devotionals to a devotional book being coordinated by the Africa-Indian Ocean Division and has a deep interest in women's ministries. Apr. 17, Oct. 25, Oct. 27.

Rachel Nyirabu is presently a housewife and wife of the Tanzania ambassador to the United States. She has served the church as a deaconess and Community Services director, and is on the General Conference Women's Ministries Advisory Committee. Her special interests are gardening and community service work. Aug. 13.

Hephzi Ohal was born in India and came to the United States in 1962. She and her husband have three grown children. She is an executive secretary at the International Monetary Fund in Washington, D.C. She has served as a deaconess and enjoys reading and traveling. Feb. 7, Aug. 11.

Rose Otis is the director of the General Conference Office of Women's Ministries, a department created at the 1990 General Conference Annual Council. Prior to her present election, Rose spent two years working with her husband representing the General Conference in the former Soviet Union, helping to organize the church into a division and negotiating with government officials. She and her husband have two grown children. Feb. 9, June 14, June 25, Oct. 26, Dec. 30.

Pamela Palmer, a public high school teacher, was born in Jamaica. She and her husband have two grown children and make their home in Maryland, where she is the head elder and the Sabbath school superintendent at her local church. She enjoys tennis, reading, piano, and volleyball. June 26.

Rachel I. Patterson is an editorial assistant in the North American Division Church Ministries Department and the NAD coordinator of Shepherdess International. She and her minister husband have two grown children. Rachel has written numerous articles for Christian magazines and enjoys writing, reading, antiques, and traveling. Mar. 9, Nov. 12.

Julia L. Pearce is a consultant in women's health services (R.N., Ph.D.) and has written articles regarding women's health issues. She makes her home in California, and is the coordinator of women's ministries in her local church. She enjoys women's history, reading, sewing, and giving women's medical presentations. **Apr. 14, Dec. 7, Dec. 15, Dec. 29.**

Christene Perkins is a registered nurse with a master's degree in nursing and is presently on a sabbatical leave to help care for her 87-year-old mother. She has written articles and books on health-related topics, is actively involved in her local church, and enjoys reading, bird-watching, gardening, sewing, baking, woodworking, travel, and people. **Dec. 4.**

Dollis Pierson, retired schoolteacher, missionary for 25 years, and widow of Robert H. Pierson, a former General Conference president, writes from Hendersonville, North Carolina. Through the years Dollis has worked in many areas of church work, compiled a book, *By His Side,* and written articles for various church magazines. Oil painting and reading are among her special interests. **Oct. 8, Dec. 16.**

Starr Piner is a registered nurse and mother of three children living in California. She is an earliteen Sabbath school leader who loves children, sailing, skiing, waterskiing, ice skating, bicycling, photography, and elderly people. **June 6, Oct. 17.**

Margo Pitrone and her husband love living in San Diego, where she is a minister with a deep commitment to recovery and support groups for women who have been victimized. She is a published writer and enjoys walking, reading, and racquetball. **May 27.**

Jeanne Rasoanindrainy and her pastor husband are living in Madagascar, where she is a teacher and the health and temperance director of the Central Malagasy Mission. She is a published writer and enjoys gardening and reading. **Jan. 25.**

Betty Rayl, the women's ministries director for the North Pacific Union, is a homemaker and rancher in Oregon and the mother of four grown children. She was a schoolteacher before becoming a "midwife to cows, ewes, and mama cats, with a specialty in raising orphan lambs and calves." Her hobbies are sewing, gardening, crafts, painting, piano, reading, writing, and being a grandmother. **June 27.**

Mabel E. Richards, the widow of preacher and radio speaker H.M.S. Richards, Sr., lives in California. Through the years she worked with her husband in evangelistic crusades and in the Voice of Prophecy offices and still enjoys working as a volunteer at the Media Center preparing literature mailings. **Aug. 18.**

Mary Margaret Richards recently retired from teaching in the Los Angeles school system. She's the wife of Harold Richards, Jr., of the Voice of Prophecy. Her seven grandchildren are her delight! **Oct. 1.**

Kay D. Rizzo is a free-lance writer living in Gresham, Oregon. She is the author of 13 books. This devotional first appeared in the *Adventist Review,* Feb. 6, 1992. **June 5.**

Mindy Rodenberg is a student at Takoma Academy in Maryland, where she is the editor of the school paper. She has written for various publications and is a Youth to Youth leader. She enjoys walking, sewing, cooking, writing, traveling, and desktop publishing. **Nov. 28.**

Jodi V. Ruf, a part-time English teacher and full-time wife and mother, lives in Tennessee, where she is a church elder. She enjoys traveling, reading, music, attending plays, and watching her daughter grow. **Mar. 28.**

Leona Glidden Running is a retired professor (emeritus) of biblical languages at Andrews University in Michigan, where she still teaches several ancient languages. Three books she has written have been published. She enjoys swimming, reading, knitting, and crocheting. **Feb. 3, Mar. 7, Mar. 15.**

Deborah Sanders writes from Canada, where she and her husband and two children make their home. She was a drywall and lather construction worker until her son was born five years ago with severe mental handicaps. She has written a collection of poetry and enjoys doing community service work. **Aug. 24, Sept. 5, 6, Nov. 17.**

Sheila Birkenstock Sanders, a speech therapist, is a transitional counselor for retarded adults in California. She is a widowed mother of two and stepmother of four children, and a Sabbath school superintendent and teacher. She has contributed to the *Collegiate Quarterly* and enjoys photography, travel, reading, sewing, and singing. **Feb. 20, Mar. 17, June 18, 19, Nov. 12, Dec. 9.**

Roberta Schafer is a minister's wife, mother, and homemaker living in Canada. She is the director of women's ministries for the Maritime Conference, is actively involved in youth ministries, and enjoys crewel stitchery, reading, and exercising. **Feb. 15, Apr. 10, Aug. 20.**

Cheri Schroeder, whose father was an American Indian, came out of spiritualism and the occult. She is an apartment building manager and home schooling mother living in New Hampshire, where she teaches an adult Sabbath school class and gives Bible studies. She enjoys painting, needlework, reading, hiking, and gardening. **Feb. 12, Feb. 21, Sept. 19.**

Marion Simmons is a retired educator who spent 50 years in Seventh-day Adventist church work at the elementary and college level, and in departmental work at the local, union, and division levels. She is a published writer and enjoys traveling, public speaking, reading, and promotional work. **Feb. 19.**

Janice Smith, the mother of four preschoolers, is an elementary teacher (not presently employed), homemaker, and recording artist, and plans to home-school her children. She is involved in ministry to families and is the kindergarten leader at her local church in Canada. She enjoys outdoor activities with her family, sewing, crafts, and music. **Apr. 22.**

Annie Souaré was raised in Africa with a Muslim father and a Catholic mother. She, her mother, one brother, and one sister joined the Seventh-day Adventist Church through an evangelistic effort held in their community. She is now studying computer science at Oakwood college. **Mar. 8.**

Marie Spangler, founder of Shepherdess International (a support system for ministers' wives on the General Conference level), is a retired teacher, a mother of two grown children, and a minister's wife. She is a published writer whose special interests include music, memory books, people, pastors' wives, and early childhood development. **Jan. 1, Jan. 10, Jan. 19, Feb. 23, Mar. 14, Mar. 18, Apr. 28, May 25, June 13, June 28, Aug. 5, Sept. 18.**

Glenice Linthwaite Steck lives in Angwin, California, with her husband and two children. She is an administrative secretary, is actively involved in the children's Sabbath school departments at her local church, enjoys walking, and collects "Dickens' Village" lighted miniatures. **June 15, July 6.**

Ardis Stenbakken, an Army chaplain's wife for 23 years and mother of two children, has been a high school and college teacher, has held almost every church officer there is, has a regular column in *For God and Country,* and has had articles published in other religious publications. She is also a speaker for women's ministries retreats, enjoys oil painting, quilting, cross-stitch, and traveling. **Nov. 21.**

Elizabeth Sterndale, a psychiatric nurse, is a general field secretary and the director of women's ministries for the North American Division. She has written several articles on health topics, enjoys reading, gardening, traveling, listening, and walking. **May 13, July 21.**

Sally Streib, registered nurse, free-lance author, and part-time editor for Shepherdess International, is also a pastor's wife and mother of three children. She recently had her first book, *Treasures by the Sea,* released and has written articles for several religious magazines. Her hobbies are scuba diving, shell collecting, camping, photography, nature study, and people. **Jan. 23, Aug. 2, Aug. 16.**

June Strong, homemaker, author, and speaker, counts as one of the greatest challenges and highest honors of her career her conservative church congregation's electing her as their first woman elder. She has written six books and for 18 years has had columns in religious magazines. June enjoys gardening, people watching, tole painting, and reading. **Apr. 1, Oct. 12.**

Arlene Taylor is president and founder of a consulting and education service and director of infection control at St. Helena Hospital in California. She is a published writer, hosts a one-hour weekly radio program, *Causerie,* and is an internationally known lecturer. **Feb. 3, Feb. 6, Mar. 7, Mar. 15, Apr. 11, Apr. 24, Apr. 29, May 6, July 7, Aug. 17, Oct. 10, Dec. 19, Dec. 23.**

Sylvia Taylor, a nurse and mother of two grown children, lives in active retirement with her husband in Elanora, Australia. She and her husband were both previously widowed. She has written a number of devotional articles and stories that have been published. This devotional first appeared in the *Adventist Review,* Jan. 28, 1988. **Nov. 26.**

Abiba Thiombiano writes from Abidjan, Côte d'Ivoire, where her minister husband is the program director for Adventist World Radio. She is employed at the Africa-Indian Ocean Division. **June 29.**

Barbara Tobias, an assistant professor of nursing, is a pastor's wife, mother of two teenagers, public speaker, and seminar presenter living in Georgia. She particularly enjoys working with young people, and directs a puppet ministry for the youth of her church. Her interests include cooking, entertaining, and reading, but her interest in people and how they feel about themselves predominates. **May 3, Sept. 1.**

Katie Tonn-Oliver makes her home in California. She is a creative and commercial writer and a seminar presenter who has written 11 books and numerous articles. Katie is a recovering victim of child abuse, and currently has four major writing projects on the subject of abuse. **June 12, June 20, Aug. 10.**

Elizabeth Tribes is a conference treasurer's wife and mother of two children who just moved from England to France. She teaches music and English part-time and enjoys reading, gardening, walking, swimming, and cycling. **Apr. 6.**

Nancy Van Pelt, a family life educator, certified home economist, author, and internationally known speaker, has written 17 books on family life. She and her husband make their home in California and are the parents of three grown children. Her hobby is quilting (she has finished nine!). **Jan. 21, May 4, Aug. 1, Sept. 2, Sept. 16, Sept. 25, Oct. 22, Dec. 1.**

Junell Vance is the director of women's ministries for the Atlantic Union Conference and makes her home in New York. She is involved in music ministries and enjoys people, travel, organ, and piano. **Apr. 21.**

Evie VandeVere is the director of women's ministries for the Southern Union and Georgia-Cumberland conferences. She is a public speaker and a seminar and workshop presenter, and has had several articles published in religious magazines. Evie enjoys reading, photography, traveling, and her grandchildren. **Feb. 2, Feb. 13, May 12, June 9, June 22, July 11.**

Nancy Vasquez is an administrative secretary in the North American Division office, wife of the vice president of the North American Division, and mother of three children. Her special interests are reading, writing, crafts, shopping, and baking. **Apr. 20, June 23, Dec. 18.**

Nancy Vyhmeister is a professor of mission at the Seventh-day Adventist Theological Seminary at Andrews University in Michigan. She has written various articles for religious publications and textbooks. Nancy enjoys home-making, writing, friendships, and her grandson. **Mar. 3, Aug. 21, Oct. 15.**

Sharlet Briggs Waters, director of medical records at St. Helena Hospital, is a wife and mother of two young children and is involved in children's Sabbath school. Sharlet's interests are gourmet cooking, travel, home remodeling and redecorating, and shopping. **Nov. 19, Dec. 27.**

Dorothy Eaton Watts, a free-lance writer and speaker, is a conference president's wife in Canada. She was a missionary for 16 years, founded an orphanage, taught elementary school, held various other positions in the denomination through the years, and has written eight books and numerous articles in religious publications. Her hobbies include bird-watching, gardening, and hiking. **Nov. 1, Dec. 3.**

Marla Weidell, a pastor's wife, was the first women's ministries coordinator in the Dakota Conference, and the originator of *Bouquets,* an inspirational newsletter for women. She enjoys collecting dolls at garage sales. These devotionals first appeared in *Bouquets,* vol. 1, no. 2, 1990; vol. 2, nos. 3, 4, 1991. **July 14, July 29, Dec. 31.**

Veryl Dawn Were writes from South Australia, where she is a homemaker. She is a nurse by profession, served as a missionary for eight years, is the mother of one grown son, and has written articles for various religious publications. Currently she is involved in community service work with her husband and enjoys gardening, bird-watching, stamp collecting, and knitting. **Feb. 10.**

Penny Estes Wheeler lives in Hagerstown, Maryland, with her husband and four children. She is the acquisitions editor for the Review and Herald Publishing Association, a Sabbath school leader, and a confirmed storyteller. Penny has written eight books, and numerous articles for religious publications, and was the editor of *Guide* for three years. Her other interests are flower gardening and the ever-changing lives of her four children. These devotionals first appeared in the *Adventist Review*, Sept. 1, 1988; June 6, 1990; Dec. 5, 1991. **Mar. 2, May 15, Aug. 9.**

Ellen G. White (1827-1915) wrote more than 50,000 manuscript pages, 5,000 periodical articles, and 25 books. She is the most translated woman author in the entire history of literature, and the most translated American author of either gender. Ellen was a public speaker, mother of four children, pastor's wife, and a founder of the Seventh-day Adventist Church, who believed that she was appointed by God as a special messenger to draw the world's attention to the Holy Scriptures and help prepare people for Christ's second advent. **Feb. 27.**

Hyveth Williams, the first Black female pastor in the Seventh-day Adventist Church, is a native Jamaican raised in London, England, and lives in Massachusetts. Before becoming a Seventh-day Adventist she was the executive assistant to the mayor of Hartford, Connecticut, and produced a local television show and hosted a radio program for nine years. Hyveth is a published writer of several magazine articles and a chapter in the book *Feminine Dimensions of Adventist Beliefs.* She collects bells and miniature boxes and enjoys reading, caring for her three pets, and traveling. **May 31, July 1, Nov. 18.**

Debby Gray Wilmot, a registered nurse, homemaker, piano teacher, pastor's wife, and mother of two, lives in California. She is the church choir director, accompanist, and women's ministries coordinator, and a coordinator for the Northern California Conference Shepherdess organization. Debby enjoys acrylic painting and gardening. **Feb. 5, May 23, 24, June 16, Nov. 22, Dec. 22.**

Elinor Wilson is well known in Adventist circles around the world, having been first lady of the church for 11 years. She and her husband, Neal C. Wilson, live in Burtonsville, Maryland. She taught church school for 25 years. Elinor has two children and four grandchildren, whom she enjoys immensely. **Oct. 23.**

Halcyon Wilson and her husband live in Riverside, California, where she is the pastor for family life and counseling. She has six adult children and is a seminar presenter and a published writer. Halcyon enjoys her family, reading, decorating, and writing. **Nov. 16.**

Nancy Vollmer Wilson is a part-time physical therapist and full-time mother to three daughters. She and her husband, Ted, spent nine years as missionaries in West Africa before her husband was elected as an associate secretary of the General Conference. Nancy plays the piano and enjoys reading, traveling, hiking, baking, and gardening. **Mar. 27, Apr. 4.**

Sheila Wilson writes from England, where she is a schoolteacher. She has been actively involved in church work and spent five years in the mission field, where her two sons, now adults, were born. She has written articles for various religious publications, and her special interests are travel, equal opportunity issues, family, and friends. **July 5.**

Miriam Wood, a retired teacher, has written 15 books, has had a column in the *Adventist Review* for the past 20 years, and has written numerous articles for many religious publications. In 1990 she was awarded an honorary doctorate from Andrews University. Her greatest hobby is reading, and she is also keenly interested in the lives of her children, grandchildren, and new great-granddaughter. **Jan. 27, June 2, Dec. 6.**

Marge Woodruff has enjoyed many rich experiences as the wife of a pastor, administrator, and missionary. The Woodruffs recently returned from Adventist Volunteer Service on Guam, where Marge worked in the Adventist Book Center. **Mar. 24.**

Lindeni Xaba writes from Soweto, South Africa, where she lives with her husband and four children. She is a secretary, is actively involved in fund-raising for her local church, and enjoys cooking, baking, flower arranging, and music. **Nov. 27.**

Our thanks also to the writers of the devotionals attributed to **anonymous** (Sept. 30, Oct. 28) and *Chesapeake Partners* (June 4).

Letting Go of Clutter

*Thou wilt keep him in perfect peace, whose mind is stayed
on thee: because he trusteth in thee. Isa. 26:3.*

Happy New Year! If you were to walk down the streets of Italy
at midnight New Year's Eve, you would be startled by
suddenly seeing a battery of all kinds of personal possessions being
hurled out apartment and house windows. No, these Italians are
not angry!

Prior to this time the streets are quiet and clear of pedestrians
and traffic. But at the stroke of midnight the streets become alive,
and there are sounds of music, laughter, and fireworks. Windows
fly open, and people throw out anything that reminds them of
something that happened during the past year that they would
rather forget. As this new year begins, I'm sure that we all feel there
are some things we would like to throw out the windows of our
spiritual lives.

Conditions in the world, both inside and outside the church, are
screaming that our Lord's return is imminent. At this momentous
time we each need to ask ourselves, "What will God have me be and
do?"

Anne Ortlund's secret in *The Disciplines of the Beautiful
Woman* (p. 25) can become our challenge for the new year—a
challenge for spiritual maturity that will make this year *really* count
for Christ:

"I drop the clutter from my soul,
  Reorganized by Your control."

She also writes, "How you live your life as a woman, all by
yourself before God, is what makes the real you. Nothing on the
exterior can touch or change that precious inner sanctuary—your
heart, His dwelling place—unless you let it. And God, who loves
you very much, has tailor-made all your outer life—your circumstances, your relationships—to pressure you into becoming that
beautiful woman He's planned for you to be" (p. 125). Our
heavenly Father waits to bless us in inconceivable ways to make our
lives what we never dreamed they could be.

Johann Wolfgang von Goethe once said, "I find the great thing
in this world is, not so much where we stand, as in what direction
we are moving." As we personally take up the challenge for
spiritual maturity this new year, may we become the "beautiful
women" God has planned us to be.   MARIE SPANGLER

Never Give Up!

All the fat is the Lord's. Lev. 3:16.

If it were possible to tabulate all the New Year's resolutions the globe over, losing weight would likely top the list in frequency, don't you think?

Now, experienced dieters know all the tricks. They know that the first reading in the morning is the lowest, while the scale's springs are still tight; which direction on the tile the scale will give the lowest reading; and when they lean forward the scale will read less than when they put all their weight on their heels. The expert dieter weighs in on Wednesday to minimize the effect of a weekend mistake (Sabbath dinner splurge), and weighs first thing in the morning after removing watch, after shaving, after voiding, and before dressing and inserting contacts!

Likewise, do not many sinners go to desperate lengths to minimize the hard recognition of sin in their lives? Do we not know every trick there is to minimize its guilt and consequences—seeking to deny every evidence of its presence that we possibly can?

But wait. Is that so bad? Short of fooling ourselves or outright denial, the desperate attempts may not be that bad. They reveal that we hate sin as we hate fat. Are we not trying to coax it down and get it out of our lives with every reading? Perhaps one problem is that we become discouraged when we have lost an ounce when we wanted to lose a pound. Good! That means our goals are ever urging us onward.

When you stand on the scales in your skin, humbled before God, determined to try again, and asking for His help one more day, don't be discouraged! If you lose just one ounce a day during leap year, that is 22 and 7/8 pounds off a year. But if you gain an ounce a day, the result is 22 and 7/8 pounds more by December 31. You see, the difference is in the *trend*. And the difference between the two trends is an unbelievable 45 and 3/4 pounds!

Ellen White supports the importance of the trend of life with this passage: "The character is revealed, not by occasional good deeds and occasional misdeeds, but by the tendency of the habitual words and acts" (*Steps to Christ*, pp. 57, 58).

A sin problem, like a weight problem, rarely remains stable. We are moving one direction or the other, always. So if you are discouraged over the little progress you make, multiply it by two and inform yourself, "That's how much I *didn't* fail!"

Courage, sister. Keep fighting the fight of faith. Never give up! Jesus is coming! Maranatha!   JANET KANGAS

The Full Story

Because you have so little faith. I tell you the truth, if you have faith as small as a mustard seed, you can say to this mountain, "Move from here to there" and it will move. Nothing will be impossible for you. Matt. 17:20, NIV.

As a child and young adult I always struggled to understand how people in the Bible could be so perfect. Didn't they make mistakes? Didn't they get angry? Didn't they ever feel like giving up? It made me wonder what was wrong with me. Why couldn't I be as faithful as Job or as courageous as Esther or be set apart as a person after God's own heart? Why didn't I have faith the size of a mustard seed? I was trying for all I was worth, but I still seemingly fell short of the mark.

It was only when God led me to my own study of the Word that I realized I had not been "told" the full story. Job's story became more precious to me when I read about his human struggles with despondency. Esther became closer to me when I realized that she too had fears. David's full story helped me realize what God can do in our wretched lives.

My life changed when God showed me that the faith of a mustard seed could be just holding on to any small part of a belief or promise, until God blessed in accordance to His will. For the woman that touched the hem of His garment it took only her belief in a small touch to restore her to health. For me, it took my belief in Romans 8:28. No matter what happens to me, I know I love God, and because I love Him, all things will work for my good. One small piece of the Word, but powerful enough to move mountains.

Thank God for understanding our humanness and for giving us the "human," practical, full-story accounts of what He can do in our lives. Let's not depend on the preacher or the Sabbath school teacher, but let's study to show ourselves approved unto Him. There is strength in the Word.   DEBORAH M. HARRIS

The Advent: What It Means to Me—1

*First the Christian dead will rise, then we who are left alive
shall join them. 1 Thess. 4:17, NEB.*

If you have ever lost anyone close to you, you have a special desire
in your heart for the soon coming of Jesus. Recently I had
occasion to poll Andrews University Seminary secretaries, asking
each, "What does the Second Coming personally mean to you?"
Some of their answers reflected the inner longing each of us has for
restoration of lost relationships.

Perhaps as we grow older this desire becomes even more
meaningful. Yet as I read the letters children send in response to my
advice column in *Guide*, I've learned that even they long for the
healing of stolen relationships. One wrote, "My friend died yesterday. We were really good friends, and I was really scared when I
found out today. I was sad and crying all day. How will I get over
my friend's death?"

I responded as best I could, sharing tips on grief recovery. But
they sounded hollow to me even as I wrote them. I know that her
only real healing will come when she's reunited with her friend at
Christ's return.

One secretary I talked to confided that she hopes to meet her
birth mother. Adopted, she naturally has questions about her
biological family and hopes to become acquainted with them in
heaven.

Personally, I look forward to interviewing four great-great-
grandparents who helped organize my church. One great-great-
grandfather was converted by Adventist pioneer J. N. Andrews in
1860 and might find it interesting that I worked at Andrews
University—never dreamed of when he died in 1870.

How many of us have prayed for loved ones without the
slightest hint that they would ever give their hearts to Christ? One
of the women told me that her mother had spent a lifetime praying
for her husband (this woman's father), dying without seeing any
change take place in his life. Shortly before the husband died, a
professor studied the Bible with him. The man accepted Christ and
committed his life to God through baptism. Imagine the mother's
joy at being reunited with her husband at Christ's return!

Is there a special relationship you long to have restored? Have
you lost a parent or a husband? Do you seldom see a close friend
who has moved far away? Are you impatient to talk with Jesus

face-to-face? Just the thought of these reunions thrills our hearts. Heaven can't come soon enough, can it? MADELINE S. JOHNSTON

The Advent: What It Means to Me—2

He will wipe every tear from their eyes. There will be no more death or mourning or crying or pain, for the old order of things has passed away. Rev. 21:4, NIV.

Along with the restoration of lost relationships, the secretaries at Andrews University look forward to Christ's advent as a release from pain and suffering. One woman said, "It's when all bad things finally come to an end. Animals won't be abused anymore; children won't be left." Another said simply, "It's the great rescue."

One divorced woman shared with the group how it had been difficult for her to raise her children alone. She quickly added that she prefers to emphasize how God has faithfully supplied her needs and supported her through this trial, but deep in her heart she longs for release from the stress.

The Advent promises us release from physical, mental, and emotional pain, and even from financial pain—we won't need money anymore. It will mean the reversal of physical and mental decline—very meaningful as we grow older. It will bring release from temptation and evil, from moral dilemmas and questions, from theological debate and heresy trials!

The Advent will release us from unhealthy distinctions between people. No one will be abused because he or she is too old or too little. (Occasionally I've felt the need to call Child Protective Services because of one of my *Guide* letters; other times I've wondered if I should.) Gender biases will be gone—and I've sometimes wondered if that will ever come, short of the Second Coming.

No one will be looked down upon because of occupation. One secretary recently asked a friend if her daughter was still studying X-ray technology and the woman replied, "No, she's not doing that anymore. Now she's just a secretary, like you." Such attitudes take their toll on the self-image after a while.

Happily, the Second Coming will mean the end of racial prejudice. Never again will I hear a young Black girl who has been attending a White church school say, "No one wants to be my friend, so I usually eat alone. They say, 'You're a stupid jerk.' They tell secrets to other people, but not me, and it hurts. Nobody cares. When they aren't looking, I run off and hide and cry a lot." Nor will I again stand in the seminary lobby and hear a student proclaim, "White is right only when it's on rice."

The Advent will spell release from dysfunction in persons, in families, and in the church. For some of my *Guide* correspondents it will mean the end of sibling hostility, of harsh and dictatorial parents, of rape at 14, incest at 12, and rejection and friendlessness at any age. It will mean the end of wanting Mom's live-in boyfriend to leave but being powerless do anything about it, or wanting desperately to be baptized but having Mom (angry over her divorce) refuse to allow it.

Expectations of restored relationships and release from pain give us unspeakable joy in anticipating the Second Coming—an eager joy that makes us long for Jesus to come again, soon.

MADELINE S. JOHNSTON

JANUARY 6

The Advent: What It Means to Me—3

God has not destined us [of the daylight] to the terrors of judgement, but to the full attainment of salvation through our Lord Jesus Christ. 1 Thess. 5:9, NEB.

While I was discussing the Advent with the secretaries, our conversation turned to the topic of punishment. Confident in Jesus' promise of salvation, they expressed no fear of retribution. But unfortunately for many Adventists, retribution is their major emphasis.

Retribution is biblical. Throughout Matthew 24 and 25 we are reminded that the useless servants and uncaring people will be cast into utter darkness and burned with Satan and his angels. But that's not what God wants for us. We can lose out by focusing entirely on God's love and mercy or entirely on obedience and judgment. We need balance. But if we must be unbalanced, there is less danger on the side of love and mercy.

Those Christians who focus on God as the stern judge respond primarily with fear, dreading the Advent, wondering if they're good enough; while those who focus on God's mercy anticipate Christ's return with joy, knowing that *He* is certainly good enough.

Our daughter Beth, a nurse, once took hospital chaplaincy training with a group of seminarians. One morning in their regular small-group session, the question arose, "If you were in an auto accident and knew you had only 60 seconds to live, what would be going through your mind?" Beth and the Catholic priest said that they would be searching their minds for any unconfessed sins, so they could ask forgiveness. The three Mennonites all spoke of counting the blessings God had given them and thanking Him for the rich lives they had experienced. The supervisor pointed out that their theology undoubtedly influenced their response.

Through my *Guide* correspondence I have become increasingly aware of a distressing element in our church. There are many parents who focus on judgment and perfectionism, killing the joy their families should experience in the church and in anticipation of the Advent. To take attention off their own failure to reach perfection, they become overcritical of others. Considering it their responsibility to get all family members into the kingdom, they tighten the screws, assuming that the end justifies the means.

This misinterpretation of supposed rights and responsibilities as household heads produces a high incidence of wife and child abuse. Children write to me of rules without reasons, of Mrs. White being used as a club, of parents yelling to retain authority, of major arguments over pants, jewelry, and makeup. Will these children anticipate the Advent as retribution or release?

A young girl once told me, "I'm terrified of my parents. I've prayed about it several times, but it seems like Jesus doesn't always answer my prayers. . . . They always say something mean about the things I've accomplished or am proud of. . . . I've never heard them tell me they love me, and they probably don't." Can this child believe God loves her when she feels so unworthy of love? Can she anticipate the second coming of a God who seems not to answer her?

The Advent: What do *you* expect? What do your young people expect? — MADELINE S. JOHNSTON

JANUARY 7

The Advent: What It Means to Me—4

For the grace of God that brings salvation has appeared to all men. It teaches us to say "No" to ungodliness and worldly passions, and to live self-controlled, upright and godly lives in this present age, while we wait for the blessed hope—the glorious appearing of our great God and Savior, Jesus Christ, who gave himself for us to redeem us from all wickedness and to purify for himself a people that are his very own, eager to do what is good. Titus 2:11-14, NIV.

For the past few days we've joined the secretaries at Andrews University as they've shared what the Advent means to them personally—restored relationships, release from pain, and an escape from retribution made possible by our loving God. The women also felt that belief in the Second Coming gave them a rationale for living godly lives.

One secretary mentioned that when she looked at recent world events, she realized anew that the Advent could be very near, and she suddenly didn't want to put so much money into a new home. Her values were changing.

The Advent gives us a rationale for character development. But again we need balance so that we don't become self-absorbed. We need to remember that it also gives us a rationale for reaching outward. One secretary thought about the unreached people groups around the world and said, "I grew up with the idea that the world had been reached. Now there are all these people out there who have never heard the good news. It's not fair." This young woman and her husband have since left to take the good news to one such group.

The dean's secretary said that anticipation of the Second Coming gave her a rationale for not worrying. She said, "There is no reason to worry about what happens to me here, because I know the end. All kinds of bad things may happen, but we know that God will have the final say—so it's OK."

The Second Coming also gives us a rationale to allow God to paint a picture of Himself in our lives that is so true, so undistorted, and so balanced that our young people, our families, the older members of the church, and the unbelievers who know us will also want to see Him again.

When our Lord comes the second time, will you be there to meet loved ones you've lost? To be found by those you've prayed for? To be set free from pain and sorrow?

One *Guide* correspondent wrote me a very mature letter, saying that she was attending public high school and becoming attractive to some of the boys there. She had determined not to date them, and she sought some advice to explain this position to them without making her religion appear narrow-minded. Later, reminiscent of the one leper, she wrote a beautiful letter to thank me for my reply. She concluded, "God bless you! I'll be looking for you in heaven." Her response sums up what we all look forward to.

MADELINE S. JOHNSTON

No More Tears

He will wipe every tear from their eyes. There will be no more death or mourning or crying or pain, for the old order of things has passed away. Rev. 21:4, NIV.

As a nurse in the Shady Grove Adventist Hospital emergency room I'm a firsthand witness to a lot of pain and suffering. There's hardly a day that passes that I don't say to myself, "Jesus, only Your coming will end this suffering! Come soon!"

I've spent hours trying to bring the dead back to life while distraught family members plead with us to keep trying just a little longer. I've walked the parking lot with parents who've suddenly had their only child snatched from their lives. I've physically supported a young wife who went to work expecting a normal day only to receive a call that her husband had died of a heart attack at age 35. I've manually manipulated a human heart, urging it, coaxing it to beat again, and breathed into a tiny infant's mouth to the rhythmic sound of a mother's breaking heart. Yes, we do all we can. We're considered a top-notch medical team, but in spite of our best efforts, there's still too much bad news for waiting relatives.

Little Tommy was one example. He was 3 years old. A victim of cerebral palsy. While he and his little sister splashed in the tub one evening, their mommy tried to change her clothes for an evening out to celebrate her birthday. She needed an evening away from the responsibility of caring for a handicapped child! Suddenly she heard the water running, and when she rushed to the bathroom her worst fears were realized. Tommy had slipped and lay face-down in the water.

For 45 minutes our team made every effort to save Tommy, but eventually the doctors ceased resuscitation efforts. For the next two hours I hugged and consoled family members. I joined them in a prayer circle with Chaplain Harry Krueger, seeking to find some consolation for the distraught parents. Again my prayer was "Jesus, come quickly!"

I love my work, but I'll be glad when the day comes that my services aren't needed anymore. That day when Jesus promises there'll be no more death or tears. I'd like to be with Tommy's mom and dad again, when they're reunited with him! I'd like to share in the triumph of life over death when Tommy's parents realize that he's not only alive, but perfect in every way! HEIDI OTIS BOWEN

Heirs to the King

When thou saidst, Seek ye my face; my heart said unto thee, Thy face, Lord, will I seek. Ps. 27:8.

Imagine that you are an extremely wealthy person with billions of dollars at your disposal. You live in a magnificent mansion with many beautiful furnished rooms. You provide for your children the nicest clothing, the most comfortable furnishings, the best toys and educational materials. The time spent with your children is quality and enjoyed by all. They receive ample love, care, and attention.

Now consider this. Upon waking every morning, one of your children puts on the same ragged outfit that is kept safely under his or her pillow. Daily your child goes to the kitchen and begs for scraps of food, pausing only for a moment to speak to you, saying essentially what he or she said to you yesterday. Through the day your child toils with problems, fears, and worries. At the end of the day he or she is exhausted and falls to sleep with barely a word to you.

Are you that child? Do you live, talk, and think like a poor, abandoned, unloved child? Is your religious experience the same old garment you put on yesterday, or do you go daily to God's closet of promises to find a new victory and blessing? Are you begging for the scraps of this world's success, or do you boldly try new ventures, assured that your Father will give you aid and guidance? Is your conversation with Him the same thing day after day, or is it like that of friends who are glad to see each other again?

It must sadden the Father when He sees us struggling with problems, situations, and habits as if He has not provided for our every need. Let's consider whose we are and live like it.

"God regards us as His children. He has redeemed us out of the careless world and chosen us to become members of the royal family, sons and daughters of the heavenly King. He invites us to trust in Him with a trust deeper and stronger than that of a child in his earthly father. Parents love their children, but the love of God is larger, broader, deeper than human love can possibly be. It is immeasurable. Then if earthly parents know how to give good gifts to their children, how much more shall our Father in heaven give the Holy Spirit to those who ask Him?" (*Christ's Object Lessons,* p. 142).   WANDA DAVIS

Women of Vision

Now Saul, still breathing threats and murder against the disciples of the Lord, went to the high priest, and asked for letters from him to the synagogues at Damascus, so that if he found any belonging to the Way, both men and women, he might bring them bound to Jerusalem. Acts 9:1, 2, NASB.

Luke used the phrase "belonging to the Way," frequently in the book of Acts as a synonym for Christianity. To the pre-Christian Saul it was a term of derision—a term that, if accurately applied, could cost someone their freedom and life.

In Acts 22:4 Paul testifies to persecuting "this Way to the death, binding and putting both men and women into prisons" (NASB). Why did Paul treat even women so cruelly? I believe it's because women played an important role in the establishment of the early Christian church.

When it comes to our church, we find that many women used their talents and energies to help build the infant organization. While in Australia my husband and I had the privilege of visiting the gravesite of Maud Sisley Boyd, a woman of great vision. Her granddaughter, Nona Coombs, thrilled us with inspiring stories of God's leading in her grandmother's life.

Maud Sisley was our first Adventist woman missionary. After 10 years of service in the Review and Herald Publishing House, she asked for a six-month vacation to distribute literature in Ohio with her friend, Elsie Gates. Her accumulated savings from her 10-cent-an-hour wage at the publishing house would have to see her through this time of service.

As a single young woman Maud traveled to Switzerland to help J. N. Andrews start our first publishing branch overseas. She later married C. L. Boyd and became the first woman missionary to South Africa. After her husband's death, she was asked by Ellen White to help the workers in Australia develop Avondale College.

This woman of vision seemed to have had one purpose in life—to carry God's message both abroad and in her homeland. God honored her vision and blessed her efforts mightily. Surely as God used dedicated, selfless Christian women in the beginning of His great work on earth, He will use them in the finishing of His work. What a privilege to be a part of it! Is He calling you today?

MARIE SPANGLER

Roots

And I pray that you, being rooted and established in love, may have power, together with all the saints, to grasp how wide and long and high and deep is the love of Christ. Eph. 3:17, 18, NIV.

The very year I landscaped my yard was the year one of southern California's worst freezes came along. I was out of town when it arrived, and returned home to find that half or more of the flowers and trees I'd been nurturing for eight months had shriveled up and turned brown.

The garden section of our local paper cautioned us not to prune the dead foliage prematurely. Leave it, the paper said, to protect whatever remained of the plants from further damage. And be patient!

Regular inspection tours proved the newspaper right. One by one, the plants began reviving. In the end, only two didn't—kalanchoes I'd planted just a few weeks before the frost.

Saddest looking, at first, was a small jade plant that once had been glossy green. While the larger jades began discarding their dead leaves and renewing themselves almost immediately, this one just sat there, a withered skeleton. Finally I gave up on it. But reaching down to uproot it, I noticed tiny yellowish-green leaves growing from several of its lower joints. It too was going to make it.

"Plants do that," said a more experienced gardener-friend when I told her about it on the phone. "It's a miracle."

The miracle, as I've thought about it since then, has to do with roots. Transplanted into the soil but not yet firmly grounded, the newly planted kalanchoes didn't have a chance. With eight months' head start, the jade plants' root systems sustained them through one of California's coldest winters.

Life has winters too. Winters of loneliness, grief, and profound pain. Are you firmly grounded in God's love, sufficiently prepared to make a comeback after winter's worst? Am I? By God's grace, I hope so!   JOCELYN FAY

The Brass Bedstead

But seek first his kingdom and his righteousness, and all these things will be given to you as well. Matt. 6:33, NIV.

I'll never forget those adventurous years when my husband and I were a newly married couple living in rural Vermont. We had a large house to furnish on a small budget, and I was constantly hunting for bargains. Antiques were my passion, with garage sales and auctions becoming my favorite haunts.

Not far down the maple-treed lane lived a little old woman who took a special liking to us "young'uns." She tromped through her raspberry patch, selecting bushes for us to transplant into our fledgling garden. She discussed religion with us and often spoke of our special "holy day" that we called Sabbath. Her small house centered on her bedroom, which was loaded with well-worn books and piles of newspapers. Amid the heap of tattered quilts and unkept papers I saw a magnificent old brass bed. I ran my hand admiringly over its tarnished curves.

One day I heard that the old woman had passed away. Her relatives decided to sell her possessions at an auction. I felt a surge of excitement at the thought that maybe I'd have a chance to buy the bedstead. It was a lovely antique, but even more, it would remind me of the kindly woman who had been such a unique part of our Vermont neighborhood. I waited eagerly for the date to be set for the auction.

My heart dropped to the pit of my stomach when I learned that the auction was scheduled for Saturday. "Oh no, why Saturday!" I moaned to my husband. "Why does it have to be on the only day that we don't do any business? Couldn't we make an exception just this once? Or at least have someone else put in a bid for us?" I wanted that bed so badly—surely there could be a way.

For days I struggled with the idea of how to get that bed on my Sabbath. But after much prayer I knew that I couldn't intentionally go against God's wishes. I had to give up the idea of ever getting that brass bed. It hurt, yet I felt relieved when I made the choice.

The day of the auction came and went. I wondered with nostalgia who had gotten the bed and how much it had gone for. Some days later I asked a friend about the bedstead.

"Strange thing happened about that bed," she said. "It never came up for the auction. I guess it was supposed to go to a relative, but the person doesn't seem to want it now." She saw the wonder in my wide eyes and asked, "Are you interested?"

"Am I!" I nearly shouted. Before I knew it, I was the proud owner of the old brass bedstead. Not only did I have the bed without desecrating God's holy day, but I paid a fraction of what it probably would have gone for on the auction stand. I was bubbling with excitement at God's care for my desires, even the little "luxuries" of my life. I immediately thought of the verses that say "Wherefore, if God so clothe the grass of the field, which to day is, and to morrow is cast into the oven, shall he not much more clothe you, O ye of little faith? Therefore take no thought, saying, What shall we eat? or, What shall we drink? or, Wherewithal shall we be clothed? . . . But seek ye first the kingdom of God, and his righteousness; and all these things shall be added unto you" (Matt. 6:30-33).

I'll never be tempted to go against God's wishes for the Sabbath again. But more than that, I'll always be amazed at God's surprises!

HEATHER GUTTSCHUSS

JANUARY 13

How Much Do I Give?

One man gives freely, yet gains even more; another withholds unduly, but comes to poverty. A generous man will prosper; he who refreshes others will himself be refreshed. Prov. 11:24, 25, NIV.

A few years ago practically every church in India collected money and clothing for the victims of a terrible flood. One of the donors was a poor woman who brought an old sari and the last few rupees she owned to contribute to those in need. The pastor, knowing she was poor, kindly told her that she really couldn't afford to help. But the woman insisted that he accept her gift. "I have two saris," she said with a smile, "and I can wear only one at a time. As for the rupees, I can earn more. Please take them. Someone needs them more than I do."

I have often thought of this unselfish woman and I wonder—how much do we give? How much do we have left over after giving?

My 6-year-old grandson, Jason, listened intently as I told my daughter about a group of orphans in India. He quietly slipped out of the room and brought down his money box. Emptying its contents onto my lap, he said, "Here, Nana, take all my money and give it to those poor children." Three times I coaxed him to put his money back in his box, thinking he might change his mind later on. But he held firm to his decision. His tender heart was touched by their suffering and need. He too gave his all!

Is it possible that we have become calloused to the needs of others? Is our giving only the result of pressure? No one has ever become poorer by giving. Giving is part of the Christian's life, for by our giving someone else receives life.

The trend in our selfish world is to gather rather than give, to hoard rather than scatter. Christ said, "Whose are these things if thy soul be required tonight?" (see Luke 12:20). We must never stop giving—giving without counting the cost, and giving till it costs us something. The widow gave her last two mites, and in doing so, received Jesus' commendation, "She hath given more than anyone else" (see Luke 21:3).   BIROL C. CHRISTO

JANUARY 14

Words of Remorse

For I acknowledge my transgressions: and my sin is ever before me. Against thee, thee only, have I sinned, and done this evil in thy sight. Ps. 51:3, 4.

People's reactions to their sinful behaviors are legion. Some, not sorry for the sin, are sorry indeed for the consequences; some, not high in self-esteem, turn inward to a life of self-recrimination. The fortunate ones, recognizing the one satisfying response, turn to God.

True repentance is hard to come by. Everyone knows that forgiveness is a gift, but many people forget that godly remorse is one also.

Disconsolate, a man sat at a funeral parlor, too overcome with grief to acknowledge any sympathy. Covered with literally dozens of red roses, his wife's silver casket rested between two multiple-plant stands, each holding 10 cut-flower arrangements. But those attending the funeral didn't notice the fragrance or beauty of the flowers. Their attention was drawn to the poor man whose body shook with sobs as he held his head in his hands.

"He must have loved her very much," a woman commented to her companion. "Why, I've never seen so many red roses in my life. Poor dear. What love they must have shared."

The inconsolable husband spoke to no one, and soon most of the people left. Suddenly he got up and staggered to the casket. In an anguished voice he exclaimed, "Oh, once I almost told her I loved her!" Then he buried his face in the roses, mourning a love his wife never heard him express.

Words of remorse, gut-wrenching remorse. But King David would have understood. He knew the feeling: "For I acknowledge my transgressions: and my sin is ever before me . . ."

This husband's precious wife was dead. The "I love you" forever too late. The scent of roses bittersweet in bereavement. Unbearable remorse!

But the message of King David ends in hope. Undone by his adulterous alliance with Bathsheba, he clung to God, claiming forgiveness. And his hope gives our remorse hope too: "A contrite heart, O God, thou wilt not despise" (Ps. 51:17).

WILMA McCLARTY

JANUARY 15

Roses and Thorns

Before they call I will answer; while they are still speaking I will hear. Isa. 65:24, NIV.

When I was a thoughtless young girl in high school, I used to find the words "Life is not a bed of roses" rather amusing. It was not the sentiment that I laughed at, but rather the manner in which they were uttered by a minister who often preached on Sundays at our school chapel.

Years later I often ruefully remembered both the words and my laughter, because I knew only too well that roses do indeed have thorns.

In January 1990, as I drove to pick up my child from school, my mind was preoccupied and my heart heavy with my overwhelming problems. I made a slow turn from a busy street onto a side road. Suddenly, to my horror, a young boy ran directly into the path of my car. I tried desperately to avoid hitting him, but it was too late. He had gone down. As I climbed shaking out of the car a voice in me cried, "Lord, please help me! I cannot bear this. How can I live with myself?"

God, however, had answered my prayer before I could express it. The only injury the little boy suffered was a small cut on the knee, and he learned an important lesson in road safety. As for me, I learned that God would not give me more than I could bear at any one time, that indeed there are angels intervening on our behalf, and that there is never a thorn without a rose. ADJIKO HANSEN

Free for the Asking

And I say unto you, Ask, and it shall be given you. Luke 11:9.

He was just a bit too friendly—the smile too fake—as he strode toward us at a Nevada rest area.

"Hello. Are you folks from Tennessee?" he asked, the answer obvious from our license plate. "I used to live in Nashville . . . Say, I was wondering, could you let me have a little money?"

"What do you need it for?" my husband inquired.

"I need $7.50 for a water pump for my car. I've got a friend here who says he will take me to town."

Now, a town on that desert stretch of the Nevada interstate was 75 miles away. Besides, a water pump for $7.50? Really now.

For some reason my husband and I are often approached for handouts, most frequently at rest areas. I like to tell myself it's because we look so compassionate, but what is probably closer to the truth is that we look so naive, so vulnerable.

"I don't believe so this time, sir," my husband responded. "Sorry."

How should we respond to rest area scams, to professional leeches, to appeal-to-sympathy parasites? A slim chance always exists that a person may have a legitimate need. What should we do?

Think of Christ, daily besieged with a million prayers—asking, begging, pleading, imploring. Jesus must wonder Himself at times what to do as He looks at weary travelers in the rest areas of life with their innumerable requests. So many prayers are selfish; so many a substitute for work; so many downright harmful if answered as asked. But Jesus *did* say, "Ask, and it shall be given you."

My husband and I felt sad, really, after we refused the requested $7.50. We were haunted by the possibility of its being a real need. And Jesus must also feel sad, when He can't answer all prayers as asked, especially when we tend to lose faith when our requests aren't answered to our satisfaction.

The next time we claim the "Ask, and it shall be given you" promise, we must have faith that our *words of asking* will be answered to our best advantage.

"When we have asked for His blessing, we should believe that we receive it, and thank Him that we *have* received it. Then we are to go about our duties, assured that the blessing will be realized when we need it most" (*The Desire of Ages*, p. 200).

WILMA McCLARTY

JANUARY 17

Forgiveness Is Not a Feeling

Get rid of all bitterness, rage and anger, brawling and slander, along with every form of malice. Be kind and compassionate to one another, forgiving each other, just as in Christ God forgave you. Eph. 4:31, 32, NIV.

A little friend of mine scraped her knee. It really hurt, but she quite enjoyed all the attention she received. So much so that all the time it was trying to heal she kept removing the plaster and picking the wound to make it bleed again. Understandable, I suppose; she was only 5. But what worries me is that I find adults doing the same thing.

No, not their knees, but their hurts. The devil goes around fashioning words into stinging whips and then getting people to use them on each other. On the receiving end we then lash ourselves over and over with the soul-scourging words till they're etched indestructibly on our minds and the blood flows freely.

What I want to know is why do we do it? Not why *they*—the ones wielding the whips—do it, but why we have to keep scourging ourselves all over again with *their* barbs.

We know from a Christian standpoint that we must forgive and that we probably will forgive. But sometimes we wait until we're good and ready, having picked our hurt open again and again to get maximum self-pity out of it! Now, I'm not saying I've mastered the art of not whipping myself with other people's angry words, but I refuse to go into an action-replay of the excruciating moment of hurt, then sit picking over the wound till the blood flows again. A quick prayer for the gift of forgiveness gets the wound cleaned up and bandaged immediately and gives the resulting peace of mind a chance to complete the healing process.

Recognize angry, hurtful words for what they are, the devil's weapons for tearing us apart, for working people up into his favorite state—hatred and division. Simply refuse to rehearse them over and over in your minds (or to your friends).

All we really need is to learn to forgive sooner rather than later. Forgiveness is much more effective if we don't withhold it until we feel like giving it. Where did we get the idea that forgiveness is a

38

feeling, anyway? Forgiveness is the only balm for a bruised mind, so why don't we take a cool look at the scourge marks and think for a moment of the hurt they've also done to the person who struck the blows? Once we can see them as hurting, too, the process of forgiveness is already under way, and the hurt will begin to heal.

ANITA MARSHALL

God's Touch

Yet I am always with you; you hold me by my right hand. You guide me with your counsel, and afterward you will take me into glory. Whom have I in heaven but you? And earth has nothing I desire besides you. Ps. 73:23-25, NIV.

The plane terminal was busy as I waited anxiously for my plane to board. The lady next to me seemed preoccupied, so we sat in silence, each in our own thoughts. I began thinking over the past two months of my life, which had been very difficult for me and had challenged my faith and trust in God. My thoughts were interrupted by the lady next to me, who was rummaging through a very large purse.

"Did you lose something?" I asked.

"No," she replied. "I guess I'm just nervous."

"I know what you mean. Flying makes me nervous too."

"Well, that's not exactly it," she said. She looked at me as if she wanted to say more but wasn't sure she should. I waited. Finally she looked up, glanced around the terminal, and leaned toward me.

"You don't know me. You'll never see me again. I need to tell somebody." She took a deep breath and lowered her voice to a whisper. "I'm leaving my husband. He doesn't even know it yet, but I can't take it anymore. Right now I'm headed across the country to have an affair." She hesitated, then continued, "I am not doing this because I want to. I don't want to leave my husband, but I'm so unhappy. We're both unhappy. What do you do when there are no good options?" She looked at me and waited.

I thought back over the past two months of my life. I knew what it meant to have "no good options." I searched my mind for the different answers I could give. Should I act as if everything in my life were fine and give her some pat answer to life's chaos? That's what I wanted to do. Finally, at a loss, I shared a little of my own story. I shared my frustrations and pain and how all of that had caused me to question.

"So what do you think the answer is?" she asked. She was challenging me.

"I'll be real honest with you," I responded slowly. "I don't have a specific solution for what is happening to me at the moment, but I do have a God who does, and that is very comforting for me." My words went straight to my own heart. "I have a God." In the chaos of the moment, I had almost forgotten.

She thought for a moment and then slowly began sharing about how her family had been committed Christians and had gone away from it. She talked about how she would like to get back to it. She seemed to get more excited as she talked. As she got up to board her plane, she said something about calling her husband and talking to him as soon as the plane landed. But I wasn't listening very closely, because my own words were sounding again and again in my ears, "I have a God." As my plane was announced, I got up and walked slowly toward the gate. The problems of the past two months shrank in the face of the words "I have a God." I can't tell you what became of the woman with the large purse, but I can tell you what happened to me. God touched me, and His touch made a difference.

So often we come to the world with hopes that somehow we can touch people for God. But there is something that needs to take place before we can reach out to a hurting world. We must let God touch us. That touch in our own lives will make a difference. And it is through that touch that God will touch His world.

CARLA GOBER

JANUARY 19

Do You Really Know Jesus?

I count all things to be loss in view of the surpassing value of knowing Christ Jesus my Lord, for whom I have suffered the loss of all things, and count them but rubbish in order that I may gain Christ, and may be found in Him, . . . that I may know Him, and the power of His resurrection. Phil. 3:8-10, NASB.

A 97-year-old lady received visits from her pastor. On one occasion she told him that when she was a little girl she had visited the White House and shook hands with President Lincoln. If someone were to ask you if you knew President Lincoln, you would probably respond, "Of course, he was the president of the United States during the Civil War and was known as Honest Abe." We don't know Abraham Lincoln like this 97-year-old lady did; and she didn't know him as did his son, Tad, who could burst into his dad's study at any time, jump up on his knee, and get a bear hug and kiss. The son really knew Abraham Lincoln, wouldn't you say?

Do I really know Jesus? is the ultimate question in life. While I was in college one of my professors, Marjorie Kemmerer, impressed me with her Christian life and influence. She had a close relationship with Christ, and this was evident to all who knew her. I discovered that her secret of knowing Him lay in the fact that even though her first class for the day began at 7:30 a.m., she would rise at 4:30 a.m. in order to have quiet time with the Lord. Jealously guarding a daily quiet time spent alone with Jesus, communing with Him through prayer and Bible study, is not an option. The only way Jesus knew His Father while on earth was through the same avenues open to us.

E. M. Bounds states beautifully, "In prayer, God stoops to kiss man, to bless man, and to aid in everything that God can devise, or man can need." That includes everything!

Susanna Wesley, mother of 19 children, had no place to go to meet the Lord where she could be alone. At her chosen time she would take her apron and cover her face. Her children knew never to disturb their mother when she was praying in her apron!

Jesus will make Himself known to us when we pour out our souls to Him in prayers of thanksgiving, intercession, and petition. Let us thank God for the privilege of communing with Christ in prayer and Bible study, which is the way to really get to know Him as our Friend and Saviour. MARIE SPANGLER

JANUARY 20

Precious in God's Sight

Since thou wast precious in my sight, thou hast been honourable, and I have loved thee. Isa. 43:4.

One day I was talking to a middle-aged woman who had come to my office at her doctor's request. Her physician had helped minimize her physical problems, but still she felt depressed and sad. She told me that she had wanted to care for her feeble elderly in-laws but that the rest of the family had spurned her offer and suggestions. It hurt her deeply to think that her love and service were not needed.

What wonderful peace and hope filled her heart as we read the Bible together. Knowing that she was precious in God's sight gave her new purpose and will to serve her Maker. New avenues of volunteer work opened to her. Now she felt needed, wanted, and loved. She found meaning to this favorite text of mine: "Thou wilt shew me the path of life: in thy presence is fulness of joy; at thy right hand there are pleasures for evermore" (Ps. 16:11).

As mortal human beings, we know there are times of tragedy and unexpected trials that come to us very suddenly. The tears flow fast, and we feel so helpless. It is at these times that we need to find that quiet place, near to the heart of God. He gives us strength to go forward in faith. Our Jesus, who set an example of courage, will give us the assurance that His love is boundless and that we are precious in His sight.　　　　　　　　　　　　　EVELYN DELAFIELD

JANUARY 21

Elegance—A Great Investment

Many women have done excellently, but you surpass them all. Prov. 31:29, RSV.

Two women were visiting at church when one said to the other, "There's JoAnn. She's the most elegant woman I know." What about JoAnn was so elegant? Was it stylish clothing? the classy way she walked? money? lavish jewelry? What did JoAnn possess that prompted others to discuss her elegance?

What is elegance? Can anyone have it? Is it reserved for only a few of the "beautiful people"? Should a Christian woman desire or actively pursue it?

The dictionary may help us understand the word "elegance." It means "tastefully refined; tasteful opulence; tastefully ornate in dress or furnishing; marked by grace, refinement, and simplicity." Yes, that's JoAnn, all right.

Many Christian women I know have never experienced or approached elegance. They have been taught plainness to the nth degree. As I look into their faces I can safely and sadly deduct that they have never enjoyed one moment of elegance in their entire lives!

Elegance is often construed to imply money or worldliness, but when marked by grace, refinement, and simplicity, it can, and should be, desired and pursued. Our everyday lives can be made more pleasant and elegant by adding just the right details. A single rose in a small vase adds beauty. A fragrant bowl of potpourri adds a special touch to a room. Colored place mats can make a table setting exciting and attractive.

Rather than serving yourself on any old plate, use a decorative one. Write a letter to a friend on scented stationery with a colored pen rather than a regular ballpoint. Enclose a few confetti hearts! You may never know what profound effect that little touch of elegance can contribute to brighten the recipient's horizon!

As we incorporate the concept of specialness into our daily lives, we can treat others more graciously. We each have only so much time. We can either live life in an ordinary manner, or live more graciously. Short-term, it may be easier to live the ordinary existence—a gracious, elegant life requires thought and effort. But in the long run, graciousness is a great investment. The choice is up to us.

By adding special touches to our daily lives, we are making a personal statement about ourselves—that we value ourselves, our family, our time, our home, and the material things God has given us. This provides a marvelous sense of well-being.

When we take time to make little things in our daily lives satisfying and more beautiful, disappointments and outside pressures become easier to take. By adding beauty, joy, and a touch of elegance to our lives, we are well on our way to making our stressed-out lives more bearable and enjoyable. The fulfillment it brings far outweighs the effort expended. Choose elegance!

NANCY VAN PELT

JANUARY 22

"Yes, We Can!"

Then Esther sent this reply to Mordecai: "Go, gather together all the Jews who are in Susa, and fast for me. . . . I will go to the king, even though it is against the law. And if I perish, I perish." Esther 4:15, 16, NIV.

Shyness, to many of us a lifelong acquaintance, has few virtues. It blocks the paths of Christian ministry and witnessing. It deafens our mind and will by shouting "I can't, so why try?" It stifles interest in Ingathering, giving Bible studies, teaching a class, leading a group, and praying in public. But shyness tells many lies. The truth is that God can free us from the shackles of shyness and fear. Because He can, we can!

Boldness carries a risk and often leads to leadership. And leaders get criticized, gossiped about, and misunderstood. Far too often we choose our inconspicuous and familiar ruts, safe from public view. While we may admire and applaud the courage,

43

confidence, and daring exploits of others, we think, *I can't do that*.

And why not? The Bible records the bold and daring deeds of heroes such as Daniel, Joseph, Esther, Rahab, Ruth, and Paul. Has such courage gone out of style? Has it vanished from the face of the earth? No! God has power over all fear. His Holy Spirit is waiting for us to plug into His power and do bold deeds for God, as Bible heroes did.

With God's tremendous power available, why do we give in to fear and shyness? We can deliberately replace these hindrances with courage and boldness. As we learn to know ourselves and identify and name our problem areas, we can devise ways to develop the preferred opposite qualities. And we can learn new skills and stretch our comfort zones as well.

Fear did not prevent Queen Esther from trying to save her people. Instead of panicking, she prayed, fasted, and planned what she could do. She boldly carried out her plan, although it meant risking the king's displeasure and immediate death. She refused to say "I can't." What a role model!

Do you want your life to make a difference? Then find ways to overcome fear and shyness. Strengthen your boldness muscles by using them. Stretch and grow, do and dare for God. God is our strength and wisdom. His Word tells us, "I can do all things through Christ which strengtheneth me" (Phil. 4:13).

Yes, we can!

FANNIE L. HOUCK

JANUARY 23

Rescued!

God is our refuge and strength, a very present help in trouble. Ps. 46:1.

M y friend and I walked along a wooden walkway that meandered several hundred feet out over a marshland. Wings of the white ibis caught the early-dawn sunshine and wild geese honked out their joy.

Two days earlier January gloom had seeped into my usually cheerful heart and joined the other weary thoughts that lurked there. "I'm tired," I said to my friend, Martha. "I feel like the adventure of living is more like a pit, and I'm sinking down into it. I can't face another problem or another person with one."

We made some quick arrangements and then drove south until we found the sunshine sparkling over a South Carolina marshland.

Excitement replaced gloom as I looked over the water. People and their needs seemed far away. After scanning the crisp winter sky, I allowed my binoculars to sweep over the water. There, just below us, six spiraled periwinkle shells clung to a bunch of marsh grass. Those shells just begged to be captured and examined. I stretched out on the walkway and reached down, but I couldn't grab even one of those tiny treasures.

I decided to lower myself off the platform feet first and stand in the muddy water for only a moment to grasp the pesky things. I removed my tennies, peeled off the sweat pants that covered a pair of shorts, and pushed up my shirt sleeves. I wiggled backwards, squeezing beneath the railing and allowing myself to dangle over the side. When my feet hit the cold water and sank into the mud, I sucked in a breath.

"The shells are on that bunch of grass just to your left," Martha shouted. "But I think they are still beyond your reach."

I lowered myself farther off the walkway and searched for the bottom of the muck with my feet. Suddenly the muscles in my arms screamed. They refused to hold my weight another moment. I could feel my arms slide off the walkway until only my hands clutched the edge. Freezing mud oozed up around my ankles and grabbed my legs. Still I could find nothing solid beneath them. I tried to pull myself back up to the walkway, but the mud held me fast. Even my friend couldn't drag me out of the pit.

I tried moving myself toward dry land by sliding my hands along over the rough boards. "I'll never make it," I screamed after only a few minutes. "It's just too far."

"Could you swim?" my friend asked. But we both realized before I answered that the water was too shallow to float me to shore. Fear and cold sucked the strength from my body and left my mind unable to think. My hands ached and threatened to release their hold. Then, as I realized my utter helplessness, I cried out to God.

"I have an idea," Martha said, falling down onto her stomach on the walkway. She wedged her feet between some boards on the far side. "Try to pull one leg free, place it in my hands, and push," she commanded, hanging her arms over the side and lacing her fingers together. "God will pull you out."

She was right; only God could pull me out. I twisted and turned my captured legs. Suddenly the left one loosened. I wrenched it with a burst of energy I didn't have and plunged it into my friend's hands. I pushed. To my amazement, I found myself sprawled on my face on that dry, safe walkway.

I smiled and stood up. Water dripped into brown puddles at my feet and a thick layer of gray mud clung to my body. I shivered.

We headed for the car, placed a beach towel over the seat for me to sit on, and drove to a nearby bathhouse. I scraped the mud off and tried to wash myself with the frigid trickle of water that came from a faucet attached to the outside of the bathhouse. My skin turned rosy pink. Still I didn't look very clean.

My friend rummaged in my day pack and found a soft, dry sweat suit. It looked like a treasure. I wiggled into it and plunked down against a sand dune to soak up the warm sun.

We watched as waves rushed in and tumbled upon the shore, where they fizzled into bubbly foam. A sea gull sailed over on an invisible air current, and thoughts of peace and joy tiptoed back into my heart.

Are you facing some challenge without the strength of His presence? Are you about to plunge into a muddy pit? Cry out to Him. He will rescue. He will cleanse. He alone can give you peace and joy for your journey through life.   SALLY STREIB

JANUARY 24

Created Clean

For just as through the disobedience of the one man the many were made sinners, so also through the obedience of the one man the many will be made righteous. Rom. 5:19, NIV.

Created clean in Eden
a comely man and maid
perfect from the Maker's hands
with innocence arrayed

No shadows on their walk with God
no space for shame or guilt
no ken of crime, no thought of grief
no need that blood be spilt

Until they walked the way of death
and took the taste of sin
that barred to them the Garden gate
and lasting life within.

Create me clean, O God, this day
scrub every corner white
and may the mirror of my life
for Thee shine pure and bright.   FANNIE L. HOUCK
Copyright 1988, Fannie L. Houck.

Just as I Am . . .

"For I know the plans I have for you," declares the Lord,
"plans to prosper you and not to harm you, plans to give
you hope and a future." Jer. 29:11, NIV.

Each woman has dreams and plans for the future, and she tries to realize them with all her might. But she's very often stopped in her efforts, especially in professional domains. She'd like to improve herself, but she can't. The instability of her condition—marriage, pregnancy, motherhood, husband's assignment—hinders her progress. And she feels like her life is made up of pieces of a puzzle instead of a whole picture. She was a teacher here, then a secretary there, and later a librarian over there. What kind of impression can she make after that? A woman has no future. She's but a spare wheel!

Fortunately, that's only an impression! Our text says that God has plans for each one of us and that He's preparing us for the future. So we needn't worry! Though our lives may seem like scattered pieces of a puzzle, God knows how to gather them and place them so that we have prosperity and hope for the future.

God's promise is true. Let me tell you why I'm so convinced. In 1973 my husband graduated from Andrews University, but I hadn't completed the requirements to earn my education degree. My children were still too small to be left alone while I went to class full-time. But I did receive a certificate in home economics for evening cooking classes that I attended haphazardly. Thus, when we flew back home, I had some credits in education and a certificate in home economics. I thought I was a failure.

But God had plans I didn't know about! Had I graduated in education that year, I would never have had the opportunity to be a sanitary reform teacher in our union's seminary, or to counsel members and nonmembers all over my country on diet, or to write a book about vegetarianism.

Surely God has plans for each of us, and His plans are the best for us. Isn't that marvelous? Ask Him to show you His plans, so that you may succeed in all things. Implore Him like David in Psalm 143:8: "Show me the way I should go" (NIV). As we keep our eyes, ears, minds, and hearts open, we will grasp the opportunities He puts in our path! Let's listen to His instructions and follow Him wherever He leads us! If we let God plan for our future, we'll find out for ourselves how good the Lord is.   JEANNE RASOANINDRAINY

Windows of Our Souls

Blessed are your eyes because they see. Matt. 13:16, NIV.

L ong ago, in a village near Paris called Coupvray, there lived a little lad of 3 named Louis. As the son of a harness maker, he commonly played with bits of leather and an awl. One day as he was playing, the awl slipped and punctured one of his eyes. A doctor bandaged it carefully, but the eye soon became infected. Unfortunately, the infection spread to the good eye, and the boy became totally blind.

Although peasants, Louis' parents enrolled him in the National Institute for the Young Blind in Paris. The school tried to teach the children the alphabet by means of crossed twigs, but few were able to learn by this method. Some books were developed with letters sewn into the pages with string—nine words per page. Each book weighed 20 pounds and some of the children could hardly lift them.

Louis thought there must be a better way to learn to read than that and started experimenting when he was 12 years old. By the time he was 15, he had developed a raised-dot alphabet system. Braille passed along his gift of genius, and his system has been translated into almost all tongues. As a result, millions of blind people have received light into their souls as their fingertips rove over the embossed letter punches. Ironically, Braille's system of writing required an awl, the very instrument that was the cause of his blindness.

This story always makes me think about my eyes and the importance of taking care of them. Even more, I am reminded of the importance of monitoring the information that enters into my brain computer through my eyes. In the Bible, Dr. Luke wrote that the lamp of your body is the eye (Luke 11:34, 35). When your eyes are sound, you have light for your whole body; but when the eyes are bad, you are in darkness. See to it, he says, that the light you have is not darkness. If you have light for your whole body with no trace of darkness, it will all be as bright as when a lamp flashes its rays upon you.

Metaphorically, the eyes are the windows of our souls. They can reveal whether there is light or darkness inside us. The psalmist David said that the Lord was his light, and therefore he was not afraid (Ps. 27:1). The apostle John wrote that Christ is the true Light that lighteth every person who comes into the world (John 1:9). Do you ever feel darkness in your soul? Remember that God is light. God wants to shine light into your soul—to light up your life. MYRNA MELLING

Build Your Own Rainbow

Whenever the rainbow appears in the clouds, I will see it and remember the everlasting covenant between God and all living creatures of every kind on the earth. Gen. 9:16, NIV.

All my life I have been fascinated by rainbows, and I have seen some outstanding ones in unusual places. I remember a rainbow in New Guinea and one on the island of Bali. They were sheer enchantment, as was the double rainbow over Salt Lake City, Utah, that I viewed from the mountains that overlook the city.

After one rainbow sighting I was suddenly struck with the thought of how wonderful it would be to live forever under my own constant, unfailing rainbow—to maintain that state of quiet joy that makes everything worthwhile, and nothing drab. Perhaps I could even live *in* the rainbow, with all the beautiful colors concealing the "everydayness" of life. As I pondered this idea, the thought struck me that perhaps I could construct my own rainbow—definitely a do-it-yourself project.

First of all, the "anchor" at one end of the arch would be a settled belief in the existence of God as Creator and ruler of the universe. The "anchor" at the other end of the arch would be my own firm commitment to Jesus as my Saviour. Without these essential anchors, the rainbow would have no stability—no staying power.

Now, let's select *red* as the first color and call it *organized enthusiasm*. Notice that I have qualified "enthusiasm" with the important adjective "organized." I've met many enthusiastic people who couldn't seem to focus their energies long enough to make a difference in their own surroundings, let alone the world. In Col. 3:23 the apostle Paul wants us to do everything enthusiastically, with thorough organization. The follow-through is as important as the idea itself.

Now let's add *orange* to our rainbow and identify it as *confidence*. Women have not always had many opportunities to develop confidence in themselves as leaders and doers, but this is changing. Ralph Waldo Emerson stated that "they can conquer who believe they can. A person has not learned the lesson of life who does not each day surmount a fear." How can we acquire confidence? By realizing that we are daughters of the King—we are royal. A royal person has power.

I choose to make *blue* stand for the *proper use of time*. Women need the blue rainbow band in a special way, for so much is demanded of them in life. They fill so many roles simultaneously. Often the blue band will mean that you have to make difficult priority choices, but the orange band gives you the self-confidence you will need.

Now *yellow* we'll call *single-mindedness*. Remember that the simplicity of an uncluttered life is beautiful to behold. *Green* will stand for *perseverance*. And *indigo* will represent *flexibility*. We have to have the indigo band for a special reason: women can never reach their full potential for God if they are stubborn, rigid, or close-minded. There's still a *violet* band, which certainly stands for some of the *bruises* we get along the rocky road of life. But with the Great Physician on our side, we know we'll heal rapidly.

So there is my rainbow, and yours, if you choose to construct it and live in or under it through Christ's grace and help. Our lives need never be drab again! MIRIAM WOOD

JANUARY 28

I Will Heal Thee

Beloved, I wish above all things that thou mayest prosper and be in health, even as thy soul prospereth. 3 John 2.

I was lying in the mud, my helmet still on, the dirt bike weighing on my leg. Broken in three places, my ankle hurt too much for me to talk.

"Are you OK?" "Where does it hurt?" "Here, get up." Everyone crowded around the accident. But the last thing I wanted to do was get up, preferring, for a few minutes at least, to lie on the ground in my misery.

Only after the pain subsided did I listen to any instruction: "Take your shoe off." "Wiggle your toes." "Keep this ice on your leg." "Elevate your ankle."

My reactions were typical—"Stop the pain!" says the human race. "Then give me advice if you must."

Remember the varied and often conflicting home remedies for burns you've heard through the years? One advised putting salt on the wound to promote healing and to prevent scarring. Another instructed to smear the burn with butter. Yet another said to keep aloe vera juice on the spot constantly for several days.

Now, all of these are marvelous suggestions, but they fail a major test—*they don't stop the pain!* So burned fingers and arms and feet get stuck under the nearest cold water faucet for immediate pain relief instead.

Although not a doctor, John—the beloved, the compassionate—wanted his friend to "prosper and be in health." The reason is as true now as it was then. There is a definite connection between body and mind, and when one suffers, so does the other.

Jesus, our Creator, knew better than anyone the close connection between the condition of the body and the health of the mind. Physical healing was such a part of His ministry. Imagine Him traveling through entire towns and healing everyone in them! Near Nazareth "were whole villages where there was not a moan of sickness in any house; for He had passed through them, and healed all their sick" (*The Desire of Ages*, p. 241).

Jesus' promise to us today is the same as it was in Jeremiah's time: "For I will restore health unto thee, and I will heal thee of thy wounds, saith the Lord" (Jer. 30:17). WILMA MCCLARTY

JANUARY 29

A Wife Gives Thanks

Thanks be to God for his indescribable gift! 2 Cor. 9:15, NIV.

I watched my husband critically as he stood inside the main entrance to our church in his red usher's jacket, greeting people, passing out bulletins, and welcoming newcomers.

Glancing at him as the service began, I thought, *How I wish he wouldn't wear that old tie. And why did he get his hair cut so short?*

Just then our pastor called the ushers to the altar. Four came—without my husband. He was fumbling under the seat for the basket that he'd set down while talking to a new family who had just entered the sanctuary. Hastily he retrieved the basket, stretched his steps, and caught up with the others.

I watched him with the same impatience I'd felt so often lately—wishing he were different, wishing he enjoyed traveling, wishing he'd learn to swim, wishing he'd been promoted and transferred "back home."

"Honestly," I muttered under my breath, "why doesn't he get with it?" That's when I heard the Lord speak to me. *Read Job 14:3.*

Lord, I replied, *how about if I look it up at home?* Our pastor *is speaking and getting ready to lead us in prayer.* The command came again: *Read Job 14:3.*

I hurriedly flipped through my Bible and located the scripture: "Must you be so harsh with frail men, and demand an accounting from them?" (TLB).

Tears filled my eyes. I looked up toward the altar as the pastor began reading the scripture for the day. I watched my husband amble up the aisle with those long, slow strides of his. Except for my pounding heart, everything in me became still.

Although the pastor was just introducing his sermon, the Lord had already tutored a delinquent parishioner in need of direct instruction.

As my spouse slipped into the pew and squeezed my hand, my heart cried out, *Father, forgive my silent sins against my husband. He didn't hear me, but You did. Thank You for helping me to see what I was doing.*

And Father, thank You for my husband. Thank You for the love he shows when he sets out for the bus stop each day with his lunch pail, even before the sun has risen. Thank You for the brushing he gives the dog I hauled home from the pound. Thank you for the hours he spends at the kitchen table helping our daughter with her math, or paying bills for orthodontists, prom dresses, and puppy shots.

Thank You for the times he cared for me while I was so desperately ill. Thank You for the bird feeder he built for me outside the kitchen window. Thank You for all the hours he spent with me at flea markets, loaded down with the good deals that I was unable to resist. And for the times he escorted me to musical programs and baseball games, just because I love music and ball games.

Thank You for the hikes, shared picnics beside a mountain stream, and wanderings in the moonlight to glimpse a herd of elk grazing in the long summer grass.

Thank You, Lord, for this unique man—quiet, patient, dependable. Most of all, thank You for letting me see in him a small reflection of the sustaining, unconditional, protective love You have for us.

Thank You, Lord, for helping me to appreciate him just the way he is.   NANCY HOAG

Hailstones and a New Hairdo

Or else let them come to me for refuge; let them make peace with me, yes, let them make peace with me. Isa. 27:5, NIV.

It was a hot day in January, and I was visiting in Brisbane, Australia. Some friends had invited me for the weekend and arranged to pick me up in the city. I took the opportunity to have my hair done for Sabbath, and as I came out of the salon I noticed that it had become very dark. Anxious about my new hairdo, I rushed through the underpass to the appointed rendezvous by the side of a major road.

Just as I got there, I felt some enormous drops of rain. I was standing by a tree, quickly looking in my bag for something to protect my hair, when suddenly there was an enormous clap of thunder and flash of lightning right above my head! I looked up in terror and saw a sight that made me quake. The sky was green and boiling. Although I was visiting from England, I knew what that meant—hail. In seconds the wind was howling and I was jumping from leg to leg as hailstones the size of golf balls rained down on me.

Wave after wave of thunder crashed over my head, and it felt as though the end of the world had come. Water swirled above my ankles, and every time I tried to move away from the tree, the wind threatened to sweep me off my feet. I have never known such terror in my life. The stinging lash of the hailstones combined with the shrieking wind, crashing thunder, and flashing lightning is something I will never forget. I was trapped, and all I could do was cry out loud to God to protect me and to send my friend to fetch me. The 10 minutes before he arrived were the longest in my life, and that he managed to drive to where I was standing was nothing short of miraculous.

As I lay in bed that night, bruised and battered, I gave thanks that I was still alive. As I contemplated my deliverance, I realized that had I taken the time to look up sooner, instead of being intent on my hairdo, I would have seen the signs of hail in the sky and gone to a place of safety.

As it was, I had been caught in a mini-cyclone with winds of more than 100 miles an hour, which caused $10 million worth of damage in 10 minutes. Since then I have often wondered, Do we "look up" often enough, or are we so intent on life down here that

we fail to see the signs God is giving us of the end of the world?
AUDREY BALDERSTONE

JANUARY 31

Red Sea Problems

Praise be to the Lord, to God our Savior, who daily bears our burdens. Ps. 68:19, NIV.

R ed Sea problems are problems for which we think there are no solutions. The Israelites faced such a problem after they fled Egypt. When Moses finally commanded them to stop, they found themselves up against an impassible sea with a rugged mountain to the south. Suddenly the cry arose, "Chariots! Soldiers!" Indeed, it was Pharaoh's advance guard. Was it any wonder terror filled their hearts? As far as they could see, there was no solution to their problem.

But out of this peril came deliverance. As the helpless thousands inched forward under Moses' command, they saw "their path opened through the waters and their enemies overwhelmed in the moment of expected triumph. Jehovah alone had brought them deliverance" (*Patriarchs and Prophets*, p. 288).

Your back may not be up against the Red Sea or the Egyptian army, but perhaps it is up against a rebellious teenager, an unfaithful spouse, an aging parent, an alcoholic, a coworker you just can't get along with, rent that keeps going up, or a serious illness. The list of Red Sea problems is endless. And most likely each one of us has at least one such dilemma.

Think about your Red Sea problems as you read the following: The Israelites "were weary and terrified, yet if they had held back when Moses bade them advance, God would never have opened the path for them. . . . The great lesson here taught is for all time. . . . The imagination pictures impending ruin before and bondage or death behind. Yet the voice of God speaks clearly, 'Go forward.' We should obey this command, even though our eyes cannot penetrate the darkness, and we feel the cold waves about our feet. . . . Faith courageously urges an advance, hoping all things, believing all things" (*ibid.*, p. 290).

After their deliverance, the Israelites joyously sang what we call the song of Moses: "The Lord is my strength and my song; he has become my salvation. He is my God, and I will praise him" (Ex. 15:2, NIV). This triumphant song points forward to the destruction of all our Red Sea problems. John saw the redeemed standing on the

54

"sea of glass mingled with fire," having "the harps of God. And they sing the song of Moses the servant of God, and the song of the Lamb" (Rev. 15:2, 3).

When it rains, I enjoy going up into the Appalachian Mountains that surround my house. From a vantage point on Mount Zion Road I watch as fingers of mist swirl up from the forest floor to join the rain clouds. I realize that there must be some scientific explanation for this phenomenon. But as I watch these fingers of mist unfurl and ascend, I don't particularly care about scientific explanations. Instead, I visualize the day when we too will rise to meet one special cloud—the cloud of angels bearing the Solution to all our Red Sea problems. May your soul rise and your wings stretch to rest in His embrace.　　　　　LYNDELLE CHIOMENTI

FEBRUARY 1

Sunrise Alleluia

The heavens declare the glory of God; the skies proclaim the work of his hands. Ps. 19:1, NIV.

When the sunrise paints the eastern sky
Let every heart, awaking, cry,

Alleluia to the God of Creation,
God of glory and goodness
 and everlasting love!
Alleluia to the God of Creation!
God of glory and goodness
 and everlasting love.

Let the Lord of love and light
Paint your life with joy both day and night;

Alleluia to the God of Creation,
God of glory and goodness
 and everlasting love!
Alleluia to the God of Creation!
God of glory and goodness
 and everlasting love.　　　　　FANNIE L. HOUCK

Heartsearch

I the Lord search the heart and examine the mind, to reward a man according to his conduct, according to what his deeds deserve. Jer. 17:10, NIV.

One day while the trash collector was emptying my trash can into the truck, a bottle fell out and shattered into many pieces. Picking up the broom and dustpan, I walked to the end of our driveway and began sweeping the wide area of broken glass.

When finished, I congratulated myself on a job well done, and began walking back up the driveway to the garage. For some reason I turned about halfway up the drive and looked back at our cul de sac. To my chagrin, the late afternoon sun illuminated several points of light on the pavement—more broken glass. I sighed and returned to sweep again and again. Each time I checked at the halfway mark of the driveway, and each time I could still see bits of glass reflecting light from the sun. Finally, I admitted to myself that I probably would never get every bit of glass swept off the pavement.

Walking back to the garage one last time, I thought, *This is just like my life. I think I have it swept clean of all wrongdoing, and then Jesus, through His Word, the Holy Spirit, a sermon, or some godly friend, shines His light into my heart, and I see more sin pieces that I need to let Him sweep out of my life.* I realized once again that only Christ could rid my life of sin, and David's prayer for purity became my own: "Search me, O God, and know my heart; test me and know my anxious thoughts. See if there is any offensive way in me, and lead me in the way everlasting" (Ps. 139:23, NIV).   EVIE VANDEVERE

Our Birthright

Jesus loved Martha, and her sister, and Lazarus. John 5:11.

Jesus not only associated with women of His day; He loved them. He also taught their liberation. For example, Christ taught that women are not responsible for the choices men make in terms of sexual behaviors. Not only did Christ develop loving, platonic relationships with women, but He taught that other men should be able to do the same (Matt. 5:28). Men of that society often secluded women on the basis that their presence would be a constant sexual temptation.

Christ taught that women were accountable for their *own* actions, as outlined in the story of Ananias and Sapphira (Acts 5:1-11). Women are expected to be familiar with the Bible, to understand sin, and to be fully accountable for their choices and behaviors.

Christ included women in His work and thereby elevated the place of women in the early Christian church. Women were present in the upper chamber at the time of Pentecost (Acts 1:14; 5:14). At that time in society participation in public worship was reserved mainly for men. Christ encouraged women to gather with men in religious assembly.

Christ accepted the service of women, and they played a prominent role in His work. Women assisted Christ in His mission, and cared for His material needs, and in turn He rewarded them by making them witnesses and heralds of His resurrection (Mark 15:40, 41; Luke 24:10). Indeed, He gave His most advanced information first to a woman, telling the Samaritan woman plainly that He was the Messiah.

The historic situation of women is not part of God's perfect creation, but a result of sin. The New Testament does show a better way. Perhaps the most heartening part of the New Testament for women today is the record of how Jesus treated women. He simply disregarded all artificial human barriers and customs, and with impartial kindness treated women as equals. He healed and taught them just as well as men.

Joy, joy, for Christ was born of Mary. By choosing to enter this world through childbirth, Christ forever elevated the value of women. Let us claim that birthright. LEONA GLIDDEN RUNNING
AND ARLENE TAYLOR

Staying in the Line

Be kindly affectioned one to another with brotherly [sisterly] love; in honour preferring one another. Rom. 12:10.

I was 16 years old. First driver's license. I was in bumper-to-bumper start-and-stop traffic in the seven-mile stretch from Ottawa Beach on Lake Michigan to its owner city, Holland, Michigan.

In my peripheral vision, off to the right, I saw a red car from a side street coming into view. There wasn't a *chance* he could break into the line of traffic unless someone good-heartedly let him in. I knew what my mother would do. So I stepped on the gas and watched for him to fill the empty space behind me.

But lo, a second later, I glanced in my rearview mirror and saw the red car still waiting to move. Ah, that moment of truth! There is only *one* way, be it on the highway to Holland or the highway to heaven, to let someone into the line. And that is to let him or her into the line *ahead* of you!

Now, it may be easy to conceptualize our rejoicing to step aside and let the converted nationals of the countries to which our church division sends missionaries enter heaven before ourselves. But what about each other at home?

I once heard a seminary professor from the Old Testament department say, "It's easy for me to defer to someone from the church history department or be happy for that person's success. But let me perceive that someone in my own department is getting an edge over me—and *then* I have a problem!"

Are we more apt to rebel when we feel that we don't have control of the situation? Perhaps in yielding to someone unknown we feel magnanimous, whereas if we have to yield involuntarily to a workmate we feel trampled on, insecure, or belittled.

Whatever the reason, the hymn says, "All is changed when Jesus comes to stay." The Jews couldn't handle that. When He came 2,000 years ago and told them, "The last shall be first," what was their response to this radical who turned their world upside down? They hated Him.

Let's not be so hard on those Jews. If Jesus walked into our offices this morning and said, "All right, in My kingdom all the secretaries get the chief seats and uppermost rooms I talked about in Mark 12:39," what would be our response?

One thing is certain—if we can't handle this in heaven, we

won't be there. And we won't handle it there if we can't handle it here. There is only one way not only to let someone else into the line, but also to stay in the line ourselves. JANET KANGAS

The Homecoming

How lovely is your dwelling place, O Lord Almighty! My soul yearns, even faints, for the courts of the Lord; my heart and my flesh cry out for the living God. Ps. 84:1, 2, NIV.

One summer our yearly family outing was spent camping by a lake. Some friends who owned a boat had invited us to join them for a few days of waterskiing. Blue sky, fresh air, sunshine and water, sleeping out under the stars, sharing and singing around the campfire, and an unhurried schedule all contributed to a memorable vacation.

My favorite spot of solitude was a large rock by the water's edge from which I often watched the glorious sunsets. While sitting there in the lingering twilight of the last evening, I realized how many things in life come to an end—sometimes before we are ready to let them go. This had truly been a special time for me. The peace of nature and the fellowship of friends had been unforgettable. I would miss them.

Out of those nostalgic feelings surrounding this event came a question that I have pondered frequently during the intervening years. We often speak in terms of longing for heaven or talk about the fact that we miss knowing Jesus on a face-to-face basis. But could it be that Jesus misses human beings, also? The close relationship He enjoyed with His original creation has been gone so long. Does Christ yearn to walk with us by a lake or join us at a special spot to share thoughts and ideas?

Because of Jesus' great desire to save us and to bring us back to Himself forever, He became human—identifying with our physical nature as well as with our feelings and emotions. How hard it must have been for Him to leave His followers. After several years of close association and shared life experiences they were cherished friends. I can feel the earnestness in the words as He spoke to them, expressing how much He was counting on them being with Him forever (John 14:1-3).

Today Jesus might express similar sentiments to us in the

following way:

> I really miss you and wish that you were here,
> Just to talk to you and to brush away your tears.
> I know the pain you know.
> Why can't you just let go
> Of those earthly things that bind?
> Why don't you leave them far behind?
>
> I really want to come and take you by the hand.
> We'll live together in a new and perfect land.
> We'll be the best of friends.
> There'll never be an end.
> You are a part of Me, so it's not hard to see—
> I really miss you.
>
> My love is written in the sky above,
> In sunset's evening glow.
> It's reflected in the faces of special people that you know.
> I've done everything I can, and yet I'm still alone.
> Don't you feel compelled to turn your heart toward home?
> I really miss you.

How can we resist the loving invitation of such a special Friend? My heart responds as I hope yours does also. *Come quickly, Lord. I miss You, too.* DEBBY GRAY WILMOT

FEBRUARY 6

His Hands

Because you are my help, I sing in the shadow of your wings. My soul clings to you; your right hand upholds me. Ps. 63:7, 8, NIV.

Melissa watched me as I threaded the needle with waxed yarn and showed her how to string the flowers together carefully. We were making a lei from flowers we had picked off a bush in the backyard. I pointed out the pistil and stamens in the center of the flower and explained how the needle had to go right through the calyx. Now it was her turn, but she didn't pick up the needle. She was staring at my hands. "Your hands do a lot of things, don't they?" she mused. How like her to have fixed her attention on a different aspect of the project. "They do a lot of things for me, too," she continued. "Tell me about hands."

I set the flowers aside, and we talked about hands. I explained how the left side of the brain controls the right hand and vice versa; how in each hand and wrist there were more than 25 bones and numerous muscles; and how our individual fingerprints are all slightly different from those of any other human being. Somehow we got around to discussing stories in the Bible about women and the ways in which they had used their hands—the woman who swept the floor, the woman who baked bread, the women who sewed clothes, and the women who touched the scepter.

I told Melissa that since we were made in the image of God, our hands must be something like the hands of God. That intrigued her, and we started thinking about Bible stories all over again. This time stories about Christ's hands—breaking the bread, holding the children, putting clay on the blind man's eyes, holding on to the donkey, and working in the carpenter shop.

Tears came to her eyes as we talked about the soldiers pounding nails into Christ's flesh. I had read and heard and even told that story a hundred times or more, and somehow, I had never stopped long enough or gotten into the story deeply enough to have tears come to my eyes. I had always focused on the words and not allowed myself to meditate about the feelings. We talked about being in the new earth and being able to look at Christ and see the scars from the spikes. This time I thought about those scars in a new way: with emotion as well as intellect.

We went back to making the lei. Since then, I think about the hands of God frequently. We are forever in those hands. What a comforting thought. The psalmist wrote, "Your arm is endued with power; your hand is strong, your right hand exalted" (Ps. 89:13, NIV). "My times are in your hands" (Ps. 31:15, NIV).

ARLENE TAYLOR

FEBRUARY 7

Thy Word Have I Hid in My Heart

Thy word have I hid in mine heart, that I might not sin against thee. Ps. 119:11.

It was the third time in less than a year that my car radio was stolen. Since it was time-consuming to get another radio installed, I decided to do without one for a while. And I began to fill the 40-minute trip to my office in other ways. Some mornings I planned the day's agenda, some days I daydreamed, and occasionally I would pray for friends and colleagues.

One morning I was upset, and my mind was buzzing with unpleasant thoughts. I tried very hard to shake them off, but without success. I took an old Bible with me to the car, hoping to drive them away by memorizing Scripture. I selected Psalm 103 because a very dear friend of mine often repeated the first two or three verses before she prayed. I came to the first red light, and I read the first verse: "Bless the Lord, O my soul: and all that is within me, bless his holy name." I repeated this till I memorized it, and then went on to verse 2: "Bless the Lord, O my soul, and forget not all his benefits."

I began to list God's benefits in my life. I was aware of the benefits that came with my job—home leave, education allowance for children, medical allowance, etc. What were God's benefits to me? Peace of mind, direction and purpose for life, happiness, and many others. Before long my mind was free of ugly and unwanted thoughts. Instead I was rejoicing in the benefits of God.

It took me about 10 days to learn all 22 verses. And even though it was quite an effort to memorize the Psalm, the benefits have been great. In the process of memorizing I was forced to concentrate on the meaning and sequence of the passage. It is as if I squeezed every word to get the right meaning, and understood the emotions and feelings of the author as he wrote it.

Many times since I have dug into my memory bank and retrieved this beautiful Psalm (and others that I have memorized) when I needed encouragement; when I was overwhelmed with His goodness to me; and sometimes just for the sheer beauty of the poetry. It has truly been a blessing!　　　　HEPHZI OHAL

FEBRUARY 8

Walking With Him

Whoever walks wisely will be delivered. Prov. 28:26, NKJV.

Walking carefully with my crutches, I begin what seems like another endless journey. My hands are sore from bearing my weight upon them as I move the crutches step by step, and my shoulders are tired as they act as the pivot point for my body. It's easy to become discouraged and say I can't go another step. Every little task is a challenge. My body grows weary as I make the effort to move and do my work.

It would be so much simpler just to sit and let someone wait upon me. Yet I know that I must exercise and regain my strength. The week of bed rest following surgery took its toll, and now I need to work at regaining what I lost.

I spend too much time thinking *If only* . . . As the ladder gave way and I fell, I knew that I should have spent an extra minute making certain that it was on firm ground. But I hadn't done that. So now I must spend the weeks recuperating and growing well and strong again.

In my walk with God I sometimes neglect to take the extra minutes to nourish my faith and trust in Him, and I grow weak and discouraged. Then I need to recover and again enter into His presence. I need to daily meditate upon His life.

Did Jesus feel as I do as He began the long walk to Calvary? The cruel cross He bore must have hurt His shoulder and back. The weight of the timbers in the cross caused Him to falter and fall. Yet He didn't say "If only Eve and Adam had chosen My way instead of listening to the serpent" or "If only I didn't have to do this to save humanity." He carried the burdens of my sins to Calvary and hung there for me willingly. Is it possible to love Him enough for His gift to me?

My faith and trust are again renewed and I go forth with a new awareness of His gift to me. I will draw from His love the strength I need as I walk through life.　　　　　　　　　　EVELYN GLASS

FEBRUARY 9

My God Is Real!

Trust in the Lord with all your heart and lean not on your own understanding; in all your ways acknowledge him, and he will make your paths straight. Prov. 3:5, 6, NIV.

We get a lot of gift catalogs in the mail at our house, and I have to admit that I rather enjoy browsing through some of them. One evening while I was thumbing through a few of my favorites, a large, colorful advertisement caught my eye. The heading read "The Chess Set of the Gods." *Wow*, I thought, *this has to be beautiful*. And it was! An inlaid white marble chess board with an exquisite wooden base held 32 perfectly sculptured figures of mythological gods that were made of pure white bisque and rare jet-black porcelain. Although I don't know the first thing about the game of chess, I couldn't resist the urge to know how much this elegant display of frivolous amusement would cost. But on and on the advertisement went, extolling the beauty of the set and submersing me deeper and deeper into the merits of its qualities. At last I came to the price. It said, "You will be billed for just one chess player per month at $37.50 each." I did a quick calculation and learned that 32 x $37.50 equals $1,200! Well, that settled that! No one on my Christmas list was going to be treated so extravagantly, and even if someone were, he or she would choose something other than an ornate chess game.

Since the dawn of civilization men and women have built monuments to the gods of mythology. Now, once again, here they were—lifeless, powerless figures posed on a marble board. So much for the gods of mythology!

Every day I praise my heavenly Father for the privilege of knowing that I am a child of His! What a difference understanding this reality has made in my life! It is He and He alone to whom I trust my "moves." I believe that my life is not a game of chance, but a life so valuable in God's sight that He was willing for His only Son to die that I might live! He repeatedly assures me in His Word that I can trust Him with my good days and my not-so-good ones. He has promised never to leave me, or forsake me. In fact, He has promised to make the last "move" in my behalf when He sends His Son to defend me on the great judgment day! Praise God, my God is REAL!   ROSE OTIS

FEBRUARY 10

Peace Which Passeth Understanding

Thou wilt keep him in perfect peace, whose mind is stayed on thee: because he trusteth in thee. Isa. 26:3.

In October 1989 a dream came true for me—a dream that I sometimes thought would never be fulfilled. I had the rare opportunity of having my three sisters and brother in my home for a time of happy fellowship and reunion. Unfortunately, these happy occasions had been lacking since the death of our dear father 14 years before. We were scattered over three large states of Australia and were all living busy lives. Then our chance came. We had such a happy time during those few days—a time for looking back and remembering. Little did we realize that it would be the last occasion we would have fellowship together.

A few weeks later my younger sister, Heather, had to undergo corrective surgery. The operation revealed advanced inoperable cancer. This was very sad news for all the family. At this time Heather again committed herself to the Lord of her life, trusting in

His promises. Never once did she complain or question, Why me?

Being a nurse and having spent nine years in a mission hospital in Kenya, I had seen many people face death under varying circumstances and conditions. I had watched with a sad heart the varied rites and ceremonies of their relatives looking for the evil spirits who had stolen away their loved ones. I had heard the soul-chilling calls to keep other spirits away and seen the fear and agony written on their faces. No peace was found there, no trust in a loving heavenly Father.

By April 1990 it became evident that Heather's life journey was drawing to a close. Her faith and trust in God and His divine power never wavered. She knew that the Lord could heal her if it was His will. She rested in His promises, meanwhile, doing all in her power to stay and overcome this enemy.

When hospitalization became necessary, I arranged to spend as much time with my sister as possible. During those last three weeks of her life I witnessed a greater peace, trust, and cheerful resignation to God's will than I had ever seen before. Thankful each day for the little things—the presence of her family, a soothing shower, the kind attention of the nursing staff, a beautiful flower, visits from friends—she responded with cheery smiles from a heart at peace with her Lord.

One morning as my older sisters and I arrived, almost afraid to enter her room, she smiled and said, "Please don't leave me today. Today is the day. I'd like to say one more goodbye to my family, and please, one more prayer by the pastor." The family and pastor were soon there. With a radiant smile on her face, she weakly hugged and kissed her two grandchildren, took a moment's rest, and then looked at each of us and said, "I just want you all to know how much I love you." Lifting a weary hand, she waved as a "Bye-bye" whispered from her lips.

Heather taught me that day the true meaning of today's text. We each can have this peace which passes understanding as we daily commit our lives to our heavenly Father's care and trust completely in His wonderful promises.   VEYRL DAWN WERE

A Chain Reaction

But the fruit of the Spirit is love. Gal. 5:22.

Wouldn't it be wonderful if the Holy Spirit did something really special in our church? These words rang in my mind one Sabbath as I looked fondly over our congregation. Our church included many dear people, some of whom were working actively for the Lord, but the unity didn't seem to be there. *I'd love for Women's Ministries to be instrumental in bringing us together,* I thought, *but what can we do?*

Our biweekly prayer luncheon seemed to be a good place to start. I asked the ladies what they would like to see done in our church. Their answers were as varied as their personalities.

"I'd like to see a vespers program started," said one young mother. "I hate just coming to church and then going home to close the Sabbath by ourselves. I'd like our children to see that others keep Sabbath the same way we do."

"Why don't we start a prayer vine so people can call in a request and know that many others will soon be praying?"

"Isn't there some way to show more love?" a timid voice asked softly. We stopped and thought about it awhile. "Doesn't it all boil down to that?" we wondered.

Soon one of our ladies agreed to coordinate a biweekly vespers program, and the church responded gladly. Many families were willing to plan an occasional program. Men and women alike volunteered to be "on the prayer vine" and the comfort of that ministry is now widespread inside and outside the church. "I just never knew that many people cared about me," said one brother.

One of the best things that happened was that women's ministries led out in a full quarter's midweek prayer meetings, focusing on the Holy Spirit. There had been only a sporadic trickle of members on Wednesday evenings, but attendance quadrupled during that quarter and led into a series on spiritual gifts that was well attended. People agreed that the age and gender barriers should be overcome, and many new ministries are evolving as people seek to develop and use their gifts.

Recently I watched on Sabbath morning as our members greeted each other with bright smiles of true happiness. Later that evening I attended a vespers program that closed the Sabbath with love and reverence. Afterward, a spontaneous social occasion arose. *Truly*, I thought, *the Holy Spirit* has *done something really special in our church!*

"And now abideth faith, hope, charity, these three; but the greatest of these is charity" (1 Cor. 13:13).   Lea Hardy

Love Developed

Now we see but a poor reflection as in a mirror; then we shall see face to face. Now I know in part; then I shall know fully, even as I am fully known. 1 Cor. 13:12, NIV.

Small I wandered
Before—lowly
Humbled by Your presence.
Then gradually
Became encased
In a shell
Of my own making.
Father,
I want to
Break out of this
Cocoon of
Judgment and criticism:
The hardened walls
Of pride
That reveal
Only more clearly
The underdevelopment
Of a soul.
So many changes
I want
And in that wanting
Force a reflection
In others.
But now,
I feel a pulse of
Love—
A calling out,
To burst
Through this facade

And emerge,
Wet and trembling,
Into reality.

CHERI SCHROEDER

FEBRUARY 13

A Sabbath Morning Prayer

In the morning, O Lord, you hear my voice; in the morning
I lay my requests before you and wait in expectation. Ps.
5:3, NIV.

Eternal Father,
    It is so good to be here in Your house today. I praise You for Your wisdom in creating the Sabbath. You knew how much Your children would need this time with You away from our daily busyness.

I am needy this morning, Lord. I confess my sins and ask Your forgiveness, knowing that only as I forgive others can You forgive me.

Thank You for the young people surrounding me here in Your house this day. Their presence brings me hope for the future, and I am happy in their love for You. Pour on them Your richest blessings as they continue to keep their faces turned toward You in love and service. They are a very precious heritage to many—may they become precious to all. Help me to love them as Jesus would were He on earth today.

Thank You for being with me this past week. Some of the days were good days; some were full of worry and frustration. But You supplied me with strength for my journey and brought me again to Your house of worship. I come in gratitude and praise for Your blessings, and in supplication for Your presence to give me direction and wisdom to deal with problems that Satan throws in my pathway.

Help me to have vigorous, daring thoughts for Your cause on this earth. Give me such trust in Your goodness that I will willingly walk wherever You lead; active compassion for all who enter my personal world in need of tender, loving care; and a clear vision of Your plan for me and wisdom in achieving it.

And Father, may my faith be such a happy and joyous one that others will be able to see and accept Your deep love for them, too.

In Jesus' name and for His sake, I pray. Amen.

EVIE VANDEVERE

Foreign Exchange

Come, all you who are thirsty, come to the waters; and you who have no money, come, buy and eat! Come, buy wine and milk without money and without cost. Why spend money on what is not bread, and your labor on what does not satisfy? Listen, listen to me, and eat what is good, and your soul will delight in the richest of fare. Isa. 55:1-3, NIV.

Being the wife of a career treasurer, I have had a lot of exposure to the world of finance. Often I have heard of the problems connected with foreign exchange in financing the work of God around the world. Money values fluctuate rapidly and frequently, making it hard to know from day to day what your money is worth.

Each day we are involved in some form of exchange. In our personal transactions we are interested in making the very best exchange possible, whether it be an exchange for services, goods, ideas, or relationships.

The people of Isaiah's day were trying to find happiness and security, but they were looking in the wrong places and spending their money for things that did not satisfy. Then one day Isaiah stood before them and said, "Come, all you who are thirsty, come to the waters; and you who have no money, come, buy and eat! Come, buy wine and milk without money and without cost" (Isa. 55:1, NIV).

Isaiah was telling the people about God's system of exchange—a truly foreign exchange that they were not used to. Isaiah was saying that God was offering them security, happiness, and salvation, and that it was free.

For all whose lives are burdened and made miserable by sin, He freely offers forgiveness and cleansing. In place of all that is bad and evil He offers to put that which is good.

God offers us peace for worry, love for hatred, joy for sorrow, hope for despair, freedom for bondage, courage for fear, contentment for restlessness, self-control for slavery, a new heart for an old, and eternal life for death. These exchanges God offers are free to us, but they cost God a great deal, even the death of His only Son. "Christ was treated as we deserve, that we might be treated as He deserves. He was condemned for our sins, in which He had no share, that we might be justified by His righteousness, in which we had no share. He suffered the death that was ours, that we might

receive the life which was His. 'With his stripes we are healed' "
(*The Desire of Ages*, p. 25).

This is real foreign exchange. It took someone who was a
foreigner to our sinful world, a foreigner to our sinful nature, to
make this kind of wonderful, almost unbelievable exchange possible.

God's exchange rates never fluctuate, and they are never
unfavorable. He lovingly invites us to take advantage of His foreign
exchange.   RUTH MURRILL

We Went Outdoors to Find Him

*And he said to them, "Come away by yourselves to a lonely
place, and rest a while." For many were coming and going,
and they had no leisure even to eat. Mark 6:31, RSV.*

One of the most memorable times in my life was our camping
trip in northern Saskatchewan. It was at a time when my soul
and physical being longed for rest. So when our sons displayed an
interest in camping, all other plans were abandoned. With the car
loaded with canoes, camping gear, and two teenage sons, we
headed to the great northern area of La Ronge. Parking our car in
a safe spot, we canoed Otter Lake for nearly two hours before
reaching the perfect spot. It was an island that would be occupied
by only our family. The island was covered with luscious green
moss so thick it could have served as a bed if necessary. Stately trees
and calm blue waters brought a spirit of tranquillity to my soul.
Simple food cooked over an open fire beat all the banquets I had
ever attended.

Camping had once been a favorite with our family, but with the
arrival of those teen years and the busyness of our lives, it had been
forgotten. Once more we were together without the city lights
beckoning us to some event. We had time to talk and laugh together
until dusk, when the mosquitoes appeared and sent us all scurrying
to our tents.

Sabbath was a day of quiet activity. Sunday morning we began
our tour of the area, by canoe of course. We followed the map
carefully, as we didn't wish to have an extended holiday. Nestled up
in that great northern country was the most beautiful waterfall. We
spent many hours basking in the sun and watching the water
rush by.

When Monday morning arrived, I felt refreshed and closer to

God. I had gained a different perspective on life. I knew why God had given the invitation, "Come ye yourselves apart into a desert place, and rest a while" (Mark 6:31). We, as families, need that rest and quiet time with each other and with God. May we each make that effort to "come apart . . . and rest a while." ROBERTA SCHAFER

FEBRUARY 16

Suntan

And we all, with unveiled face, beholding the glory of the Lord, are being changed into his likeness from one degree of glory to another; for this comes from the Lord who is the Spirit. 2 Cor. 3:18, RSV.

August is the time of year for vacation and suntan. Where the sun has its way, I'm brown as a toasted bun. But underneath the shorts and bathing suit areas, I'm my pale self.

There are times in which my Christian walk is like that. When I expose only a portion of my life to the influence of Christ, the Son, only a part of me is changed. As long as I keep portions of my life from Christ's radiance, I am only a shirt-sleeve Christian, not totally changed. I must continually expose myself to His love to keep my glow.

Many see their faith fade, even die, because they neglect their daily exposure to God's Son. Day-by-day exposure will keep you healthy and blessed.

God, let Your light shine on us, in us, and through us.

LOUISE HANNAH KOHR

FEBRUARY 17

Two Conversions Contrasted

To open their eyes, and to turn them from darkness to light, and from the power of Satan unto God, that they may receive forgiveness of sins, and inheritance among them which are sanctified. Acts 26:18.

Conversion can be like a falling meteor or a sunrise," Billy Graham said. Perhaps this is the best way to differentiate between the two conversion experiences—one that takes place in a crisis situation and one that happens gradually, making it difficult to determine when the day dawns. Yet even in a gradual conversion there is the instant when the sun's disc appears on the horizon and death is replaced by life.

We can see these contrasting conversions take place in the lives of two fiery fisherman who would become two fishermen on fire—John and Peter. The term *conversion* means "a turning." Jesus knew there was nothing He could do for these men until they turned from their pride.

John was first impressed when Jesus called a little child and tenderly folded it in His arms, saying, "Except ye be converted and become as little children, ye shall not enter into the kingdom of heaven" (Matt. 18:3). John began to meditate. Did this mean that he could forget about competition and pride? Is this what made Jesus so dearly special? Could he just be himself and be loved by God? If God loved him, who else or what else mattered? The ones he'd been trying to impress didn't like him anyway, since they perceived him as a threat. *Wow! This is good news! Let me learn more!* John thought.

Day by day, in contrast to his own violent spirit, John watched the tenderness and forbearance of Jesus and heard His lessons of humility and patience. He opened his heart. Self was hid in Christ. Eventually, because of his receptive spirit and confiding trust, the Saviour was able to communicate His deepest spiritual teachings through him. John's conversion was like the sunrise.

John alone stayed with Jesus at the judgment hall when Peter, after denying Jesus, rushed back to the garden. There Peter fell exhausted upon his face and wished that he might die. Why, oh, why hadn't he used his big mouth to defend Jesus instead of hurting Him so—the One who would do *anything* for him? Where had he been when Jesus' anguished weeping had soaked the earth? Sleeping! That's where he'd been—sleeping! How could he ever face the other disciples again? Better to have fled as they had than to help crucify Jesus as he had. Oh, how *could* he have done such a lily-livered thing!

When Peter finally rose from the dirt, he was a converted man. He had renounced pride and self love. The turning was complete. All he loved now was Jesus. His conversion was like the falling meteor.

Soon there will appear in the East a small black cloud that grows to surpass the brilliance of the noonday sun. Jesus at its center, arrayed in all His glory, will come for His converted people—some Timothys who were molded to Christ from birth, some Peters who were plunged into tear baths of crisis conversions, and some Johns, who discern *now* on the horizon the circle of the sun's disc.　　　　　　　　　　　　　　　　　　　Janet Kangas

Whatever Happened to Barabbas?

So Pilate gave sentence that their demand should be granted. He released the man who had been thrown into prison for insurrection and murder, whom they asked for; but Jesus he delivered up to their will. Luke 23:24-25, RSV.

We found this man perverting our nation, . . . and saying that he himself is Christ, a king," (Luke 23:2). Angry, tired, and anxious to be done with Jesus, the chief priests present their accusations to Pilate and wait impatiently for his solution.

Pilate realizes that their accusations stem from their jealousy of Jesus and his examination of the case doesn't yield a guilty verdict. But what should he do? There is still a raging mob before him and an innocent Man beside him. Ah, yes. There's that old custom. And it just might help him secure Christ's release.

The Desire of Ages, page 733, tells us that at Passover it was a habit to release a prisoner of the people's choosing. "The Roman authorities held a prisoner named Barabbas, who was under sentence of death. This man had claimed to be the Messiah. . . . Under satanic delusion he claimed that whatever he could obtain by theft and robbery was his own. . . . By giving the people a choice between this man and the innocent Saviour, Pilate thought to arouse them to a sense of justice. . . . So, turning to the crowd, he said with great earnestness, 'Whom will ye that I release unto you? Barabbas, or Jesus which is called Christ?' "

We know how the mob answered Pilate's question. We know what happened to Christ. But whatever happened to Barabbas? What did he do after his release? Did he watch Pilate flog Jesus? Did he listen to the soldiers mockingly hail Jesus as king of the Jews? Did he stumble up the path to Golgotha with the others to observe history's most singular event? How did he react to the innocent Jesus taking his place?

But even more important, why should we care about the answers to these questions in the first place? Why? Because Barabbas represents sinful human beings. Because in many ways, you and I are like Barabbas.

First of all, Barabbas was held prisoner under sentence of death. We too are prisoners—prisoners of sin. And the penalty for such is the same sentence Barabbas faced—death. But Barabbas did not die. He went free because Jesus, an innocent Man, took his place.

Likewise, we needn't die, because He who knew no sin died for our sins.

We are also like Barabbas because there are times when we too claim to be a messiah. How often we try to save ourselves! How often we twist the words of the song, saying "I, but not Christ." Which one of us has *never* pursued our own righteousness by trying to be good? Which one of us has *never* forgotten that we are helpless, and that when we walk on water we should always keep our eyes on Jesus?

Yes, you and I are like Barabbas. So I can't help wondering, Whatever happened to Barabbas? LYNDELLE CHIOMENTI

FEBRUARY 19

Thy Word

But he said, Yea rather, blessed are they that hear the word of God, and keep it. Luke 11:28.

Years ago I had a speaking appointment in a large city. It was in the days before we flew in airplanes, and I had taken the train from my hometown. Arriving in the city exhausted, I hailed a taxi and instructed the driver to take me to a hotel. As I recall, there were no Sheratons or Marriotts then, or any of the now popular hotels we know around the world.

The bellhop took my bags and showed me to my room. In one quick glance I surveyed my tiny habitation. To my disappointment, I discovered that the room's only window opened out onto a fire escape. I felt apprehensive. The porter's look was not to my liking, and the window couldn't be locked.

After the porter left and I had bolted the door, I glanced over at the dresser and noticed a Gideon Bible. Immediately I felt better — more secure. While the devil is very active everywhere (and this includes hotels), it was good to know that the owner or manager had allowed Bibles to be placed in the establishment.

I walked over to the dresser and picked up the Bible. As I leafed through its pages, my eyes caught several things people had written who had evidently stayed in the room. Some were curses, some filthy words. These have long since been erased from my mind, yet I have never forgotten what someone had penned just inside the front cover: "This Book will keep you from sin, and sin will keep you from this Book."

How true these words are! When we are indulging in sin, we are not studying God's Word. And when we are reading and studying the Bible, sin is not appealing to us. We come to abhor it. The psalmist wrote for us in these sinful days, "Thy word have I hid in mine heart, that I might not sin against thee" (Ps. 119:11).

MARION SIMMONS

FEBRUARY 20

Jesus, Rose of Sharon

Thanks be to God, Who in Christ always leads us in triumph . . . and through us spreads and makes evident the fragrance of the knowledge of God everywhere, for we are the sweet fragrance of Christ [which exhales] unto God, [discernible alike] among those who are being saved and among those who are perishing. 2 Cor. 2:14, 15, Amplified.

As a child I can recall the wonderful odor of an after-shave lotion that my father used to wear called King's Men. It came in a beautiful gold-colored bottle shaped something like a crown. I liked it so much that I used to sneak into the bathroom and dab some of it behind my ears. I thought it smelled better than anything else I had ever encountered.

Second only to King's Men was the incredibly delectable odor from the cookie factory near one of the freeways in our town. On the afternoons that I drove along that freeway, I never missed an opportunity to roll down my window and inhale the smell of lemon cookies baking.

What a lovely idea that we can be a fragrance for Christ; a fragrance that is easily identified. In Ezekiel 20:41 the Lord tells the children of Israel that He will accept them as a pleasant odor when He leads them out from the peoples and gathers them out of the countries in which they have been scattered. Their allegiance to Him as the one God amid heathen nations that worshiped many gods must indeed have been a sweet aroma to Him.

Ida A. Guirey wrote the words to a lovely hymn entitled "Jesus, Rose of Sharon." The words of her song sum up what Christian living is all about—and I cannot think of a flower with a fragrance more sweet than a rose.

"Be full of love for others, following the example of Christ who loved you and gave himself to God as a sacrifice to take away your sins. And God was pleased, for Christ's love for you was like sweet perfume to him" (Eph. 5:2, TLB). There you have it. The ingredients to this perfume are neither secret or closely guarded. God is

75

very plain about what pleases Him and how we can learn to wear His perfume so that all can recognize it as belonging to Christ.

It is my daily prayer that my life will be a lovely fragrance to God and to those whose lives I touch. SHEILA BIRKENSTOCK SANDERS

Strong Dust

Come to me, all you who are weary and burdened, and I will give you rest. Take my yoke upon you and learn from me, for I am gentle and humble in heart, and you will find rest for your souls. For my yoke is easy and my burden is light. Matt. 11:28, NIV.

L ook up, little woman,
From the dust
Whence you came."

"It is not so easy, Lord.
See the small flecks
Of interest flashing."

"Seek Me first."

"But Lord,
The dust weighs heavily."

"Cast your cares on Me."

"But how quickly
The dust runs
Through the hourglass, Lord!"

"Come out, little woman,
From this
Clay prison of time—
Walk with Me."

"But Lord, dust is weak
And shifting.
How can I be
What You say?"

"I am your strength
And your foundation.
Lean on Me.
I love you."

Then I turned my autumn face
To His
And in the Son-light
I grew.

CHERI SCHROEDER

FEBRUARY 22

The Path to Higher Life

God resisteth the proud, but giveth grace unto the humble.
James 4:6.

One of the five finalists in a beauty pageant was being interviewed in the last round of appearances before the judges' big decision. She was asked: "What characteristic do you consider to be the most important one for the winner to possess?" The young contestant replied, "I believe the most beautiful characteristic a woman can possess is humility, because humility, of all the characteristics, is the one characteristic that the possessor is unaware that she has."

Although I am not promoting beauty contests, I like to think that this woman's response was the deciding factor that won her the contest; no other finalist offered so rich a response to the same question.

Humility takes many different faces. Frank, a 90-year-old widower, received a framed letter from the president of the United States in honor of his work in the community, which included delivering meals on wheels to senior citizens 25 years his junior. Along with a dozen other awards, it lies hidden in a drawer rather than taking its place on the wall. Frank just doesn't feel comfortable displaying something in his home that broadcasts his good deeds to the world. He simply helps people because they need it, and the only reward he expects is the good feeling that always comes when he reaches out to others.

Compare, for a moment, the beauty pageant winner's response, "Humility is the one characteristic the owner doesn't know she possesses," with a remark by Muhammad Ali: "Tonight I'm goin' to be humble. I'm goin' to do it. Because there's nothin'—just nothin'—that I can't do!"

The comparison leads us to agree with Andrew Murray: "Just as water ever seeks and fills the lowest place, so the moment God finds the creature abased and empty, His glory and power flow in to exalt and bless. . . . Here is the path to higher life. Down, lower down!"

JANET KANGAS

FEBRUARY 23

One of a Kind

For Thou didst form my inward parts; Thou didst weave me in my mother's womb. I will give thanks to Thee, for I am fearfully and wonderfully made; Wonderful are Thy works, and my soul knows it very well. Ps. 139:13, 14, NASB.

A daughter with a good sense of humor decided she would play a trick on her mother, who was an impeccable seamstress. The mother had informed her that when gift time came around she wanted something her family had bought—not just made for her. The fun-loving daughter had noticed a dress in a store window she thought her mother would like for her birthday. After purchasing fabric and sewing the dress, she clipped a designer original label out of one of her dresses and sewed it to the garment she had just finished making for her mother. When the mother opened the package on her birthday, she excitedly put the dress on and strutted before the mirror, not knowing that her daughter had actually made it. She respected the workmanship and design of the dress because of the label.

God sews His label in every person He creates. We are of eternal value because all of us are His "originals." He never intended for us to lose that identity, and certainly never wanted anything to spoil His workmanship. He knows us as individuals, not as a collective mass of people. Furthermore, He has a specific plan for each one of our lives. Some people question the reason for their existence. Such thoughts especially trouble us when we encounter disappointment or cope with depression. A major reason God gave us the Bible is to remind us that each one of us is His "special" person, and that He created us for a specific purpose.

The *Good News Bible* makes verse 13 of our text especially pointed: "You created every part of me; you put me together in my mother's womb" (TEV). Not only did our Lord create every cell in our bodies, but He even knows our particular life span: "His days are determined, the number of his months is with Thee, and his limits Thou hast set so that he cannot pass" (Job 14:5, NASB). God even decided the good that only you as an individual could do. "For we are His workmanship, created in Christ Jesus for good works, which God prepared beforehand, that we should walk in them" (Eph. 2:10, NASB). Thus He created you for a purpose and has a plan for your life. Never doubt that you are special—one of a kind. Why not thank God for your uniqueness and your specialness, for you belong to Him, both by creation and redemption.

MARIE SPANGLER

FEBRUARY 24

Was It My Guardian Angel?

The angel of the Lord encamps around those who fear him, and delivers them. Ps. 34:7, RSV.

It was just a few days before Christmas, but instead of feeling festive this holiday season, I felt overwhelmed by depression. Only a foreigner studying in a Western country can identify with the frustration and discouragement I had been experiencing lately. I'd been tempted many times to quit my study at the hospital laboratory where I was doing my practicals and go home.

I stood on a corner waiting for a friend who was attending an evening class close by. As I watched the shoppers rushing frantically to buy their last-minute gifts, I thought of how hectic and demanding my own life had become. The sound of Salvation Army bells and tired, crying children faded into the distance as my mind turned toward God. I hadn't troubled anyone with my dreary feelings today, but God knew how I felt. Somehow I wished He'd reach out to me to brighten the darkness that filled my heart.

Suddenly, a woman I had never seen before embraced me tightly and whispered into my ear, "Be of good courage. Cheer up!" It all happened in a flash. Before I came to myself, she was gone, lost in the passing crowd.

Who was this woman? I wondered. How did *she* know how I was feeling? Was it my guardian angel? I'll probably never know who she was until Jesus comes, but the important thing is that I was comforted. That strange yet precious experience was my stay throughout the years I spent there. It made me feel confident that the Lord was with me.

Now when I run into a difficult situation that vivid experience comes to mind, bringing with it strong assurance that God is near and that He cares.

THELMA NORTEY

The Blessings of Solitude

Be still, and know that I am God. Ps. 46:10.

I stood inside an empty apartment that an acquaintance had suggested I consider renting. I had been thinking of moving from the large house I shared with another tenant. Oh, to have a kitchen of my own again and freedom to move about without considering the routines of another person!

The apartment was located in a complex of units rented by singles and young couples. It had plenty of space for my belongings, extra storage, and a sunny kitchen. Yet as I stood there looking around, something made me feel uncomfortable. What was this uneasiness?

Returning to my current living quarters, I sat in silence in my favorite chair. Looking out into the parklike backyard, I asked myself, "Why was there unrest in the other apartment? What was the difference?"

I watched as squirrels explored a grove of trees where foliage gently swayed in the wind. The sun made sparkles on the granite patio where cats lazily stretched out to bask in the warmth.

Then I heard it—the silence. No vehicles rushing by, no doors slamming, no blaring music, no television. God's restful silence of nature. Birds called soft messages among the rustling leaves, and scurrying squirrels dropped occasional acorns and pieces of bark. It was a restful place to quiet the mind and to be still; a place to experience God. What a perfect location to practice, in silence, knowing God and recognizing the divine voice. I would miss this peaceful experience if I moved.

The Bible speaks of quietness and stillness, especially in connection with the calm after upheavals and wars. Many descriptive words point out the restful, quiet lifestyle that is promised as God's gift to those who will inhabit the land reclaimed by our King-Deliverer. Until that time we are admonished to be still and know God. Let's make it our goal to spend quiet time with Him each day. As we do, He will reveal His will and love to us.

LORNA LAWRENCE

Herstory

Restore to me the joy of your salvation. Ps. 51:12, NIV.

The warmth of the New England autumn day startled me. It had been cold and damp for weeks, and the Indian summer weather was delightful. I walked down the street to my parked car with a bounce in my step, catching every playful breeze I could in my hair.

Then I saw her. A woman walking alone in the park, oblivious to the bright sunshine and the blaze of color in the trees above her. Her gaze seemed vacant, as if deep unmet needs or a hidden wound absorbed her total concentration. Wrapped tightly in her woolen coat, her hunched body reminded me of a fetus. It was as if she had curled herself over her past, as if she were protecting herself from her present, hugging her heart to reduce the chill. How could I expect her to stand tall and recognize a summer day when winter was the only season she ever knew?

She reminded me of another stooped woman who had great needs and who was fortunate enough to find Jesus within her reach. In His healing touch He gave hope to all of us who carry cavernous hurts that impede our lives, that we too will be healed. He knows our pain. He recognizes our needs. He will restore us. His care is not withheld.

Recovery reaches some of us sooner than others. Like the woman healed by Christ's touch, some of us may have healing deferred many years. In the meantime, herstory does not allow us to diminish the certainty of our own healing:

"Just then a woman who had been subject to bleeding for twelve years came up behind him and touched the edge of his cloak. She said to herself, 'If I only touch his cloak, I will be healed.' Jesus turned and saw her. 'Take heart, daughter,' he said, 'your faith has healed you.' And the woman was healed from that moment" (Matt. 9:20-22, NIV).

GILLIAN GERATY

How Shall We Keep the Sabbath?

Then he said to them, "The Sabbath was made for man, not man for the Sabbath. So the Son of Man is Lord even of the Sabbath." Mark 2:27, NIV.

God is merciful. His requirements are reasonable, in accordance with the goodness and benevolence of His character. The object of the Sabbath was that all mankind might be benefited....

"In order to keep the Sabbath holy, it is not necessary that we enclose ourselves in walls, shut away from the beautiful scenes of nature and from the free, invigorating air of heaven. We should in no case allow burdens and business transactions to divert our minds upon the Sabbath of the Lord, which He has sanctified. . . . The Sabbath was made for man, to be a blessing to him by calling his mind from secular labor to contemplate the goodness and glory of God. It is necessary that the people of God assemble to talk of Him, to interchange thoughts and ideas in regard to the truths contained in His Word, and to devote a portion of time to appropriate prayer. But these seasons, even upon the Sabbath, should not be made tedious by their length and lack of interest.

"During a portion of the day, all should have an opportunity to be out of doors. How can children receive a more correct knowledge of God, and their minds be better impressed, than in spending a portion of their time out of doors, not in play, but in company with their parents? Let their young minds be associated with God in the beautiful scenery of nature, let their attention be called to the tokens of His love to man in His created works, and they will be attracted and interested. . . .

"All who love God should do what they can to make the Sabbath a delight, holy and honorable. . . . We should devote time to interesting our children. . . . We can walk out with them in the open air; we can sit with them in the groves and in the bright sunshine, and give their restless minds something to feed upon by conversing with them upon the works of God, and can inspire them with love and reverence by calling their attention to the beautiful objects in nature.

"The Sabbath should be made so interesting to our families that its weekly return will be hailed with joy. . . . Parents, make the Sabbath a delight, that your children may look forward to it and have a welcome in their hearts for it" *(Testimonies,* vol. 2, pp. 582-585).
                                                          ELLEN G. WHITE

Cast the First Stone

Jesus looked up and said to her, "Woman, where are they?
Has no one condemned you?" She said, "No one, Lord."
And Jesus said, "either do I condemn you; go, and do not
sin again" John 8:10, 11, RSV.

This story is very familiar, but you're probably used to looking at it as a spectator. For a few minutes I want you to stand in the bare feet of the woman.

Only minutes ago you were safe in your cozy, seductive room. Now you've been dragged through the streets and must face the penalty for your crime. All your senses are screaming against what is coming. Alongside the anguish is the terrible feeling of injustice. The man who was with you has gone slinking back to his wife. You feel desperately alone, with no one to defend you—to explain about your childhood spent in loveless poverty or the lack of a dowry to attract a decent husband.

Suddenly you're catapulted from the rowdy mob and flung to the ground in front of the last Man on earth you want to see at that moment. You've heard Jesus of Nazareth speak and you *know* He's a good man. They're asking *Him* to judge you! Shame and terror wash over you in sickening waves. You can't meet His gaze, so you fix your eyes on His feet and wait for Him to confirm the death sentence.

Then you notice that everything has grown quiet. And in the stillness you see His finger writing in the dust. Then you hear Him say, "Let him who is without sin cast the first stone." He continues writing, and you hear stones dropping to the ground and feet shuffling away.

You can hardly breathe. *He* is without sin, some say. Does He intend to carry out the sentence by Himself? You steel yourself for the first blow. Maybe He intends there to be only one—a mighty blow to the head. The day you listened to Him He spoke of mercy and justice. That would take care of both—a quick death.

But you don't want to die! You're still young. You love life. If you could just have one more chance, you'd live a better life—a *clean* life . . . But you've sinned a terrible sin. He knows it. He's sinless. He's picking up the stone now. He's coming toward you. You grit your teeth, willing yourself not to go out screaming and begging for mercy.

Then you hear, "Woman, where are those who accuse you?"

You hardly dare to look around, but it's just you and He and the question: "Does no one condemn you?"

You hear your own whisper, "No one, Lord."

Then the most beautiful words you'll ever hear: "Neither do I condemn you; go, and do not sin again."

Relief floods over you. You want to kiss His feet, but He knows what you are—*have been.* You can't touch perfection with sinful lips, but you can show Him that His mercy and goodness can do for you what man's hatred couldn't do. One day you'll give Him the honor He deserves.   ANITA MARSHALL

MARCH 1

The Pivotal Question

Where is the one who has been born king of the Jews?
Matt. 2:2, NIV.

In one version of the legend of the Holy Grail, Percival, one of King Arthur's knights of the Round Table, traveled far to visit the kingdom of the Fisher King in order to obtain the secret of the Grail (believed to be the cup used by Christ during the Last Supper). When he arrived, however, he found the entire kingdom in utter ruin and life at a standstill. The king was incurably sick, and the palace, gardens, and towers were crumbling. Even nature was inoperative; the animals would not breed and the trees refused to bear fruit. To make matters worse, there was no one in the kingdom who dared to ask what the matter was. But Percival fearlessly strode right up to where the king sat slumped on his throne. "Where is the Grail?" demanded the courageous knight. The question rang throughout the kingdom and suddenly everything came to life again.

What was it about that question that produced the miracle? It was a question about the supreme reality, the sacred source of life and immortality. The Wise Men asked a similar question of Herod when they innocently asked the haughty king, "Where is the one who has been born king of the Jews?" Even as it unleashed persecution, this fundamental question opened heaven's treasure trove for all the human race. A world languishing in the death throes of sin heard that question ring across the sphere, and suddenly, eternal life was available to every living soul. Searching for God always implies that life-giving question that, when asked out of a fervent desire to know God, will bring boundless joy and life.

Jesus must have had this in mind when He likened the kingdom of God to a woman who had lost a valuable coin. She lit a lamp, swept the whole house, and searched relentlessly until she found it. Her joy was so great that she called in her friends to celebrate with her. Isaiah invites us to "Seek the Lord while he may be found; call on him while he is near" (Isa. 55:6, NIV). The implication here is that there may be a time when we will call on the Lord, but to no avail. The time for seeking is now, while there is time to do so. The psalmist assures us that "those who seek the Lord lack no good thing" (Ps. 34:10, NIV). The promise is that we will never be disappointed when we ask that pivotal question in our heartfelt search for God. LOURDES E. MORALES GUDMUNDSSON

MARCH 2

The Waiting

He who testifies to these things says, "Yes, I am coming soon." Rev. 22:20, NIV.

They stood next to the car, a bouquet of little girls, begging me not to leave. "Don't go, Mommy. Please don't go."

"When are you coming home?"

"Take me with you."

I looked helplessly at my husband, Gerald. The trip was necessary. Unavoidable. We would be gone a mere week, and my father had come miles to stay with our daughters. They would be fine. They would stop crying.

I gave each one a final hug and turned toward the car, but the 8-year-old clung to me, tears raining down her cheeks. At last I pried her arms away, trying to brush away her tears with promises of return. Time means little to a child, and she would not be comforted.

Gerald started the car. We backed up, turned, and slowly drove away while my father shepherded the girls toward the house. Noelle stopped, digging her fists into her eyes. I saw her lips move, but I couldn't hear her words. Then I let my own tears fall, vowing that I'd never leave a child that heartbroken again.

It was nearly midnight when we arrived in Washington, D.C. In the motel room I called home, even as I kicked off my shoes. Dad said that the children were fine. They were asleep, of course. I shouldn't worry.

The days passed, the hours packed with meetings, questions, and problems. Each evening when I fell into bed, my mind traveled backward, across black ribbons of highway, down the Shenandoah Valley, across Virginia, through the Smoky Mountains and middle Tennessee to our own four acres and tree-covered ridge, my morning glories, and three little girls who counted the days until our return.

Not that they missed me every moment. I knew that, no doubt, my thoughts turned to them more often than they thought of me. Their grandfather was a good baby-sitter. He'd buy popsicles and potato chips for them, walk with them in the woods, push them in the swings. He could be persuaded to talk about the olden days and would probably let them stay up past their bedtime. Mostly I thought of Noelle. I could not erase the feel of her arms around my neck, and I knew that she especially was waiting for me to get home.

Finally the time came for the trip back. We packed our suitcases, got up early, and headed south. Traffic was light, the sun bright. It felt good to be going home.

And yet 700 miles is *700 miles,* and the 55 m.p.h. speed limit made them drag. The sun climbed, hung directly above for a short while, then began its descent, faster, faster, until lavender shadows bathed the distant hills. Then darkness. We were still a long way from home.

Somehow, with the falling darkness, I felt desolate. My children were waiting, and through no fault of my own I wasn't there with them. If sheer will could have bridged the distance, if love could have erased the miles—but it couldn't. Three little faces etched in my memory called me home. Three little children waited, and we were late.

In the darkness, the car slowly covering the miles, my mind wandered beyond this homecoming. Could it be for Christ, as for mothers throughout history, that the pain of separation is all the more intense because He knows His children are anxiously awaiting His return? Could Christ's heart possibly ache as badly as mine did then, wanting to will the miles away, mentally clasping each landmark to my heart, so glad to be nearing home? Or does Christ have an infinite capacity for longing, for love?

Perhaps that is why we are told that "it is of the Lord's mercies that we are not consumed, because his compassions fail not" (Lam. 3:22) and "the Lord is not slack concerning his promise, as some men count slackness; but is longsuffering to us-ward, not willing that any should perish, but that all should come to repentance" (2 Peter 3:9).

PENNY ESTES WHEELER

On Being Ready

Therefore you also must be ready; for the Son of man is coming at an hour you do not expect. Matt. 24:44, RSV.

Three-year-old Alex and his parents will be arriving tomorrow from Africa. We've done a lot of preparing. Beds are made; the refrigerator is full. We bought a stool for Alex to stand on so he can reach the sink. I've put a few precious items away from inquisitive fingers. On our last shopping trip Grandpa bought the largest bucket of Lego blocks in the store! I've been putting food out for the raccoons and skunks so they'll be used to coming for supper— Alex likes animals! We've borrowed a van for the trip to the airport. We've fastened a car seat in it.

We've been serious about our preparations because we fully believe Alex and his parents will come. We've prepared well because we're thrilled to have them come. We're excited!

Jesus promised the disciples He would return. But He warned them that they could not know for sure *when* He would come. His followers were to trust and know that if He went away, He would also come back, and take them to be with Him in the heavenly mansions (John 14:1-3).

To be sure they were ready at the right time, Jesus said His followers should live in readiness—that they should not *get* ready, but *be* ready. Christ said, "You also must be ready; for the Son of man is coming at an hour you do not expect." I've been thinking about my readiness for Christ's second coming as I've prepared for Alex's arrival. Being ready to receive family from afar takes time and effort. Being ready to receive Jesus also takes time and effort. Time to study, pray, serve; effort to not become weary in well-doing.

True, I do not know when Jesus is coming. But I can't delay my preparation. I must be ready, not only because I don't want to be left behind, but because living in readiness is exciting. "Even so, come, Lord Jesus!"   NANCY VYHMEISTER

The Cross and I

But far be it from me to glory except in the cross of our Lord Jesus Christ, by which the world has been crucified to me, and I to the world. Gal. 6:14, RSV.

I once took part in an ecumenical Easter symposium that asked each of the participants to answer the question "What does the cross mean to you?"

My answer: *Everything!*

The cross means everything to me, for without it I have nothing that is vitally important in this life, and without it there is no life to come. The cross has made all the difference. It has made the difference between guilt and forgiveness; between separation from God and reconciliation with Him; between fear and peace, despair and hope, defeat and victory.

In this life, in short, the cross means freedom from guilt, anxiety, and bondage to my own worst enemy, self. As Paul exults in 1 Corinthians 15:57: "Thanks be to God which giveth us the victory through our Lord Jesus Christ."

"If in this life only we have hope in Christ," Paul says, "we are of all men most miserable" (verse 19); for the cross means resurrection. It means hope for the future—an eternal future with freedom from pain and death and the dominion of darkness. It means a hereafter in which I can live the life God meant for us all to live, in the perfect conditions of Eden.

What does the cross mean to me? Ellen White says it best: "Christ was treated as we deserve, that we might be treated as He deserves. He was condemned for our sins, in which He had no share, that we might be justified by His righteousness, in which we had no share. He suffered the death which was ours, that we might receive the life which was His. 'With his stripes we are healed' " (*The Desire of Ages*, p. 25).　　　　　　　　　　JEANNE JORDAN

Facts Without Truth

And Abraham said of Sarah his wife, She is my sister: and Abimelech king of Gerar sent, and took Sarah. . . . And Abraham said, . . . they will slay me for my wife's sake. And yet indeed she is my sister; she is the daughter of my father, but not the daughter of my mother; and she became my wife. Gen. 20:2, 12.

Have you considered that there can be a difference between fact and truth? Abimelech, king of Gerar, knew there was. And when Sarah and Abraham had finished righting the wrongness of their plot to conceal her full identity, they both knew there was.

A high school teacher once told me he got tired of warning and rewarning several fellows in his class not to bring any more knives to school.

"The next one that brings any weapon to school will have it taken away," he promised. Two days later Jim brought a large jackknife to class and the teacher took it from him, telling him he could have it back at the end of the week to take home.

But the teacher was so disgusted with Jim's persistence in breaking the weapon rule that he threw the knife into the bathroom wastebasket. The school janitor, of course, dumped the wastebasket's contents—knife and all—into the large incinerator. As expected, Jim was waiting at the teacher's office Friday afternoon at 3:15.

"I've come for my knife, sir. You said I could have it at the end of this week. I promise I'll take it home and leave it there this time. Promise!"

"Sorry, Jim," the teacher replied. "I haven't seen your knife for several days. I don't know where it is now. Too bad." He faked a look of concern. As the teacher told me the story, he seemed quite pleased with himself.

"You see," he chuckled, "I really didn't know exactly where that bothersome knife was—it was probably out in the city dump by then. I just told Jim the truth, that's all." But had he?

Rather than confronting the issue, he resorted to word games. Rather than face the consequences of his mistake, he retreated into subterfuge semantics, purposely failing to define his terms. In short, rather than tell the truth, he told the facts.

Abimelech was shocked that Sarah and Abraham would have plotted to deceive him: "Thou hast done deeds unto me that ought not to be done," he accused (Gen. 20:9). Partial truths he could not accept.

Christians today have no more right than Abraham and Sarah did to confuse intentionally, being merely factual when others think they are also being truthful. If they do, one day God will say to such, "Thou hast done deeds unto me that ought not to be done."

WILMA MCCLARTY

MARCH 6

The Morning Son

But they who wait for the Lord shall renew their strength, they shall mount up with wings like eagles, they shall run and not be weary, they shall walk and not faint. Isa. 40:31, RSV.

Last night as I crawled into bed I said to myself, "I dread tomorrow." Only a mother could understand why I was feeling that way. You see, last night was our Revelation Seminar banquet. It was wonderful meeting all the precious people I'd heard about for so long. The food was delicious, and it was fun transforming the little church basement into a banquet hall.

But now I was home. It was very late when I tucked the children in—so late that I envisioned tired, grumpy children to live with the next day. (My boy promised me it would not be so. Precious optimism—I love it!) But I also had visions of the laundry room. To say the least, things had gotten a little out of hand with our washing machine on the blink. Piles of laundry had become mountains of laundry. The nursing home laundry was scheduled to be done tomorrow too.

We were low on bread, so baking had to be a priority tomorrow. There were dirty dishes in the sink. Waiting stacks of Sabbath school material and Horse Club material cluttered the countertop. Boxes of banquet fixings sat on the floor. The news-letter needed to be done. My assignment for Natural Remedies class needed to be done—it was due tomorrow. It seemed humanly impossible to meet the demands of the coming day.

Then tomorrow dawned. Sunlight flooded the world, and the birds filled the earth with their singing. Mother Nature was literally bursting with new life. It was a gorgeous morning that I opened my eyes to. I looked out our bedroom window toward the pasture, and six deer were bouncing along the canal road, all bathed in the golden sunlight of the sunrise. My spirits rose as I rose for the day.

I couldn't help joining the birds in singing praises to God. I too felt new life pulsating through my veins, and I was eager to tackle the tasks of the day before me.

What made the difference? What is the difference between night and day? The sunshine, of course. I suddenly thought of the disciples that dark night that Christ lay in the tomb. Their banqueting time with Him was over, and things were in a real mess. How discouraged and overwhelmed they felt—how they dreaded their tomorrow. But when morning dawned and the Sun of righteousness rose in all of His brightness and glory to everlasting life—their hearts burned within them. They felt revived, and they too could face their tasks of tomorrow.

"Then spake Jesus again unto them, saying, I am the light of the world: he that followeth me shall not walk in darkness, but shall have the light of life" (John 8:12).

May every day of yours be sunny, filled with the life-giving Sun of righteousness. And remember—after every dark night comes the dawn of a new day!   GERITA LIEBELT

MARCH 7

Improving the Lot of Women

There is neither Jew nor Greek, slave nor free, male nor female, for you are all one in Christ Jesus. Gal. 3:28, NIV.

Her voice rang out across the foyer. "Paul must have really hated women! Why else would he have written so many things against them—telling them to be silent in church?" I tried to make my way through the throng to explain that while Paul was alive, women were active in church life to a degree that is unthinkable in many of our churches today; to tell her that he readily accepted women as comrades in his work—but she was gone.

Here are some of his eye-opening admonitions:

Paul encouraged equality in marriage, stating that wives had the right to demand sexual faithfulness from their husbands (1 Cor. 7:3, 4). Paul lived in a time when marriage was not held in high esteem. In fact, classic Greek philosophy stated that true love was to be found between men.

Paul encouraged mutual submission in the marriage relation. Rather than adopt the view that women were to submerge themselves in marriage, the husband was instructed that he too must give himself up. In patriarchy, the woman had to leave her family and reside with the husband's relatives. Paul encouraged couples to follow Christ's example, who left heaven to be with the church. "For this reason a man will leave his father and mother and be united to his wife, and the two will become one flesh" (Eph. 5:31, NIV).

Polygamy was discouraged with instruction that a woman should not have to share her husband with another woman (1 Tim. 3:2, 12). Marriage, when it did occur, had degenerated into a condition that was male-dominated. Both polygamy and concubinage were accepted forms in society, which had created absolute chaos in the area of morality.

Divorce was discouraged in an effort to protect the rights of women (1 Cor. 7:10, 11). Among Jews and Romans alike, divorce was unilateral and exclusively under the control of men. Only the father was considered to be a "parent" to the offspring. Divorce for a woman meant separation from her children as well as disgrace. Paul spoke out against marriage as a game of musical chairs.

Singleness was identified as a state both pleasing and acceptable to God (1 Cor. 7:8). This profoundly affected a woman's perception by society. It meant (and means) that women do not have to marry and bear children in order to fulfill God's plan for their lives.

Relationships between unmarried persons of the opposite sex were defined as desirable, but they were to be characterized by purity and propriety (1 Tim. 5:2, 12). There were many single people in society during the early days of the gospel (unlike the Old Testament times, when nearly every Israelite was married). Paul writes about the value of deep friendship with members of both genders—always stressing sexual purity.

Many do not take into account the fact that Paul wrote against the backdrop of his current culture. As such, his rights and responsibilities for women were revolutionary and freeing. He wrote to improve the lot of women. He valued their assistance and association, and called them by name. Perhaps Paul rose to his finest insight when he wrote that, as a result of Christ's coming, there is neither male nor female—for we are all one in Christ Jesus.

LEONA GLIDDEN RUNNING AND ARLENE TAYLOR

MARCH 8

"The Lord Is Not Slow About His Promises"

The Lord is not slow in keeping his promise, as some understand slowness. He is patient with you, not wanting

anyone to perish, but everyone to come to repentance.
2 Peter 3:9, NIV.

We're all familiar with Genesis 3:4, which says, "But the serpent said to the woman, 'You will not die' " (RSV). Our theology has explored the meaning of this text and commented in depth on the impact of the lie the devil told our first parents. Satan said these words more than 5,000 years ago, but the belief in the immortality of the soul is stronger than ever as we come closer to the end of the world. It seems that the lie is updated to suit people's superstitions, values, and knowledge.

Today we have witnessed an invasion of Oriental religions, parapsychology, and supernatural phenomena. No one can estimate the suffering some people go through because of their belief in communicating and interacting with the dead!

What is it about this lie that invariably causes it to seem true? It is the faithfulness with which our enemy invests time and energy to disguise his old lie, "You will not die." He does everything and anything to keep it alive.

But God has done everything to enable us to believe in the truth that sets us free, in His promises of love and saving power. He has invested all heaven for the redemption of His children.

For God so loved the world that He gave His only Son to save us and give us eternal life. And He didn't stop showing His love for us on Calvary. Each day we enjoy the presence and the comfort of His Spirit, the protection of the angels, and material blessings that He personally bestows upon us.

If God loved us so much that He sacrificed His Son to save us, shouldn't we be able to trust His every promise? I stand in awe when I think of what He did and what He does for me.

Father, I know that You are trustworthy and able. Help my unbelief when the boat of my life rocks. Teach me to trust You more.
ANNIE SOUARÉ

MARCH 9

Happiness Is Keeping God's Law

You shall not covet your neighbor's house. You shall not covet your neighbor's wife, or his manservant or maidservant, his ox or donkey, or anything that belongs to your neighbor. Ex. 20:17, NIV.

The Ten Commandments have received a lot of bad press over the years. Many people assume they are an arbitrary list of prohibitions that keep them from enjoying total freedom. Much of present-day Protestantism goes to great lengths to prove that the Ten Commandments are no longer valid or binding on born-again Christians.

I might be more inclined to listen to their arguments if experience had not proved the timelessness of the counsel. The first four laws give guidelines to keep my worship pure, and the Sabbath gives me a constant reminder of my Creator-God.

At the very heart of His counsel is the home. The children were to be disciplined in such a manner that they would respect and honor their parents. Adults raised in this environment would understand the authority of God and respect the property of others. This fifth commandment on the home would be the foundation on which each new generation would build its response to the first four commands and also to the next four commands in Exodus 20: 13-16.

Commandments six through nine govern our treatment of one another and are so basic that few argue with their inherent rightness even when they are in the process of breaking one of them. Most people will concede that the world would be better off if there were no killing, no immorality, no stealing, and no lying, but they often rationalize that their situation is unique. The grief and illness caused by ignoring these instructions can never be measured. But it's the tenth commandment that really convinces me that God loves me. He really does want me to be happy. No one knows if I covet my neighbor's house. It doesn't hurt my neighbor. Now, if I kill my neighbor and take the house then I am guilty of killing and stealing. Even the laws of the land would punish me for this deed. But only God and I know when I covet.

Coveting can destroy every happiness. If we work outside the home, we covet the time of those who stay at home. If we stay home, we covet the respect given those with careers. If we are rich, we covet the carefree, bohemian existence. If we are poor, we covet the worry-free life of the wealthy. The list goes one. There is simply no station in life in which all our desires can possibly be met when wants are goaded by a covetous spirit. On the other hand, if we heed this counsel, there is simply no station in life that can break our spirit of contentment.

Before any of the other commandments are broken, I must break this tenth one and covet the authority or possessions of another. This command is not only the safeguard of my soul. It is the promise for my complete happiness and contentment. Happiness is keeping God's law in my mind, where only God and I know.

RACHEL K. PATTERSON

94

Nothing More

Truly, I say to you, this poor widow has put in more than all those who are contributing to the treasury. Mark 12:43, RSV.

Your aging mother falls and breaks a hip. A few weeks later your husband loses his job after 25 years of working for the same corporation. But that isn't enough. Your daughter calls to tell you she's divorcing her husband and wants to move back in with you.

Or five minutes before quitting time your boss asks you to photocopy 10 copies of a 40-page document. Then just as your computer loses a day's amount of work (including detailed graphics), your daughter calls to remind you that when you get home you have to make three dozen cookies for the Pathfinder bake sale.

Whatever our lives are like, there will always be times when we feel as though we have nothing more to give. But wait. Is that the sound of money tinkling in an offering box?

Yes, it's the widow's two mites. How can her generosity urge us on when we feel that we've given life all we've got? Listen further, for the sound of her money tells a story of strength and courage.

Mark 12:42 describes the widow as "poor." The Greek word used here means "one in extreme want," or one "lacking in anything." In reference to the same woman, Luke 21:2 uses yet another form of this Greek word that means "one who lives a hand-to-mouth existence and who must work each day just to have something to eat the next."

Commentaries tell us that one mite is worth only a fraction of one U.S. penny and that in the time of Christ two mites equaled less than 2 percent of a day's wages. For a person who lives a hand-to-mouth existence, giving just one mite would have been more than generous.

What did this hardworking widow know about the cause she loved that prompted her to sacrifice tomorrow's food? Perhaps she had heard from someone, somewhere, that the Messiah would risk the riches of heaven even if she were the only one who required salvation.

The widow and Jesus. Two people who literally gave everything they had. Now, how about you? Dig deep. With His help, through the gift of His power, you also have two mites to share.

LYNDELLE CHIOMENTI

That's Why!

We ought to obey God rather than men. Acts 5:29.

Three-year-old Penny was visiting Grandmommy who was spoiling her good in grandmommy ways. How Grandmommy enjoyed teaching her how to plant the flower seedlings and then showing her how to stand on the little Playskool step to reach into the sink and rinse away the mud but not the memories. As cute as Penny was, it was even more fun to observe Grandmommy enjoying her.

But suddenly the tone changed. Penny wanted the patio door shut, and Grandmommy wanted it open. Penny was determined, and Grandmommy was just as determined. The scene was positively a power struggle. Penny kept demanding, *Why?*

"Because *I said so*. That's why!" Grandmommy, exasperated, finally quipped. "And I'm the big mommy around here and you are just a little girl! *That's* why!"

A previous scene flashed from my memory. Grandmommy (Irene) had queried me as to why Adventists observe the seventh day as the Sabbath. Like any good Adventist, I explained that God had commanded it and nowhere in the Scriptures could we find reason to believe He had changed it. Furthermore, He had stated that His law could not be changed.

"Well, I don't see why it should matter," Irene had responded. "So long as we keep one day in seven—what's the difference?"

I had explained that God requires obedience. Naaman could have disobeyed and washed himself in any one of the clean rivers instead of dipping in the dirty Jordan. He could have asked, "What's the difference in a river?" Likewise, what's the difference in a day?

God decreed it—that's the difference. Naaman was healed of his leprosy because he obeyed. We can be healed of sin if we obey. Even the most loving creature who exists expects to be obeyed. I wondered now if Irene would have understood it if I had said it her way: "Because He *said so*—that's why! And *He's* the big Creator around here and we are just little creatures. *That's* why!"

Obedience is important to God for He says "If ye love me, keep my commandments" (John. 14:15). But the verse also reveals that our obedience is based on our love for Him. Likewise, His commandments are based on His love for us and are actually the principles of His kingdom. God is merely saying, If you love Me, here is how to become *like* Me!

David apparently understood this, for he wrote that he delighted in the commandments, loved them, and longed for them (Ps. 119:47, 127, 131)!

Ellen White assures us that the commandments are the life of God's people (*Testimonies*, vol. 9, p. 251), that they are adapted to our necessities (*ibid.*, vol. 2, p. 169), and that obedience is for our best interests (*The Sanctified Life*, p. 76). She summarizes the matter like this: "When the requirements of God are accounted a burden because they cut across human inclination, we may know that the life is not a Christian life. True obedience is the outworking of a principle within. It springs from the love of righteousness, the love of the law of God. The essence of all righteousness is loyalty to our Redeemer. This will lead us to do right because it is right—because right doing is pleasing to God" (*Christ's Object Lessons*, pp. 97, 98).

Neither God nor Grandmommy want a power struggle merely to show who's boss. Grandmommy waits for the eventual day when Penny will close the patio door happily—just for love. God waits for the day when Irene will keep the seventh-day Sabbath—just for love.   JANET KANGAS

MARCH 12

Leave the Waterpot

> *The woman said, "I know that Messiah" (called Christ) "is coming. When he comes, he will explain everything to us." Then Jesus declared, "I who speak to you am he." Just then his disciples returned and were surprised to find him talking with a woman. But no one asked, "What do you want?" or "Why are you talking with her?" Then, leaving her water jar, the woman went back to the town and said to the people, "Come, see a man who told me everything I ever did. Could this be the Christ?" John 4:25-29, NIV.*

We have often heard the story of Jesus interacting with the Samaritan woman at the well. Embedded in this story is perhaps the greatest testimony to the influence of women being used of God. Jesus first wants us to know through this story that it doesn't matter what race we are, how poor we are, or how sinful we are. He can use us if we are willing. Even when we are not aware of our own willingness to serve God, He knows our worth and will seek after us in order to give us the opportunity to drink from the living waters. Thus was the case of the Samaritan woman.

Jesus sought after the Samaritan woman, and in so doing defied many Jewish customs. But He had a plan for her life, and as a result many were saved. Jesus is also seeking many women today and can use us to save souls, but we must learn to leave the waterpot, as did the Samaritan woman. This woman had come to the well with the intent of leaving with her waterpot full of a necessary, life-sustaining substance. Instead, when she learned of the living water, Jesus Christ, and what He could do, she left her waterpot and returned to the town praising His name and inviting others to come see the Messiah. Her waterpot and its contents became secondary to the joy she felt in knowing Christ had come to save her.

We also have waterpots that we have filled with life-sustaining substances, but we must be willing to leave the waterpots in our lives as well. This is not to say that we must forsake our responsibilities, but we must not allow our waterpots to get in the way of God's plan for each of us. Our waterpots are filled with our homes, our cars, our children, our mates, our clothes, and much more. These items must become secondary to our desire to drink from the living water, Jesus Christ.

Herbert Lockyer in *All the Women of the Bible* tells us that the Samaritan woman was considered the first Samaritan woman evangelist and she laid the foundation for the Samaritan Pentecost. Saved by the living water, this sinful, adulterous woman was fulfilling God's mission for her life. Her love for what Jesus had done for her was enough for her to respond to His call. If we love God, then we must, as He admonishes us in John 21:15-17, feed His sheep.

When we leave our waterpots, we will achieve the unimaginable through Jesus Christ. History has not seen what we would be able to accomplish. Leave your waterpots and go tell the world what God has done for you. DEBORAH M. HARRIS

MARCH 13

The Lord Is Near

I want you to be happy, always happy in the Lord; I repeat, what I want is your happiness. Phil. 4:4, Jerusalem.

My mother would sit contentedly on the beach watching the five of us swimming in the lake. Although she'd rarely go in herself, she enjoyed the day thoroughly just by observing her children splashing and diving in the water.

But I could never understand how Mom could possibly be happy just seeing us having fun. "Come on in and swim too," I'd urge.

For me just to sit on the sand and watch others swimming would have been worse than staying at home. No, I didn't understand then, but I do now. Why? Because I too am a parent, more than content to cheer my son's baseball game or to ride in the boat as my daughter skis.

I've come to believe that being able to say "What I want is your happiness" is a mark of maturity, parental maturity in some cases, spiritual maturity in others.

Paul wanted so to emphasize his desire for his friends to have joy that he said, "I repeat." Ellen White manifested the same spirit when she wrote to someone needing encouragement: "Again I say: Rejoice in the Lord. Rest in Him. . . . I want you to have heaven. . . . Whatever you lose here, be determined to make sure of eternal life. Never become discouraged."

Now, it's one thing to give advice to "never become discouraged," but to tell someone how to follow that counsel demands more insight. Mrs. White not only gave the advice; she showed her friend what he could base his confidence on: "Many times I have seen that the everlasting arms were round about you, when you did not seem to realize or appreciate the great condescension of heaven" (*Testimonies*, vol. 8, pp. 130, 131).

Have you admonished the newlyweds, "Have a happy life together!" Have you instructed the mourners, "Don't be sad!" Have you told the lonely, "Have a merry holiday season!" Have you advised the sin-sick, "Don't be depressed." Did you then give them the reasons your counsel made sense? Did you show them how? Did you tell them why? Paul did.

After telling the Philippians twice "to be happy," he told them why: "The Lord is near" (Phil. 4:5, NASB).

And could there have been given a better reason?

WILMA McCLARTY

MARCH 14

The Prayer of Relinquishment

Father, if Thou art willing, remove this cup from Me; yet not My will, but Thine be done. Luke 22:42, NASB.

Barbara Nelson, in telling the story of her son Dwight's close brush with death, shares what it means to surrender. When Dwight was a child, he was in a waterskiing accident that fractured his skull. He lay motionless before his parents. Emergency measures were taken, and soon a helicopter whisked him to a hospital far away. There was room in the helicopter for only the pilot, a medical assistant, and Dwight. As Barbara prayed and relinquished Dwight to the Lord, peace flooded her soul just as the sunbeams outside broke through on that cloudy day. She felt the assurance of God's love and presence no matter what the outcome might be. Her trust in God was rewarded, and today God is using Dwight in a powerful way as a minister.

Nothing could disturb the peace of mind Jesus possessed, because He always made it His practice to relinquish everything to the Father. This habit reached its zenith in Gethsemane. It was not a matter of selfishly wanting to avoid drinking the cup of death. Rather, it was His dread of separation from His Father. His struggle was more intense because of His perfect love for His Father. No person on earth has ever suffered as Jesus did in praying His prayer of relinquishment. When we relinquish all to the Father and live as Jesus did, we too can have peace and security.

To relinquish, according to Webster, is to surrender, to let go, to give up. Today we hear much about being our own person and maintaining our rights. Seminars teach us how to win and how to get ahead. We even have seminars that teach us how to intimidate others. Wouldn't it be wonderful if we could have seminars that taught us how to relinquish? But total surrender is not part of our vocabulary. In the morning we pray, "Lord, I give myself to You today. Work out Your life in me." But how often we get up from our knees and take control, instead of waiting for God to lead. For a peaceful life in Christ, there must be a total surrender on our part, a giving up of ourselves completely to the will of God.

Remember, God does not expect us to surrender in our own strength or by sheer power. He is more than willing to help us. Pray for trust in Him and believe in His power to help. "For it is God who is at work in you, both to will and to work for His good pleasure" (Phil. 2:13, NASB). God's full blessing is realized in *total* surrender.   MARIE SPANGLER

Restoring Harmony

Now I want you to realize that the head of every man is Christ, and the head of the woman is man, and the head of Christ is God. 1 Cor. 11:3.

The telephone rang, and Joyce* tearfully explained that she wouldn't be able to attend the Christian women's retreat after all. Her husband felt that it was her job to take care of the children (ages 11 and 14), and that he certainly couldn't do that while she was "off meeting with a bunch of women." The clincher of his argument was that Genesis 3:16 indicated that men should rule over their wives—and he, for one, intended to do just that.

I replaced the receiver and thought about the untold misery and wasted opportunities in the lives of countless women because of misunderstanding of Scripture. In the first place, the word translated as "rule over" would be more accurately translated from the original as "resemble." As the woman would experience travail in childbirth, so the man would resemble her in that he would suffer painful toil.

In the second place, the story of Creation (Gen. 1) stresses equality with no distinction in terms of superiority or subordination. Adam means both man and woman, and both were made in the image of God. Neither gender in itself mirrors the character and personality of God—only the species does.

When God saw that the man needed a "helper suitable for him," or as the original Hebrew word really means, a "counterpart" (a complementary equal), the woman was created. She was created not from his head to rule over him, nor from his feet to be trampled underfoot by him, but from his side—as a symbol of equality. God uses the same word "helper" to apply to Himself, so it does not imply inferiority. They were both given dominion over the earth which also implies equality. In addition, it was the man who was to leave his parents and "cleave to his wife," which implies more of a matriarchal rather than patriarchal organization.

Even the order in which human beings were fashioned does not imply man's superiority or woman's inferiority. Rather, they form a ring composition, an *inclusio*, in which the man (created first) and the woman (created last) correspond in importance. Creation would not have been complete without woman.

* Name changed

The story of the Fall, as told in Genesis 3, accounts for the disruption of the harmoniously balanced relationship between the genders. The curses mentioned are not God's prescriptions of the way that things should be; they are descriptions of the way things often would be as the result of sin's entrance. They cannot be used to support male domination and supremacy in all spheres of life.

Neither the Old Testament nor the New Testament supports the idea of the woman as reduced to a blindly obedient slave of a despotic husband. Paul indicates that the man is head of the woman as the Father is head of Christ—and They are equal in the Godhead.

Christianity was supposed to restore the broken original relationship and harmony. How comforting to realize that the model Paul uses to describe mutual submission in the marriage relationship is based on Christ as Saviour of the church (Eph. 5:23)!

LEONA GLIDDEN RUNNING AND ARLENE TAYLOR

MARCH 16

This Thing Is From Me

Thus saith the Lord, Ye shall not go up, nor fight against your brethren the children of Israel: return every man to his house; for this thing is from me. 1 Kings 12:24.

King Rehoboam may have been Solomon's son, but he didn't seem to inherit much wisdom. In some ways he was downright foolish. A test came in the early days of his reign when he could have easily won the hearts of Israel if he had not insisted on being so arrogant and stubborn.

The people had been heavily taxed when Solomon frittered away his wisdom and reveled in earthly treasures and pleasures. Now, as Rehoboam took the throne, they wondered how they would fare. Solomon's counselors tried to guide the new king, but Rehoboam was egotistical and willful. Had taxes under Solomon been heavy? His would be heavier!

Israel had no more patience with extravagance. The kingdom split. Israel crowned Jeroboam king and responded to Rehoboam, "What portion have we in David?" (Or of his house, for that matter.)

Well, Rehoboam wouldn't stand for rebellion. He assembled an army. And just before they could strike, God sent a message—the one in today's text. "This thing is from me." You have been foolish. You did not listen or call upon Me. You were confident in your own strength, so I'm taking it all away. Your great kingdom is

102

gone. Only a small portion remains. Now depend on Me.

Where are you today? Have your plans been upset? Are you bowed down and weary of trying to make a go of it? God says, "This thing is from me," for you made your plans without Me, then came asking Me to bless them. Trust Me to plan for you—I'll accept all responsibility.

Are you facing money difficulties? Is it hard to make ends meet? God says, "This thing is from me," for I am your purse-bearer, and would have you draw from and depend on Me. My supplies are limitless. (See Phil. 4:19.) Prove My promises. Let it not be said of you, "In this thing ye did not believe the Lord your God" (Deut. 1:32).

You may be surrounded by people who do not understand you, who reject you, who mistreat you, or who do not seem to appreciate you. Sometimes God may allow earthly friends or even families to fail you. If your best friend disappoints you—one you have opened your heart to and confided in—remember, the best friend to have is Jesus. He will hear when you call; He will keep you lest you fall.

If you are passing through a night of sorrow, know that God is a man of sorrows and acquainted with grief. If tragedy strikes, if death comes, turn to Him, and you will find everlasting help, consolation, and comfort.

When you are in difficult circumstances, when temptation assails you, and the evening comes in like a flood, remember, your weakness needs God's might. Your safety lies in letting Him fight for you.

This day, take His promises into your hands. Believe them. Use them freely. See Jesus and His possibilities in all things. Set your heart on the Word of God. It is life. "This thing is from me."

CHESSIE HARRIS

MARCH 17

Speaking From the Heart

Pleasant words are as an honeycomb, sweet to the soul, and health to the bones. Prov. 16:24.

Your voice tells people a great deal of information about you as a person. It reveals whether you're male or female and hints at your approximate age. It's an indicator of your intelligence and may also give a clue as to the region of the country from which you came. It may tell about your socioeconomic origins, your educa-

103

tion, and in some cases your occupation.

Your voice also tells the listener whether you're feeling in a good mood at the moment or whether you're angry, sad, fearful, or depressed.

Luke tells us that, the "good man out of the good treasure of his heart brings forth what is good; . . . for his mouth speaks from that which fills his heart" (Luke 6:45, NASB). There is no doubt that our mood and feelings are reflected in our voices as we speak. Our voices can become powerful instruments used for witnessing to others about what Jesus has done for us in our lives.

Because we take speaking for granted, we rarely stop to think about how effective our voices might be as a witnessing tool. Some people have been given unusual talents in music, painting, or literature, but we all have been given the gift of speech. We should develop this talent to the best of our ability as a witness to others for salvation. Try listening to yourself on a tape recorder. After you have said, "Oh no, I don't really sound that way," listen to the basic pitch of your voice. Do you have a nice melody to your voice and use lots of inflection? Are you difficult to understand because you speak too rapidly? In the English language it's easy to slur or run sounds together. A little practice in front of a mirror can do much to help some of these problems.

"Well," you say, "I've done all these things; now what?" Now it's time to ask the Lord to help with the rest. Ask Him to change you in such a way that His love and character will be reflected in your voice quality as well as in the words you speak. We are promised in Ezekiel 36:26 that we can have a new heart and spirit. Our heart of stone can be changed to a heart of flesh. Our new heart will be reflected in our voice. Merry hearts cannot help showing up in people's faces and voices. Whether you're an exuberant, outgoing extrovert or a more sedate introvert, your witness for the Lord and how you present it will flow from your heart right through your vocal cords to the ear of your listener.

"Pleasant words are as an honeycomb, sweet to the soul, and health to the bones." "A gentle answer turns away wrath, but a harsh word stirs up anger" (Prov. 15:1, NASB). How well Solomon understood the power of words as well as the underlying way that the words are spoken. Thank God that we all have the potential to have our words and voices be like "apples of gold in settings of silver" (Prov. 25:11, NASB). SHEILA BIRKENSTOCK SANDERS

Busyness

Thus I considered all my activities which my hands had done and the labor which I had exerted, and behold all was vanity and striving after wind and there was no profit under the sun. Eccl. 2:11, NASB.

Many people erroneously feel that they must appear busy at all times. Ethel Renwick, who spent a lifetime studying international lifestyles, wrote, "One of the great ills of American society is that they make outrageous demands upon their bodies by overwork. The work ethic, being at the very core of America, is taken to an extreme and rationalized as worthy, even noble." She particularly points her finger at Christians who "live as though God depended on them alone and had no other way of getting things done" (in Sybil Stanton, *The 25-Hour Woman*, p. 95).

A professor from Fuller Seminary, who was invited to the North American Division evangelism council in Florida several years ago, made an interesting observation about the busyness of Seventh-day Adventists. He said, "When I came to Daytona, the first thing I did was drive down on the beach to see the ocean. Since I was attending a Seventh-day Adventist convention, I knew this would be my only opportunity to see God's kingdom of nature." Then he added, "Undoubtedly you folk teach the correct Sabbath, which is the seventh day of the week, but I wonder if you know what it means to experience and enjoy the rest that is inherent in the Sabbath!"

Have you ever visited a park and watched children on the merry-go-round? Someone keeps the large wheel spinning, making it difficult to get off. Most of the children clutch the bars for dear life while whirling in circles until they feel sick or someone rescues them. As children grow, they keep going back for more of this type of activity, until at some point in their lives they conclude, "I don't need this anymore!" There will always be a merry-go-round in life, but you don't have to be on it! If you are discouraged, tired, and disheartened, perhaps this is one of your problems. Perhaps you haven't been able to distinguish between the urgent and the important. Get off the merry-go-round and start changing your world!

George Bernard Shaw once said, "People are always blaming their circumstances for what they are. I don't believe in circumstances. The people who get on in this world are the people who get up and look for the circumstances they want, and, if they can't find them, make them." "Man can shape circumstances, but circumstances should not be allowed to shape the man. . . . We are to master them, but should not permit them to master us" (*The Ministry of Healing*, p. 500). Aren't you thankful that God requires us only to do our best, never to overdo? He is the one who has invited us to come apart and rest awhile.   MARIE SPANGLER

MARCH 19

Hope

Be ready at all times to answer anyone who asks you to explain the hope you have in you, but do it with gentleness and respect. 1 Peter 3:15, 16, TEV.

Not long ago I attended a seminar in Vermont that changed my life. Months before, when I had first heard of the seminar, I had felt God impressing me to go. As soon as I got there, I knew why. Three Spirit-filled days of prayer, instruction, laughter, and new friends refreshed me both spiritually and physically.

In one of my classes I was asked to take a Bible verse and use it to write a sermon. I chose 1 Peter 3:15, 16 and I'd like to share with you the thoughts I wrote down.

"My heart is a garden of hope. Before planting, I need to clear the ground by pulling out the weeds of fear, loneliness, and despair. I have a large space now to use the hoe of compassion to break up the hard clumps of unforgiveness and dislike. With prayer I rake out smooth areas so that God can plant seeds of kindness, tolerance, forgiveness, patience, helpfulness, unselfishness, understanding, and gentleness.

"The Holy Spirit waters my garden with the dews of righteousness and rains of compassion. I put supports of Bible study near each plant. God opens the doors of heaven and lets His sunshine of divine truth and promises cascade down upon my garden.

"Every garden has weeds that need to be destroyed, such as bitterness, jealousy, discontent, and self-pity. I need to spray the bugs of lies, deceit, faultfinding, criticism, and gossip with a liberal amount of Bible reading.

"God produces the fruit. The good deeds in my garden have grown and spread. I can harvest the fruits of the Spirit from my garden of hope. Joy, peace, gladness, and freedom are the fruits. Flowers grow and blossom giving a sacrifice of sweet-smelling savor to my Lord.

"This is my heart's garden, a promise of our blessed hope in Jesus. Jesus will reap the harvest of my garden of hope when He comes." DORIS E. EVERETT

MARCH 20

Garbage Pail Words

Death and life are in power of the tongue. Prov. 18:21.

Sticks and stones can hurt my bones, but names will never harm me." *Wrong!* Ask any acne-blemished teenager who endures being told to "go bag your face." Ask any late-developing girl who hurries down the hall, pretending she doesn't hear "Hi, Turnpike—no curves in sight" as she walks to class. Ask any brainy but not brawny student who hides his A English compositions to keep from being called "Teacher's Pet" by the school jocks.

Toy manufacturing is a multimillion-dollar enterprise pushing for profit hundreds of playthings, all guaranteed to entertain—even educate—for hours of "innocent" amusement. Innocent? Well, not quite.

One of the most harmful toys ever marketed camouflages its demeaning message in vivid hues. I'm not thinking of a violent video game, nor a toy gun, nor a comic book. The winner of the "Most Damaging Toy Award" is . . . Garbage Pail Kids—wallet-sized, brightly colored, inexpensive trading cards. These cards picture children with deformed bodies and faces, their abnormalities heightened by clever artistic distortion. The kids are captioned "Gory Cory," or "Deaf Geoff," or "Lucas Mucus"—all degrading rhyming labels intended to bring awareness to disfiguring.

The good news is that a Christian group was concerned enough over the dehumanizing messages of the cards to start a protest. Consequently, the sales of Garbage Pail Kids, which were popular enough to go through several series, are now being curtailed. Ironically, the curtailment of these cards will most likely increase their value; the first series of cards are already coveted collector items.

But the bad news remains: people themselves have not quit categorizing each other. "Death and life are in the power of the tongue," Solomon reminds us (Prov. 18:21). And words become weapons of death when used to degrade, to dehumanize.

Garbage Pail people simply do not exist. The words of a children's gospel song have it correctly: "God don't make no junk!" WILMA McCLARTY

MARCH 21

The Parable of the Lost Daughter

So then she got up and started back to her parents. She was still a long way from home when her parents saw her; their hearts filled with pity, and they hurried, hugging their daughter and kissing her. See Luke 15:20, TEV.

There was once a daughter who, having received her education and begun making her own way in life, decided to move into a relationship that was not held in approval by either her church or her parents. Her parents pointed out future difficulties with her decision and suggested other options open to her, but to no avail. Upon her insistence to follow her own plan they helped her move, although they were burdened with heavy hearts.

After a period of time she came to the rude awakening that her freedom was on a short string, both financially and emotionally. She was not even able to go places with her friends. Her parents had continued to keep in touch with her regularly, and as they saw signs of her deteriorating relationship they let her know they would always be there to help. Her mother told her that if at any time she felt unsafe or fearful to call day or night and help would be provided.

Finally one Friday evening after her mother had gone to bed, the call came. Her mother arose, dressed, loaded up the family car with empty boxes and suitcases, and went out to meet the daughter. Together they filled the car and returned home, where the daughter would stay with her parents temporarily. The parents' prayers had been answered, and there was great rejoicing in their household.

PEGGY HARRIS

MARCH 22

Show the Signs and Wonders

I thought it good to shew the signs and wonders that the high God hath wrought toward me. Dan. 4:2.

As I stepped into the elevator with my bellhop in tow, I was enjoying the flow of conversation with this young man as he helped me with my luggage.

"This place used to be a zoo to work for," he told me.

"What made the difference?" I asked.

"We're under new management," came his quick reply.

"Under new management? Oh, the very same thing happened in my life! It too was a zoo, but now I'm under new management!" I joyfully responded.

That's all it took to have his full attention. He wanted to know all about my "new management."

When he found out that I had surrendered my less-than-perfect heart to Jesus Christ and accepted His new management, he was all ears to discover what a magnificent change it had made in my life. I in turn was delighted for the opportunity to show this fellow the wonders God had wrought for me.

He confided that he had tried a lot of denominations, but had yet to find one that followed the Bible 100 percent. Well, did I have good news for him! That opened the door wide for me to share my experience with the church I know follows the Bible 100 percent: the Seventh-day Adventist Church. I invited him to attend one of the local Adventist churches the following weekend, and I could tell by his smiling eyes that the invitation was well received.

Granted, I was weary as I walked into that hotel, but could I pass up the opportunity to share the wonders that God had done for me? I'd never have that opportunity again with that man.

When you pray for opportunities to witness of the signs and wonders God has done for you, be prepared to fasten your safety belt and embark on the trip of a lifetime—under new management!

JUDY COULSTON

MARCH 23

The Pleasure of His Presence

You have let me experience the joys of life and the exquisite pleasures of your own eternal presence. Ps. 16:11, TLB.

Flowing through our property is a quiet, spring-fed creek—home to beavers, ducks, and herons. Raccoons, fox, moose, and deer, along with the cattle, drink of the waters of Cyr Creek. The fresh smell of earth wet with moisture reminds me of the wildness of the area. I enjoy the spongy feel of the ground as I walk through the grass. At the base of a spring-fed water tank the minnows gather by the thousands every spring.

Leaning over the creek's banks is a pussy willow that awakens to spring very early because of the warmth it draws from the sun and the nourishment it draws from the creek. From it I gather branches of the newly opened buds to decorate my home each spring. Continuing on its way, Cyr Creek meanders on through the neighbor's pastures and empties into the Red Lake River, quietly sharing its water as it flows on its way.

Every part of the creek is in harmony with nature as it shares its bounty. It gives peace and protection to all who come seeking it. The beavers have found it a comfortable environment to make their dens and raise their young. The minnows spend their time gaining strength before they swim on to their new homes. Waterfowl find pleasure and food as they swim in the cool water. The roots of the trees lining its banks reach out for the lifegiving water.

Here is where I go early in the morning to drink in the goodness of life. As I listen to the birds singing their early-morning songs of praise my heart is lifted to God. I meditate upon His gifts to me as I wander along its banks. At evening time, as the sun is setting, I choose to sit quietly on a tuft of grass and just drink in the beauty of my surroundings. Nature undisturbed by human beings, a little quiet place in this busy world.

"Thank You, Lord, for a quiet place to experience the exquisite pleasures of God's eternal presence and to meditate upon the joys of life. It is here that I come to be renewed and to be reminded of life's blessings. Leaving behind all the cares of a busy life, I seek the same perfect harmony with You that nature reveals."

I leave Cyr Creek refreshed, ready for the challenges of a new day, having experienced the pleasure of His presence.

EVELYN GLASS

MARCH 24

Happiness Digest

And the Lord will guide you continually, and satisfy your desire with good things, and make your bones strong; and you shall be like a watered garden, like a spring of water, whose waters fail not. Isaiah 58:11, RSV.

I happened on an old friend recently and got reacquainted. Well-read books are like friends, don't you think? They are comfortable, reassuring, and familiar. One knows what to expect rather than feeling uncertain about what a first encounter might bring. So instead of a hot-off-the-press best-seller, I'm recommending a dear old classic, *Steps to Christ*. It was a godsend to me.

While George took a three-week island itinerary, I developed a diarrhea that wouldn't quit. The screening nurse at our clinic gave me a regimen that might help. Nothing but water for one day, only certain fruit juices and water the next day, a bland diet for three days or so. I lost weight, tired quickly. Then the flu bug hit.

I couldn't eat, and felt achy, feverish, and alone. What could I do besides gargle and take medicine? *A good book would sure be nice*, I thought, but we had brought only our clothes and two down-filled pillows to Guam.

Fortunately, previous occupants of this Adventist World Radio apartment left some magazines on the coffee table's lower shelf. Among them I found *Happiness Digest*, the modernized paperback edition of *Steps to Christ*.

How I love that first chapter about God's love and its revelation in nature! Many familiar sentence or paragraph gems flashed off the pages.

And I have learned something new about the book. A temperance worker told me that its chapters closely parallel the AA and Al-Anon Twelve Steps. Then I remembered my Nancy saying that she told her Al-Anon group that these steps were not new to her, that she had been brought up by those principles. This angle opens a new avenue for distributing and sharing the gospel.

When did you last reach for this volume? Being small and tucked in beside the larger "red book," it's easily overlooked. May you enjoy happy sessions with this good friend. MARGE WOODRUFF

MARCH 25

The Seven Last Words of Christ

It is finished. John 19:30.

The composer took for the name—and content—of one of the most popular religious oratorios, "The Seven Last Words of Christ." He could have chosen "The Seven Last Miracles" or "The Seven Last Trips" or "The Seven Last People He Saw." But no, Theodore Dubois selected the seven last words—sentences, actually—that Jesus spoke, and in so doing gave artistic permanence to Jesus' final utterances.

Actually, anyone's dying words are valued as some of the most significant ones the person has spoken. After a death, the loved ones want to know whether a note was left, whom the person talked to last, what the person said. A soldier's last lingering comment before going off to war is indelibly etched in his family's memory. The final phrase a lover whispers before leaving is what is most treasured.

Lawyers make a living from writing up in permanent form a client's last will and testimony, being paid handsome sums to make the words legal. Law offices, high-voltage places in general, often get unusually intense when wills are read. Who will get the business? Who will get the house? Who will get the money? One rich old lady abolished all hopes of her heirs getting wealthy when she left all but one dollar to her cat!

In Jesus' last will and testimony, His seven last sentences, whom did He remember? Were you in it? According to Dubois' Oratorio, Jesus' final words were as follows:

"Father, Father, forgive them, for they know not what they do." And Jesus remembered His tormentors.

"Verily, thou shalt be in paradise with Me. Amen, so I tell thee." And Jesus remembered a hardened criminal.

"See, O woman! Here behold thy son beloved." And Jesus remembered His mother.

"God, My Father, why hast Thou forsaken Me?" And Jesus remembered His knowledge of the terribleness of sin.

"I am athirst!" And Jesus remembered His humanity.

"Father, into Thy hands I commend My soul." And Jesus remembered His faith in God.

"It is finished!" And Jesus remembered His mission, to this earth and to all others besides.

"To the angels and the unfallen worlds the cry, 'It is finished,' had a deep significance. It was for them as well as for us that the great work of redemption had been accomplished. They with us share the fruits of Christ's victory" (*The Desire of Ages*, p. 758).

Oh, wonderful irony—Jesus' dying words became words of life for the entire universe. His death utterances gave hope of immortality. We are all in His will. WILMA MCCLARTY

MARCH 26

Help!

Then they cried to the Lord in their trouble, and he delivered them from their distress. Ps. 107:13, RSV.

When our youngest child gets frustrated and doesn't understand something, she cries out desperately just one word—"Help!"

I have tried to get her to say quietly, "Mom, would you please explain this to me?" or "Would you help me with this particular problem, please?" rather than just "Help! Help!"

Recently I was taking a walk, when suddenly I looked up into the sky and cried, "Help, Lord, help!" Things were so overwhelming in so many different areas that I couldn't even put my thoughts into words. Immediately I understood how my daughter feels at times!

Unlike me, God never gets impatient of hearing that cry for help. Have you read Psalm 107 lately? The next time you are at your wits' end, read this wonderful chapter. And as summer warms our earth, may these promises in God's Word bring warmth and new life to each of you. Remember, the war is almost over, and victory awaits those who "endureth to the end."   GERITA LIEBELT

MARCH 27

Wandering

A soft answer turns away wrath, but a harsh word stirs up anger. Prov. 15:1, RSV.

The girls were rapt with attention and full of questions as we studied the fall of Adam and Eve. It all seemed so clear to us as we read the account in *The Story of Redemption*. God told them not to eat of the tree of knowledge of good and evil. He warned them of Satan's intent and even told them the area where Satan would be confined. Why, then, had Eve been so blind? Why hadn't she trusted God and believed what He had said? In love He had given her plenty of warning, yet she had chosen to believe a beautiful snake instead. We wondered in awe at the issues that seemed so clear to us but that had confounded and tricked Eve into losing all that she had.

Later it hit me. Am I not as blind, shortsighted, and distrustful of God as Eve was when I speak impatiently to one of my daughters who is evading her piano practice; stay up too late at night working; eat that second piece of chocolate angel pie; worry about accomplishing all 17 "to do" items on my list; share a "juicy" social item with a friend; covet my neighbor's financial freedom to stay at home; or reply harshly to my husband?

God has told me that a soft answer turneth away wrath, that I

113

shouldn't covet, that my body is the temple of God, and that I shouldn't gossip or speak ill of others.

Why don't I trust my Creator, who knows more than anyone else what I need and what will make me happy? In my morning devotions, don't I commit my day and all that it brings to Him? He who emptied heaven so that I could one day spend eternity with Him and my family woos me with an unfathomable love, giving me every reason to trust Him—just as He did Eve.

Lord, help me remember what You've told me in love the next time I'm tempted to "wander" in my daily life. Help me to remember Eve, and to trust You!   NANCY VOLLMER WILSON

MARCH 28

When Will Jesus Come?

Behold, I am coming soon. Rev. 22:7, RSV.

People have been waiting for Christ's second coming ever since He first gave His promise to return. Hope has been inspired by Bible texts and Ellen White passages that use the words "soon" and "near." But as the years pass the meaning of these words can fade into doubt and we ask, "How soon is soon?"

Time is a relative idea, and the word "soon" can mean many different things to us. So what does "soon" mean to God? I'm not sure, but studying the Bible shows that God often has a different perspective on time than we do.

Many times He seems to take His time, when we, as humans, would probably hurry up. One example is the Flood. Here was this old man named Noah predicting a "soon-coming" Flood year after year. After a while people scoffed at his warning. But their laughing scorn didn't prevent the Flood. In that case, "soon" meant 120 years.

A rather dramatic way to think about time is to realize how much our human perspective on it has shrunk. Adam lived 930 years! Our lifespan of 70-80 years means we have lost more than 90 percent of our perspective since Adam. To us, the 150 years since our 1844 disappointment seems like a very long time, but to Adam those years would certainly seem relatively short. The difference in Adam's life and ours can help us realize the vast difference between God's perspective and our very limited one.

Someday our perspective on time will mesh with God's, but we may not understand until *after* it happens, just as we don't realize how fast our babies grow until all of a sudden they are adults and we marvel at how the years have flown by.

But what are we to do until our ideas of time match God's? Let me answer that with another question. If Jesus was coming tomorrow, what would we do? Would we pray? Would we find time to study His Word? Would we mend that relationship with our parent or spouse? I think we would. I think if we knew Christ was coming tomorrow, many of us would say, *Wait!* Please give us a little more time!

And that's just what God has done. He has given us this gift of a little more time. I don't know if it's a one-day gift or a 50-year gift, but I am sure that God wants us to use it to become closer to Him and closer to each other. What would you like to do before Christ comes to take us home? Whatever it is, do it now. Let's not put *Jesus* off any longer. Just as He has promised to come again, He has promised to be in our hearts every day. And if Jesus is at home with us here on earth, then I am willing to trust His perspective on when it is time to take us to our real home in heaven.   JODI V. RUF

MARCH 29

Many Mansions for Very Few?

Ye do always resist the Holy Ghost: as your fathers did, so do ye. Acts 7:51.

Ellen White tells us of a dream in which she saw a sentinel at the door of an important building. He held a measuring line in his hand and asked of everyone who came to the entrance, "Have ye received the Holy Ghost?" She tells us that "very, very few" were admitted (*Selected Messages*, book 1, p. 109). One wonders why so few qualify to receive the Spirit when the blessings are so great and the four conditions are so clear: confession, humiliation, repentance, and earnest prayer (*ibid.*, p. 121).

God's gifts are free, but they are not freebies. Yet Ellen White assures us, "We need not worry about the latter rain. All we have to do is keep the vessel clean and right side up and prepared for the reception of the heavenly rain, and keep praying" (*The Upward Look*, p. 283). She was very specific regarding what to pray. She says we are to ask, "Let the latter rain come into my vessel. Let the light of the glorious angel which unites with the third angel shine upon me; give me a part in the work; let me sound the loud proclamation; and let me be a colaborer with Jesus Christ" (*ibid.*).

All four of these points center on infiltrating the world. This helps us to better understand her statement "We shall be entrusted with the Holy Spirit according to our capacity to receive and our ability to impart it to others" (*Review and Herald*, May 5, 1896).

This revival of true godliness (seeking the Holy Spirit) "should be our first work" (*Selected Messages*, book 1, p. 121). But since God is more willing to bestow His Spirit on us than parents are to give good gifts to their children (Matt. 7:11), why is it work—especially in light of this passage: "The sinner may resist this love, may refuse to be drawn to Christ; but if he does not resist, he will be drawn to Jesus" (*Steps to Christ*, p. 27)?

It is human beings who make work of it by resisting. "The reason why men and women today do not believe the truth is because it condemns their life practices. They see that the truth calls for a reform, and they fight it because they hate the work involved in sanctification" (*The Upward Look*, p. 140). "If men would only give up their spirit of resistance to the Holy Spirit . . . God's Spirit would address itself to their hearts" (*ibid.*, p. 51).

Jesus did not plan on "very, very few" receiving the Holy Ghost, for He is building "many mansions" (John. 14:1-3). Let us not find "For Rent" signs in heaven. JANET KANGAS

MARCH 30

Looking for Jesus

As a hart longs for flowing streams, so longs my soul for thee, O God. Ps. 42:1, RSV.

The last thrust of winter has blasted us with chilling sleet, but the calendar promises that spring is ready to descend. I'm ready! I can't wait for the end of cold weather and the blossoming of fragrant shrubs, trees, and flowers.

Making my way across a large patch of ice during a recent storm, I thought longingly of spring and wondered, "Am I as eager for the return of Jesus as I am for spring?"

We claim to long for our Lord's return, but sometimes I feel we don't spend enough time thinking about and hungering for it. When things go smoothly, we don't sense our need for something better. When January was warm and sunny, spring lost some of its appeal. But when winter lashed out in March, we pleaded for spring—now!

Dear friend, let's spend time contemplating the beauty of our Lord's return even when things go right. Let's hunger for His eternal presence much more than we long for the flowers of spring. ELLEN BRESEE

The Ultimate Home

Let not your heart be troubled: ye believe in God, believe also in me. In my Father's house are many mansions: if it were not so, I would have told you. I go to prepare a place for you. And if I go and prepare a place for you, I will come again, and receive you unto myself; that where I am, there ye may be also. John 14:1-3.

When I was a child, I built a crude A-frame and strung string around the perimeter from the top to the ground—then I planted morning glories. As they grew, they covered the A-frame, providing me with my own private world—a pretend home. It was a lot of fun, and the morning glories were beautiful!

Do you ever wonder what kind of home God is preparing for you? Do you suppose it will be brick, frame, or stucco? Maybe it will be a beautiful bower of grapevines. Whatever it may be like, it must be really "out of this world" because we are told, "Eye hath not seen, nor ear heard, neither have entered into the heart of man, the things which God hath prepared for them that *love* him" (1 Cor. 2:9).

But the heavenly mansions that God is preparing will be inhabited only by those who love and obey Him. To some, this may seem like too high a price. They don't want to deny themselves now for whatever long-term gain there may be. There are so many temptations in this world to keep our minds off eternal things. When we stray onto the enemy's ground, our thinking becomes clouded and we cannot comprehend spiritual things. Like Esau, we sell our birthrights for a mess of "pottage."

Sometimes in this world we sacrifice for college, a trip, or a car, but how much are we willing to sacrifice for eternal life? May we keep foremost in our minds that the goal is to inhabit that mansion that God has prepared for our everlasting joy. To lose our inheritance is a loss for eternity!   PAT MADSEN

Stumbling Upon Unexpected Glory

The joy of the Lord is your strength. Neh. 8:10, RSV.

It had been a hot summer with little rain. I knelt in my garden tugging at weeds whose roots were anchored firmly in the dry, baked soil. A short distance away a sprinkler flung water in a wide-arching spray over another section of the garden. The droplets pattered on blue-green hosta leaves with a refreshing cadence.

Another familiar sound, a gentle whirring, fell faintly upon my ear, and I halted my work to seek out its source. A tiny humming-bird moved methodically along the rose impatiens spilling over the edge of the lawn, lifting now and then to a pink phlox or scarlet snapdragon. Eventually, it came within range of the sprinkler's pseudo shower. It lost interest in the flowers. Their bright colors were no longer enticing. Their nectar failed to seduce. It wasted no time attempting to determine where this shower was originating on a clear, sunny day. Neither did the bird worry that the shower's range was unnaturally limited (actually it was just about humming-bird size). It rose into the mist in utter ecstasy and for about 10 minutes I watched it hover and bounce about in the strong spray. I did not have to be a hummingbird to tell it was having a wonderful time, that on this hot morning it had stumbled upon an unexpected glory.

At last, it flew away, sparkling like a tiny gem in its wetness. I felt lonely when it left, robbed of something hard to define. I'd shared, vicariously, in the most innocent, dancing joy. My own cares had not once entered my mind, so entranced had I been by the bird's obvious delight.

As I sat cross-legged on the thick grass, pondering, it occurred to me that I too had stumbled, years ago, upon an unexpected glory when I met Jesus Christ. A glory so intense that I lost all interest in the things that had, until then, consumed my energies and atten-tions. I lived in an atmosphere of spiritual ecstasy. Others saw the transformation and marveled.

But what about now? Was I still radiating joy? Were those about me eager to determine its source? Was my life a daily singing witness to my eternal expectations? Were people, even those who'd never bent the knee, drawn to share this new and shining wonder from the morning of my life? Was it still fresh and obvious?

"Let me never lose it, Lord. May the hummingbird's reminder linger ever in my heart."

"We are made a spectacle unto the world, and to angels, and to men" (1 Cor. 4:9).   JUNE STRONG

Speaking Heavenese

I am crucified with Christ: nevertheless I live; yet not I, but Christ liveth in me: and the life which I now live in the flesh I live by the faith of the Son of God, who loved me, and gave himself for me. Galatians 2:20.

Several years ago when we were getting ready for a trip to Europe, I purchased several language books that were supposed to help us communicate with people in the countries we would visit. But I found that it was a bit tricky pulling out the book and looking up what I wanted to say. And if I was lucky enough to get my message across, it was even more difficult to understand the reply. As I look back on the experience, I wish I had anticipated how much preparation I would need and started getting ready earlier.

I have often liked to speak of the language of heaven as "heavenese." What kind of language will be spoken there, do you suppose? Will we need to be prepared to speak it when we get there, or will we be blundering along with our guidebook in our hand trying to bluff our way through? First of all, I think everyone that speaks fluent heavenese will have had a true conversion experience. The first thing that is needed is to get rid of that problem we all have with self. When self stands in the way, we have cut our communication with heaven and we are on our own, which most of us have found to be a pretty scary situation.

"The Christian life is a battle and a march. But the victory to be gained is not won by human power. The field of conflict is the domain of the heart. The battle which we have to fight—the greatest battle that was ever fought by man—is the surrender of self to the will of God, the yielding of the heart to the sovereignty of love. The old nature, born of blood and the will of the flesh, cannot inherit the kingdom of God" (*Thoughts From the Mount of Blessing*, p. 141).

"The warfare against self is the greatest battle that was ever fought" (*Steps to Christ*, p. 43).

I want to learn to speak fluent heavenese, and I want to spend every precious moment getting ready so that in the glorious day of eternity's great dawn I will feel perfectly at home. My heavenese will flow as fluently as if it were the only language I had ever learned. PAT MADSEN

APRIL 3

Termites!

Great peace have they which love thy law: and nothing shall offend them. Ps. 119:165.

Have you ever seen termites at work? They work quietly, behind the scenes, unnoticed by the casual observer, but nonetheless the results of their labors are devastating!

We had just moved to a new district and went for a drive to find our church. It sat on the corner in an older middle-class neighborhood. It was a stone structure with beautiful stained-glass windows that seemed to invite all who passed by to enter. Inside, the sanctuary had exposed beams that gave it a cozy yet reverent atmosphere.

Years went by and we enjoyed our church. One day as I stood in the foyer greeting visitors, I noticed some small holes in the doorframe and made a mental note to mention it to my husband the next day. When a pest control company lifted the sanctuary carpet to inspect the damage, they found that much of the wood floor needed replacing. Doors and doorframes had been damaged as well.

There are some spiritual termites that eat away at our spiritual life if we are not on our guard. Some of them are resentment, hatred, anger, an unforgiving attitude, stubbornness, self-righteousness, and jealousy.

I have had some termites to get out of my life. I had the termites of resentment and anger eating away at my spiritual life structure. I actually became physically ill over the situation! At first I didn't even want to give those feelings up, so I became more and more ill. It wasn't until I asked God to make me willing to surrender those feelings and I turned them over to Him that I could begin the healing process. I began claiming the promise for peace found in today's scripture. Praise God, He has given me a peace that passeth understanding! Whatever termites we might have in our lives, God has promised us the victory! CELIA CRUZ

Seasoned With Grace

Let your speech always be with grace, seasoned, as it were, with salt, so that you may know how you should respond to each person. Col. 4:6, NASB.

It had been my busiest workweek yet, and now it was Thursday evening and I was exhausted. One more day of work and I could collapse. I was busy trying to finish my paperwork on the patients I had seen that day when the phone rang.

"Mother, it's for you," Emilie said as she brought me the phone.

"Hello! I'm calling from *Highlights for Children* and was wondering what your children like best about our magazine."

"I don't really know." A long pause. I was hoping she would terminate the call. "They're right here. Shall I ask them?" Elizabeth and Catherine were reading books nearby.

"Girls, she's calling about *Highlights for Children*. What do you like most about the magazine?"

As soon as I repeated their answers to my caller, she quickly proceeded to tell me that if I bought a three-year subscription *now*, I would save $16.95—a real bargain, "especially since you have three children who will benefit."

I was weary, thinking more of progress notes than subscription bargains. Once more I put the phone down on my lap and with frustration and irritation said to my mother who was visiting, "This lady is struggling to be a saleswoman." I was too tired to make a decision and only wanted to end the conversation.

"No, I don't think we're interested."

Replying in a steady voice, my caller said, "I just want you to know that I'm not struggling to be a saleswoman; I *am* one!" and hung up.

I was stunned. How had she heard my comment? It wasn't kind, and I'd had no intention of her hearing it. I felt terrible, and all of a sudden it wasn't important to get my paperwork finished. I wanted to tell her that I was sorry and didn't mean to hurt her. If she had known I was a Christian, would she ever be interested in knowing more of Christ?

Words . . . they flow so freely, but do they reflect our allegiance? "Lord, forgive me. Live within me and help me to be so full of Your love that I will rightly represent You even when I'm tired, even when I'm delayed. May Your love make the difference in me today—even when I think no one will see or hear."

NANCY VOLLMER WILSON

APRIL 5

Grow Me Like a Tree

They will be called oaks of righteousness, a planting of the Lord for the display of his splendor. Isa. 61:3, NIV.

Grow me like a tree, my Lord,
Thick roots plunging deep;
Tapped into Your ceaseless well
Where countless blessings sleep.

Train my boughs to offer shade
To those who come my way;
Grace each leaf with Your desires
And brace when gales would sway.

Trace the faces that I touch,
What seeds I sow abroad;
Let leaves and pollen fly in wind
That others know my God.

Grow me where You've planted me,
Bring bloom in Your own time;
Ripen only Spirit-fruit
Maturing in Your clime.

Gently prune the sucker limbs,
Shape me as You please;
Trim the deadwood with Love's knife
And cure of sin-disease.

In Your season transplant me
With Your redeeming hand
To thrive and grow eternally
In Your unblemished land.

FANNIE L. HOUCK

Be Thankful

In the name of our Lord Jesus Christ give thanks every day for everything to our God and Father. Eph. 5:20, NEB.

Not long ago my husband and I were dealt a very heavy blow, the consequences of which will follow us for several years. Whatever the specific circumstances, these kinds of experiences are always full of anguish. The tunnel is very long, very dark, and very humiliating. Why this? This is the question that spills out again and again through the tears.

I knelt by my bed when the children had gone to school and poured it all out to our heavenly Father. Remembering Paul's counsel to be thankful in *all* things, I thanked God over and over, until I really meant it, for the experience and the valuable and necessary lessons it was teaching us. I pledged myself to do everything in my power to resolve the problem, and asked Him to send me the means. I got up from my knees with peace in my heart.

It would have been possible to search for and find solutions myself, but to the detriment of my home and the family. I waited for the Lord to provide, in His wisdom and love, the means to resolve the problem that would allow me to remain the homemaker I felt it was my privilege and responsibility to be. I couldn't believe that He would want us to learn lessons in one area of our lives by making us neglect responsibilities elsewhere.

I didn't have to wait long. Possibilities almost immediately began to present themselves, miraculously (there is no other word for it), and they continue to do so. The tunnel has an end, and it is no longer dark, because He is walking right beside us to guide us through. We are stronger in our weakness, richer in our knowledge of God, and more conscious of our complete dependence on Him. "The Lord's true love is surely not spent, nor has his compassion failed; they are new every morning, so great is his constancy" (Lam. 3:22, 23, NEB).

ELIZABETH TRIBES

Perhaps an Angel

*For He shall give His angels charge over you, to keep you
in all your ways. In their hands they shall bear you up, lest
you dash your foot against a stone. Ps. 91:11, 12, NKJV.*

It had rained all night, freezing rain that covered everything with
a glaze of ice. Trees and bushes sparkled as if covered with
diamonds, but our road was a wide ribbon of glaring ice. The steep
hill I live on intersects a busy highway at the foot of the hill. No one
would be able to use the hill until it was sanded.

I thought about my dentist appointment for that morning and
how if Dana, my husband, were still alive he would never let me go
on icy roads. He would always protect me by taking me himself.
Now I am on my own, with God to help me. Soon I heard the sand
truck go by and watched as the whirling blades on the back of the
truck threw sand across the road. *It should be safe to leave now*, I
thought.

After leaving my driveway, I put the car into low gear and
started my slow descent down the hill. All went well until I realized
I was gathering speed and needed to slow down to avoid a quick
stop at the intersection, which was bound to be slippery. Very
gently I touched my brake, and immediately my car spun in a
complete circle. I tried to steer in the direction of the skid as I'd been
taught, but I succeeded only in making another complete circle in
the opposite direction. I hit a patch of ice and flew out into the
center of the highway, where I made another complete circle. So far
I had been too busy trying to control the car to remember to pray.
As I felt the car starting another circle I cried out, "Please, Father,
help me!" When I did, it felt as if giant hands picked my car up,
turned it around, and set it down on the other side of the
intersection—pointed in the right direction. Just a split second later
a huge truck went roaring by, followed closely by another big truck.
There was no way they could have stopped in time had I still been
in the center of the road. Coming around the corner, they would
not have seen me until they were on top of me.

I sat there praising our Lord and thanking Him for answering
my prayer. I believe He sent angels to carry me to safety and to save
my life.

DORIS E. EVERETT

God Does Care

The angel of the Lord encampeth round about them that fear him, and delivereth them. Ps. 34:7.

Gail left home early one cold winter morning for church, nine miles away. Although there were two or three churches nearer, she'd kept her membership in the town where she stayed before her marriage.

It was her turn to be organist that day, and she needed to practice, since she wasn't familiar with one of the hymns. She collected the keys for the church just after 8:00 a.m., drove to the church, and parked next to the low wall near the entrance to the church grounds. She unlocked the two locks of the front door and went in. Since she was a bit later than usual, she decided to leave the front door unlocked. The secretary would be arriving in just a few minutes anyway.

Gail walked down the aisle to the organ, placed her books on the top, and checked the switch. Then she went into the vestry and switched on the main lever. As she came back to the organ, she slipped off her boots. She pressed a key to check the tone, and it was then that her very sensitive ears picked up the heavy tread of footsteps. She was petrified. She distinctly heard someone trying to unlock and open the front door, which she knew she'd left unlocked. It didn't open!

Through frosted windows she saw someone in a white and blue track suit top passing toward the side door. The person had a key or keys, and tried to open the security door of the small room—without success. He then proceeded round the back to the vestry door. The jingling of keys was heard, again without success. The man came down that side of the church. He went to the front door again, which he tried to open for the second time, but it still wouldn't open. He went to all the doors around the church again. Gail was now standing in a corner at the back of the church with her heart pounding heavily.

Finally, she heard the footsteps receding. When she thought it was safe, she went and locked the front door, breathing a sigh of relief and a prayer. She was too drained to practice. About 10 minutes later the church elder and his family arrived, and not the expected secretary. They had planned to visit another congregation, but plans had changed at the last minute.

Gail is indeed grateful that her guardian angel kept that front door closed. PHYLLIS DALGLEISH

His Listening Ear

Never will I leave you; never will I forsake you. Heb. 13:5, NIV.

More times than I care to count, I have been confronted with a challenging situation and pursued a solution—sometimes successfully, sometimes not—and later thought to myself, *Why didn't I think to pray?* When the "big" problems come, it's easy to remember to pray. But it's just as easy to overlook praying about the "small" everyday challenges. We need to remember that God is interested in our everyday experiences, too. He covets our frequent communication.

Several years ago I participated in a support group. One night a student from Pepperdine University related how she learned to "talk" with the Lord. She often would talk aloud with Him while driving her car. She was happy for her car phone because she could hold it to her ear while she communicated with God and people driving by wouldn't wonder if she was talking to herself!

But some people don't feel comfortable talking with God. My husband visited an elderly gentleman who was lamenting his failing eyesight, loss of hearing, and inability to get around. While there were things he could no longer do, he could and did pray. And since he could still write and read large print, my husband was impressed to suggest that he make a prayer list and pray for people in need. But the man replied, "I've never been one to worry the Lord." I felt sad when I heard that. I know the man prayed, but I think it was more a formality than a conversation with God.

Bill Hybels *Too Busy Not to Pray* has been an inspiration to me. I was impressed with the thought the author presented on Hebrews 13:5, "Never will I leave you; never will I forsake you." He says it is not necessary to remind God to be with us. "Instead, we need to pray that we will be aware of His presence, that we will be confident because of it" (p. 43).

Reflecting on this sentence, I realized my prayers had consisted of a lot of "be withs." Now I pray, "Make me aware of Your presence today," and "Thank You for promising to reveal Yourself to me in a special way."   BETSY MATTHEWS

A Mother's Prayers

Surely, thus says the Lord: "Even the captives of the mighty shall be taken, and the prey of the tyrant be rescued, for I will contend with those who contend with you, and I will save your children." Isa. 49:25, RSV.

Emilie had carefully raised her son to love the Lord. She had followed God's instructions, putting Him first in every aspect of their home. Morning and evening the family raised their voices to God in prayer and praise! But upon entering his teenage years, her son turned his back upon God and the church.

Emilie's dreams were shattered. The burden, and sometimes guilt, that a mother feels when she sees her child take that final step against God's love and leading can seem unbearable.

Each day this mother faithfully presented her son's name before the Lord. Many years went by. At times she wondered if she would live to see this promise fulfilled in the life of her son.

God was faithful, and after 40 years her son gave his heart to the Lord. Truly God tenderly holds in His hand our loved ones who have turned their backs on Him.

Our prayers give God permission to act against Satan and release those whom he is holding. By claiming the promises of God's Word, you can use the sword of the Spirit to limit the power of evil forces effectively.
ROBERTA SCHAFER

Receiving Is Part of Giving

Freely ye have received, freely give. Matt. 10:8.

As a child I took the words of this scripture to heart and tried to implement them in my daily life. Over the years I became very comfortable giving to others, but I never understood that part of *giving* involves *receiving*.

The Lord has often used dear friends to gently teach me some of the lessons I needed to learn.

Nell Thompson and I had met for lunch and were enjoying the

stimulation of one-to-one sharing. I finished eating the last mouthful of mouth-watering pasta—fettuccine Alfredo, a particular favorite of mine—and we prepared to leave. Even though we both faced busy schedules, we lingered to savor the last few moments of our time together. The waitress brought the bill, and I opened my wallet, expecting to split the tab as we usually did. Instead, Nell reached out and picked up the bill, saying, "Today is my treat."

"Oh no," I quickly protested, "your treat was in giving me some of your time. You can't pay for my lunch, too."

"But I want to do this," she answered. "It will give me a great deal of pleasure."

I continued to protest, "But you are on a fixed income while I am earning a salary."

Maintaining her grip on the bill, Nell looked me straight in the eye and said kindly but firmly, "Arlene, you know how to give; you need to learn how to receive—graciously." I was stunned, and had the words come from someone else within whose affection I was less secure, I might have felt crushed. What did she mean? Surely it is always more blessed to give than to receive (Acts 20:35)!

Nell continued, "Do you remember the story of Mary and the alabaster box of oil of spikenard?" (Luke 7:36-50). Of course I did. "Christ did not need Mary's gift," she explained, "but He graciously accepted it so as not to deprive her of the pleasure and the blessing that comes from giving." She went on to draw an analogy. When people are comfortable only with giving and uncomfortable with receiving, the potential giver and receiver are both deprived. One loses the blessing of giving and the other loses the blessing of receiving. She said that giving and receiving were like two sides of a coin and that they must be in balance in our lives. I had never thought of it in that light before.

How many times, I wondered to myself, had I deprived others of the pleasure of giving because I was uncomfortable with receiving? Even though Christ "did not come to be served but to serve" (Matt. 20:28, NIV), there were times when He allowed others to give to Him (Mark 15:40, 41).

It is so important to maintain equilibrium in our lives—including a balance between giving and receiving. The Lord, no doubt, is pleased with gracious receivers as well as with generous givers. Furthermore, there are times when we need to receive even an admonition graciously. This was one of those times, and the gift I received far outweighed the price of many lunches. It has remained with me all these years.

While my first instinct is sometimes still to remonstrate with a prospective benefactor, appropriate words come more easily now (thank you; that's very thoughtful of you; I appreciate your kindness) because I hear Nell's voice in memory reminding me that receiving is part of giving. ARLENE TAYLOR

The "Words" of Body Language

But Jesus said unto him, Judas, betrayest thou the Son of man with a kiss? Luke 22:48. And the Lord turned, and looked upon Peter. Luke 22:61.

A ctions speak louder than words," the proverb says. And body postures, facial expressions, hand movements, and gestures communicate such undeniable messages that they have been classified as body language.

Those with expertise in translating what all these movements mean claim that these physical motions provide us with several psychological insights.

A knowledge of body language permits a listener to detect differences between the actual words a person says and what that person really means. For example, differences between fake and genuine smiles can be unmasked by noticing cheek movement and lines around the eyes—not the mouth.

In addition, arm and leg positions during an interview can reveal attitudes of caution, tentativeness, or uncertainty. Certain postures connote hostility and fear, while others connote acceptance and openness. Skilled body language communicators can detect a speaker's real message more accurately and can also make sure their own body language matches their words, to prevent sending out mixed messages.

Body language as a science is a relatively new concept, but society has long recognized the power of nonverbal communication. A thumbs-down signal speaks as clearly as any "no" that could be spoken.

Body language has not only a social, but a spiritual dimension: "By a glance of the eye, a motion of the hand, an expression of the countenance, a falsehood may be told as effectually as by words" (*Patriarchs and Prophets*, p. 309).

Two thousand years ago, on history's most infamous Friday, body language sent the Saviour to His death: "But Jesus said unto him, Judas, betrayest thou the Son of man with a kiss?" On the darkest of nights, the cock having crowed after Peter's third denial, Jesus' head and shoulders moved to face His disciple in one of the most poignant postures in the Bible: "And the Lord turned, and looked upon Peter." O wordless rebuke! O voiceless grief!

Then the Crucifixion, the most telling of postures. "The spotless Son of God hung upon the cross, His flesh lacerated with stripes; those hands so often stretched out in blessing, nailed to the wooden bars; those feet so tireless on ministries of love, spiked to the tree; that royal head pierced by the crown of thorns; those quivering lips shaped to the cry of woe" (*The Desire of Ages*, p. 755).

So Jesus gave Himself. His whole being suspended between heaven and earth is the most powerful of symbols, the ultimate body language. "And the Word was made flesh," and we killed Him (John 1:14). The broken body of Christ . . . O powerful language of love!   WILMA MCCLARTY

APRIL 13

Eyes That See

Then Elisha prayed, and said, "O Lord, I pray thee, open his eyes that he may see." 2 Kings 6:17, RSV.

When I was a young girl I didn't enjoy books, and did very poorly in school. It wasn't until I was 10 years old and in fourth grade that a teacher finally realized that I was straining to see the blackboard. She sent me to the school nurse for a simple eye test. You know, the kind in which you stand about 20 feet from a large poster featuring letters of the alphabet, cover one eye at a time, and read the letters. When I took the test I couldn't see any letters from the second row down. The nurse sent a note home telling my parents to take me to an eye doctor. My eyesight was so poor that I was legally blind!

I'll never forget the first time I put on my new glasses and looked around. I could see things across the room! I looked out the window and could see birds flying, leaves on the trees, blades of grass, and flowers. I had never seen a bird fly before. The people walking by on the sidewalk had faces and expressions I could see. I went to school the next day and endured the taunting chants of the children calling me "four eyes," and didn't even care. I could see, and that was all that mattered. The blackboard, the teacher, the students, the bulletin board . . . everything was in focus. A whole new world opened up to me!

I was so excited. I just couldn't see enough, fast enough. I was hungry to take everything in. I have often contemplated that experience and thanked God again for the gift of sight.

Sometimes we become "out of focus." We do a delicate balancing act between our families and careers. We struggle with problems with toddlers and teenagers, communication with our husbands, trying to "keep up with the Joneses" while living within our budgets—and the list goes on and on! We look inward and allow our personal problems to blur our spiritual vision. May our daily prayer be "O Lord, keep me in focus. Help me to keep my priorities straight. Open my eyes that I might see!"   CELIA CRUZ

Invited to Dinner

Jesus said to him, "There was once a man who was giving a great feast to which he invited many people. When it was time for the feast, he sent his servant to tell his guests, 'Come, everything is ready!' . . . So the master said to the servant, 'Go out to the country roads and lanes and make people come in, so that my house will be full.' " Luke 14:16-23, TEV.

Imagine being invited to a great feast in the home of the rich and famous. We often have a fascination with the rich and wonder what it would be like to stay at such a place or eat dinner in grand style, perhaps sitting next to a celebrity. The place settings would be elegant, the linen especially beautiful, and the conversation stimulating. No doubt we would tell our friends about this great invitation and all that went on.

Jesus tells us that the invitees in His story were too busy to attend and had all manner of excuses to offer—real estate, prior engagements, family concerns, household needs. Are their responses typical of our own? Do we invest time in the trivia of the day and get bogged down in chores that seem important at the moment? God calls us to a grand feast! He has the table all ready and anticipates our companionship. Haven't we experienced disappointment when someone we invited and planned for was unable to come? We looked forward to the meal and how to make it pretty, longed for the conversation and close fellowship, and then felt the pain of loss when it did not happen. We cannot know God's feelings, but we may experience in a small way the disappointment of rejection when our company does not come.

Think about the ideal invitation we'd all like to have—some great occasion when the printed formal invitation comes followed by a phone call with particular instruction on attire: "This is a black-tie affair. The women will be wearing very dressy black gowns. Oh, the parking will be in a private garage. Limousines will drive up to the entrance on the north side." As you enter, you notice the beautiful clothes and hear a grand piano being played. You are directed to the area where people are signing the guestbook and to the second floor where sumptuous food and fine entertainment await you. Are we really awake and in this wonderful place? Do we fit in?

Think of going to God's house. The invitation has already been received, the place and menu are prepared, the limousine will be calling in about an hour. It may be hard to imagine that God truly wants us not only to come to the grand feast but to *stay* in His house! We must be getting ready to go to this feast—anticipating the meal and eagerly awaiting meeting the guests and being part of God's *full house* (John 17:24; 14:1-3).   JULIA L. PEARCE

APRIL 15

Windows of Blessing

Prove me now herewith, saith the Lord of hosts, if I will not open you the windows of heaven, and pour you out a blessing, that there shall not be room enough to receive it. Mal. 3:10.

When I was 16 years old, my one great desire was to study at Newbold College, England, to become a Bible instructor. Thirty years later as I look back over the passage of time, I am reminded of how God has provided for my every need and indeed poured out many blessings.

I came from a relatively poor family in good old England. My father had made many sacrifices in order to remain true to the Sabbath. Money was in short supply, and there was no money to pay my college fees. I was accepted as a student at Newbold College on the condition that I had sufficient money for my fees. I therefore began to work (I earned £3 per week) and also applied to the local government education department requesting a scholarship for my studies. Many people reminded me that it was very unlikely that I would receive a scholarship to take such a course of study; it had never been done before.

Our family prayed hard those few months. One day I received the long-awaited letter and hesitated in opening the envelope for fear it contained bad news. You can imagine my joy and gratitude when I read the contents, learning that I had been granted not only full scholarship (all fees paid), but also an allowance for books, travel, and pocket money. God was good indeed! He truly knows when to open the windows of heaven.

Let us be faithful stewards and trust God, for He will open the windows of heaven and pour out a blessing at the right time.

EUNICE M. MASON

APRIL 16

Bending the Knotted Oak

David would take his harp and play. Then relief would come to Saul; he would feel better. 1 Sam. 16:23, NIV.

I sat in the dim, quiet coolness of the great cathedral. Beams from the late-afternoon sun streamed in through the stained glass and warmed my heart, if not the chill in the air. The high Gothic arches, the massive stone pillars, and the gigantic pipe organ promised a musical treat par excellence. However, I found myself waiting half in expectancy and half in dread for the program to begin. I had developed a pattern of avoiding church musical programs at Christmastime as much as possible because the familiar old carols brought tears and pain of something as yet unremembered from childhood. Even though I knew the tears might come again, I joined friends for the annual Christmas concert at Grace Cathedral.

The crowd hushed and from a distant balcony I heard the pure, clear voice of a child singing "Silent Night," and then a different musical rendition of "Away in a Manger" than I had learned as a child. I listened to the program with reverence, in awe of the magnificence of the total experience. I felt quite pleased with myself that I had made it through the program without crying as we stood to sing the three closing carols together. But as our voices swelled to reach the heights of the glorious cathedral, the tears began to wash down my cheeks and splash on the printed verses on my program. I stopped singing and asked God where this pain began and how I could be healed from it. As I embraced the pain, allowing it to rise to its fullest, the memory of a very deep loss at Christmastime long past burst into my mind. And slowly, with the music and the tears, some of the pain washed away.

Congreve was right: "Music has charms to soothe a savage breast, to soften rocks, or bend a knotted oak." I felt the music and also felt relief.

Music has a mysterious power over the soul. It motivates us to clap our hands, tap our toes, or sing along with it. It stimulates the nerves in our brains, helping us to feel more alive. It allows us to heal from the pain of the past.

The program was over, and I silently thanked God for, as

William Walford put it, the "sweet hour of prayer." The music, a form of prayer, had called me from my world of care. My soul had found relief from its distress and grief.

I mentally thanked the musicians for sharing their talents that had helped me feel the spirit of the season and assisted me in coming closer to God. Their gift of beautiful music and God's gift of His Son had both changed my life.

The last notes faded as the rays from the setting sun merged themselves into the coming night. And I, carrying the melodies in my heart, was ready to begin another day of growth in my own life.

MYRNA MELLING

APRIL 17

Reunion

For the Lamb in the midst of the throne will be their shepherd, and he will guide them to springs of living water; and God will wipe away every tear from their eyes. Rev. 7:17, RSV.

A few days ago I visited the church where I grew up and was thrilled to see a couple friends for whom I'd been deeply concerned.

They had both married non-Adventist husbands and for quite a while it seemed like the devil used their marriages as a weapon against them. For about 15 years one of them had cried to the Lord to touch her husband's heart and convict him, and it seemed her prayers were never to be answered.

These women had been humiliated and treated badly because of the faith they proclaimed. Yet they never became discouraged, because they knew in whom they believed. They were aware that their "light and momentary troubles [will achieve] for [them] an eternal glory." They fixed their "eyes not on what is seen, but on what is unseen" (2 Cor. 4:17-18, NIV). And the Lord honored them, and answered their prayers. He won their husbands' hearts.

I felt unspeakable joy that Sabbath as I watched one of these men preach the sermon and the other sing in the choir. Tears ran down my cheeks as I praised God in my mind then and as we met after the service to recount how good the Lord is. The devil places a lot of hurdles in our path, but with God, our victories are sure.

That was a reunion that renewed our faith in God. It draws my mind to the final reunion in our heavenly home, when all of God's children from far and near, who have won victory through Christ our Redeemer, will meet to sing their untold experiences on earth in the Song of Moses and the Lamb.

As I praise God for those who are still in the race, I think of those we have left behind, and I pray that the Holy Spirit will renew their strength so that they may gain the victory that is in Christ Jesus. It will be a terrible thing for any of us to be missing on that great day. Will I be there? Will you be there?

"The Lord, your God, is in your midst, a warrior who gives victory; he will rejoice over you with gladness, he will renew you in his love; he will exult over you with loud singing as on a day of festival" (Zeph. 3:17, RSV).   CONSTANCE C. NWOSU

APRIL 18

Asking Forgiveness Affectively

And [Jacob] bowed himself to the ground seven times, until he came near to his brother. And Esau ran to meet him, and embraced him, and fell on his neck, and kissed him: and they wept. Gen. 33:3, 4.

Did you think I meant *effectively?* Well, no, I meant affectively (influencing emotions), but I believe that to be affective is to be effective. So adjust the spelling if you must!

There are six words usually spoken in an apology: "I'm sorry. Will you forgive me?" Unless accompanied by some pretty strong paralanguage, these six words satisfy only the cognitive (intellectual) domain.

Asking forgiveness is one area in which Jesus, having never sinned, left us no example. And while the Bible contains instances of prayer repentances to God, there are precious few instances of asking forgiveness of another individual. Probably the most revealing one is Jacob's repentance to Esau. Note the steps above and beyond the actual apology:

1. Jacob prepared a present of more than 500 animals for Esau (Gen. 32:14-16).
2. Jacob referred to himself as servant and to Esau as lord.
3. Jacob bowed seven times before Esau.
4. The two brothers embraced, fell on each other's necks, kissed, and wept.
5. Jacob insisted that Esau accept the present when Esau declined. You can read this touching scene in Genesis 32 and 33.

Like Jacob, the prodigal son also took the identity of a servant when he approached his forgiver. In their deep remorse, both were willing to come crawling.

Neither had the attitude "I'm Christian enough to confess; you should be Christian enough to forgive." Neither cast the slightest innuendo of reflection upon the forgiver, such as "Let's talk this through calmly; you knew that God Himself declared the birthright was to go to the younger" or "You knew that giving me all that money was like turning a 2-year-old loose with car keys."

Unlike Jacob, the son had only his humility to submit. It was the forgiver who became generous. Note his responses:

1. Had compassion, fell on his neck, and kissed him.
2. Dressed him with the best robe, a ring, and shoes.
3. Ordered a veal dinner for everyone with music and dancing.

Forgiveness, then, is recorded as very emotional in the Bible. All four men—Jacob, Esau, son, and father—were involved in embracing and kissing.

Although the son could not present gifts like Jacob, the father could not resist. Although Esau's response was not like the father's, Esau could not resist.

Jacob could never make restitution for his grave mistake, but he left nothing undone to make Esau feel better about him. His was a far different approach from one we often hear: "Well, what do you expect me to do about it now?"

Perhaps you are remembering something you did that didn't seem so bad—at least not bad enough to stimulate all the heartfelt repentance you perceived was being sought. You may think the whole issue was exaggerated. Is that what matters?

Jesus did leave us an example in this area. Jesus did not make a rational, cognitive decision that He had no business being on that cross in the first place. His death on the cross, the greatest decision ever made in the universe, was *affective*—"for God *so loved* the world" (John 3:16)!

Which will it be for you today—cognitive confessions or affective forgiveness?   JANET KANGAS

APRIL 19

The Power of a Song

Speak to one another with psalms, hymns and spiritual songs. Sing and make music in your heart to the Lord. Eph. 5:19, NIV.

It is common knowledge that singing brightens life and that spiritual music is able to elevate the human heart to God. Many Christians have received comfort through spiritual music, but spiritual songs can impress godless people as well. They can even banish evil, with divine assistance. I experienced this in my early youth.

It was the year 1945 at the end of World War II. I was a 16-year-old girl when the Russian Army advanced toward Vienna. Because of the bombing raids, my parents had fled with me to the countryside, where we were living in a small village near the Danube. We knew about the advance of the Russian Army, and one evening we saw Russian tanks on a nearby wooded hill. The inhabitants hoisted white flags on the roofs. Everyone wanted to escape alive and hoped that the war would soon be over.

After evening prayer we went to sleep unsuspecting of all that would happen during the night. In the morning there were violent knocks at our door. My father opened it, and Russian soldiers stormed in to thoroughly search the house for weapons, wine, and valuables. As my frightened mother saw the menacing look on the soldiers' faces, she motioned to me to play at the harmonium. With trembling hands I played the only two hymns I knew by heart, and hoped that the music would somehow impress these wild-looking fellows.

And then the miracle happened. One after the other, they left the house. Then others came in, listened for a while, and disappeared. I don't remember how many times I played these two hymns over and over, but God helped us through a time when we were unaware of our tragic situation. While we were sleeping that night, strong angels must have guarded our door, for the surrounding people suffered terribly from looting, beatings, shootings, and rapes. God had given my mother the idea that the spiritual songs could soften the rough spirits, and He literally "shut the lions' mouths," as was the case with Daniel.

Oh, that we would use the spiritual songs more often! Words and melody are meant to comfort and uplift us, and to elevate our minds toward God. Many people have had encouraging experiences with these hymns.   SUSANNE HATZINGER

APRIL 20

Fine Tuning

Finally, brethren, whatever is true, whatever is honorable, whatever is just, whatever is pure, whatever is lovely, whatever is gracious, if there is any excellence, if there is

*anything worthy of praise, think about these things. Phil.
4:8, RSV.*

I was just a half block from work one morning when one of my
most "unfavorite" songs blared out from the car radio. Normally
I would have changed the station, but since I would be turning the
car off in just a few minutes, I let it go. A half hour later I realized
my mistake when I found myself humming the tune of that awful
song. I stopped in mid-measure, shocked at my own behavior. But
the horrible tune kept playing over and over in my mind. Imperceptibly I was being changed. The next time it came on the radio it
was not quite as offensive. I tuned it out consciously, but my
subconscious embraced it. Eventually I could even listen to it
without being offended. But what was really scary was when I
actually started liking the song.

Perhaps some of you have gone shopping with your teenagers,
as I have, and have had to listen to some of the subtle (and
not-so-subtle) lyrics of the music played in the teen shops. The same
situation happens. First, rejection. Then passiveness. Finally, acceptance.

Does this have to happen? King David said, "Thy word have I
hid in mine heart, that I might not sin against thee" (Ps. 119:11).
This, I decided, was the key to counteract this unwanted influence.
So, with a slight modification of the "word," I picked a hymn,
learned all the verses, and hid it in my mind. Then I was ready.
Whenever an unwanted tune began playing around in my head, I
mentally pulled out my "weapon" and began the counterattack. It
worked! I won the battle. But the war was not over. It took
perseverance. And the war still rages. But every time I encounter an
unwanted tune creeping into my mind, I mentally, and sometimes
audibly, start singing "my tune." And everything turns out fine.
That has to be "fine tuning." NANCY VASQUEZ

APRIL 21

In His Presence

*And when Jesus saw her, he called her to him, and said
unto her, Woman, thou art loosed from thine infirmity.
Luke 13:12.*

While reading this text, I was immediately reminded of the song
"He Touched Me." The verse reads "Shackled by a heavy
burden, 'neath a load of guilt and shame, then the hand of Jesus

touched me, and now I am no longer the same."

I remember too the stories in the Bible about the women who suffered from illness. Both women had spent a number of years shackled by heavy burdens. One for 12 years, the other 18. Both women had carried the stigma of guilt and the reproach of shame. Then along came Jesus.

One saw Him as her last hope and reached out her hand to just touch the hem of His garment. The other could not even lift herself up, but Jesus laid His healing hands on her, and she too was made well.

One was healed by touching, the other by being touched. The key factor was that both were in the presence of Jesus. They were found in the Master's company.

O friend, "are you weary and troubled? No light in the darkness you see?" Then "Turn Your Eyes Upon Jesus"! Like the two women, be found in the Master's presence. Be found in His presence always, day by day, hour by hour, moment by moment. There is healing there, for in His presence is the balm in Gilead. In His presence is joy forevermore, and in His sweet presence all darkness flees.   JUNELI VANCE

APRIL 22

Focus on the Positive

For the Lord shall comfort Zion: joy and gladness shall be found therein, thanksgiving, and the voice of melody. Isa. 51:3.

The other morning as I drifted into awakeness, my ears slowly became aware of two very small voices lustily singing "With Jesus in the family, happy, happy home . . ." They weren't always in the same key. They were often out of sync with each other and the words didn't always match, but at that dreamy moment all I could focus on was how beautifully touching it was to be awakened by my two youngest children spontaneously singing praises to their friend Jesus.

There is always more than one way to focus on the daily situations that parents face (and family life is always daily). It becomes vital to use our God-given willpower to choose to focus on the positive aspects of our circumstances.

Choose to focus on the wonderful blessing it is that your child has two hands and 10 fingers to explore with, rather than on the oatmeal plastered behind his or her ears. Choose to be grateful that

God instilled inquisitiveness in his or her small being, rather than getting frustrated by nose- and finger-prints on the windowpanes. Choose to be thrilled that there's a wellspring of happiness flowing from your children, instead of getting angry that they burst out singing while you were on an important business call. Choose to be cheered by the progress that now the puddle gets as far as the bathroom before forming, instead of feeling depressed that it didn't get in the toilet. Choose to be touched and awed by the dependence that they feel on you to help them get out of "stuck situations," instead of being wearied by the pleas for help with stuck zippers and knotted shoelaces.

It is very important for children to be trained to sing quietly during phone calls, eat neatly, tie their own shoelaces, and master a host of other simple and complex tasks that will aid in their developing into responsible adults. But more important than the rote learning of details (a dog can be trained not to put nose and paws on windowpanes) is the attitude in which details are taught. That choice of attitude is what creates the atmosphere that surrounds us at all times. And the atmosphere that surrounds us will be indelibly imparted into our children's inner beings—to be reproduced now, and later.

Yes, I am going to teach my children to sing on tune, in the same key as their accompaniment, and to match the words and rhythm with their partner. That's an important part of growing up. It will come in time by means of my example and my loving, patient instruction. But for right now, and always, I want them to feel an atmosphere of appreciation and praise emanating from my heart for my Creator and for His gift to me of my children and the beautiful songs they sing. — JANICE SMITH

APRIL 23

Just a-Passin' Through

Truly, truly, I say to you, unless a grain of wheat falls into the earth and dies, it remains alone; but if it dies, it bears much fruit. John 12:24, RSV.

There we were, 100 women singing the children's ditty "The Word of God is like a little bitty seed scattered all around." We had come together for a weekend of praise, hoping to find community and belonging.

As we sang, I thought of the scattered seed and the rooting process that allows for a seed to grow and mature. I thought of the importance of people having roots, of belonging to a place and community with one another.

Then another song, "This world is not my home, I'm just a-passin' through," floated through my mind. It is no secret that we have all been touched by brokenness. It is no secret that we live in a scattered, fractured world.

Can we have roots and a sense of belonging in this world in which we are just "a-passin' through"? Yes indeed! It is through the Holy Spirit that we can be wonderfully connected to one another. It is in the sharing of our stories and in the taking into our inner beings the moment-by-moment encounters with one another that we have what will give us a sense of belonging to one another.

JOYCE HANSCOM LORNTZ

APRIL 24

The Miracle of Sound

Speak, Lord, for your servant is listening. 1 Sam. 3:9, NIV.

Radio has always fascinated me. Television hadn't been invented yet when I was a child. We did have a radio, however. One with shortwave capabilities. Sometimes my father, Leslie Warren Taylor, would sit down beside the radio in the evening, turn the dials, and suddenly we would hear voices from Iceland, Alaska, or some other distant land. Dad told me that the sense of hearing is based on a code system, and he was correct; not dots and dashes like the famous Morse Code, but vibrations. He explained that the pitch of a sound depends upon the frequency of the vibrations carried on the airwaves, while the intensity of the sound depends upon the size of the sound waves. I was able to understand the comparison when he said that sound waves, originating from a vibrating object and resulting from the alternate compression and decompression of air, were carried through the air much like waves travel on water—to be picked up by our radio receiver.

About 20 percent of the people in our culture prefer to pick up information through the sense of hearing. Many people (especially music lovers) cherish the sense of hearing almost as much as the sense of vision. Benjamin Disraeli once said, "There is no index of character so sure as the voice."

The brain is able to decode sounds that enter it by either ear. In the average person, however, the right ear prefers to receive informational language input which is decoded in the lower left brain quadrant (in Wernicke's area). When competing verbal material is presented to both ears, the right ear will tend to pick up the material faster. The left ear prefers to receive musical and emotional messages, which are decoded in the lower right brain quadrant.

Knowing this can help you to maximize the brain's decoding ability. If you telephone a friend to ask for directions to his or her home, hold the receiver to your right ear. This will give the edge to logical, linear, sequential skills and allow you to write down the correct directions more easily and accurately. If you telephone a friend to offer condolences because of a death in the family, hold the receiver to your left ear. This will give the edge to caring, harmonizing skills and can help you to relate more empathetically.

Women tend to hear better and to have more accurate auditory recall. They are much more sensitive to noise, however, and are less tolerant of loud noises than men. Women tend to concentrate better when the environment is quiet. They score higher on IQ tests, for example, when there is no noise or distraction in the room.

God wants to speak to us, too: "Hear, O my people, and I will speak" (Ps. 50:7). Often this is a still small voice, and sometimes we are too busy to listen for it or too tired to hear it. We need to think of the miracle of sound; to listen to the voices of those we know and love; to speak a gentle word of encouragement to someone else; and above all, to be still and say, "Speak, Lord; I'm listening."

ARLENE TAYLOR

APRIL 25

Of French Fries and Root Beer

Except ye be converted, and become as little children, ye shall not enter into the kingdom of heaven. Matt. 18:3.

Gramma!" shouted my 4-year-old granddaughter. As I entered the door she jumped into my arms. Tammy, my only grandchild at the time, could always talk me into doing what she wanted. "French fries and root beer, Gramma. Let's go!"

I laughed, and looked at her mother, who responded, "Well, it is suppertime. Why don't you two run along? I've got things to do."

We soon climbed into my car and were off to the nearest french-fries-and-root-beer place. The cheerful waitress took our order: two root beers and one order of fries. Tammy looked at me. "Only one french fries, Gramma?"

"Yes, honey, that's all," I answered. I knew that she would never eat a whole order, and the thrifty side of me had decided we would share. *No need to explain*, I thought.

The waitress soon filled up the tray, and we found our way to a table where we sat down to feast upon this delicacy of childhood. I placed the french fries between us. Tammy looked longingly at them, then reached for the ketchup bottle. "Careful, dear," I said as I picked a french fry off the plate.

She stopped in midair, looked at the french fries again, then looked me straight in the eye. "Gramma, you don't like ketchup, do you?"

This was my chance to teach a little temperance (never mind that we were eating greasy french fries), and I began, "No, dear. I don't eat ketchup because it has vinegar in it and it's really not . . ."

The temperance lecture would be a lost cause for that day, for there she was, carefully pouring the ketchup, covering *every* french fry. I watched in astonishment. Gramma would eat no french fries from that batch—and Tammy knew that she would have them all to herself! (Who says 4-year-olds don't understand?)

Openly, innocently, without guile or deceitfulness, she had done what she thought she had to do. In her childlike way she had solved her problem and taught her grandmother a lesson. No scolding, no condemnation, no asking why. But we both knew that next time I would order my own french fries!

"Except ye . . . become as little children" acquired new meaning for me that day. PATRICIA A. HABADA

APRIL 26

One More Spiritual Gift

I caused the widow's heart to sing for joy. Job 29:13.

The truth that music is the universal language became evident when I heard our familiar hymns sung in Spanish in Southern Mexico. How I identified with the expressions and meaning even though I didn't understand the words. I could penetrate beyond the sounds, and identify perfectly with what the singers were feeling and thinking right then.

I was especially touched when I was told that I might not recognize some of the melodies. "The people here see their pastor very infrequently, since he pastors 22 churches," my interpreter explained. "So if they like the words, they might just make up a melody of their own!" (in which case the translator overlooked that I would not recognize either).

Imagine my surprise later in Europe, when I heard one of the same melodies, unknown to me in English, being sung. The Adventist Church is truly a "world church"—the Spanish and the Danish singing the same hymn, unknown to me! The transplanting of the message truly did not all come from the United States!

A couple months before, I had experienced the same bonding through music with my spry 92-year-old grandfather. Before I moved from schooling in Michigan to my job in Maryland (12 hours away), he had chosen, for our last day together in Michigan, to go dune buggy riding!

The return ride from Silver Lake took about two hours. We were somewhat weary from a full day, plus downhearted as we were counting down the last two hours before distance would separate us. Lurking in the back of our minds, unspoken, was the nagging thought that death would separate us before we could meet again. How I wished my call to the General Conference had come after that event so that I wouldn't have to leave him behind.

And then, rather suddenly, Gramps got a grip on the situation. "You know, the fun we had today makes me think of that old song our quartet used to sing," he said as he began to beat out his base part. I joined in and was sure that only the holy angels were in the car with us, because no evil ones could have survived in that atmosphere!

Glad for the upbeat tempo, I asked, "Know any more, Gramps?"

"Well, there are some we used to sing at camp meeting," he said, and so we continued. Suddenly here we were enjoying an experience that closed the two-generation spread between us. These songs meant the same to him as they did to me! And there were no slow, pensive hymns like "Nearer, My God, to Thee," or "Just As I Am." Oh, no! The songs he chose were the liveliest I've known: "I Have the Joy, Joy, Joy, Joy Down in My Heart!"; "Brighten the Corner Where You Are!"; "He Lives!"; and "Lift Up the Trumpet!"

Each piece seemed to remind us of three more, and before we knew it we were at his home in Kalamazoo. Our souls were vibrant, and the joy bounced in our hearts. What could have been a tearful farewell ended with just a big hug and a beaming promise, "I'll write tomorrow!"

I am not sure why Paul never included music as one of the spiritual gifts in his three lists (Eph. 4, 1 Cor. 12, Rom. 12). Music crosses every barrier: language, age, or loneliness. Why not try it today?

JANET KANGAS

Flowers of the Field

As for man, his days are as grass: as a flower of the field, so he flourisheth. Ps. 103:15.

To flourish as a flower is a wonderful challenge. What a pleasure it is to plant the seeds, to nourish and water the buds. Man does so little, but the Master Artist displays all the lovely shades and colors to delight the eye at the proper time and season. If we human gardeners neglect to give water and attention to the soil, we cannot expect beautiful results. Life is like that. As we study the beautiful life of our Jesus, His example of labor and love is most encouraging. We too can spread beauty and hope to those who don't know our Lord.

This statement suggests ways of growing like the flowers of the field and to blossom as a rose: "When the love of Christ is enshrined in the heart, like sweet fragrance it cannot be hidden. Its holy influence will be felt by all with whom we come in contact. . . . Love to Jesus will be manifested in a desire to work as He worked for the blessing and uplifting of humanity. It will lead to love, tenderness, and sympathy toward all the creatures of our heavenly Father's care" (*Steps to Christ*, pp. 77, 78).

Planting seeds in human hearts brings great rewards to your own soul. I learned this as a heartbroken child after my parents divorced. Fortunately my mother encouraged me to make short visits to a nearby nursing home to sing to the lonely patients and bring them small bouquets of California wildflowers. It was there that I learned the joy of service—a lesson I want to keep fresh in my daily walk with my Jesus, who did so much for me.

EVELYN DELAFIELD

Unconditional Acceptance in the Lord

For while we were still helpless, at the right time Christ died for the ungodly. Rom. 5:6, NASB.

Nothing is more helpless than a newborn baby. A tiny infant contributes nothing to a family in terms of financial or physical help. From a human standpoint the greatest example of unconditional love is that of a mother who night and day cares for a helpless, nonprofitable nurseling.

An infant would never think of "doing" or "being" in order to gain acceptance and love. Such a concept enters our minds only when we are old enough to think and act for ourselves. Unfortunately, we live in a society that tells us that we are more valuable if we behave in a certain way, that we are really loved only if we are successful. Love thus becomes conditional. Rarely do we think that we can be accepted or loved without doing something to deserve it.

This notion spills over into the spiritual realm. We feel that we must do everything right and be perfect before we can experience God's approval or love. But doing things in order to win love and approval from either God or society is like eating a potato chip or salted peanut. Who can stop with eating just one? "No matter how many 'badges of love' you collect, they are never enough, because they are empty of real nourishment and cannot seem to feed the hunger gnawing deep inside. So you keep doing more, working a little harder, hoping this time it will take the awful emptiness away" (Sue Monk Kidd, *God's Joyful Surprise*, p. 24).

Our text makes it clear that God loves unconditionally. Can you imagine anything more wonderful than to know that we are in God's loving embrace regardless of what we have done? He loves us for who we are, not for what we do. God doesn't wait for us to become perfect. Rather He loves us now, fully and completely. How do we know this? "The value of all the world sinks into insignificance in comparison to the value of one human soul" (*Counsels to Writers and Editors*, p. 126). Grasping the reality of God's unconditional love converts the heart and causes us to respond in obedience to His will.

We can understand our worth only as we go to Calvary. Only in the mystery of the atonement of Christ can we place a true estimate upon ourselves. Each of us must be very valuable to God for Him to create us and then to redeem us from Satan's clutches. God gave His Son that we might live now more abundantly and with Him forever when He returns. May we accept ourselves through the eyes of our Saviour as He unconditionally accepts us.

MARIE SPANGLER

Surprise Me!

Taste and see that the Lord is good, Ps. 34:8.

My little friend Melissa was visiting me for the day. Looking at life through her eyes every now and then gave me a glimpse into my own childhood (we were alike in so many ways), and her fresh outlook always gave me something to think about.

It was late afternoon and time to fix our dinner. She usually perched herself upon the counter and visited with me while I cooked—and helped, too. Today, however, she was *playing* the piano, and I could hear her creating a little tune of her own. Partway through the process, Melissa skipped into the kitchen to ask me if I had been listening. I had been. We talked about music for a while, and then I asked her, "Would you like to know what we are having to eat tonight so that your mouth can start watering ahead of time?"

She giggled. "OK, tell me one thing we are having," she said, as if it were a game.

"Pasta primavera," I replied, and when her eyebrows almost reached to her hairline, I proceeded to describe it for her. Partway through the description she informed me that she knew what I was talking about but she called it *spaghetti and veggies*. I continued, "We are also going to have . . ." but she stopped me.

"No, don't tell me anything else. That way, when I get to the table there will be a surprise."

Now it was my turn to laugh. "OK, Melissa. I won't tell you any more, so you can have a surprise. But just suppose you don't like the surprise? Then what?"

She pondered that for a moment, cocking her head to the side as she so often did. Finally, in all of her 7-year-old wisdom, she said solemnly, "That won't matter. It will still be a surprise."

In metaphor God prepares a table for us here on this earth. How often I have wanted not just the assurance that there would be something on the table, but to know in advance exactly what it would be and whether or not I would like it. In actuality, however, there have been many times when I have had to get right up to the table before the Lord let me see what was there. Sometimes I have even had to sit there a few minutes and wait—and at those times, I have often squirmed in my chair.

What a lesson in trust I find in Melissa's response. According to her philosophy, it's not important (or even desirable) to know ahead of time everything that will be on the table. God calls us to come, sit down, and trust. We know our bread and water will be sure—but the rest is a surprise. And if we have a mind-set to look for the lesson in everything, all of the surprises will have a pearl tucked away in them.

Melissa and I pulled our chairs up to the table and bowed our heads a moment to return thanks to God. She was expecting the pasta primavera; the éclairs from a *real bakery* were a surprise. This time she liked everything—but even if she hadn't, there would have still been the surprise.

"You prepare a table before me. . . . My cup overflows" (Ps. 23:5, NIV). ARLENE TAYLOR

APRIL 30

Words Made Memorable in Song

Sing together . . . for the Lord hath comforted his people. Isa. 52:9.

The aged lady was near death, the reason for her frailness never definitely established. Some thought Alzheimer's disease; others guessed severe depression. But whatever the reason, both body and mind showed irreversible signs of decline.

She occasionally came out of her stupor when she heard religious songs. She would sing the old hymns by memory that she had learned as a child, and their comforting words and happy rhythms would bring her back—at least momentarily—to reality. But once the music stopped, she would slip back into senility, once again feeble, depressed, dying.

The power of music is no secret, and it's exploited or used for numerous evil or beneficial ends. As any ad agency knows, the words of advertising slogans catch in the minds of would-be consumers much more quickly if put to a snappy tune. Mental hospitals recognize the value of songs as therapy for their patients. Politicians know the value of patriotic tunes. And religions too make use of the spiritual impact of sacred music. In fact, the first book printed in the Colonies was the *Bay Psalm Book*, a publication of the early Puritans to set the Bible psalms to music and hence enhance their memory.

Mood music didn't get its name by accident; the name was given in recognition of music's ability to dominate any environment it's used in.

Singing is mentioned often in the Bible, too, as a favorite outlet for occasions of thanksgiving, praise, and worship, and celebrating victories. Music, when coupled with words, makes these expressions more intense, more captivating, and hence more memorable.

Early on, Jesus recognized the positive power of song in His own life. Often He expressed the gladness of His heart by singing psalms and heavenly songs. "Often the dwellers in Nazareth heard His voice raised in praise and thanksgiving to God. . . . As His companions complained of weariness from labor, they were cheered by the sweet melody from His lips" (*The Desire of Ages*, p. 73).

Next to Jesus, Satan must know as much about music as anyone, since he was at one time the archangel. How he must delight to see the followers of Christ misuse the powers of song. Let's pledge to sing "the songs of Zion" instead. WILMA McCLARTY

MAY 1

"Sonkist"

An honest answer is like a kiss on the lips. Prov. 24:26, NIV.

While I was picking raspberries early one morning, my attention was attracted to a family a few rows over. The four children, mother, and grandmother were all picking berries with enthusiasm. The mother praised her children often; she thanked them for getting up early. "Picking berries for the freezer is hard work," she said. "Grandma and I could never have done all this without you!"

Every once in a while I would hear one of the children yell "Sunkist" when an exceptionally big, beautiful berry was found. Evidently the Sunkist ad had made a big impression on them!

I was so blessed that I walked over to where this special family was picking and praised the mother for her pleasant and kind words, her sweet spirit. I told her that she had beautiful children and that they were all special gifts from God; that they too were Sunkist. Then she did something I did not expect. She called her children over and said, "This lady has something to tell you; please listen! She has a word from God."

I told them that God loved them very much and that each of them was Sunkist, just like the berries. They were more beautiful, sweeter, kinder, and more appealing because they were "Sonkist"—kissed by the Son of God!

I explained that God had a special work for each of them to do because they were Sonkist. Their smiles of appreciation brought me great joy, and as the tears trickled down the mother and grandmother's cheeks, I knew they too had been touched.

The children ran to pick more berries, and I turned to leave. Their mother stopped me and said, "How can I thank you for the insight and blessing you have brought to us?"

"I'm the one who has been blessed by meeting your wonderful family," I answered. I shared with her the scripture I had read that morning for my devotions: "An honest answer is like a kiss on the lips."

She thanked me; we hugged and said goodbye. Then I realized that I too had been Sonkist—kissed by the Son of righteousness, refreshed by His presence, and made aware of His love!

Lord, let my lips give an honest answer. Let my words today be as pleasant to the one who hears as a kiss on the lips. HAZEL BURNS

MAY 2

Of Low Means, but High Hopes

There shall be nothing in the city which is evil; for the throne of God and of the Lamb will be there, they shall see his face and his servants will worship him . . . And there will be no night there . . . ; and they shall reign forever and ever. Rev. 22:3-5, TLB.

In the late 1940s I was born into a Hispanic family of poor means. I can remember as a little girl my father working 16 hours a day under the hot sun in the lemon orchards of Del Mar Ranch. I can almost feel the hot dusty days when my mother and seven brothers and sisters walked up and down the dirt rows picking whatever fruit was in season: strawberries, apricots, oranges, prunes, grapes, even walnuts. From the hot humid farms of Fresno and Gilroy, California, to the fertile fields of Ventura, my family migrated, seeking work for survival. Our family's struggle reflected the hard life for the Mexican in the United States during the 1950s.

In spite of the obstacles, my parents had a positive philosophy: "We are a family of low means but high hopes." Although we were physically deprived, we were encouraged to grow mentally and spiritually, and were awakened to the possibilities of building a better world.

The idea of building a better world reminds me of the recent celebration of Columbus's discoveries, and Bush and Gorbachev's "better world" view. But it also sends my thoughts to a world beyond human comprehension. A world in which there will be life beyond the grave, life free of emotional pain, life in which all are of equal value, life that promises joy, peace, and love.

The promises of a better world here are bound by human limitations. But the promises of a better world *mas alla del sol* ("beyond the sun") are of eternal worth. And like my parents, you too can say, "Here on earth I am of low means but high hopes . . . in Christ." Remember that Jesus loves you and cares for you; He designed you with all your special gifts and talents.

He has also designed a special purpose for you! Get to know Him, and as a woman you will begin that "better world" of peace, joy, and love here on earth today.　　　　RAMONA PEREZ GREEK

MAY 3

"I Like Myself, but . . ."

For we dare not make ourselves of the number, or compare ourselves with some that commend themselves: but they measuring themselves by themselves, and comparing themselves among themselves, are not wise. 2 Cor. 10:12.

The young church usher gazed into a full-length mirror, lamenting over those aspects of her reflection that were less than pleasing to her critical eye. Her thoughts turned to the church secretary, who seemed to be almost perfect. The young woman sighed and said, "I like myself, but I am too tall and thin and my hair is too curly. I wish I could be poised and elegant like the church secretary."

The church secretary paused before her full-length mirror, and her thoughts turned to the young church usher who seemed so bubbly and cheerful. "I like myself, but I am too short, and my hair is hard to manage. I wish I could be as bubbly as the church usher."

Comparisons. We compare shoe size, body measurement, and weight. We compare the ability to cook, sew, decorate, and organize a home. We compare not only our own abilities or lack thereof, but also the abilities of our husbands, children, and even our pets! We compare our worst characteristics with another's best attributes. We set ourselves up for disappointment and dissatisfaction and then exclaim, "I like myself, but . . ."

Scripture speaks very clearly about this habit we have of comparison. We are told that comparing ourselves with others is not a wise practice. Another human being is an insufficient measuring rod for beauty, accomplishment, or success. In addition, it is not wise because comparison sets up an adversarial relationship with others and is counter-productive to spiritual as well as emotional growth and development. Comparison ignores God-given strengths while assuming another's blessings are better.

As one author stated: "We are not hen's eggs or bananas, or clothespins, to be counted off by the dozen. Down to the last detail we are all different. Everyone has his or her own fingerprints. Recognize and rejoice in that endless variety. Rejoice today in the uniqueness of yourself. Learn to enhance your God-given strengths and gifts of others and learn to say, 'I like myself because . . . !' "

BARBARA TOBIAS

MAY 4

Appreciate Your Worth

And we, who with unveiled faces all reflect the Lord's glory, are being transformed into his likeness with ever-increasing glory, which comes from the Lord, who is the Spirit. 2 Cor. 3:18, NIV.

Charlie Brown is a perfect example of someone who doesn't like himself. He can't throw a ball or do anything right. Nobody likes him. He has no talents. He fails at everything he tackles. Charlie Brown's popularity revolves around our identification with him!

Many women feel like Charlie Brown. They wonder why they don't have more friends. Why the phone doesn't ring. Why others have so much talent. Why they are so incredibly plain or unattractive. After everyone else is asleep they lie awake shedding tears over the emptiness inside.

Through God's grace it is possible to reprogram negative feelings of worth. God will give you the power to carry out His purpose as you behold Him through His Word. One woman hated herself because she was overweight. Turning her low self-esteem over to God, she finally captured the essence of 2 Corinthians 3:18. Each day she would repeat to herself transforming affirmations such as: "I can do all things through [Christ] who strengthens me" (Phil. 4:13, NASB). "Greater is he that is in [me] than he that is in the world" (1 John 4:4). She also continually reminded herself: "One with God is a majority." "I am a beautiful person in God's eyes."

Within a matter of weeks her negative feelings and level of functioning had taken a 180-degree turn for the better! Her story

152

dramatically illustrates the truth that anything fed directly into the subconscious mind is accepted as truth.

It's hard for some of us to let go of past attitudes and habit patterns. But if you hold on to negativity and failure, you can't progress. You will keep spinning in an endless cycle of self-depreciation, which will press you down, bind, and defeat you. Letting go can actually become a beginning.

Leaving behind a lifetime of self-hate won't happen all at once. You simply can't undo 20, 30, or 40 years of disapproval in one step. You can, however, begin taking small steps to free yourself of the past. Begin now by choosing and repeating a biblical affirmation that has personal meaning for you. — NANCY VAN PELT

MAY 5

A New Vision

Before they call, I will answer; and while they are yet speaking, I will hear. Isa. 65:24.

I need a change!" My work was beginning to feel humdrum and I needed to do something to boost my energy level and spirit. I thought about some former classmates, now teaching at a college in the Far East, and, without thinking of the time difference, picked up the phone and called them. Sleepy voices greeted me and forgave my intrusion at 3:00 in the morning. They invited me to visit Asia for a few weeks during the summer and do some traveling.

Passports, visas, physical examination, specified injections—all were completed quickly. By exchanging my apartment for a house-sitting job, I saved extra money for my trip. A large yard sale left me with a skeleton of furnishings for my planned return to new living accommodations—with a fresh outlook.

Then one month before my departure, my mission friends were transferred to a new location in a nearby country. They asked if rather than just visiting for the summer, I would consider coming there to teach their children on a permanent basis. Almost immediately, my answer was yes. Because of my previous preparations, the General Conference wheels (which usually take six months to turn) were able to complete everything in just one month.

School started with five children enrolled. This soon swelled to seven with the addition of two who belonged to a Micronesian couple who enrolled at the college. One of their children, a fifth-grade boy, could not read at all (it looked like he was having trouble even seeing things on the page) and was at the second-grade level in math. Black was his favorite color.

Pulling from my prior teaching experience with dyslexic and learning disabled children, I designed a special program for this student and explained it to his parents. We were able to arrange for him to receive an eye examination (a difficult journey to the nearest city), and he was fitted with glasses.

Within six months this boy was well on his way to scholastic improvement. He was moving rapidly enough to complete three grades of reading by the end of the school year and was experiencing success in most subjects. And now his favorite color was pink.

At a parent-teacher conference his parents explained that before they had made the decision to enroll in college, they had prayed diligently for guidance; they needed to find someone who could help their son. They felt that God had indeed answered their prayers—through me. He had met their needs according to His glorious riches in Christ Jesus (see Phil. 4:19).

I stared at them, stunned. *Oh,* I thought, *I came here to help out some friends and to find a change for my own life.* But before they called, God was planning a solution for them. Although my agenda had been totally different, God had used me to answer someone else's prayer. This was a slightly new concept for me—being used of God to help others without my being aware of any part of the process.

As long as we are willing to be who God created us to be and if we place our talents and our lives in His hands—He can use them to answer the prayers of others. Although you may never know it, you may be the answer to someone's prayer.   LORNA LAWRENCE

MAY 6

The Fragrance of God

They have . . . noses, but they cannot smell. Ps. 115:6, NIV.

While human noses don't equal those of some animals, either in shape, size, or performance, they do perform valuable services for us. The nose leads the body and is the first step of the complex respiratory system that supplies oxygen for the body and eliminates carbon dioxide and other waste products. The interior structure of the nose contains a special heating system to warm the air that passes through it, a system to moisturize the air, and a filtering system.

The nose is responsible for sniffing out more than 10,000

154

different smells, using its several hundred tiny genes or odor receptors. When odors drift into the nose, they are believed to slip into certain genes like keys into a lock. Identifying scent may not be done in the brain; it just may be a "nose job." Associating the scent with a memory, however, undoubtedly takes place in the brain. The stronger the odor (extremely pleasant or extremely unpleasant), the more likely it is to evoke memories.

Scientists have known for nearly a century that every few hours one nostril opens up to let air flow easily, while the other takes a bit of a rest. Later on, the rested nostril takes over. One study measured brain waves and nasal flow in 43 volunteers for several hours. Researchers found that when the right brain hemisphere is dominant, so is the left nostril; when the left hemisphere is dominant, so is the right nostril. By covering the dominant open nostril and breathing through the other for 10 or 15 minutes, brain dominance can actually be switched, as measured by EEGs. The change may last an entire cycle—about 90 minutes. This phenomenon has led some to recommend that if you want to create a symphony, maybe you should breathe with your left nostril for a while. On the other hand, if you want to balance your checkbook, better breathe through your right nostril.

When I think of the sense of smell, I think of the Bible story about Mary Magdalene and her alabaster jar of oil of spikenard, that marvelous and expensive fragrance that probably represented the equivalent of a year's income for the average laborer back then. The fragrance of her offering has lingered over the centuries because wherever the gospel story is told, her story is also told, in memory of her grateful and creative benevolence (John 12:1-7; Luke 7:46-50).

When Mary broke the alabaster container, the unusual and sweet-scented perfume filled the room. Everyone at the feast recognized the value of her gift. Mary's gift of love, her faith, God's acceptance and forgiveness of her, and the peace in her heart are all wrapped up together in this experience. She made the best use of what she had at hand, which is what God expects of each of us. This special story challenges us to fill our lives with the fragrance of God—so that we can share that exquisite bouquet with others.

ARLENE TAYLOR

MAY 7

God's Precious Affirmation

O Lord, you have searched me and you know me. . . . You perceive my thoughts from afar. . . . I praise you because I am fearfully and wonderfully made. . . . How precious to me are your thoughts, O God! Ps. 139:1-17, NIV.

From the time we were born we have experienced people's reactions to us, felt their approval or disapproval. We have listened to a conglomerate of voices—parents, relatives, siblings, peers, teachers—telling us who we are. How we view ourselves today is an internalization of those messages.

For the most part people hang on to the negative messages that have been given to them through the years. A few are fortunate to have had supportive, affirmative words of worth to cherish inside and to feed the soul, words to pull out and derive nourishment from again and again.

Mary, the mother of Jesus, was given messages of positive reinforcement from several sources—shepherds, angels, Simeon and Anna, the Wise Men—to hide in her heart and contemplate as she raised the Son of God in an unaccepting world. God supplied these early nuggets that sustained her.

A friend of mine once told me, "We teach people how to treat us." What a shock it was to realize the truth in that statement. When people feel inferior about themselves, others pick up that message and treat them, for the most part, at that same level of self-worth.

As I began to work on my own self-worth, I found that a supply of affirmations from my Creator and Saviour were essential for my daily sustenance. I began a search for God's view of my value. The Scriptures are full of wonderful gems of our specialness; we are deeply loved, redeemed children; valuable people in process with a purpose. I found many promises of God's constant care and sustaining love.

To discover how God values you individually, look at some of these texts: Deuteronomy 7:6; Ephesians 1:6; Isaiah 43:21; Jeremiah 9:24 and 31:3; John 15:16; 1 John 3:1; Joshua 1:9; 1 Peter 5:7; Psalm 55:22.   LORNA LAWRENCE

MAY 8

Life's Filters

This is the confidence we have in approaching God: that if we ask anything according to his will, he hears us. And if we know that he hears us—whatever we ask—we know that we have what we asked of him. 1 John 5:14, 15, NIV.

Recently I encountered a bubbly, rambunctious black-and-tan puppy on my front lawn. I was concerned for his safety since the road in front of our house is well traveled. He looked much like the boxers I had known as a child. Since I knew my neighbor's boxers had recently parented eight pups, I figured one had gotten out of the backyard.

I headed to my neighbor's house, determined to return this pup to his home. I was met at the door by two people I had never seen before. Holding the affectionate mite, I told them of my plight. They spoke no English! In a hurry, and failing entirely in my communication effort, I finally just opened the screen door and put him down inside. Later, speaking with the homeowner, I found it had not been his dog! Since no harm had come, we laughed at the mistaken identity. But this experience reminded me of how our own insights may seem so correct to us when in reality they are colored by our perception of fact.

Life is a filter. The human life experience colors each person's future encounters. I place enormous value on life after experiencing a plane crash. I value friends following the death of my best friend, my husband. I survey the sparkle of a sunset on crystalline ocean waves quite differently after viewing the framed image through a camera lens. The quiet gratitude of a family receiving an overflowing Thanksgiving basket can be fully appreciated only by the person who has also received one during a difficult time. Deep emotion while singing the "Hallelujah Chorus" can be known only by the person who has experienced heartfelt gratitude and thanksgiving for the gift of God's Son.

When Jesus fed the 5,000, there were those who sat in judgment of His wisdom and His purpose. When He cleared the Temple of those whose greed defiled it, there were those who failed to understand His protestations. There are several verses in the second chapter of Proverbs that detail the design of God regarding finding His knowledge and understanding. In the seventh verse we find, "He layeth up sound wisdom for the righteous: he is a buckler to them that walk uprightly." Correcting our perception of God as more than Santa Claus, as being who He is—our Father—allows us to lie back into His arms. He is there for each of us. JUDI WILD BECKER

MAY 9

What Do You Have in Your Hands?

Raise your staff and stretch out your hand over the sea to divide the waters so that the Israelites can go through the sea on dry ground. Ex. 14:16, NIV.

What is in your hands?

When a Ghanaian in a remote village says "Nobody lives by the river and goes thirsty," that means it is a privilege to live by the river. It means we must acknowledge the existence of the river and drink its sparkling water. Then and then only can we enjoy it and be refreshed.

I can imagine old father Moses clinging to his shepherd's staff and trembling in the presence of the I AM. Moses has held his staff for so long that he has taken it for granted. It is his ordinary old staff, only meant for shepherding his helpless flock. He has therefore failed to realize its potential.

However, Moses was obedient. Thank God that the doubting Moses by faith obeyed God's command, threw the staff on the ground and, presto, it turned into a snake! The Bible says Moses ran, but he came back and followed God's instructions. It is the power of God through this ordinary staff that liberates the Israelites from bondage to freedom. This is no fairytale. The Bible says, "For I can do everything God asks me to do with the help of Christ who gives me the strength and power" (Phil. 4:13, TLB). The same Bible confirms this by saying, "For if you had faith even as small as a tiny mustard seed you could say to this mountain, 'Move!' and it would go far away. Nothing would be impossible" (Matt. 17:20, TLB).

Yes, we can achieve the seemingly impossible. Why then do we underestimate what God can do through us? Do we take our capabilities for granted through lack of faith or merely through idleness? Martin Luther, the great Reformer, says, "If I rest, I rust." We have too many wonderful talents buried deep in us to rust or rot.

God is inviting us to use melodious voices, power of speech, loving care, and all the other graces He has bestowed on us that we have taken for granted. By faith these will put the devil on the run, and God's people will perform wonders. Like the Israelites, we shall, indeed, be free from bondage. Remember: Talents + Faith = Great Miracles.   NORA AGBOKA

MAY 10

Remembering Yesterday

This is love: not that we loved God, but that he loved us and sent his Son as an atoning sacrifice for our sins. Dear friends, since God so loved us, we also ought to love one another. No one has ever seen God; but if we love one another, God lives in us and his love is made complete in us. 1 John 4:10-12, NIV.

Mother's Day. What a flood of memories that evokes. Thoughts of my own mother, whom I am still privileged to have. We have lived so far apart for so many years now. But even the time apart and the miles between cannot erase that special bond of love and memories, some pleasant, some not so pleasant.

The not-so-pleasant memories are of the times I hurt her—especially as a teenager. Alas, one cannot change yesterday. The unkind words and actions are there to stay, set in concrete. However, I can apply the lessons learned to my own teenager. I know that my mother is forgiving—and has probably long ago forgotten my unkindnesses. Now that I'm a mother, I've learned that forgiveness is part of being a mother—learning to forget what ought to be forgotten and to recall only the things that do not sting. Remembering our own teen years helps us to be more understanding. Relationships were sometimes rocky, but in the end Mom's steady love and prayers won my heart back.

Sometimes we mothers of teenagers have moments of relapse, when we tend to forget the beautiful and concentrate on the hurt of the present moment. When self-pity takes over, it's time to turn one's thoughts over to God. He then helps us look deeper into the hearts of the ones for whom we care, understanding their secret wishes and the load they bear. Then we begin to search for lovely things. Love must learn to dwell on pleasant memories, like the note one 13-year-old wrote: "Mom, sometimes we differ, but you're still my best friend."

Love sometimes isn't easy to recognize—it doesn't always come wrapped inside a dozen red roses. Sometimes you're not sure it's there at all. Then we cry out to God, "Lord, I'm not doing so well. You have a lot more love and know-how, so please take over." With His help we can accept today and leave tomorrow in His gracious hands. Any motherly sacrifice will appear small compared with the sacrifice Christ has made for us. ELLEN BRESEE

MAY 11

Use It!

His master replied, "Well done, good and faithful servant! You have been faithful with a few things; I will put you in charge of many things. Come and share your master's happiness!" Matt. 25:23, NIV.

159

D octor, I can't take this pain in my arm any longer," I moaned. "Since last fall it's hurt too much to move it at all."

"How high can you lift your arm?" he asked.

Slowly and painfully I lifted my right arm. I could barely get my hand as high as my head. My shoulder joint felt locked in place like a well-rusted hinge. Why hadn't I dealt with the pain months before? Why hadn't I realized my shoulder could "freeze" if not used?

"Doctor," I worried, "will my shoulder be all right again?"

He shrugged. "We'll have to wait and see." Then he showed me some exercises that might help.

I had heard nurses say, "Use it or lose it." Suddenly I knew that meant joints, too, not just muscles. Had I permanently lost the free use of my arm? In Matthew 25 Jesus told of three servants who also learned to "use it or lose it." Before taking a trip, their master put them in charge of his assets. On his return he called for an accounting.

Two smiling servants proudly reported, "We invested your money and doubled it. Here it is!"

The master beamed. "Excellent! Excellent! I will promote you." But he frowned when the third servant returned only the original portion to him.

"I was afraid," this servant confessed, "so I buried it in a safe place. I knew you'd be terribly angry if I lost or mismanaged it."

"You know how I do business," the boss exploded. "I wanted you to use it and show a profit. You could at least have earned bank interest on it! But you did nothing. You're afraid!"

What is the difference between users and losers?

Despite risk, users responsibly and energetically use their assets. Using what they have increases their ability to manage it. Users are dependable; users are winners.

Losers, however, fear risk and responsibility. They deep-freeze their assets instead of using them. For lack of practical experience they fail to learn and grow and qualify for greater service. They lose both opportunity and reward.

Every woman's day of reckoning will come, as it surely did for the three servants, and for me after I had failed to exercise that painful arm. (Fortunately, my shoulder responded well to physical therapy.)

As servants of God, we are responsible for the way we use our God-given assets. Whatever they are—a knack for art, music, leadership, friendliness, encouragement, or whatever—we are unworthy of our Master's trust if we hide them or fail to develop them. He is well pleased when we use even our tiniest talent to honor and glorify Him.

FANNIE L. HOUCK

The Gift of Hospitality

Do not forget to entertain strangers, for by so doing some people have entertained angels without knowing it. Heb. 13:2, NIV.

On a late July afternoon back in the seventies our family of six pulled into a campground near Oregon's Mount Hood. As my husband and son began setting up our camper by the proverbial babbling brook, a woman appeared at my side and asked, "May I watch your camper being set up? I've always wondered how they work."

We began visiting while she watched them. When they finished, I invited her into our traveling "home" for a closer inspection. As she was leaving, she asked if we would be in Portland the next day. We said we planned to visit the zoo and rose gardens. "You've been riding so much; why don't you come to our house when you are through sightseeing? I'm sure your children would enjoy swimming in our pool. I'll write out the directions for you." She left, but not before calling back, "Please come; I'll be looking for you."

Her gracious invitation was accepted, and we did indeed enjoy her hospitality. To this day a warm feeling comes over me when I think of the wonderful hospitality shown our family by this kind woman to whom we were total strangers.

When I was a child, every Friday found my mom preparing extra food for Sabbath dinner. Usually no formal invitations were extended until after church, but often our guest would be a stranger visiting our church for the first time, a new member, a lonely friend, a minister or missionary. Though the various places we lived were often humble, I felt free to invite people home. My parents always welcomed them, and no matter how bare the pantry was, Mom always managed to prepare wholesome, appetizing meals.

In spite of that early training, I've sometimes failed to be hospitable because my house was not "spotless." And I know I've missed some very special times with friends. For it is not the house but the spirit that pervades that makes it a hospitable home. It's the companionship and conversation, the feeling of acceptance and enjoyment derived from being together and sharing a meal—even if it's just soup and crackers or fruit and sandwiches.

Hospitality is also going the second mile in entertainment—not as a return favor, but simply for the joy of sharing. "But when you give a banquet, invite the poor, the crippled, the lame, the blind, and you will be blessed" (Luke 14:13, 14, NIV).

I believe Jesus was speaking not only of physical handicaps, but spiritual and social handicaps as well. And I believe the promise He gave after His admonition to be hospitable: "And you will be blessed."

EVELYN VANDERVERE

MAY 13

My Curse—a Fountain

She left him and afterward shut the door behind her and her sons. They brought the jars to her and she kept pouring. When all the jars were full, she said to her son, "Bring me another one." But he replied, "There is not a jar left." Then the oil stopped flowing. 2 Kings 4:5, 6, NIV.

Have you ever been down to your last dollar? I have. And so had the widow whose story is told in the fourth chapter of 2 Kings. A poem from *Eve's Version,* by Nova Schubert Bair,* tells the widow's story.

"What Do You Have in the House?"

Elisha asks me. Does he not hear?
My husband has died; a creditor
stands ready to lead my two sons
away as slaves. Nothing is left
to buy their freedom—unless my favors?
I shrink from his words. "Just something
in the house," the prophet reassures.

"Only a pot of oil," I answer.
He bids me borrow vessels.

Now they are standing ready. I close the door.
My curse becomes a fountain as I pour.

Isn't that beautiful? The presumed curse became a fountain. The widow was told to sell, pay her debts, and live!

There was a time when I had not one dime left over in any week. Then someone asked me to give a weekly Bible study with a

---

* "What Do You Have in the House?" by Nora Schubert Bair, appeared in *Eve's Version: 150 Women of the Bible Speak Through Modern Poets,* and is used by permission of the author and Paramount Publishing Company.

family that lived 20 miles away—40 miles round trip. My miles were measured by the cost of gasoline. Could I do the study? The Lord said that I could.

For one year I went the extra 40 miles through the city and gave the study without one penny increase in gasoline cost. It was as if there were no extra miles. The person with whom I studied that year gave his heart to the Lord, as did one of his sons. My lack of money did not prevent God from creating a fountain for hungry souls.   ELIZABETH STERNDALE

MAY 14

Channels of Blessing

For I was hungry and you gave me something to eat, I was thirsty and you gave me something to drink, I was a stranger and you invited me in, I needed clothes and you clothed me, I was sick and you looked after me, I was in prison and you came to visit me. Matt. 25:35, 36, NIV.

God puts us in positions where we can be His instruments of blessings to those around us. In 1972 a sick woman came to my house at 6:00 a.m. with a large abscess on her buttock. I was the college nurse, but was also working in a food industry, and my schedule was tight. Should I ask her to go, or help her and maybe be late to work? My minister husband encouraged me to help her. The passage from Matthew rang in my mind. The thought came to me that God may have placed me there to be a channel of blessing to this woman. I treated her, and like the woman of Samaria, she told others, and the next day three people came seeking help. This trend continued, and eventually we established a clinic which now serves hundreds of patients.

God has placed every man and woman in the position they find themselves in, high and low alike, to be His channel to bless others. It can be by giving alms, giving a ride, praying with the afflicted, counseling the troubled, or inviting the less privileged or disabled to your home.

What is your position? A housewife? Mother? Storekeeper? Nurse? Bus driver? If you are willing to be used by God, He will provide opportunities for you to reach out to others. Every case of need we see is a unique opportunity to respond, to provide for the needs of others, to be the channel to bless others.

VERTIBELLE AWONIYI

163

Be Careful

Have I not commanded you? Be strong and courageous.
Do not be terrified; do not be discouraged, for the Lord
your God will be with you wherever you go. Joshua 1:9,
NIV.

I stand, the telephone to my ear, talking to my father. It's late, and he's leaving for Texas at 6:00 a.m., planning to drive the 1,300 miles in two days. He is 78 and I worry about him.

I ask if he's finished packing. I tell him to say hello to assorted relatives. I make him promise not to pick up hitchhikers. His voice is deep, dear, precious. I don't want to let go.

The conversation lags, but I keep him close with my questions. I want to hold on to him, to ride the long highway with him, keeping him safe and bringing him back.

"I guess I'll watch the 11:00 news and go to bed," he tells me. "OK."

A pause. "Well," he says, "see you in a couple weeks."

"OK, Daddy. You be careful."

I open her bedroom door in the predawn darkness and tiptoe across the room. She'd asked me to wake her before I left for the airport, so I bend down to touch her arm. "Goodbye, Noelle. I'm going now."

It's snowing outside, and I'm a little worried about the drive to Baltimore. She stretches, my 17-year-old daughter, and I touch her hair. "Goodbye. It's 5:45 a.m. I'm leaving."

Eyelids flutter. " 'Bye, Mommy. Have a good trip."

"I will."

"Be safe."

I promise to be safe, as if I had any control over slick highways and airplane flights. This is the downside of travel. Leaving those who love me. She squeezes my hand. "Be careful."

We're putting her on a British Airways jetliner, our eldest daughter, sending her—no, *letting* her—fly across the ocean to Newbold College. She is wearing a new green coat and dark-green leather gloves. Her eyes sparkle. She loves England and the school there. She is utterly happy, and I am utterly desolate.

A voice announces that her flight is ready to board. I hug her, and she laughs. "Are you going to let go of me?"

Now I laugh. "Of course! You have a good flight." I walk with her a few more steps. One more quick squeeze. I let her go, and she gives me a smile of pure radiance.

Caught up in the crush of people, she reaches the flight attendant and hands him her ticket.

"Robyn!"

She turns for a heartbeat.

"I love you. Be careful."

I love you.
Be careful.
In our family the phrases are interchangeable. They mean the same thing. *I love you. So take good care of yourself. Be careful.*

You are precious to me. I can't bear to see you hurt. Part of my heart and soul, *you are cherished beyond words. So be careful. I love you.*

My thoughts turn to God, our all-loving Father, and to Jesus, who became one with us, forever bound to us by a human body. They know, far more than we, the hurt and harm that merely living brings to Their earth children. And so They sent us the loving message, repeated in a thousand different ways: *Be careful. I love you.*

"Be firm and brave, never be daunted or dismayed, for . . . God is with you wherever you go" (Joshua 1:9, Moffatt).

"Be careful," God pleads. For "your enemy the devil prowls about like a roaring lion looking for someone to devour" (1 Peter 5:8, NIV).

"Be wise."

Keep the laws I have given you, these 10 rules that will safeguard you against a thousand dangers. "Watch and pray so that you will not fall into temptation" (Mark 14:38, NIV).

"Be careful," God says. "I love you."   PENNY ESTES WHEELER

MAY 16

The Ultimate Transaction

I delight greatly in the Lord; my soul rejoices in my God. For he has clothed me with garments of salvation and arrayed me in a robe of righteousness. Isa. 61:10, NIV.

My mother has a unique knack for telling the most tear-jerking stories as matter-of-factly as if she were relating tomorrow's weather forecast. Her voice devoid of emotion, she relates all the galling details, then walks off into the kitchen to start the potatoes. Left gaping on the couch, my sisters and I shake our heads in disbelief, yelling after her, "But what happened next?" She rarely remembers.

One of her choicest stories, never failing to produce a scene of intense melodrama in our living room, concerns an incident that occurred when Mom was about 8 years old. The story begins with Mom—back in a day when 25 cents bought a lot more than a call at the corner phone booth—receiving two quarters from a generous relative.

The silver was tucked away and spent mentally on every conceivable joy an 8-year-old girl could imagine. But one day Mom took out the two precious quarters, dusted them off, and slipped them into her skirt pocket for a very special occasion: a carnival had come to town.

Reluctant to part with her treasure, Mom wandered happily through the fairgrounds, content just knowing that the brightly colored displays were all hers, should she want them. When it was almost time to leave, a vendor of mysterious packages began making his way through the crowd.

"Gifts from all over the world," he called out in a cunning voice. "Just 50 cents, and you can own the most beautiful things humans can imagine: dazzling rings, sparkling glassware, lovely vases . . ."

Mom's heart raced as she reached out to grab the man's coat, which seemed to be all too rapidly flapping by her. The transaction was a quick one. Two quarters. One plainly wrapped package. And then the voice, above her, booming out into the nameless crowd, "This young lady just won a beautiful watch!"

Little fingers fumbled with the prize, a small heart bumped rapidly in anticipation. And then the box was open before her, revealing its contents: an empty, broken perfume bottle. "Oh, sir," came the trembling voice, "there's been a terrible mistake. Oh, sir . . ."

But the man promising the world had disappeared into its farthest reaches.

Empty glass; an empty promise. A broken bottle and a broken dream. The exchange of a treasure for a cheap fraud. One of life's unfortunate inequities.

Sometimes it seems as if our entire existence is made up of exchanges. We exchange our singleness for a lifetime partnership. Some discover the joy of being two; others face a lifetime of emotional abuse and misery. We exchange our time for a career. And with that transaction may come creative challenge and fulfillment . . . or the feeling of being caught in a relentless machine, merciless in its demands. We exchange our money for luxuries, and so it goes, and so we live. Sometimes winning; other times, standing openmouthed, staring into an empty, broken perfume bottle.

Christ tells us He will give us His righteousness in exchange for our filthy rags. And that is the ultimate transaction. Life can bat us around, rob us of the tangibles and the intangibles, until we feel we have nothing much left to offer. Yet Christ is still waiting, with a spotless robe of pure white. And the best part of it is, we don't even have to relinquish the two quarters. SANDRA DORAN

MAY 17

To the Greater Glory of God

We have different gifts, according to the grace given us. If a man's gift is prophesying, let him use it in proportion to his faith. If it is serving, let him serve; if it is teaching, let him teach; if it is encouraging, let him encourage; if it is contributing to the needs of others, let him give generously; if it is leadership, let him govern diligently; if it is showing mercy, let him do it cheerfully. Rom. 12:6-8, NIV.

I love exploring cathedrals. It's not just the size of them that's fascinating, but what men found to fill them with. Stained-glass windows so beautiful they take your breath away, vaulted ceilings that pull your eyes skyward, creepy crypts, imposing pulpits, curiously carved choir stalls and chaste chapels of prayer, bold bell towers, intricately tiled floors, needleworked kneelers, saintly statues, prayer books, and perfectly preserved Bibles.

Cathedrals are not places to hurry through. If you're like me, you stay for hours until the last detail has been looked at, until you've used up all your store of wonder.

Whenever I go into a house of God, I speak to Him before I begin searching out its secrets. As I meditate, the mystery of the place begins to move into my mind, and I'm aware once again of the *awe-ful* task that the men of the Middle Ages took on gladly—to *build* to the greater glory of God.

Even the great-great-great-great-grandchildren of the men who built to the greater glory of God didn't always see the vision of their forefathers come to fruition. And *we* moan if our tasks take a minute longer than we'd imagined they would. Which brings me to this question: When did you or I build anything to the greater glory of God?

We have cathedrals enough. What I'm talking about are daily deeds done despite discouragement, hours spent in homely pursuits that help another human being, ditches of division filled in, work done without wasted words, quality of work put before quantity of ease; cheerfulness in carrying out church activities.

Every day is an opportunity to build for the Master Builder bright new visions to inspire the uninspired, work miracles with the humdrum, and breed wonder where there was boredom. We can face the world fearlessly despite doubts and dangers, knowing that we are safe in the all-sufficient arms of the Saviour of souls. We are privileged to keep His commandments in a couldn't-care-less society, love the unlovely without respect for reward, and discover in someone the image of their Maker when it's marred by the spots of human sinfulness. There are endless possibilities of ways in which we can build, each day, to the greater glory of God.

To the greater glory of God. It's a phrase to set the mind soaring to discovering the many ways it's possible, each day, to do something of eternal significance. — ANITA MARSHALL

MAY 18

Interruptions

All things work together for good to them that love God.
Rom. 8:28.

Sometimes the plans of God's created beings have been disrupted by choices over which they had no control. The events of this world disrupt our plans, and God interrupts our plans.

Paul is a Bible character who had his plans interrupted. He was one of the most energy-filled Bible characters. He slept, ate, and lived what he did, even when he was killing Christians. When Saul became Paul, he could have redirected that energy to studying the scrolls and the Scripture. He could have gone back to Gamaliel and said, "You were my teacher. Why didn't you teach me these prophecies? Why didn't you show me that Jesus was coming?" He could have been angry with the people who inspired him to go out and kill the Christians. But instead, Paul decided to use his energy for taking the message of Jesus to other parts of the world.

As with each of his journeys, Paul meticulously laid out plans for the second missionary journey. He planned to visit the churches that had been started earlier, which he did. But his long-range plan—that which made him really excited—was to go to Asia. He really wanted to be the first one to go start the work there. But when Paul set out to go to Asia, the Bible tells us his way was blocked. Paul didn't understand what was going on, and he just kept pushing to go to Asia. Finally in the third city he was beaten and left for dead. Then, he was receptive to the message that God gave him: "I want you to go to Macedonia."

Paul wasn't too excited about going to Macedonia. He wanted to go to Asia. He could have said, "Look, Lord, I'm going to Asia. I've made all my plans. I'm going." But he listened to the message from God, changed his plans, and went to Europe.

Sometimes Paul is pictured as a man who worked against other men, who trained leaders. But when he arrived in Macedonia, he found only a handful of women. Again, Paul could have been upset: "Women, Lord?" And to make things worse, they were Jews, not Gentiles. Paul wanted badly to witness to Gentiles. But he worked with them because they were receptive to the message that God had given him. Lydia was baptized, and the first church in Europe was established.

Sometimes the events of this world disrupt our plans. Sometimes God interrupts our plans, as He did Paul's. Disruption is difficult to accept, and it is difficult to explain. The challenge is to be prepared to direct our energy into positive action with each interruption that God sends or allows, believing that "all things work together for good." CAREL SANDERS CLAY

MAY 19

Heavenly Letters

Thy word have I treasured in my heart, that I may not sin against Thee. Ps. 119:11, NASB.

We were on our way out the driveway when I began going through the mail. As I idly flipped through the envelopes, pausing to open bills and examine other correspondence, I gasped. "Oh, Curtis," I exclaimed, barely able to contain my joy, "he wrote to us!" "He" referred to my stepson, Omar, away at college only two weeks. Although his new home was only a two-hour drive for us, it felt like a million light-years away.

Each day Curtis, my husband, and I asked each other about the mail—never daring to verbalize the unspoken question: Was there a letter from Omar?

In response to my excited outburst my always calm and collected husband beamed from ear to ear, and I noticed a faint misting in his eyes. "Well!" he demanded as I fumbled to open the missive. We hung on every word, as I read the letter out loud in the car, and we stopped to reflect or comment frequently. After the first time through we heartily agreed a second reading was in order and very possibly a third. No doubt each of us would also enjoy a quiet and private fourth reading while we formulated our response.

All subsequent letters have been met with no less enthusiasm. Every word devoured, savored, and thoroughly digested.

In my scrapbook reside other significant letters from my life, including a note from my dad while I was at college, letters from my stepchildren written while vacationing with their mother, love epistles from my dear husband, and cards from family and friends for all sorts of occasions.

One other book in my house is full of wonderful letters. These messages, sent from the most precious source imaginable, contain words of encouragement, ideas for better living, and glimpses of the past and future. They are exciting, imaginative, innovative, provocative, and fun. Whenever I read these letters I am filled with awe.

The psalmist puts it this way: "I rejoice at Thy word, as one who finds great spoil" (Ps. 119:162, NASB). The Bible is God's wonderful love letter to us, our greatest treasure here on earth. Despite efforts to destroy the Holy Word it has always been preserved. As a child I studied about the Waldenses and their dedication to carrying the message of the Bible. In spite of persecution, these devoted people carried bits of the Bible sewn inside their clothes.

In the twentieth century we are fortunate to have the freedom and education to read God's Word ourselves. If one translation does not meet our need or explain a text sufficiently, we turn to an alternate version for clarification or further study. God has protected His Book down through time. His message is so precious that He wants everyone to read it and enjoy. Each time we open its pages we are opening ourselves to the words of our dearest Friend.

Make time in your busy schedule today to read God's wonderful words for you. Taste, savor, and digest every thought. God longs to communicate with you. "Thy words were found and I ate them, and Thy words became for me a joy and the delight of my heart" (Jer. 15:16, NASB). CAREL SANDERS CLAY

MAY 20

I Can Do All Things

Commit thy works unto the Lord, and thy thoughts shall be established. Prov. 16:3.

Writing has always been an impossible task for me. I make it impossible because I don't even try. It is an area of my life in which the Holy Spirit has been trying to help me grow for years. My usual response to someone who asks me to write an article is "Sorry, that's not my gift." Or "You don't know me—I can't write."

I wonder how Jesus would have responded if Peter or James or John had said, "No, Jesus, You've asked the wrong person. I'm a fisherman." Jesus said, "You will be My witnesses." Because of their love for Him and their great desire to communicate to everyone that Jesus was Lord, they gladly wrote what they had seen, what they had heard, and what they had known about Him. They were able to do this through the promised Holy Spirit.

I have asked for the Holy Spirit to be in control of my life for years, but I still held firm to my inability to write. I think a good label for it is *pride*. I don't want to make a fool of myself. I don't want to expose my ignorance or lack of skills in choosing the right descriptive words.

I have spent hours mixing colors so that I would have just the right blend for an oil painting or watercolor that I was working on. It was worth the time spent because those who viewed the picture were as inspired as I was with the finished product. You might say they entered into the experience with me. I have always viewed writing much like painting a picture. The words that you use are like paint. You must know how to choose, mix, and blend words to bring the reader into your experience.

This past year many people told me I should write my experiences down or keep a journal. My response was that I have written them down. Pride, however, keeps them in my possession. Just recently I prayed, "Lord, You have delivered me from the fears of public speaking, You have delivered me from the fears of leading small group Bible studies, and from leading in women's ministries. Why, Lord, haven't You delivered me from the fear of failure in writing?" I felt the Lord was saying to me, "I haven't needed to, because you haven't done anything yet." The scripture "Commit thy works unto the Lord, and thy thoughts shall be established" came immediately to my mind.

I knew the Lord had spoken to me in a still, small thought-voice. He seemed to say to me, "I will deliver you when you need Me. I will part the water when you get your feet wet. Call upon Me, and I will show you great and mighty things that you know not. I have called you to the burning bush, but you have failed to take off your shoes."

"O Lord, forgive me! I have limited Your witness by my control." I am excited with the new freedom I now have in Christ. The enemy no longer has chains on my hands (Jer. 40:4). Thank God I'm free! I, like the disciples, must write what I have seen, heard, and know about Jesus. I sought the Lord and He heard me, and He delivered me from all my fears! HAZEL BURNS

MAY 21

I Fared Better Than Jonah

And the word of the Lord came unto Jonah the second time, saying, Arise, go unto Nineveh, that great city and preach unto it the preaching that I bid thee. So Jonah arose, and went unto Nineveh, according to the word of the Lord. Jonah 3:1-3.

It was only two months to graduation. The final two weeks of practice teaching was all that lay between me and a final grade. So I tackled those two weeks with total dedication. Creating kindergarten aids often took me into the midnight hours. But I enjoyed teaching and felt rewarded when the children clearly grasped the essence of the topic presented.

Then I read the supervisor's final assessment of my work.

"Your discipline is weak" provided the first blow. Great improvement was needed in several areas, and she listed them. Her final blow to my fragile self-esteem read: "If you improve on these and other weaknesses, you should become a *fair* teacher."

My despair notwithstanding, my grade was evidently sufficient to allow me to graduate. My first appointment was to a one-teacher school deep in the forests of Western Australia clear across the continent from home and my aging parents in the east. At this time the Second World War was raging, and little civilian transport was allowed across state borders during the war. There would be four state borders between my home and my appointment.

So, reflecting on my supervisor's assessment of me as a teacher, and the appointment that appeared like banishment and terminal separation from my parents because of the war, I did what Jonah did. I said, "No, I am not going to take that appointment." I intended to present my resignation at the evening session of the Annual Council. I sincerely hoped that no one would select that guilt-inducing hymn, "I'll Go Where You Want Me to Go."

Thirteen years, a second graduation, a marriage, and three children later we visited the forest schoolhouse where my husband was to preach and where the appointee teacher had failed to show all those years ago. We wondered if the congregation who worshiped there might say, "So you're the one who failed to teach our children in 1943"? But they received us warmly, graciously over-

172

looking the past and giving thanks for the ministry of the day.

It was at an aboriginal native school of which my husband was appointed as superintendent that God touched me on the shoulder and said, "You have fared better than Jonah did when he refused My call. I'm calling you again to teach. There is a teaching emergency at Karalundi School, and no one but you can resolve the dilemma."

It had been 18 years since I had graduated with a teaching diploma, and I still felt the pain of inadequacy. But the same Lord who asked the reluctant Moses, "Who made your mouth?" reminded me also that He was still completely adequate, and I would be also, if I trusted Him.

After a week's refresher course from the retiring teacher, I finally stood before 30 small aboriginal students. Opportunities to fill emergency teaching roles have continued to open ever since, and the Lord reminds me not to say no.

Jonah's recollection of his experience strengthened me greatly. "When my soul fainted within me I remembered the Lord: and my prayer came unto thee into thine holy temple" (Jonah 2:7).

I suspect that the Lord might well have said, "Why didn't you pray that prayer earlier when your problems seemed so crushingly insurmountable?" But His gentleness prompted me to serve as a teacher at last, and His grace won my heart.   EDNA HEISE

MAY 22

When Opportunity Calls

Philip . . . told him the good news about Jesus. Acts 8:35, NIV.

Ten years ago I stopped at an office at break time looking for a particular person. He was out on an errand at the time of my call, but there was a young man at his desk reading the book *Health and Happiness*. After a short conversation, I discovered that he was very interested in what he was reading, but unfortunately the book was not his. It was clear that he would like to own a copy of the book. The next day I took a brand-new copy to his office at break time, gave him the new copy, and asked him to write his name in it. He was surprised. It then occurred to both of us that we had not even introduced ourselves the previous day. I told him where my office was and gave him my telephone number.

After this first acquaintance, I gave my "office son" other books and magazines, some of which we discussed, until one

Sabbath morning there he was in church smiling at me.

He and his two sisters and a friend are now baptized members of the church. He is a choir director in one Adventist church, while his sisters belong to a singing group and the friend is a deacon in another SDA church. They are all on fire for the Lord, have won others to Christ, and are giving Bible studies in many homes.

Because I was willing to witness, my "family" has increased by two daughters, two sons, a daughter-in-law, two grandchildren, and another grandchild on the way. They all turn to me for counseling, guidance, and love. Together we are one big happy family in the Lord. The opportunity? Only a simple statement and question: "You seem to be enjoying what you are reading. Is it good material?"

Opportunities for witnessing are all around us. May the Lord open our spiritual eyes to see them and enable us to use them to the glory of His name. When opportunity calls, may we, like Isaiah of old, answer, "Here I am; send me." CONSTANCE M. LARYEA

MAY 23

Of Kindred Spirits

Before they call I will answer; while they are still speaking I will hear. Isa. 65:24, NIV.

Everyone likes to be listened to. The prophet Isaiah (49:1) called upon the islands to listen to him, and James (1:19, NIV) said: "Everyone should be quick to listen." Perhaps that is why God created human beings with only one mouth and two ears—to encourage us to listen twice as much as we speak.

I have a young friend who has been going through a great deal of turmoil in her life. Although my role has been somewhat that of a mentor because of our age difference, it has been interesting to discover that we are kindred spirits. There is an ease in the flow of language between us (verbal and nonverbal) that makes our conversations effortless and rewarding. Sometimes we don't even speak in complete sentences, and yet we understand exactly what the other means. Sometimes we don't even use words, and yet we feel what the other is feeling.

Unlike many men, women need to "process" their thoughts out loud. They need other women friends to talk with, listen with, share with, and feel with. My friendship with this young woman has reinforced this truth for me. I have discovered anew how important it is to "listen." Many times I have no solutions for her. The only thing I can offer is the gift of listening as she expresses things that are meaningful in her life. Sometimes they involve pain, confusion, and disappointment; other times joy, personal growth, and affirmation. Regardless of the sentiments expressed, I have been rewarded through her gift of trust in me as a listener and through the opportunity to practice the art of listening.

Recently it occurred to me, as I was thinking about our friendship, that sometimes we develop skills in areas where we ourselves have had a need. If we have craved someone to listen to us, for example, perhaps it makes us more sensitive and more willing to give others that gift. One day while I was musing about this, the following words came to my mind:

> Listen well—
> For I am speaking with something far more expressive than
>   words,
> The language of the heart,
> Often so silently eloquent, begs of you to
> Listen gently—
> Interpret what I cannot say with a sensitivity my soul will feel,
> The sweet understanding of kindred spirits
> Flashing warm within your eyes, assures me you will
> Listen always—

God listens to us, always—wherever we are and whatever we are doing. He listens gently and understands that we are speaking with more than words; with the longing of our inner hearts that do not know where to go. God is willing just to listen—but He is also willing to do much more than that. The beauty of our relationship with God is that He has solutions for us. Sometimes we are not ready to look at those solutions. It can take time for us to be willing to look at some of God's solutions, but He doesn't rush us.

Perhaps the task for us to learn is that while God listens to us, He wants us to listen to Him. "He who has an ear, let him hear" (Rev. 13:9, NIV).

DEBBY GRAY WILMOT

MAY 24

The Song of My Heart

And we, who with unveiled faces all reflect the Lord's glory, are being transformed into his likeness with ever-increasing glory, which comes from the Lord, who is the Spirit. 2 Cor. 3:18, NIV.

Joan Hughson asked me if I would write a theme song for our pastors' wives group. She said I could use any topic I chose, but she wanted to have it completed by the spring of 1991 so it could be introduced at the annual retreat. It is sometimes difficult to write on demand, and sure enough, nothing came to my conscious mind. Weeks and months went by, and still nothing happened. Many times, when I recalled her request, I would toy with different ideas, but nothing ever jelled. The subconscious mind, as designed by our Creator, is marvelous, however; and with the help of the Holy Spirit, it sometimes creates things for us.

A few weeks before the deadline I was performing one of those unglamorous daily grooming routines—brushing my teeth. As I looked at my reflection in the mirror, it started me thinking about my desire to reflect the life of Jesus in my own life. Suddenly the words that I needed for the theme song came to mind. Putting down my toothbrush, I grabbed pencil and paper and could hardly write fast enough to stay ahead of my thoughts. These words flowed out on the paper:

> Give me Your mind, Lord, serve through my hands,
> Help me respond in love to all life's demands.
> Let every word I choose be what You would say,
> May someone see Jesus in my life today.
>
> I am Your servant, teach me Your will,
> Your special promises in my life fulfill.
> Help me reflect Your love to others, I pray,
> May someone see Jesus in my life today.

I set the words to music and practiced the song so I could introduce it at the annual spring retreat. When the day arrived, I got up to sing and explained to the other ministerial wives how the song came to be written. "Many songs have glamorous stories around their origins," I told them. "This song was written during one of the most routine and mundane of activities—toothbrushing!" Upon reflection, however, I had come to the realization of just how appropriate the setting was. We are to reflect God's love not only in the spectacular and staged events of life but in all of our activities. We are to be a looking glass, as it were, to mirror the love of Christ to others.

Christ came to this earth to show us what God was like, and He was so sure of the connection He had with His Father that He could say with confidence, "Anyone who has seen me has seen the Father" (John 14:9, NIV). In a similar way, we are on this earth to help others see who Christ is. The Lord wants us to reflect the likeness of Christ with ever-increasing glory. How wonderful if people can say of us, "I have seen Jesus reflected in your life today."

DEBBY GRAY WILMOT

Under Whose Control?

Now the man's name was Nabal, and his wife's name was
Abigail. And the woman was intelligent and beautiful in
appearance, but the man was harsh and evil in his dealings,
and he was a Calebite. 1 Sam. 25:3, NASB.

The name Abigail in Hebrew means "father is rejoicing." In the
Greek it means "source or cause of delight." A most fitting
name for Abigail. What a contrast we see in her name and her life
to that of her husband's name and life. David had planned to
destroy Nabal, whose name meant "fool," and his clan for the rude
treatment received. When interceding with David, Abigail spoke of
Nabal as being a "worthless man . . . for as his name is, so is he"
(1 Sam. 25:25, NASB).

Abigail's behavior revealed a beauty of character. Her Spirit-
filled life radiated through her personality. Although married to a
cantankerous man, she did not allow his behavior to tarnish her
character. His despotic ways could not change her from being a
tactful, peace-loving, kind, charming, and courteous woman. Nor
did Nabal's harsh dealings intimidate her.

Abigail knew the secret of happiness even though outward
circumstances were anything but desirable. She and the Holy Spirit
were close friends, and the result was a close daily walk with God.
Because of this walk, her life exerted a powerful influence for good
in the home, church, and community.

This episode teaches two important lessons that we need today.
The first is found in the marked contrast between the characters of
Abigail and Nabal—vivid illustrations of what a person can
become under the Lord's control and under Satan's. Those who
serve God and those who don't serve Him have character traits and
personalities that are as different as lemonade is from lemon juice.
Those controlled by God's Spirit inevitably develop qualities such
as kindness, patience, and long-suffering. The longer and closer we
walk with God, the more Godlike characteristics we develop. It is
as simple as that! On the other hand, if we are under the control of
the evil one, the longer we live, the more we develop Satan's
attributes.

The second lesson is that we are all under the control of one of
the two powers—Christ or Satan. Although this is a frightening
thought, understanding that there is no neutral ground should drive
us to our knees and the Word. We can choose to be controlled by

God's Spirit. If we make the right choice, Abigail's experience of developing a beautiful character can be ours! MARIE SPANGLER

MAY 26

Lessons From Long Ago

And he said to them, "Men of Israel, take care what you do with these men." Acts 5:35, RSV.

One thing is certain. The days following Pentecost were anything but ordinary. The fearful, cowering, self-absorbed ones who had been so concerned with the best place in an earthly kingdom finally got glimpses of the heavenly One, and it set them on fire. Peter and the apostles were born anew, born of God's Spirit, and they wanted the world to know.

This was not exactly what the Jewish Council leaders had in mind. With Jesus "out of the way," this little movement was supposed to die out. Instead, those in the little band who scattered from Gethsemane in the night were now preaching, teaching, and healing boldly—in the light.

The council members couldn't take it. When intimidation didn't work, they used a heavy-handed power play. Peter and the apostles were sent to a "common prison" (verse 18).

But prison was not what God had in mind. An angel was sent. The bonds were loosened. The heavy doors and locks offered no resistance. The apostles were free, and the angel told them to go preach at the Temple itself. What provocation! No escape route, or quiet flight to a hideaway. The Bible says they went to the Temple at daybreak. And when first light hit the gorgeous Portico of Solomon, the apostles were already busy, doing God's bidding.

Perplexity at the bolted prison doors gave way to rage in the council when the preachers were found. At the very least, the apostles could have followed the orders to remain silent. But Peter and the others put the matter into correct perspective. They were following God, not humans.

One man, Gamaliel, the speaker in today's text, saw the light. "Take care," he cautioned. "You might even be found opposing God!" (verse 39, RSV).

And the lessons for us? Are there parallels? Yes and No. Church leaders of today should not be reduced to or characterized as a vengeful band with murder in their hearts! They are not.

However, in many cases, women who hear God's call and who want to heed Him have been imprisoned by a social form and order

178

that is not necessarily spiritual. This reading isn't about the ordination debate, though it should be and will be resolved. This is about service.

If women, who could offer a wellspring of service, are truly appointed by God, they will not stop. Their ministry will not die. First light will find them preaching, teaching, and healing on the very Portico of Solomon. — KYNA HINSON

MAY 27

Called to Differing Roles

A woman who fears the Lord is to be praised. Give her the reward she has earned, and let her words bring her praise at the city gate. Prov. 31:30, 31, NIV.

As Seventh-day Adventist Christians today, how do we solve the dilemma of motherhood versus career?

Those women who are mothers and choose to stay at home often feel less valuable to society because they *just* work in the home. Those who have children and work outside the home often feel guilty for leaving their children. Those who choose not to have children are made to feel as if they are abnormal for not wanting what every woman should want. And those who want to have children, but cannot, feel an emptiness within whenever they see a woman pregnant, or listen to sermons that praise motherhood.

Sometimes there is friction between mothers who choose to stay home and women who choose to become professionals. Both women may feel that somehow they are not doing what they are supposed to. Motherhood seems second-best in a society that has educated us to equality with our male counterparts. And a career seems second-best in a Christian community that has educated us in a manner that says women are called to be mothers and wives first of all.

I believe in the principles of Proverbs 31. And I believe, therefore, that there is another option available for dealing with the issue of motherhood verses nonmotherhood. I believe that our church can, and should, be a place of peace. A place where we encourage women to be what God created them to be, human beings with individual gifts: some the gift of singleness, some the gift of healing, some the gift of mothering along with other gifts.

We do not need to fight over which gift is the best gift; they are all of equal value and necessity to the building up of our Christian body. We, as women, need to encourage and nurture one another in whatever gift we feel God has called us to use. We need to encourage men to use their gifts as well. We are not to separate believers into groups, men versus women, mothers versus careers, Black versus White, or rich versus poor. Let's make Galatians 3:28 our motto: "There is neither male nor female: for ye are all one in Christ Jesus."

Motherhood is necessary, good, and praiseworthy. We need to stop saying, when asked what we do, "Oh, I'm just a housewife and mother." But we need to remember that motherhood is not the only calling God may have given women. The principle of Proverbs 31 is that a woman who takes seriously her calling—be it minister, truck driver, seamstress, doctor, secretary, mother, or a combination of these—is a virtuous woman. We need to rise up and call all women who do this "blessed." MARGO PITRONE

MAY 28

A Second Chance

Thou hast granted me life and steadfast love; and thy care has preserved my spirit. Job 10:12, RSV.

While serving as a missionary in Cameroon, I caught a serious viral hepatitis. It took a turn for the worse, and I had to leave my husband and three children in order to return to Europe to get better medical care. The doctors took care of me, but I was so sick that they informed my parents that there was no hope for my recovery. My brother, who was in charge of an elementary school, told the schoolchildren, who spontaneously formed a prayer band. Miraculously, my health began improving.

A well-known evangelist, who had cancer, was in the same hospital where I was being treated. In spite of all the medical care and prayers, he died a few days after his arrival. His son, whom I knew well, had heard about my admission to the hospital and also that I was slowly recovering. He came to visit me. "You see, he has completed his work, and God wants to give him some rest," he told me. "As for you, the Lord certainly entrusted you with a task, a mission that He wants you to carry out."

These words made me think, and now I consider each day of my life as a blessing given to me by the Lord to serve Him. Each one of us is alive for some sort of mission, however humble it may be. We may have a lot of reasons to complain, but every single part of life is meant for service and praise to our Lord. As we become aware of this, our life will be brightened by a new light.

Remember Mordecai's words to Esther? It may be asked, Were you brought to this place for just such a time as this? Whatever our family, social, or professional responsibilities may be, we must consider life as a blessing granted to us by God for a very special task.   TANIA LEHMANN

MAY 29

Promises for Those Who Serve

No temptation has seized you except what is common to man. And God is faithful; he will not let you be tempted beyond what you can bear. 1 Cor. 10:13, NIV.

One of my work assignments as a young person was to stoke the old steam boiler with coal. The hot water built up tremendous pressure, and we had to keep close watch on the pressure gauge. Should the pressure increase so that the boiler was in danger of blowing up, we pulled the lever and released some of the steam.

Our lives are like a steam boiler. As we fuel them with work, study, and recreation, we get into situations of tremendous strain. Sometimes we may not sense the pressure building up. There are also various kinds of tests that come to us, such as health problems, parenting problems, and relationship problems. We need strength in order to pass these tests successfully. We do not want to give in to the temptation to do wrong, so we need power to resist.

God has made provision for us to live as His children in this world of sin, so there is no need for us to be overcome by pressure and to yield to the temptation of temper, criticism, and intolerance of others. The Bible is full of promises like this one: God keeps faith and will not allow us to be tested above our powers. He has assured us that He will provide a way out.

We should notice that the promise is not that we be taken away from the trial. The promise is that when we are tested and tempted we will be able to bear it.

Jesus has provided us with an example of how to overcome temptations and to be victorious. Peter states that Christ has left us "an example" and that we should "follow his steps" (1 Peter 2:21). If we heed this advice, we will find a "way out" of every problem, trial, and temptation. Here is how to find the way out: "Watch and pray, that ye enter not into temptation" (Matt. 26:41). Ask, "What would Jesus do?" Yield your will to Jesus every morning. Occupy yourself with doing good, as Jesus did. Unite with other Christians for prayer and fellowship. Take time to read the Bible every day.

JOYCE FORTNER

MAY 30

The Easy Life

Rise up, ye women that are at ease; hear my voice, ye careless daughters; give ear unto my speech. Isa. 32:9.

Here, speaking to the inhabitants of Jerusalem, Isaiah turns from the Assyrian attack to the description of local peace and then the glories of heaven. He is speaking here to the pampered women of Jerusalem, but if the rest of the chapter applies in a prophetic sense, why not verse 9?

Compared to women in the past, we are a pampered generation. My mother washed her clothes in a wringer washer run by a gasoline engine, and then hung them outside on clotheslines looped from tree to tree. In winter they froze so stiff they'd stand by themselves. After bringing them inside, she'd stand them around the stove to dry. (I especially enjoyed the long johns standing there in various degrees of relaxation!) Some of the clothes were rolled while damp to await her irons, which she heated on the wood stove. The other day I threw some clothes in the automatic washer, and later switched them to the dryer, from which they emerged soft and fluffy and almost wrinkle-free! We're pampered.

"Rise up, ye women that are at ease; hear my voice." Does it ever occur to us to praise God for the fact that we, as women, are called to hear God's voice? If we listen, we can hear Him speak to us. He will tell us how we can best serve His cause and glorify His name.

Rise up! Glorify God! Determine today to serve Him well. I'm praying for you. LEA HARDY

MAY 31

Seeking the Lost

What do you think? If any man has a hundred sheep, and one of them has gone astray, does he not leave the ninety-nine on the mountains and go and search for the one that is straying? Matt. 18:12, NASB.

I recently visited some friends in California, and we took a few days off to enjoy the Santa Barbara beaches and sunset. Unfortuately while we were away, the newest addition to the family, a beautiful, playful kitten, slipped away into the darkness of the lost. Even though there were other pets—a much-loved dog and a very classical dowager cat—I couldn't believe the overwhelming sadness of the family.

That night, as I lay in my bed in the guest room adjoining the front door, I could hear the children's mother, calling the kitten's name, making familiar sounds hoping to attract his attention, hoping to find and bring him home again. Sometimes she'd drive around, calling the kitten. She hardly slept that night. Early the next morning, just as dawn began to pierce the thin layer of smog, I saw her standing at the half-open front door anxiously peering out, calling, calling, hoping the kitten would hear and come home. I couldn't help thinking about how Jesus acts much the same way toward those who are lost. Perhaps the time has come for all who belong to the family of God to become concerned—no, worried— and motivated to action. Like that mother, we need to leave the warmth of our comfortable churches, to be up before dawn and out late in the evening seeking lost kittens.

I don't believe that we need to go into bars and brothels to find them. Many are in our own homes, in our workplaces, on the streets where we live, in the malls, at the fast-food centers, perhaps even in the mirror you looked into this morning.

Let us make a determination today to seek the lost.

HYVETH WILLIAMS

JUNE 1

How Soon Are We Going to Heaven?

"Behold, I am coming quickly! Blessed is he who keeps the words of the prophecy of this book." . . . He who testifies to these things says, "Surely, I am coming quickly." Amen. Even so, come, Lord Jesus! Rev. 22:7-20, NKJV.

Every time I read these words I remember an evening when my youngest child was 3 years old. That day for worship we had been talking about heaven. Later, when I was rocking him to sleep, Kenneth started asking questions:

"Mommy, where is heaven?"

"Heaven is way up, Kenneth."

"Up? How far up? Is it higher than the sun?"

"Yes! It is way beyond the sun!"

"Mommy, do we really have a home way up there? a home we can live in?"

"Yes, son. Jesus has a real and beautiful home for us there."

Then, with mounting excitement, he asked, "Mommy, when are we going to heaven?"

"Soon. Very soon."

"What is soon, Mommy? Is it tomorrow? Oh, Mommy, I want to go now!"

How can you explain to a 3-year-old that Jesus *is* coming soon, but that He is not coming *tomorrow*? For him, any time later than tomorrow is not soon! O, Lord, I don't want him to lose the sense of expectancy! Then I started thinking: *Do I feel that same yearning for heaven? Do I feel it so strongly that I want to go now? Has my mind been so busy with everyday cares that I am not looking "way beyond the sun"?*

But wait, are not those everyday cares precisely the ones that should make me want to go to heaven now? Today Kenneth fell down and had a very badly scraped knee that made him cry a long time. What mother does not want to take away the pain of her child? In heaven "there shall be any no more . . . pain" (Rev. 21:4). A friend called, devastated because her mother is dying of cancer. In heaven "there shall be no more death" (verse 4). We are struggling to pay all the bills, keep the boys clothed, and help a student in need, all on a Third World salary. But in heaven we are promised that we "shall inherit all things" (verse 7). I am tired of trying to think up ways of supplying my family with nutritious and attractive but inexpensive meals that will keep them healthy. But in heaven, we will have the varied fruits of "the tree of life" (Rev. 22:2). Two days ago we went to Monterrey, 40 miles away. I forgot to take the thermos with drinking water, and although we were very thirsty on a 98-degree, sultry day, we did not dare drink the city's contaminated water. But in heaven we will drink from the "pure river of water of life" (verse 1).

Oh yes, Lord! Like Kenneth, and like John of old, I too want to say, "Even so, come, Lord Jesus!" Come *now!* Keep the fire of hope and yearning kindled in my heart! Don't let me forget that my home is up there, "way beyond the sun"!   ADA GONZALEZ DE GARCIA

Eagles or Caterpillars: The Three-winged Life

Ye have seen . . . how I bare you on eagles' wings, and brought you unto myself. Ex. 19:4.

At one point in my life when I was feeling especially burdened by responsibilities, I listened to a Sabbath school teacher who made a statement that I have never forgotten. "The hardest thing in the Christian life is to live above 'everydayness,' " she said. And I immediately thought of example after example of how the brightness of the day is clouded, the joy of the Christian life is obscured, and the peace that is ours by right is destroyed by little things, "everydayness." Women have always seemed especially afflicted by this malady, because of their awesome responsibilities in so many areas. When one is rushed, the longest line at the store checkout counter is always chosen; unexpected guests always arrive upon the heels of departing guests; traffic jams occur in the midst of rushing to an important committee meeting; the computer goes "down" when there is a pile of urgent work that simply must be done. Patience is taxed to the utmost, and living on anything but the most mundane level seems impossible. The struggling Christian woman sometimes surrenders to words of complaint and harsh, impatient feelings.

But there's a solution in God's plan for "everydayness." I think it lies in what I shall call the "three-winged life." In other words, women can be eagles, or they can be caterpillars. A crawling, caterpillar-like soul will very likely be crushed by "everydayness," while the eagle soul soars above the mountaintop in the pure blaze of God's sunshine. The soul on wings just flies over the world and the trials in it that drag down the spirit.

We can overcome in our lives, I believe, with these three "wings": (1) surrender to God, (2) trust in God, and (3) interest in others. The precious, quiet moments just before the busy day begins are exactly right for breathing a prayer: "Please take all of me today, Lord—my tongue, my actions—and make me Your loving, devoted child." When the first touch of "everydayness" hits, the silent prayer can ascend like lightning to God's throne: "You can handle this, Lord, and I turn it over to You." When real or imagined injustice comes our way, the cure is instant. Self-pity can't live in an atmosphere of concern for others—for all those who are suffering, who are bereaved, who are living in parts of the world where there is no hope of a better tomorrow. And there is usually someone only a few feet away who needs just what a caring Christian woman can give in love and concern.

In *The Christian's Secret of a Happy Life*, Hannah Whitehall Smith makes this statement: "It is not worthwhile to cry out 'Oh, that I had wings and then I would fly,' for we have these wings already, and what is needed is not more wings, but only that we should use those we have. The power to surrender and trust exists in every human soul, and needs only to be brought into exercise. We shall not mount up very high if we surrender and trust only in theory, or in our especially religious moments. We must do it definitely and practically about each detail of daily life as it comes to us."

We do not have to be defeated caterpillars; we can be triumphant eagles. We can, through God's help, live the "three-winged" life.   MIRIAM WOOD

JUNE 3

Caught in the Storm

And behold, there arose a great storm on the sea. . . . And they went and woke him, saying, "Save us, Lord; we are perishing." And he said to them, "Why are you afraid, O men of little faith?" Then he rose and rebuked the winds and the sea; and there was a great calm. Matt. 8:24-26, RSV.

Perhaps now it will cool off," my mother wished out loud as the thunder rolled across Lake Michigan. It had been oppressively hot and humid for several days.

A bright sizzle of lightning beckoned my father to the window. And that's when he saw the tornado floating across the sky. From one side dangled a tail that gyrated up and down and side to side. It was meandering toward Grand Rapids, where my brother was headed that very minute.

Fortunately for us, the tornado was not touching down when we saw it. But the next morning, I could hear my father talking as I left my bedroom. "Blown into the field," "hay swirling everywhere," "ran to the ditch," "a piece of wood through her eye."

These phrases were bits and pieces of terrifying stories. While he was driving to Grand Rapids, my brother noticed the tornado in his rearview mirror. And this time it was touching down. He screeched to a halt and ran over to a ditch to lie down. As he peeked over the rim, he saw a barn explode. Hay and wood swirled through the air like thousands of toothpicks.

The tornado moved on to destroy not only my father's cousin's house, but his wife as well. They didn't find much of the house. But they found his wife in a nearby field with a piece of wood through one of her eyes.

Thus it is that the story in Matthew 8:23-27 amazes me. The storm mentioned in these verses must truly have been tumultuous in order for men who earned their living from the sea to be frightened. Mrs. White uses phrases like "dense darkness," "roaring of the tempest," "howling winds," and "lightning's glare" (*The Desire of Ages*, pp. 334, 335).

No wonder the disciples were terrified. Who wouldn't be? But Jesus wasn't. He was sleeping.

The disciples' lack of faith is mine. I'm bailing out the water and screaming right along with them. The lightning flashes, and I can't believe what I see! While the wind is blowing the world apart, Jesus is sleeping!

When the disciples' cries finally do awaken Him, He asks what seems to me an incredibly stupid question. "Why are you so afraid?" (verse 26, NIV). But then something even more stupendous happens. Jesus stands up in a boat that is ready to capsize. And above the roar, He commands the storm to stop.

And it does.

We find ourselves asking, "What kind of man is this? Even the winds and the waves obey him!" (verse 27, NIV).

"What kind of man urges us to remain calm when life threatens to swamp our boats with fear, uncertainty, bigotry, and injustice? What kind of man will stand up for us and denounce the sin that causes these tornadoes to rush upon us?"

Jesus' answer is this. "I am God become human. I love you so much that I came to this earth to show you how to live, how to die, and how to live again. I, who brought calm to Galilee, can bring calm to your soul. Peace, be still."

LYNDELLE CHIOMENTI

JUNE 4

Beautiful Attitudes

Blessed are those who keep my ways. Prov. 8:32, NIV.

How blessed is that woman who knows her need of God, for only then can others find a bit of heaven in her presence.
Blessed is that woman who finds in sorrow the comfort of a

187

living God, who learns that although life is burdened with unhappiness, a heart overflowing with gratitude can seek and find such fullness of joy that all bitterness is crowded out.

Happy is the family of the woman who possesses a gentle spirit. Her husband will place his world at her feet; her children will come often to her door. She truly listens and surely hears.

How blessed is the woman who yearns for justice and does something about it—shares her home with the homeless, her food with the hungry, her joy with the desolate—yet cares for the needs of her own family, including them in the sharing.

Happy is the woman who knows how to forgive, who cannot hold a grudge, and asks others for forgiveness. Divine forgiveness shall be hers.

Happy is that woman whose heart is pure, swept clean of self-pity, nagging, and complaints. In her heart is abundant love for her husband. So happy will her marriage be that others will see God in her home. Even their children shall behold Him.

How blessed is the woman who is a peacemaker, sharing neither gossip nor faultfinding. She studies her children to learn how to bring peace to them. She has self-esteem because God is her Father. Her children respect her because she is fair and just. She teaches them how to become members of God's family. Heavenly peace shall dwell deep within her soul.

Can this woman be happy when she has been misunderstood, mistreated, unappreciated? Yes, for she has exchanged her will for God's peace, joy, and love, and she will be given God's crowning gift—heaven! CHESAPEAKE PARTNERS

JUNE 5

Of Lace and Love

Does a . . . bride forget her wedding dress? Jer. 2:32, TEV.

As the mother of a recent bride, I can tell you that it will never happen. From the moment Mark proposed to my daughter, Kelli, my sane little world dissolved into a maelstrom of bridal magazines, bridal patterns, bridal salons, bridal fashion shows, bridal satins and laces at the local fabric shop. On one fact mother and daughter agreed. Kelli would need a wedding gown. Neither considered anything less.

On our first day of "just browsing," Kelli found her dream dress. She tried it on. One look in the three-way floor-length mirror and she announced, "This is the dress." One glance at the price tag that read $2,300 and I announced, "Not on your life, sweetheart."

At this point I realized I had four choices: buy the dress—only if we sold the family car; settle for something less—and endure the pathetic look of agony on my daughter's face for the next 50 years; use my VISA card—and view my eventual grandchildren behind prison bars; make the dress myself. Of course, there was a fifth—however ludicrous—option. Perhaps the person who designed the dress would feel compassion for my dilemma and out of the goodness of her heart just give me the dress? Naw! I was back to solution number four.

Three months later I found myself sitting cross-legged in the middle of the living room floor at 2:00 in the morning sewing tiny transparent sequins onto volumes of Belgium satin and Venetian lace while the rest of the family slumbered in their beds. Sloshing about in my own self-pity, I mumbled something about being a victim of my own ill-advised choices. "There must be a lesson in this somewhere."

That's when I remembered reading about another wedding and another wedding garment. "But when the king came in to see the guests, he noticed a man there who was not wearing wedding clothes. 'Friend,' he asked, 'how did you get in here without wedding clothes?' " (Matt. 22:11, 12, NIV). While the garment in question was not that of the bride, it was a wedding garment nonetheless. I wondered about the man thrown out of the banquet hall for not being properly dressed, especially when Bible scholars point out that the king supplied the garments for his guests free of charge. Free—a gift! Solution number five.

I looked down at the crumple of lace and satin in my lap for a moment, and thought of the gracious King in the story—Jesus. In His hands is a garment of exquisite purity—my robe of righteousness. I recognize my need. I know what I want. I understand my options.

Like many throughout history, I could try to buy the garment. But the price tag of Calvary is too high. I could charge it—you know, pretending to myself and the world that I own the garment, while the bank of heaven holds the title. Or I could settle for a lesser quality garment. But both the King and I would know the difference.

Of course, I could make it, like I was doing with Kelli's gown. At this point the analogy falls apart faster than a poorly stitched hem. Because when it comes to my robe of righteousness, I've tried the do-it-yourself project for righteousness many times and failed. At least for me the seams are never straight and the stitches never come out even, no matter how carefully I follow the directions. Another option would be unthinkable: I could attend the wedding without a wedding garment, like the fool in the story—and find myself thrown into outer darkness.

Fortunately, my Jesus, a person of unmeasurable talents, has designed a robe of righteousness especially for me. It is guaranteed to fit perfectly, whether I wear size 2 or 22. Best of all, this custom-made wedding garment comes gift-wrapped in God's redeeming love. But I must accept it—and wear it. I must put complete trust in God's love. — KAY D. RIZZO

JUNE 6

Does God Sleep?

My heart is not proud, O Lord, my eyes are not haughty; I do not concern myself with great matters or things too wonderful for me. But I have stilled and quieted my soul; like a weaned child with its mother, like a weaned child is my soul within me. Ps. 131:1, 2, NIV.

In the darkness, the 10-year-old child knelt to pray. The prayer was similar to that of most children—with one very personal addition. "Dear Jesus, please be with Mommy and Daddy, Grandma and Grandpa, Aunt Mary and Uncle Jerry, and all the other people who need Your love. Most of all, Jesus, remember me tonight. Please don't let me wet the bed! I love You, Jesus. Amen."

Some nights the prayer was effective, and when the child woke in the morning a prayer of thanksgiving went up. More often than not, in the middle of the night or in the early hours of the morning, sleep would be interrupted with that warm, wet feeling. Slowly the child would begin to be aware of a cold dampness. What a disappointment to wake to the feeling of a wet bed! Did God sleep too soundly last night also?

Many remedies were tried to cure the bed-wetting problem. An old folk remedy, one spoonful of honey at bedtime, did not work. No fluids after 3:00 in the afternoon produced only very realistic dreams of a soda pop bottle tipped to drink—only nothing came out. Alarm clocks were set and a tiny body tried to be awake, but was still asleep—perched on the cold gray toilet. Nothing worked; it was useless. Still the child prayed. It wasn't until well into adolescence that the warm, wet awakenings subsided and finally disappeared.

There have been many other times in this child's life that prayers were answered slowly or maybe not at all. There have been enough times that an answer has come so swiftly, however, that this child has learned that God is really listening. The most important lesson, though, is that through all of life there has been a God who offers love, support, peace, and an assurance that He is always near. And this child learned to keep talking with God in prayer (Phil. 4:6, 7). May the peace of God be upon you today.　　STARR PINER

JUNE 7

Saying Goodbye

For you know the grace of our Lord Jesus Christ, that though he was rich, yet for your sake he became poor, so that by his poverty you might become rich. 2 Cor. 8:9, RSV.

B reakfast sat in my stomach, hard and cold like the kitchen floor beneath my feet. I had to leave. It was too late now to change my mind.

It's only for a few days, I tried to console myself. But it was no use. I always felt this way before a business trip.

I moved into the warmth of the family room. As I settled on the couch, Mocha, one of our two keeshond puppies, snuggled across my feet. How soft her fur felt. And her hazel eyes, like pools of liquid trust, shone in the light of a single lamp. Her sister, Silver, lay nearby, fixing her gaze toward the corner of the forbidden bookshelves that she frequently chewed.

"Silvey," I whispered, "come here, girl." But she only stretched and yawned. Would Peter be able to practice obedience training with her while I was gone? She was going to need it! I'd have to discuss it with him on the way to the airport. Right now he was asleep.

I thought about him lying there—my favorite person. He said he'd miss me, of course, but he didn't mind my going too much.

I sighed. I really didn't want to leave any of this, not even for a few days. But as I rested my head against the back of the couch, the thought struck me: *What did Jesus leave behind when He made His trip to earth? Was there a favorite object in His Father's house that He loved to look at, to touch, to think about the history of?*

Maybe He had a pet. A favorite animal that He Himself created. Did He wonder how it would fare while He was gone for 33 years? How it would react when He returned?

What were His thoughts as He said goodbye to God? Did They hug and cry? Did They discuss what They would do in each other's absence? My mind staggered. *He who was verily God left behind all the glories of heaven to come to earth. He who traveled from star to star, from world to world, without the aid of mighty jets,*

191

traveled to earth in order to save us.

How could I possibly know what Christ left behind?

I questioned my own feelings about leaving home as I looked around the family room. The 100-year-old treadle organ sat along one wall, a solid-oak testament to a craftsman's faith from a time gone by. My mother's baby picture hung above it. And accenting the coffee table was a music box from my childhood.

What would I leave behind as my plane roared into the sky? Not much, I realized, as I felt Christ's love flow around me—a love that relinquished all the magnificence of heaven just so I could live there too. And what little I would miss would someday pale in the light of the most wonderful possession anyone could have, and never have to leave—our Lord and Saviour, Jesus Christ.

LYNDELLE CHIOMENTI

JUNE 8

The Zoo of Life

The Spirit of the Lord is upon me, because he has anointed me to preach good news to the poor. He has sent me to proclaim release to the captives and recovering of sight to the blind, to set at liberty those who are oppressed, to proclaim the acceptable year of the Lord. Luke 4:18, 19, RSV.

A teacher once dismissed an essay of mine with the comment: "Too much imagination!" She was probably right. I couldn't be told about even the smallest injury without my mind supplying all the blood and pain!

I hope I've learned to put that imagination to better use, but recently I found it running riot in a zoo! When we arrived, the sun was shining hazily through the heat mist, and it was snowing. Well, not actually, but there were fluffy white catkins all over the ground, inches deep in places, and masses of others were busy getting airborne in the rather boisterous breeze. The seed heads clung together and drifted in snowlike clumps across the large, roomy compounds, lodging themselves in fur and feather alike.

That wasn't the last time my imagination took over during that happy day. One of its more ridiculous meanderings produced a camel high up in a tree. It turned out to be an enormous orangutan, but anyone can make a mistake.

In bed that night my imagination wouldn't let me rest. A parable was trying to be born. I saw the world as a zoo. The

Designer planned a zoo without bars or cages, and at first it was perfect. Then trouble broke out, and the animals could no longer be trusted not to hurt each other—or themselves. So the Designer of the zoo provided a Keeper. By now cages had been made. Not by the Designer, but by the animals! The bars and locks were sins. The Keeper did what He could to show the animals how to live safely and happily without the bars, and some of them listened to Him and went free. Others left for a little while but couldn't handle the freedom, so they rebuilt their cages and locked themselves in.

Then the Keeper took all the bars and fences and put them around Himself until He couldn't move. The locks and bolts cruelly cut into Him, digging and bruising, while He pleaded with the animals to learn to live without the bars built by sin.

Some listened then, seeing the bars for what they were, but there were still some who clung to their cages, and there was nothing more the Keeper could do. Agoraphobia stalked the zoo, and it seemed there were very few who could cope with the promised freedoms. An Attendant came when the Keeper was forced to leave, and He's been working with the animals ever since.

Rumor has it in the enclosure, however, that the Keeper is coming back one day to get rid of all the fences and barriers once and for all.

As I dropped off to sleep, I couldn't help wondering if He'll find us humping our cages about with us, or if He'll find us free, helping others to shake off their shackles too.   ANITA MARSHALL

JUNE 9

A Light for My Path

Your word is a lamp to my feet and a light for my path. Ps. 119:105, NIV.

I was about 12 years of age and attending a friend's 4H club meeting in the country. A visit to the country was always a treat for me, a city girl.

This particular evening after the meeting we were to walk down the road to the next farm for our ride home. We began walking. It was a beautiful spring evening. The moon wasn't out, but the stars were—they seemed so close you could almost reach out and touch them.

Then someone said, "Let's run," and we were off. I remember how wonderful it felt; the cool breeze on my face, the wind pushing my hair back. It seemed my feet had grown wings and were barely touching the ground as I ran. After all these years I still remember that feeling of lightness and freedom.

But that glorious feeling was short-lived. Not being familiar with the area, I turned into the driveway too soon, fell on a cement culvert, and had to be carried into the house. Fortunately my injuries were not major, just a huge multicolored bruise and some soreness.

I needed the moon that night. I needed light.

God has promised me light for my spiritual journey with Him. His light is His Word, my flashlight for my walk toward eternal life. When I forget to use this light, I find myself tripping over unseen do-it-myself rocks and stubbing my toes.

God says, "I will instruct you and teach you in the way you should go; I will counsel you and watch over you" (Ps. 32:8, NIV).

God's Word gives joy to the heart, light to the eyes (Ps. 19:8), and understanding to the simple (Ps. 119:130).

God's Word—a lamp for my feet, a light down the path to Him.

EVIE VANDEVERE

JUNE 10

A Modern Version of the 23rd Psalm

The Lord is my Pacesetter, I shall not rush.
He makes me stop for quiet intervals,
He provides me with images of stillness that
restore my serenity,
He leads me in ways of efficiency through
calmness of mind,
And His guidance is peace.

Even though I have a great many things to
accomplish each day, I will not fret,
For His presence is here;
His timelessness, His all-importance, will keep
me in balance.
He prepares refreshment and renewal in the
midst of my activity.
By anointing my mind with His oils of tranquillity,
My cup of joyous energy overflows.

Truly harmony and effectiveness shall be

the fruits of my hours,
For I shall walk in the peace of my Lord,
And dwell in His house forever.

TOKIO MEGASHIE

JUNE 11

Finding "Home"

Then I saw a new heaven and a new earth; for the first heaven and the first earth had passed away, and the sea was no more. Rev. 21:1, RSV.

I was flying six miles high and more than 500 miles per hour, going home after a two-week stay in my childhood home. I had just left home. Yet I was on my way home. Or was I? Where really is home?

The previous night I had snuggled down in "my" bed, in "my" room in the home my parents, brother, and I had moved into some 40-plus years earlier. It had been home until my Prince Charming had come and whisked me away to the life of a nomad (minister). Since then I had lived on the West Coast, Midwest, South, and now the East Coast.

This trip to my parents' home had not been a happy occasion. I had received sudden word that my father was dying. I left my East Coast home to fly to my West Coast home to be by Dad's bedside and to console Mom. There were days of little hope and days of possible hope as my gentle father tried valiantly to rouse from his unconsciousness. He wasn't going to give up without a struggle. Our hearts would quicken as we held his hand and felt it feebly squeeze in response to our comments, or saw him weakly open his eyes and nod ever so slightly. A wiggle of his toe would delight us.

Long hours stretched into days, until it became apparent that his tired body could struggle no longer. He gave one long tired sigh and was gone. As my mother, brother, and I stood by his bedside with arms encircled and tears flowing, we knew home would never be the same again.

I returned to my present home, happy to be with my husband and willing to resume my duties. But home began to mean something different. I realized it could never really be here on this foreign planet. Though I have often longed to put my roots down deep, to live in one town and one home, I now know home is not in Washington, Texas, or Maryland. Everything here will always be temporary. Home is where my heavenly Father is.

195

I have lost my earthly father, but I have not lost my heavenly Father. He is preparing a permanent home for me where there will be no more moving, no more saying goodbye to a loved one. No more goodbyes at the airport, knowing Mom is going home to only a little black dog who can't understand why his master no longer sits in his favorite chair and holds him.

Yes, I definitely know now where home really is, and I'll never be fully satisfied until I get there!   ELLEN BRESEE

JUNE 12

Never-Shaken, Always-Steady Love

Love is patient, love is kind. . . . it is not proud. . . . It always protects, always trusts, always hopes, always perseveres. 1 Cor. 13:4, 7, NIV.

Love is not love
Which alters when it alteration finds,
Or bends with the remover to remove.
O, no! it is an ever-fixed mark
That looks on tempests and is never shaken.
—William Shakespeare

That excerpt from a sonnet is posted on the bulletin board in my study. Below it hangs a bright-pink heart in which are the words from 1 Corinthians 13 (NIV).

All too often I forget that the attributes of love penned by Paul the apostle and Shakespeare the bard are the attributes of God, who embodies love (1 John 4:8). When I forget that God is love, I also forget the unconditional qualities of God's specific love for me.

When I forget God's love for me, I forget how to love myself. And as a self-defensive measure, my ability to love my neighbor as myself is impaired. At such times God calls me back to love.

I find that God uses anything to make love live. I pick up a box of beautiful postage stamps; my hand slips. Scattered from their categories by picture and denomination, the stamps fall in a fluttered heap on the floor.

My working stamp collection includes recent love stamps, the world shaped in a heart, and some leftover love stamps—the ones with two stylized bluebirds nearly kissing above a red heart and L-O-V-E spelled out across the top. When L-O-V-E spills out all over the floor, I am reminded of God's love for me.

Sometimes it takes a major catastrophe, sometimes a minor

one, to bring out the love in my life. The love of God spills down to carpet the ground on which I step, reminding me that no matter what, I am loved.

God, please help me to love myself and others as much as You love me! — KATIE TONN-OLIVER

How Do You Value Yourself?

For through the grace given to me I say to every man among you not to think more highly of himself than he ought to think; but to think so as to have sound judgment, as God has allotted to each a measure of faith. . . . And since we have gifts that differ according to the grace given to us, let each exercise them accordingly. Rom. 12:3, 6, NASB.

A speaker once lectured a group of senior citizens on the subject of liking yourself. When she finished, an elderly man approached her and said, "I discovered something this evening that has always troubled me. All my life I have been critical of others and wondered why. After what you said tonight, I realize I have never really been pleased with myself. In fact, I cannot tell you one thing I like about myself."

The elderly are not the only ones to suffer from such a problem. People of every age struggle with self-esteem. Someone has observed that "our attitude toward ourselves influences the quality of our relationship with God and others."

We can depreciate ourselves in countless ways. Have you ever heard anyone say, "I'm only a teacher," "I'm only a minister's wife," "I'm only a layperson," "I'm just a secretary," or "I'm just a student in school"? The words "only a" or "just" reveal that we feel we are not what we want to be or that we are measuring ourselves by what others are or do. But this is putting a low value on the gifts God has given each of us. What would happen if we didn't have all types of people to carry all the various responsibilities in the church? What would happen if we had no young people to bring new ideas, creativity, or enthusiasm?

The importance of a correct sense of self-worth cannot be overestimated, for it affects our behavior, attitudes, productivity, and ultimate success. A lack of it has caused countless adults as well as young people and even children to feel miserable about themselves, to be unable to get along with others, to take a wrong course in life, and to make wrong decisions.

True appreciation for our God-given talents and abilities will never allow us to think ourselves better than others. In fact, Paul admonishes us to "be devoted to one another in brotherly love. Honor one another above yourselves" (Rom. 12:10, NIV). But that does not mean that we should disparage ourselves, either.

How can we value ourselves properly? "Christ paid an infinite price for us, and according to the price paid He desires us to value ourselves" (*The Ministry of Healing,* p. 498). In fact, "the Lord is disappointed when His people place a low estimate upon themselves. He desires His chosen heritage to value themselves according to the price He has placed upon them" (*The Desire of Ages,* p. 668). Praise God for the priceless value He has put on your life.

MARIE SPANGLER

JUNE 14

Live in the Lavender!

And be not conformed to this world: but be ye transformed by the renewing of your mind, that ye may prove what is that good, and acceptable, and perfect, will of God. Rom. 12:2, NIV.

It was Sabbath, and my husband and I were worshiping with our believers in the Crimea, just a short drive from the Black Sea. We had stayed at the church to greet our members before coming to the pastor's house for a home-cooked Sabbath meal.

Now, after several courses of wonderful dishes, we pushed back from the table to try to catch our breath. I was always overwhelmed by the effort that my Ukrainian sisters put into a meal. I had taken note of the well in front of the house where the family drew their water to cook meals, bathe, and do the family wash. I remembered the rough dirt road that we had traveled to reach this home. Now I watched as the eldest son of the family sat quietly in the background. He was home for the weekend from a sanitarium; he had tuberculosis.

I sat quietly, trying to absorb my surroundings. The room was alive with the generous spirit of this family, but the hardships of their daily lives lurked in the shadows, including the pain of a bright young son with a crippling disease. No, life wasn't a "bed of roses" by any stretch of the imagination!

On either end of the food-laden table, rose-colored drapes flapped in the breeze. "What is that I smell?" I asked.

"Lavender," my host replied.

"It's wonderful!" I hastened to add.

In a flash the pastor's young daughter was up and out the back door. Moments later she returned with a handful of the sweetest smelling lavender I'd ever smelled. Over and over I held the blossoms up to drink in nature's perfume, while across the table from me the pastor's wife sat beaming. She was obviously pleased that they'd produced something that I was so enthused about. "Yes," she said with a broad smile, "we're so fortunate to live in a field of lavender!"

How her words tugged at my heart. I would remember her convincing smile long after I'd left the warmth of her home. I vowed that in the future, even when circumstances were less than perfect, I too would choose to live in a field of lavender!   ROSE OTIS

JUNE 15

Claiming God's Promises

He will call upon me, and I will answer him; I will be with him in trouble. Ps. 91:15, NIV.

The telephone on my desk rang, and when I answered it the voice on the other end told me that my 12-year-old daughter had been involved in a bicycle accident. She was being sent by ambulance to the emergency department at the hospital where I worked. The details were sketchy, but apparently the front tire of her bike had hit a rock, throwing the bike and her off balance. The sideways fall had knocked her unconscious, and she was bleeding from the right side of her head.

I hung up the receiver and sat quietly for a moment, trying to gather my thoughts before going down to meet the ambulance. All kinds of horrible possibilities vied with each other for space in my brain. Would she die? Would she be brain-damaged? "O God," I breathed silently, "help me to get through this. And take care of my daughter—my only daughter."

The next few hours passed in a blur. X-rays were taken of her skull. Yes, she had a concussion. I explained the situation to her little brother, who was afraid his sister would die. I made arrangements for someone else to cover my work responsibilities. My husband and I tried to sort out what had happened during the accident, and conferred with the doctor over her prognosis.

I spent all that first night in her hospital room, watching the right side of her face swell and her eye turn a bright purple. As I sat by her side in the darkness, I thought about the past—I had so many cherished memories of her as a baby, a small child, a kindergartener, and a young girl who was very close to becoming a teenager. There was not much I could do to make her more comfortable, but she didn't want me to leave her side. I was frightened—oh, so frightened.

In the silence, broken only by her occasional moan, the words of Psalm 91 came to mind. God promises that if we call upon Him, He will answer and will be with us in trouble (verses 14, 15). Somehow those words seemed more real to me than ever before. I claimed those promises, and finally, just as the dawn was beginning to break, I dozed off for a few moments of needed rest.

Thankfully, within a few weeks she had recovered and was back to being her usual self. Every so often, however, I remember that still, quiet hospital room; recall my terror and her pain; and shiver with the understanding of how quickly our comfortable little worlds can be shattered. And I claim anew the promises of God. We can dwell in the shelter of the Most High; we can rest in the shadow of the Almighty. God is our refuge and fortress; in Him we can and must trust. Just as my daughter wanted me to stay beside her in the hospital, God wants us to stay close to Him.

GLENICE LINTHWAITE STECK

JUNE 16

Through My Tears

And God will wipe away every tear from their eyes. Rev. 7:17, NIV.

Some time ago I read an article in the *Adventist Review* by a woman who had spent years living with misconceptions about God. Some of these had to do with personal trials—why we experience them and whether God brings them to us. In the end she came to the conclusion that trying to figure out all the whys and wherefores was of lesser importance than the realization that God was standing next to her, in all of her trials and tribulations—weeping with her. Her willingness to be vulnerable, to share part of her real-life experience with us, was of great encouragement to me. The concept of God standing next to us made a great impact upon me, and it helped me to realize anew that God is a personal being. When I hurt, He hurts with me; when I rejoice, He rejoices with me.

We all need to have the sense that our earthly friends understand and empathize with us. How much more important to realize that God understands and empathizes with us in an even more personal and complete way. In my enriched understanding, I created a song as my way of expressing these sentiments.

> Sometimes it's so hard, Lord,
> To have the faith You're in control,
> When I view the broken pieces of my life.
>
> Scattered dreams reminding me
> That even when I try my best,
> In this world there's heartache and strife.
>
> Yet through my tear-dimmed vision
> I sense Your presence near,
> Telling me that You will see me through.
>
> I want to claim the promise—
> Help my unbelief,
> In my need I'm crying out to You.
>
> Father, dry my tears,
> Take Your gentle hand
> And touch the pain.
>
> Let me feel the peace
> That flows into my life
> From Your unfailing heart of love.
>
> Do You cry with me?
> When I look into Your eyes, Lord,
> It's then I realize,
>
> You're there through sun or rain,
> You can make my heart rejoice again.
> Father, O, my Father, dry my tears.

We have all experienced broken pieces of our lives: situations that we feel are out of our control. A prayer book from 1662 contained the following words:

"Turn our captivity, O Lord, as the rivers in the South. They that sow in tears shall reap in joy. He that now goeth on his way weeping and beareth forth good seed shall doubtless come again with joy, and bring his sheaves with him."

How comforting to know that God sent Christ "to bind up the brokenhearted . . . to comfort all who mourn" (Isa. 61:1, 2, NIV). When I have this view of God, no matter what comes into my life I can see Him through my tears and realize that He is weeping with me. Not helplessly weeping, however, but weeping empathetically. He is not only willing but able to comfort me as I mourn; He will bind up my broken heart. I rest assured that in the end God and I will come out of the experience rejoicing together.

DEBBY GRAY WILMOT

JUNE 17

Indispensable Visitor

Ye are the light of the world. Matt. 5:14.

Zipping my jacket and pocketing my keys, I stepped outside into crisp, cool, slightly damp air. I walked briskly past silent houses, hurrying to reach the open fields where I would be able to see her clearly when she came.

Like furry white blankets, wispy patches of low fog clung to the ground here and there, dimming the outline of shrubs and distant trees. But except for a few thin cloud fragments strewn about the eastern horizon, the sky above was clear.

From someone's chimney I caught a faint hint of burning wood and other early-morning odors. Then the houses fell behind me. As I crunched down the graveled path entering a field, I smelled the pungent fragrance of damp earth and grass seed.

At the far edge of the field near a deep ditch I stopped. To my far right the field ended in a distant clump of trees and bushes still half concealed by the ground fog. Beyond me stretched another field. And to my left the highway divided the land, separating fields and houses from the runways and hangars of a small airport. Behind me the houses and trees stood sleepily. I turned to look at them.

I thought about her. Wherever she went she brought warmth and happiness. Healing and health. Comfort and life. She added color to everything she touched. No wonder some worship her. No wonder that some, like me, come out in the early chill to watch for her coming. Even nature seemed to be eagerly anticipating her arrival.

The sky turned from light gray to deep blue. A thousand birds gathered along telephone wires and in the nearby trees, filling the air with a cheery welcome.

The earth threw off its misty blankets of ground fog. Choppy cloud fragments at the eastern horizon dressed out first in pink, then fiery orange, then a brilliant burnished gold.

She was here! As she touched them, summer flowers unfolded

202

in delicate colors. Without her they could not live—nor could the birds, the trees, nor I. She is indispensable.

When I turned toward home, retracing my steps through the field, Jesus' words came forcefully to my mind: "Ye are the light of the world" (Matt. 5:14).

If I am the "light of the world," then I must be willing to dispel darkness, bring warmth, happiness, health, comfort, color, and beauty to all that I touch, just as the sun does.

As the sun shone warm upon me, I thanked God for another new day—and insight by which to live it. LOIS FITCHEN

JUNE 18

The North Star

Whether you turn to the right or to the left, your ears will hear a voice behind you saying, "This is the way; walk in it." Isa. 30:21, NIV.

We all have developed a perception of who we think we should be. When we do not fulfill our expectations or reach the standard, we can become depressed. Frustration and anger over our imperfections can turn inward as we chastise ourselves for not reaching our goal. We often see ourselves as weak, worthless, and without hope of attaining the goal.

Some of us grew up in the era when looking good on the outside was stressed. Regardless of how we felt on the inside, we were expected to portray a perfect and Christlike image. This is a heavy burden at best, but when one feels worthless and like a fake on the inside, it is impossibly heavy. Depression can result from the dichotomy of feeling one way on the inside and being expected to act a different way on the outside.

The airline pilot prepares a flight plan, and the instrument panel helps the crew to keep the plane on course. It would be ideal if the plane could remain on course at all times. With headwinds, air pockets, and updrafts, however, this is not possible. It takes continual correction and readjustment to arrive safely at the destination.

The Bible contains a sample listing of individuals who lived by faith (Heb. 11). They heard the voice of God calling them to readjust their course. They accepted the lessons, learned from their errors, and continued in the direction of God's ideal.

Those who have been lost at sea or in the wilderness have often looked to the North Star for direction. Keeping it constantly in sight, they have gotten back on course. What a joy to know that when I am lost and off track, I can listen for God's voice to help me travel in the right direction. If I am willing to allow others to watch this process in my life, they can gain courage from my experience. They can learn to listen for God's directional voice in their own lives. God can help us to work out our salvation and still portray to the world a realistic picture of ourselves—one that will encourage them that remaining on course is worth it.

I cherish a wonderful poster that shows a child, bat in hand, standing in front of a broken window. Underneath the picture are the words "I am a precious, fallible child of God." Today I know that as a precious, fallible child of God, whenever I veer to the left or to the right, the infinite voice of God will call me back on course. In this process, I know I will not reach the ideal today, or even tomorrow. But as long as I listen to God's voice and continually correct my course, I can be assured that I am exactly where God wants me to be at this stage of the journey.

SHEILA BIRKENSTOCK SANDERS

JUNE 19

Sweeter Than Honey

Taste and see that the Lord is good; blessed is the man who takes refuge in Him. Ps. 34:8, NIV.

Webster's dictionary tells me that to taste is to test the flavor of something by putting a little of it into my mouth. Today, when fast food is the culinary fare of many Americans, tasting has become almost a lost art. Everything is done quickly, including eating the food. Even in restaurants quantity seems to be more important than quality. We are guilty of eating too much too fast. The opportunity to taste and savor seems to have vanished.

The Lord does not ask us to gulp down or overindulge in what He has to offer, but to taste, see that He is good—and then try more. God gave us five senses to use together to enhance our living as well as to keep us in touch with the environment around us. After all, we enjoy looking at some foods, and without our noses, tasting would be a futile effort.

It still makes me smile when I recall introducing new foods to my children when they were babies. I always told them that this new food would be "yummy in the tummy." Sometimes, after they sampled the tidbit gingerly, they would agree and want more, and sometimes they would make an unforgettable face—one that only babies can make—and the food would be spit out onto the tray of the high chair.

Most people take similar steps when they are about to taste something for the first time. Initially we anticipate that this new experience will be good; then we mentally prepare to evaluate what is coming; and after the taste, we decide if we would like to have more. Tasting is a well-ordered event. It requires thought and decision while we test for texture and flavor, deciding if it is sweet, sour, salty, or bitter. When the Lord invites us to "try it, you'll like it," He knows that what we receive will be in the right amount—and perfectly seasoned.

We like the taste of taking refuge in Him. David said "How sweet are Thy words to my taste! Yes, sweeter than honey to my mouth! From Thy precepts I get understanding" (Ps. 119:103, 104, NASB). There are words of comfort, instruction, and encouragement in the Bible to fit every occasion.

Jesus must have been talking about our ability to taste when He told us that we are the salt of the earth (Matt. 5:13). We all know how flat and unpalatable food that has not been salted is. It does not take much salt, either, to change the taste of food completely so that it becomes edible and delicious. It is my prayer that the Lord will help me to be the kind of "salt" in the lives of others that will make them want to "taste and see" that the Lord is good.

SHEILA BIRKENSTOCK SANDERS

JUNE 20

Betrayed Trust

For [Christ] is himself our peace. Gentiles and Jews, he has made the two one, and in his own body of flesh and blood has broken down the enmity which stood like a dividing wall between them; for he annulled the law with its rules and regulations, . . . thereby making peace. This was his purpose, to reconcile the two in a single body to God through the cross, on which he killed the enmity. So he came and proclaimed the good news: peace to you who were far off, and peace to those who were near by; for through him we both alike have access to the Father in the one Spirit. Eph. 2:14-18, NEB.

When someone betrays my trust, I grow angry. Like a small, hurt child, I want to wail and lash out. I feel extreme dislike. If the hurt is deep enough, I feel hatred. Then I feel guilty and chagrined. Aren't Christians supposed to love? Always?

It may take moments or years to get past the place of anger that comes when trust is betrayed. When the pain is deep and life-threatening—when it hurts so badly I wish I had never lived—my head might want to be forgiving, but my heart wants to strike back, to hurt as much as I have been hurt.

I do not like to admit that I have such strong "negative" emotions. But after time has passed, I realize that unless I do admit they exist—admit their ability to control me, admit they affect my attitudes and behavior—I remain unhealed. Only confession can open me to accept the reality of forgiveness and cleansing for me (1 John 1:8-10). Only through admission of the hurt and the anger can I be healed.

More than anything, I am helped by remembering that God, who is love made incarnate in Christ Jesus, "always trusts" (1 Cor. 13:7, NIV). If God trusts me, always, can I not also come to trust another in God's name? Miracles do happen! They have!

O, Lord, help me to trust You—and yes, the one who has betrayed my trust—as much as You trust me.   KATIE TONN-OLIVER

JUNE 21

The Ticket

They will fall by the edge of the sword, and be led captive among all nations; and Jerusalem will be trodden down by the Gentiles, until the times of the Gentiles are fulfilled. Luke 21:24, RSV.

I was anxious to get home. It had been only a few days, but I knew my desk was piled high, the garden would be out of bounds, and the mail would be something else. Getting home couldn't be too soon for me!

As I stood in line with the other airline passengers to check in, I went over in my mind all the things I would do the minute I got home. I noted each item and laid my plan of attack. Then it was my turn at the counter, and I reached into my purse for my airline ticket. It wasn't there.

"Where is that pesky thing, anyway?" I mumbled. "I thought it was right here, in this pocket." Then I spotted the envelope from the travel agent hiding behind a book I had been reading. With a triumphant smile I handed it to the ticket agent.

She opened the envelope. It was empty! I was stunned. The agent was as surprised as I was. I began to rummage in my big purse, silently talking to my Guide. *Lord*, I prayed, *what next? I can't imagine where that ticket is.*

The search went on while people waiting behind me heaved heavy sighs. I took everything out of my purse—brush, compact, Day Timer, pen, package of leftover chips, and a half-used pack of Kleenex—and laid them on the counter.

While the clerk tapped her pencil, the disgruntled passengers one by one shifted to the other foot. Another attendant came to help relieve the congestion at the counter.

I removed the small picture of my family and the "love notes" some of the women from the retreat had stuffed into my hand at the last minute. The additional agent fixed an incredulous stare on the mounting pile of stuff that came from my purse. It must have been my small flashlight or the safety pin that did it, for he called out in a raspy voice, "That's it, lady. It's too late now, no time for any more. Get another ticket."

Then I remembered. I had had my ticket in my hand in the taxi. That's where it was—in the taxi! How I hated to lose that ticket. It was as good as cash and gone for sure. But like the man said, it's too late now.

So I shoved all my stuff off the counter and into my empty purse and turned in the direction of the security check area. I hadn't gone far when the same raspy voice called, "Hey, lady, is this your ticket?" Beside the agent stood the man who had driven my taxi, out of breath. Of course it was my ticket! There was a quick exchange of tip-for-ticket and smiles all around. And from my mouth, right out loud, "Thank You, Lord! You've done it again. You are amazing, You are *wonderful* in my sight."

On the flight homeward I couldn't help thinking of how everybody needs The Ticket to get Home. Some know of their need, and some do not. Some of us are very smug, thinking we have The Ticket in a safe place. But there is so much extraneous stuff in our lives that The Ticket has been misplaced or lost.

Our Ticket for the trip Home is Jesus, of course. There's no way we can make the trip without Him. Let's pitch that extra baggage out of our lives and make more room for Him. We're just about to leave. I can hardly wait to get Home! VIRGINIA CASON

JUNE 22

A Joyous Choice

Then the angel said to me, "Write: 'Blessed are those who are invited to the wedding supper of the Lamb!'" Rev. 19:9, NIV.

One day a king planned a very special reception to honor his son. The guests would be given a beautiful garment to wear. And, as is most usual in these large affairs, an RSVP was requested of the guests. The coordinator in charge could not believe the number of guests who sent in their regrets, and she was indignant at the flimsy reasons given: "I have to clean my living room," "I must go see my great-aunt." Furthermore, the replies were rudely stated. One reluctant guest came but refused to wear the special robe. The king noticed her, and asked how she got into the reception without the special robe he had provided. When the guest could not answer, the king had her thrown out into the street (Matt. 22:2-13).

In the summer, city parks frequently blossom with banners hung from trees proclaiming "Hankins' Reunion" or "Potters' Reunion" in that particular spot in the park.

These reunions are wonderful opportunities to see grandparents, aunts, uncles, and cousins; to catch up on family news; to eat such great home-cooked food that transports you back to Grandma's table in the old homeplace; to watch babies and the ball game, and reminisce of days gone by.

Imagine how wonderful the heavenly reunion will be that God has planned for us. To sit at Jesus' table and hear Him bless the food, to see again our loved family members and friends restored to perfect health and happiness, to talk with our guardian angel.

William Barclay states: "To think of Christianity as a gloomy giving up of everything which brings laughter and sunshine and happy fellowship is to mistake its whole nature. It is to joy that the Christian is invited: and it is joy he misses, if he refuses the invitation."

The wedding supper. A joyous time for honored guests. Choose today to attend this reunion with Jesus.   EVIE VANDEVERE

JUNE 23

A Matter of Perspective

He who is faithful in a very little is faithful also in much; and he who is dishonest in a very little is dishonest also in much. Luke 16:10, RSV.

There's a sign on a desk I pass each morning on my way to work. It says "I could do great things if I weren't so busy doing little things." At first I smiled at the humor of it. But as I passed the sign day after day, I began to realize that it contained a sad truth, candy-coated with humor.

Why is it that the multitudinous, ordinary things generally consume so much of our time and energy that we have little or nothing left to give to our grand aspirations in life? Unfulfilled dreams seem to beckon us in vain while we are bogged down in the mire of "busyness." We find ourselves scratching out our existence with the chickens, when we could be soaring with the eagles.

On the other hand, there is an opposing but equally valid philosophy that is hidden in the humor of the sign. While "doing little things" *faithfully* we can actually prepare ourselves for the "great things" for the brief moment when opportunity for larger things presents itself. Some of the by-products of faithful preparation are patience and contentment. So time spent in doing "little things" is not wasted, but productive in the long run if used as experience gainers. Our motto should be "I am preparing to do greater things while I am patiently doing little things." God watches for those who faithfully fulfill the small tasks, and He rewards them with greater ones.

So how we view the "little things" can very easily be the deciding factor of whether or not we will later be doing "great things." It's all a matter of perspective. NANCY VASQUEZ

JUNE 24

The Grass Is Greener on This Side of the Fence

Not that I speak in respect of want: for I have learned, in whatsoever state I am, therewith to be content. Phil. 4:11.

I believe that a philosophy of the Christian life can be summarized in the phrase "The grass is greener on this side of the fence." There are two components to this philosophy.

The first is to be content with what you have. This can be accomplished through the second component: if you have turned your life over to God, you are exactly where He wants you to be at this precise moment. Contentment comes from being in partnership with God and realizing that "the grass is greener on this side of the fence."

It is so easy to be envious or jealous of others on the other side of the fence. I believe this is true for women who are successful in the business or the professional world. Women are not treated equally or as fairly as they should be. More is expected of women than of men in similar situations. This situation has improved markedly over recent years, but it does still exist. It is very easy to fall prey to jealousy, pride, envy, and ambition.

These were the sins of Miriam, and this is probably why I have always felt such a kinship toward her. Miriam is one of the few single women described in the Bible. In spite of being a single woman, she was the true mother of her nation and the first woman to be of national interest and have a patriotic mission. She attained a level of leadership unknown for women at that time and unequaled for centuries to come. Unfortunately, she began to feel that "the grass was greener on the other side of the fence." She felt neglected, she was jealous, and she was not content. Her sins of pride, envy, and ambition resulted in rebellion and physical manifestations of leprosy. Fortunately, Moses intervened on her behalf and begged the Lord to forgive her. She was truly repentant and was forgiven, but it is tragic that she had to succumb to discontent and not what God wanted for her at a particular time, in a particular place.

The contentment described in Philippians is always clearly visible. We all have seen people who have had this deep serenity and radiate this unusual peace and joy. One of the most memorable events of my life took place in a tiny bedroom in Shanghai, listening to a retired minister of the gospel. With difficulty we extracted from him his story. For 15 years he had been in prison, unable to communicate with his family in any way. He was mistreated at the hands of his captors and all his worldly goods were confiscated. But there was not one word of complaint from him nor one tinge of pity for himself. For him the grass had been greener on his side of the fence, whether he was in prison or a free man. An inner contentment radiated from him and was infectious to observe. May we each have such an experience; may the grass always be greener on our side of the fence.   JOAN COGGIN

JUNE 25

Behold the Revelation of Your Destiny

Make good use of every opportunity you have, because these are evil days. Eph. 5:16, TEV.

I scanned the opened mail my secretary had laid on my desk. A couple personal notes caught my attention first, and then I quickly thumbed through the remaining pieces, sorting out the "junk mail." From the highly reputable Franklin Mint came an invitation for me to own my personal crystal ball. The catchy title read "Behold the Revelation of Your Destiny!" Underneath was the name of America's most widely read psychic/astrologer, Jeane Dixon.

A chill ran up and down my spine when I read Ms. Dixon's attached letter, which praised God for her psychic powers. "Like few others in history," she wrote, "I have been blessed with the God-given gift of prophecy, and I am honored to share it with others. I am grateful to God for bestowing upon me the gifts He chose for me," she concluded the letter.

For years, whenever I thought about end-time events, I wondered what kind of scheme Satan would devise to captivate the minds of ordinary men and women with spiritualism. People like your next-door neighbors and mine. The people we stand next to in the grocery line, and whose children our children play with at the pool. The Scriptures clearly tell us that the evil one has such a plan, and the Spirit of Prophecy enforces this. "Spiritualism is about to take the world captive. . . . Few have any idea as to what will be the manifestations of spiritualism in the future" (*Evangelism*, pp. 602, 603).

Sitting at my desk, in familiar surroundings, it seemed somehow surreal. But it was happening! Call it spiritualism, astrology, New Age, or any number of other names, but it was happening, and I was a living witness to the fulfillment of prophecy. I didn't need to order a crystal ball from the Franklin Mint to recognize it. In God's Word He makes it very clear how this world will end, and in the same book of Revelation He paints some beautiful word pictures about the world to come (Rev. 21). I need to read these descriptions more often. I want to be able to close my eyes and visualize a world without sin, sickness, death, or sorrow of any kind. I want to picture every child with a full tummy, a mommy and a daddy, and hope for the future. I want to let my mind dwell on a world free of AIDS and cancer and every other crippling disease that robs us of those we love. I need to memorize the song I'll sing with heavenly angels at the coming of my Lord. After all, I don't want to be the only one singing from music!

Jeane Dixon may have been named the "Most Admired Woman in the World" for three consecutive years, but I won't look to her to reveal my destiny. My present and future life is committed to the One who holds tomorrow while reminding me, "Do not be terrified; do not be discouraged, for the Lord your God will be with you wherever you go" (Joshua 1:9, NIV).   ROSE OTIS

"My Grace Is Sufficient for Thee"

And he said unto me, My grace is sufficient for thee: for my strength is made perfect in weakness. Most gladly therefore will I rather glory in my infirmities, that the power of Christ may rest upon me. 2 Cor. 12:9.

We are not told just how soon after his conversion Paul began praying for the removal of the thorn in his flesh, and how long it took for him to realize the answer that God's grace was sufficient for all the adversities that would be his lot as a follower of Christ.

It took more than 30 years after my baptism to learn God's purpose for the heartaches He allowed me to experience. Now I know that the times I had to face much more month than money with a young family, dependent on one church school salary, my heavenly Father's grace was sufficient. With hindsight, I realize that the clouds did not completely hide the sun. True to His promise, my God supplied enough grace to see through those trying times.

Then times changed. The children grew up, and the financial crises did not occur as often. But my need for my Father's sufficient grace remained.

It appeared that one of the children had lost his way by making the pursuit of a political career a greater priority than his relationship with God and the church. In my distress and utter helplessness I sought God's unfailing grace. My Father saw my tears, heard my cry, and kept His promise to contend with the enemy and save my child. Today my prodigal is home and gives evidence of settling into the truth.

A year ago when my mother succumbed to the ravages of cancer of the cervix, lungs, and brain, I was plunged into the blackest night of grief. So far, this has been my greatest test of the grace that is sufficient. God's grace was sufficient to end my 20-year wait for my mom to join me in accepting Christ as her Saviour, sufficient to give her the victory over her 35-year smoking habit. That same grace will see me through this night of sorrow, and sustain me through future tests and trials until the glorious day when with my mother and I, the other members of my family shall see our Saviour face-to-face. Then we'll thank Him for His grace, which has been sufficient to effect our eternal salvation.

Trials continue to face me each day, but I know from whence comes my help. How about you? Trials are placed in our lives to bring us to the place of oneness with Christ that we pray for but can attain only as we live by the motto "His grace is sufficient for me."

PAMELA PALMER

JUNE 27

Storm Clouds

Even though the fig trees have no fruit and no grapes grow on the vines, even though the olive crop fails and the fields produce no grain, even though the sheep all die and the cattle stalls are empty, I will still be joyful and glad, because the Lord God is my savior. Hab. 3:17, 18, TEV.

Black clouds were boiling over the mountains as I drove off the scales at the elevator. The old blue truck roared up the hills and creaked around the corners as I raced the storm back to the ranch where my husband, Johnny, waited in the combine with another hopper full of wheat.

Fat drops of rain were pelting down before the last of the grain was spewed from the spout into the truck. Then, scurrying around like cartoon characters in fast forward, we battened down the combine and the truck groaned up the hill to shelter in the barn.

Later, soaked like drowned rats, we laughed as we dried off in the house. Looking through the rain pouring off the roof in sheets was like viewing the world from behind a waterfall. The driveway was fast filling with puddles, and the dust was turning to slippery gumbo.

"I won't be combining anymore for quite a while. This is really soaking things up. Vacation time, and it's only the second day of harvest." Johnny grinned.

Thirty years of farming teaches you to take things as they come. Rain had slowed down harvest before. Getting upset wouldn't help any.

The black clouds that had obscured the sun seemed lighter. The wind picked up and the drumming of rain on the roof turned to sharp pounding. We rushed to the dining room window. It wasn't rain that was wind-driven against the glass. It was hail!

The horror I felt was mirrored in Johnny's face, ghostly pale beneath his "farmer tan." No grin; the joke was over.

The storm lasted 15 minutes and again bright sunshine smiled down, this time on desolations. Only minutes before, the grain had stood tall and firm like fields of golden brushes. The heads of wheat had hung down plump with promise. Now the sodden stalks were

213

bent and broken, their fruit pounded into the mud. Our crop was gone. A whole year's work for nothing.

But God was still there. Although for a while we really had to search to find Him.

There are other kinds of storms that come: sickness, death, tragedies of all kinds that can wipe the smiles from our faces. Sometimes you don't even see the black clouds until suddenly, like a bolt of lightning and a clap of thunder, they shower down around you.

I don't like storms. But it's been during the stormy times that I have really felt God's presence. I learned that Jesus is not just a fair-weather friend, and when I search closely I can see His face, looking down with love, through the blackest clouds. "I will still be joyful and glad, because the Lord God is my savior."   BETTY RAYL

JUNE 28

Criticism

When there are many words, transgression is unavoidable. But he who restrains his lips is wise. The tongue of the righteous is as choice silver. Prov. 10:19, 20, NASB.

Early in life I became impressed with the importance of never criticizing another person. The husband of one of my family's beloved elderly friends had passed away. My parents and I drove over to their home to express sympathy. As I stood beside the casket, the wife came up and began reminiscing about her husband. Among the many good things she mentioned about him, one particularly caught my attention: "Of all the years we lived together, I never heard my husband say an unkind thing about anybody." Instantly I thought, *What a wonderful thing to be said about a person,* and decided it would be a good policy to follow.

But it isn't easy to keep from saying something against someone who has hurt you or who you really do not appreciate. Before we even realize it, we can put someone down in order to make ourselves look good. Without thinking of the devastating results, a person casually criticizes something his or her spouse has said or done or slips into a negative attitude toward the pastor or some other church leader.

One of our former General Conference presidents, Robert Pierson, tells the story of a new missionary full of zeal and eager to begin his new assignment. The first evening in the new country he listened to a steady stream of criticism about those in the mission field and the General Conference. Months later he became so discouraged as he reflected on the shortcomings of others that he asked for a permanent return to the homeland. He eventually left denominational employment and even the church itself.

Criticism can gnaw away at the very core of our being until we become hollow and destroyed, just as a tiny beetle can topple a mighty tree by boring into its core until it falls to the ground.

Acceptance is a basic human need, and we must learn to accept each other at face value. If we are looking for the bad in someone else, we will surely find it. But if we search for the good, we can find that too! "If sympathy, kindness, forbearance, and love are abiding principles in your life, you will be a blessing to all around you. You will not criticize others or manifest a harsh, denunciatory spirit toward them; you will not feel that their ideas must be made to meet your standard" (*Testimonies*, vol. 5, p. 650). Let us look for the good in people today and restrain our lips from criticizing.

MARIE SPANGLER

JUNE 29

More Than Conquerors

Who shall separate us from the love of Christ? Shall tribulation, or distress, or persecution, or famine, or nakedness, or peril, or sword? . . . No, in all these things we are more than conquerors through him who loved us. For I am sure that neither death, nor life, nor angels, nor principalities, nor things present, nor things to come, nor powers, nor height, nor depth, nor anything else in all creation, will be able to separate us from the love of God in Christ Jesus our Lord. Rom. 8:35-39, RSV.

In September 1983 we left Burkina Faso so my husband could study theology at the seminary at Collonges-sous-Salève, France.

While we were there, my daughter Anita, 7 years old, started her second year of swimming, part of the school curriculum. In spite of a few misgivings, the day the swimming lessons were to start she enthusiastically went to the Vernet swimming pool, in Geneva, with her brother. It was 1:30 p.m.

About 30 minutes later as he did his homework, my husband heard the terrible news. Anita had drowned in the swimming pool! He first went alone to have a look at the accident, then came back to break the terrible news to me while I was visiting with a neighboring family. My heart broken by unspeakable grief, I went, with my husband and the president of the seminary, to the Geneva Cantonal Hospital where our daughter lay lifeless, suddenly torn from our lives. Our daughter—our only and irreplaceable Anita! The only daughter the Lord had entrusted to us had just been suddenly snatched from us.

What did this mean? Had we made a mistake in what we thought was the Lord's call to go to school in France? Had we failed in anything so that God had to withdraw His blessing? Many questions filled our minds, questions that remained unanswered. In spite of the compassion of our brethren and sisters in Collonges, this heart-wrenching trial was extremely hard to bear. But in spite of our deep pain, we never lost sight of our Saviour. Our decision was made and never changed.

The accident occurred on Tuesday, January 15, 1985, and the funeral took place on Friday, January 18. On Sabbath, January 19, a mother approached us: "Brother and Sister Thiombiano," she said, "your daughter did not die in vain! After this tragedy, my daughter decided to give herself to the Lord. She said, 'Anita was ready, but if it happened to me today, would I have been ready?' "

This young lady sealed her covenant with Christ in June of the same year. What appeared to be a defeat of God's love and mercy turned into a victory. What appeared to be a loss He transformed into a gain.

Discouragement, which is Satan's favorite weapon, did not have the victory. We remained in Collonges, and my husband successfully completed his theology classes. Today, he is in charge of the programs of the Adventist World Radio in the Africa-Indian Ocean Division, Abidjan, Côte d'Ivoire. The strength and faith the Lord gave us during this trial encouraged many at the Collonges Seminary.

We pray the Lord to keep our spiritual daughter, Anne-Marie, strong in the faith until His coming. In our family worships she has replaced Anita, and we trust the Lord will reunite us in His everlasting kingdom.

Indeed, "we are more than conquerors through him who loved us" and strengthens us. In our hardest trials the Lord Jesus is more than ever on our side and gives us victory over Satan. Praise to His name!   ABIBA THIOMBIANO

Lessons From a Lonely Spider

He cares for those who trust in him. Nahum 1:7, NIV.

A spider had woven a silken web just outside my breakfast room window. I saw it the first thing when I wakened this morning. The dew had touched it to silver.

At the southern end of it a spider waited patiently for its food, a picture of patience, faith, and trust. There is no guarantee any bug will find its way into the web. The spider simply trusts that it will happen. This is why it puts so much effort into building and rebuilding the web. It believes in the web as the best way to survive.

That says something about how I need to develop my own network of trust and faith in the Lord. Through all the changes of life, and as I pass from one life season to another, I must put my trust in God and wait for Him. He has promised that He will provide for all my needs. Not all my wants, maybe, but all my needs.

Sometimes our web of life gets torn up and holes get poked in it so that it loses its effectiveness. Then it is time to evaluate our life, to get busy repairing and rebuilding it, and to continue to trust God, who has made us in His image and holds life in His hands. He has ordained life to be whole and wants to help us make it that way.

I am thinking of all those whose lives are changing, whose lives are being disturbed and torn, of those who are trying to rebuild their web of life and network of relationships. Let these words of God from the psalmist's pen rest within your heart:

"When my spirit grows faint within me, it is you who know my way" (Ps. 142:3, NIV). "I spread out my hands to you; my soul thirsts for you like a parched land" (143:6, NIV). "Let the morning bring me word of your unfailing love, for I have put my trust in you. Show me the way I should go, for to you I lift my soul" (verse 8, NIV). With God there are always new days and bright mornings.

LOUISE HANNAH KOHR

Never Worn

I advise you to buy from Me . . . white garments, that you may clothe yourself, and that the shame of your nakedness may not be revealed. Rev. 3:18, NASB.

FOR SALE: l. Beautiful white Southern belle style wedding dress, size 8—$300 (never worn). 2. Hat and veil—$50 (never worn). 3. Gloves, white elbow—$18 (never worn).

The card was posted at the reception desk of a women's dorm. The passion and pathos conveyed in this brief announcement caught my attention, and I wondered about the person selling those items marked "never worn." Was she jilted at the altar or did her fiancé die suddenly before the wedding day? After examining the message I concluded that it was the former. The terse sentences had the ring of rejection, the despair of deferred dreams, and the heartache of dashed hopes that accompanies the remorse of being jilted.

As I identified with the pain of my anonymous sister, I could not help considering the plight of another rejected love. A Bridegroom who loved His bride so much that He gave His life to purchase white garments for her to wear, not only daily, but especially at the greatest event humanity will ever witness—the inauguration of His everlasting kingdom of peace. I thought about how often we reject His overtures of love and acceptance, how reluctant we are to wear the white garments of converted characters.

Jesus, the Bridegroom, says: "Come, buy white garments without money" (cf. Isa. 55:1)! These are precious and priceless, bought with a dear price, and wearing them will empower us to glorify God in our bodies (see 1 Cor. 6:20). Why do we spend our wages for what does not satisfy to cover our shame, to hide our pride, to fill our emptiness and destroy our fears, when there are white garments offered free of cost (Isa. 55:2)? Why do we so carelessly reject these white garments that will never wear out, guarantee peace of mind, and promise eternal satisfaction?

The tragedy of our times is that too many are willing to work hard for their salvation, to pay for the white garments. Many ultimately become skilled in doing Christian things rather than being Christian people who are determined to know nothing more than Jesus Christ and Him crucified. As a result, Jesus has to write alongside His own notice recorded in Revelation 3:18 the following: FOR SALE: 1. Gold refined by fire, that you may become rich— no cost (never worn). 2. White garments, that you may clothe yourself and that the shame of your nakedness may not be revealed—no cost (never worn). 3. Eyesalve to anoint your eyes, that you may see—no cost (never worn).

I hope that the words "never worn" will not appear next to our white garments, but instead our Saviour may write in big bold letters EVER WORN! HYVETH WILLIAMS

JULY 2

The Secret to Strength

Neither be ye sorry; for the joy of the Lord is your strength. Neh. 8:10.

As I wing my way from California to British Columbia, the view from my 727 jetliner window seems a perfect backdrop for contemplating the meaning of one of my favorite passages.

As our airplane has ascended higher and higher into the brilliant sky so radiant with God's sunshine, the city details below have become smaller and smaller in dimension, until they are out of view entirely, replaced with the serene blending of earth and sea as we approach western Canada.

By the time of Christ's second coming, our "heaven consciousness" will have to be so heightened, with earthliness so torn away from us, that we will be fit for the society of angels and of God Himself.

That purification process is going to take major strength to endure. And we must endure to be saved. "He that endureth to the end shall be saved" (Matt. 10:22). Where does such strength come from? As with every good and perfect gift, it comes from above, from our Father of love who withholds no good thing from His children.

How is such enduring strength imparted to us? Through the vehicle of joy, the joy of the Lord. Have you ever equated joy with strength? The two are not synonymous, yet work in perfect tandem for our good.

Have you been feeling sorry about something lately? "Sorry" implies feeling sorrow over something. If you cannot change that "something," our verse for today lights the way to how to pick up

219

the pieces and go on living on a greater and higher plateau than ever before.

If the enemy of our souls can rob us of our joy, then he has robbed us of our strength. Don't give him that power. It's yours to withhold. As long as you maintain the joy of the Lord, your strength will remain intact. What a power is found in the joy of the Lord. Clearly the choice is yours.

Our plane has now landed, taxiing toward the terminal. I've made my choice before deboarding: I choose the joy of the Lord as my strength.

Will you join me in making that exciting decision?

JUDY COULSTON

JULY 3

Now Is the Time

My grace is sufficient for you for my power is made perfect in weakness. 2 Cor. 12:9, NIV.

I stood beside the car at the gas station. The sound of the gasoline pouring into the tank was suddenly punctuated by a loud voice asking directions from the attendant. The conversation went something like this:

"Can you please tell me how to get where I am going?"

"Where do you want to go?"

"Well, I'm not sure. I think up north."

"Where have you come from?"

"Well, again, I'm not positive."

"Well, I can't give you directions until you know where you have come from and where you want to go," replied the exasperated attendant.

It is very difficult to arrive at a destination when you are unsure of where you are headed and unclear about where you have come from and what has happened to you along the way. Unfortunately, many human beings do just that—sometimes with their entire lives. The process of finding out where you have been so that you can figure out where to go is sometimes called "family of origin work."

I believe in the value of family of origin work for several reasons:

It can help you find out how and what you were taught. Your current responses to life are directly related to your childhood. It can help you find out whether there are better, healthier, or more functional ways to act and to live life.

It can help you to reparent yourself in areas in which you are not achieving desired outcomes. Instead of continuing to muddle through life, sometimes successfully, sometimes despairingly, you compile the information that can give you direction for change.

It can help you to model healthier, more functional living patterns for the next generation, so they can have the option of learning how to achieve better outcomes for all their expended efforts.

Blame has no part in this family of origin work. We must be willing to risk doing this hard work without blame, and with the view of becoming all that God wants us to be so that we can live to bless others.

The Bible admonishes, "Behold, now is the accepted time" (2 Cor. 6:2). Now is the time to develop a personal relationship with God and to allow your heavenly Parent to help you do the hard work of looking at yourself against the backdrop of your family history. Now is the time to let Him heal the wounds caused by an impaired ability on the part of people in your past to take healthy action or to perform functionally in some area of daily living. With the apostle Paul we can claim the assurance that God's grace is sufficient to help us learn to identify our wounds, and sufficient to heal our wounds (see 2 Cor. 12:9). Looking back in love can help us to look forward in love, as well as to that time when the family of God will embrace all of us together.

MYRNA MELLING

JULY 4

The Metamorphosis

Instead of the thorn shall come up the fir tree, and instead of the brier shall come up the myrtle tree: and it shall be to the Lord for a name, for an everlasting sign that shall not be cut off. Isa. 55:13.

Every fall I become one of those snuffling, bleary-eyed figures that you hoped and no doubt assumed you had forever left behind in kindergarten. I owe my plight, not to preschool exposure to the pantheon of viruses nor to a pervasive seasonal sense of gloom and doom, but to the effect of the lowly, lacy ragweed on the hollows in my head. Like freshets in a spring thaw, my eyes and sinuses herald the annual advent of ragweed.

I first learned the toxic nature of our relationship as I watched a hot, itchy, crimson, ragweed tide flow down my arm and overwhelm other potential allergy-causing culprits during a skin

221

test at my allergist's office. At that time I had no mental picture of this plant with the highly allergenic pollen and the exotic genus misnomer *Ambrosia* (Greek for "immortality"). I simply hated it in absentia, so to speak, until the miserably hot, humid day I met my antagonist face-to-face in Chattanooga, Tennessee.

Taking a break from working on the new house in which my family was earning sweat equity, I wandered outside to glance despairingly at the 200-foot-long, thigh-high stand of weeds that had sprung up along the path of a drainage ditch through our unseeded yard. Noticing me, our neighbor, no doubt displeased with the adjacent eyesore, strolled over and remarked, "Quite a crop of ragweed, isn't it!"

"Ragweed! Is *that* ragweed?" I exclaimed, my resolve hardening rapidly. Thereafter, whenever an errant rainsquall battered our weed patch with a sodden incentive to rank new growth, I charged into the muck with a shovel and a large red wheelbarrow to rain counterblows for control of the turf. In one instance when the combined might and sweat of two of us finally managed to topple a six-foot-tall ragweed plant, the thought struck me forcibly, *This stuff is like sin! If someone doesn't uproot it immediately, it becomes a hardy, hefty plant almost overnight. I certainly can grow it well, but it's beyond me to bring it down.*

I have to face the facts. I need the Master Gardener. Ragweed and dandelions flourish naturally in the garden of my heart; philodendrons and phlox do not. Thus I am rooting for God to eradicate the weeds, and transplant seedlings of His choice from the heavenly nursery to my plot, where the Master Gardener Himself has promised to nurture the growing plants and bring an abundant yield. "But now being made free from sin, and become servants to God, ye have your fruit unto holiness, and the end everlasting life" (Rom. 6:22).

These developments I am eager to celebrate with both a taste and a whiff of ambrosia, the *real* immortal stuff.

ANDREA KRISTENSEN

JULY 5

Your Space or Mine?

They will build houses and dwell in them; they will plant vineyards and eat their fruit. No longer will they build houses and others live in them, or plant and others eat. Isa. 65:21, 22, NIV.

I live in a society in which it is not customary for people to build their own houses. Although I have heard of people who have been unable to keep up house payments and have had their homes repossessed, and people who have been dispossessed for political reasons, today's text had no impact on me until I heard that a patch of garden I was cultivating had, with the owner's permission, been given to someone else without a by-your-leave.

My family and I had been digging the patch by hand for three or four years. Every year every clod of soil was carefully examined for noxious roots. We had planted one section with strawberries, and the soft fruit that already existed on the patch had been cut back and pruned. Our friends shared a good supply of fruit with us each summer, and we enjoyed our fresh vegetables. Now, all of a sudden, all that my family had helped me work for was gone.

Every time I passed the patch I noted progress on the land. The new gardener had vegetables growing in no time at all. He did not need to bring his family to clear the root system, since we had done that, and the soil was in good condition because of the previous treatment. The gardener had a "land flowing with milk and honey" at my expense!

It was true that the land had only been lent to me, and that I had not been assiduous in cultivating it that year. I know that the incident was the result of human error rather than malice, and I held no grudges.

Nevertheless, the whole incident gave deeper meaning to the last part of today's verse: "No longer will they build houses and others live in them, or plant and others eat." I'm looking forward to my home in heaven!   SHEILA WILSON

JULY 6

Being Like Jesus

The meek will inherit the land and enjoy great peace. Ps. 37:11, NIV.

The afternoon was warm and sticky, as early summer days can be. Each of us fifth graders wished we were anywhere but cooped up in school. Our teacher, Bobbie Jane Van Dolson, began talking about the Beatitudes. She told us about Jesus going up onto a mountainside with His disciples and teaching them in the outdoors. My mind wandered. I had visions of stretching out beneath the shade of a live oak tree and feeling the breeze cool my face and ruffle my hair.

223

I came back to reality in time to hear my teacher say, "Blessed are the meek: for they shall inherit the earth" (Matt. 5:5). She continued, "Can any of you give me a definition for the word 'meek'?" One of the boys shot his hand into the air: "Glenice." The children laughed; I blushed and wanted to crawl under my desk. I was absolutely mortified (a new word I had just learned) to have everyone's attention focused upon me, and I was not sure that being called meek was a compliment! The remainder of the school day passed in a blur, and I left for home feeling crushed. Not only had I been called "meek," but everyone had laughed at me, and that was not a pleasant experience for a shy 11-year-old.

After school I talked with my grandmother, as I often did when something bothered me. I told her everything that had happened at school, and ended by saying "I'm never going back to that school again." She pulled me over to her, put her arm around me, and said, "Glenice, that was a great compliment." I didn't understand. She told me about Moses and that the Bible says he was the meekest man on the face of the earth (Num. 12:3). She reminded me that although one definition of the word "meek" involved being tamely submissive and servile, the word actually had many positive and desirable connotations. It meant that the person was gentle and kind; not easily provoked; ready to negotiate rather than to cause trouble. Moses was certainly an assertive, creative, competent leader; and he was meek in his pattern of relating to others.

Perhaps I didn't look completely convinced, because she ended up by saying that to be called meek meant that I was learning to be like Jesus—the most precious example of all. She reminded me that Christ had said about Himself, "Learn of me; for I am meek" (Matt. 11:29). As her soft voice flowed over my little bruised spirit, I began to see that my schoolmate might have meant his comment to be a compliment. Even if he hadn't, I now saw the experience of that afternoon in a new light. Rather than continue feeling embarrassed and indignant, I began to feel humbly pleased.

Over the years I have noticed other references in the Bible that talk about the meek and mention how the Lord cares for and sustains them (Ps. 147:6). My grandmother's wise explanation and encouragement have motivated me to try to develop characteristics ascribed to the meek. She planted in my heart the desire to be like Jesus in the way that I relate to others. GLENICE LINTHWAITE STECK

Jumping to Conclusions

Do not judge, or you too will be judged. For in the same way you judge others, you will be judged, and with the measure you use, it will be measured to you. Matt. 7:1, 2, NIV.

Elvitia (not her real name) was a faithful Christian and a regular churchgoer. One weekend her presence was missed in church, and another member decided to drive by Elvitia's residence on her way home to see if anything was amiss. Upon rounding the corner, she noticed Elvitia's car in the driveway. The trunk lid was up, and she saw Elvitia, lugging several bulging bags in each arm, climbing the front steps. The woman watched a moment while Elvitia went indoors, and then drove on home.

In a few minutes this woman was on the telephone calling her friends. "I noticed that Elvitia was not in church today, so I went by to see if anything was amiss. I shouldn't have bothered. Do you know what I saw? Elvitia had just returned from a shopping trip and was carrying parcels into the house. I certainly thought her Christian experience was deeper than that. Skipping church to go shopping on the Lord's day. Imagine!"

The next weekend when Elvitia attended church again, she was puzzled by the lack of cordiality on the part of some of the other members. This went on for several weeks before Elvitia finally asked someone, "What is wrong? Why do you turn away when I say hello? Why didn't you invite me to the annual potluck?" Then the story came out. Elvitia didn't know whether to laugh or cry.

On the day in question she had been ready to leave for church when a neighbor called to say that a good friend across town had just suffered a fire in her home. Fortunately, not all the rooms had been burned, but all her belongings had to be evacuated before repairs could be made. Elvitia agreed to store some of the woman's things in her home. She was making one of several trips back and forth when the member from the church had seen her—and jumped to an erroneous conclusion. That judgment had caused Elvitia puzzlement, pain, and discomfort—all of which could have been avoided.

Unfortunately, some of us do have a tendency to jump to unwarranted conclusions. We fail to realize that every time we make a judgment, a comparison, or a negative assumption about someone else, that criticism registers within us at some level. When we devalue others in this way, we always devalue ourselves. That is why the Bible so clearly says that the Lord is to be the judge (Heb. 10:30; Rom. 14:10).

The next time you are tempted to jump to a negative conclusion and judge someone else by mere appearances (John 7:24), remember how much healthier it is to ask questions if we really are concerned about another's behavior. Let us accept others just as they are, and give them "the benefit of the doubt," in the same way that we would like to be treated.   ARLENE TAYLOR

JULY 8

It's Free

The Spirit and the Bride say, "Come." And let him who hears say, "Come." And let him who is thirsty come, let him who desires take the water of life without price. Rev. 22:17, RSV.

I'm not what you'd call an avid mountain climber, but I have climbed a few hills. There were the oak-studded ones around my girlhood home, the ones at junior camp, and Two-Bit, the hill behind La Sierra College. But it was a different climb in a faraway place that really affected my life.

We had ridden a bus for a couple hours from Jerusalem. Then we began the climb up the long ramp on the back side of Masada,* which was steep and full of switchbacks. It was hot and dusty, and before very long everyone in our climbing party was sweating and beginning to huff and puff.

The hours dragged on. Some of us had small canteens of water that we shared with the others, but there wasn't enough for all of us to have our fill. Many of the hikers began to wonder out loud if this was a wise thing to do. Others spoke of turning back.

It was the middle of the afternoon when our weary group struggled up over the edge and onto the flat top of this incredible mound. The view of the Dead Sea area was stupendous. It took my breath away. As I fumbled for my camera, I spotted a clump of joyous hikers some distance away. Curious, I walked closer. And then I saw it. Above the happy people was a small sign, which I could almost read. Could it be? I walked closer. Yes. It *was.*

"Hey, people!" I called to our group. "Water!" They were so

---

* Masada is an ancient mountaintop fortress in southeast Israel, the site of the Jews' last stand against the Romans in the revolt of A.D. 66-73. The name means "stronghold, fortress." You can read the thrilling story in an encyclopedia.

busy with picture-taking they hardly noticed me. So I yelled again. "Ya-hoo, this way. Water!" At that, they came on the double.

Sure enough. A water spigot with a battered tin cup fastened to it by a long chain was the center of all the excitement.

Not one person said, "Oh, no. I don't have a cent with me. I can't drink!" Not one said, "I'm so dirty and dusty. I'll wash first, then I'll have a drink." Down to the last straggler, everybody said, "Water? Oh, wonderful. I'm so thirsty." After a swallow or two, each one said, "It tastes sooo good." We were thirsty, and we drank cup after cup of the wonderful water.

Jesus holds out to us the Water of Life today. He says, "Whoever will, let her take the water of life . . . freely." Are you thirsty? Has the climb been hard and long? Are you dirty and dusty and exhausted? Are you about to give up and go back to where things are a lot easier?

Or is it the common cup that troubles you? I'm sorry, but the water is for everyone. Whoever. Come on, you're thirsty. Drink deeply. With the Living Water, you can scale any height. And it's free! VIRGINIA CASON

JULY 9

Will the Bears Come?

Verily I say unto you, Except ye become converted, and become as little children, ye shall not enter into the kingdom of heaven. Matt. 18:3.

Traveling across Wyoming on a freezing cold midwinter night, we missed a turn and suddenly found ourselves stuck tight in a snowbank. We had just returned from years in a tropical mission field, and we had only flimsy mittens, light jackets, and one pair of boots between us. And we were miles from anything on the map.

We kicked and clawed at the hard ice packed around the car's wheels, making not even a dent. "We can't get these chains on," my husband said. "I must find help." I handed him my jacket and shivered my way back into the car. Thankfully, the children were asleep in the back seat. I revved up the motor and turned on the heater. The gas tank was one fourth full. How long would it last? I prayed that the car wouldn't stall. It was so cold I was sure we would freeze quickly.

I worried about my husband. Would he get lost? How long could he hold out? Would help get back to us in time?

With these concerns weighing heavily on my mind, I noticed the children stirring. They sat up, puzzled, surveying the scene around them. I didn't want to betray my anxiety.

"We're stuck in the snow right now," I said, a bit too brightly. "Daddy's getting someone to pull us out."

A long minute passed. Then: "Mommy, will the bears come out of the woods and eat us up?" my 5-year-old asked.

I had to smile. I hadn't noticed how close we were to the forest. "No darlings, angels are guarding our car. No bears can hurt us."

Satisfied and trusting, both children snuggled down again and went back to sleep.

Oh, dear God! Of course! What's wrong with me? I am YOUR child! I too can trust those angels. How could I have forgotten?

As the first streaks of daylight fingered the horizon, a large farm truck bumped into view. We were quickly out of the snowdrift and on our way. And we still had one-eighth tank of gas.

AILEEN LUDINGTON

JULY 10

Take No Heed of What You Shall Eat

Do not be like them, for your Father knows what you need before you ask him. Matt. 6:8, RSV.

It was Friday. I didn't have much cleaning to do, since we were temporarily living in a very small house. I didn't have much to cook—the pantry was bare, and our purse was empty. My husband offered to do the weekend shopping even though he had just enough for only a few bananas. He inquired if I needed anything else. Jokingly I gave him a list that included powdered milk, cheese, cornflakes, and flour. We laughed together as he glanced at the list, and off he went to town on his bicycle.

Evening came. Our four children were scrubbed clean and ready to welcome the Sabbath. After a meager meal, we climbed onto our bed for sundown worship. (Beds were the only furniture we had at the time.) After singing a few hymns and choruses, I told the children a couple stories. In the midst of worship we heard a knock. We seldom had visitors in this new city, where my husband was assisting a missionary pastor conducting a crusade. When he opened the door, the missionary couple stepped in with a large carton. Setting the box down they said, "We felt impressed to bring you a little gift. We too have been through difficult times." The children could hardly wait for them to leave, and when they did, we hurriedly opened the box. To our surprise, everything I had written

228

on the shopping list was there! In our excitement we even forgot to thank God for taking note of our joke.

It seemed as if the angels had read the list and made sure that we received what we needed and more. Since then, we have never doubted God's promises and His sense of humor. He is able to fulfill our every need. That Sabbath was a special one in the life of our family. The children have grown up and have families of their own, but they can never forget the Friday when our loving heavenly Father took note of our need. — BIROL C. CHRISTO

JULY 11

Powerful Women of God

For God did not give us a spirit of timidity but a spirit of power and love and self-control. 2 Tim. 1:7, RSV.

It was the cover that attracted my attention; a grid of women's faces covered the magazine cover. I recognized some of them, but several were unfamiliar. Picking up the magazine, I noticed the heading on the top of the cover. "Never Underestimate the Power of a Woman." Above the pictures were the words "50 of the Most Powerful Women Today." The editors had made their choices on the bases of fame, notoriety, wealth, intellect, and husbands.

According to the accompanying article, one wise woman scoffed at the idea of her "power." She replied that it was only borrowed power; when her husband was no longer in high political office, her "power" would disappear.

There are women in the Bible who could have qualified as "most powerful woman," but not because of their fame, fortune, or husbands. Their power came from the Holy Spirit's presence in their lives, giving them love for others, and self-control evidenced in their actions. Judge Deborah, Widow Ruth, Mother Hannah, Queen Esther, and Prophetess Anna were all women of power in their personal worlds.

As I looked at the pictures on the magazine cover and thought about why they were chosen, I thought of women I have known with love and self-control, women whose power of influence has made an impact on my life.

My grandmother, Bessie, who left a legacy of caring when she died at 91; my mother, with her wonderful sense of humor and love that always reaches out to me; an elderly Sabbath school teacher who taught and lived God's Word beautifully; academy and college deans and teachers who taught me eternal values; a mother-in-law

229

with optimistic and encouraging ways; older women who mentored me in kind, supportive manners in child care and being a wife; and my daughters and daughters-in-law who give me warm, loving friendship that I cherish highly. They are truly God's women.

So I would say to the editors of this particular magazine, "Never underestimate the power of the Holy Spirit in a woman's life."   EVIE VANDEVERE

JULY 12

The Lord Knows

A wise man's heart guides his mouth, and his lips promote instruction. Pleasant words are a honeycomb, sweet to the soul and healing to the bones. Prov. 16:23, 24, NIV.

Munich in 1947—what a time and place for a young married couple! We lacked food and clothes, and there was nothing to buy in the stores. To our delight, it was announced one Sabbath that our brothers and sisters in America had sent a big shipment of clothes and shoes to Germany. The following Wednesday we were to come to the church to pick up the garments. Full of expectation, I pedaled my bike to the church. The deacon greeted me, and I signed in and waited for the curtain to open so I could receive my garments. As I waited, I overheard a voice speaking behind the curtain. Very unkind, accusing (and untrue) words were being said about my husband and me. The poor deacon coughed, trying to get his wife's attention, but she was too preoccupied with gossiping.

By the time my turn came, I was totally outraged and refused to take any items. The other woman there, who had known my husband from childhood, persuaded me to take the clothes and not relate the incident to my husband. I assured them that I would never set my foot in that Adventist church again. When I arrived home, my gentle Christian mother persuaded me to sleep on it overnight. That night I dreamed I tried to enter my childhood church on Sabbath morning. I heard the congregation singing, but as I tried to enter the entrance hall I found it was full of raw sewage. I longed to enter the church, but I did not want my Sabbath clothes to be soiled, so I hesitated on the threshold. Then I heard a voice, clear as a bell, saying: "If you want to be saved, go through. It will not stick on you." I then woke up.

Through the years this dream has helped me over hurt and disappointment with my brothers and sisters in Christ. How grateful I am for His wonderful love and understanding. If you are hurt, remember, it will not stick on you; His grace is greater.

SOPHIE KAISER

JULY 13

To Do—Or Not to Do?

But seek first his kingdom and his righteousness, and all these things shall be yours as well. Matt. 6:33, RSV.

You may be one of those people who like lists—highly organized, visibly productive. Able to make out your schedule for an entire month at a time—and actually know that at 3:05 p.m. on Tuesday, August 17th, you will be completing "x" task and taking on number 12 from your list. But I doubt it!

In today's world one phone call can reroute an entire day. But there are still a number of things we feel we must accomplish, so it's very easy to feel overwhelmed as you try to fit everything in.

How many times have you started your day by launching a desperate prayer heavenward, "Lord, help me get everything done today!" Until children joined our household, this was my daily petition. I soon realized that although this had never really been a plausible goal, now it was no longer even an option. I needed to make some changes. This was not an easy job for someone whose personality has never been content with doing one project if two could be jammed into the same time space. So rather cautiously I turned myself over to God for remodeling. Although the Lord has helped me come a long way in this area, I certainly haven't arrived. Here are some questions that help me to prioritize my day. Maybe they'll be of help to you too.

What's the *most important* thing I need to do today? If I believe God is number 1 in my life, will I put time with Him first on my list? If I could accomplish only one thing today, what would it be? What statement am I trying to make by the things I choose to do? How will the things I do affect me, my family, or others? Will I think the things I choose to do today are important in a week, a month, a year? Will I even remember them? Am I trying to impress others or myself, or prove something by the things I do? And last, but certainly not least, how does what I do stack up next to eternity?

Looking at life in this way is changing my perspective on efficiency. And God is slowly changing me. Hopefully, if time should last, my epitaph won't read "She accomplished 7.6 percent more than the average person," but rather "She did the things that counted, and that made all the difference." JEANNE HARTWELL

231

The Penguin Lady

Truly, I say to you, as you did it to one of the least of these my brethren, you did it to me. . . . As you did it not to one of the least of these, you did it not to me. Matt. 25:40-45, RSV.

It all seemed so unlikely—an unlikely mother, an unlikely baby in an unlikely place. As I watched her tenderly caress her strange, tiny baby wrapped in red, I wondered. I know I must have stared, but she didn't seem to notice, she seemed to be absorbed in her own world of motherhood.

We had stopped for breakfast at McDonald's in the Black Hills of South Dakota last summer while on vacation. I sat waiting, looking forward to a simple breakfast "out," when she caught my eye. She was probably about 60. I noticed her tenderly caressing, patting, and talking quietly to something lying on the table, something too small to be a child. Then she held it to her shoulder and gently patted it again. That was when I saw the small stuffed penguin.

I watched this strange wonder in shocked silence. A loving mother, a stuffed penguin the object of her nurture. What could it mean? Had she suffered a loss so great that fantasy had taken hold and now offered solace? Could it mean that no one had nurtured this woman? What hole in her heart was this stuffed penguin filling?

It's summer again, and I wonder about myself. There are empty spaces in my heart too. How have I filled them? Though God has so richly blessed my life with real children who fill many holes in my heart, and a husband who supports me and nurtures my needs with his love, there are still gaps. I am checking to see how I fill them as I picture again the fantasy world of this "penguin lady."

Some of my gaps show up in self-imposed compulsive work and busyness instead of faithfulness in the little things, the facade of perfection—of looking good, and playing the part, rather than being honest about my weakness; playing the "Hi, how are you?"/"I'm fine!" game, while never sharing that I'm not always "fine." I too have holes in my heart, empty places, gaps I need Christ to fill through honesty, caring, vulnerability—through you and your experience.

What has Christ taught you that might help to fill the void in me? Can I risk telling you where I am hurting and what He's doing for me as I sometimes faithfully (too often unfaithfully) walk the unpaved, stony path of this life, looking forward to heavenly streets, smooth and paved with pure gold?

Sharing, caring, reaching out in honest, open love to one another . . . would it have made a difference to the "penguin lady"?

MARLA WEIDELL

JULY 15

I've Got to Be Something

See what love the Father has given us, that we should be called children of God; and so we are. The reason why the world does not know us is that it did not know him. 1 John 3:1, RSV.

What are we doing, Mommy?" questioned my towheaded, dancing-eyed 5-year-old as he trudged up the stairs behind me. "What are we doing?"

"Company is coming to stay with us a few days, Roddie. There will be a girl and two boys with the mommy and daddy, so you will have some new friends," I answered as I dropped the fresh sheets and pillowcases on the chair. "There, put those pillows here, son. Thanks for your help." I paused as I looked down at his concerned face and realized that he was already anticipating my next words. "The older boy is just about your age so we will let him sleep in your bed and you can sleep on the floor on these cushions in this corner. OK?"

Visiting missionaries in the house for a few days was nothing new to this little lad, and neither was having visiting "friends" in his bed. In Taiwan, where we had lived since long before he could remember, entertaining guests who were moving in to the area to begin work or who were just passing through on their way to an assignment was part of the normal program. His 5-year-old mind understood that. But now again, so soon after he had given up his bed the last time?

"Mommy"—rebellion edged into his voice—"why do I have to sleep on the floor? Can't this new boy sleep there and let me keep my bed? I'm older than he is."

"No," I answered gently, "he's older than you are. He's 7."

"Then I'm bigger than he is," came the quick and determined retort. "I'm bigger."

"No, son, I'm afraid he is bigger than you are, too."

"But Mommy . . ." Desperation cracked his little-boy voice.

233

"But Mommy, I've got to be something!"

The cry of every human heart. Whether 5 years old or 50, we all understand that desperate wail, "I've got to be something." To feel worthy, to feel loved, to be important to someone—this is a basic, heartfelt need of every person. And God, who put that need in every soul for a reason, longs to fill it in your life and mine.

What greater honor, what more soul-satisfying privilege, could God give me than to make me His child, a daughter of the King? Today, as every other day in my life, He reaches out His arms, welcomes me to His family, and reminds me again through John, the disciple who knew Him best, "Beloved, now we are children of God, and it has not appeared as yet what we shall be. We know that, when He appears, we shall be like Him, because we shall see Him just as He is" (1 John 3:2, NASB). CAROLE SPALDING COLBURN

JULY 16

Lessons From My Passport—1

For it is by grace you have been saved, through faith—and this not from yourselves, it is the gift of God. Eph. 2:8, NIV.

A passport is indispensable to international travel. Crossing borders—legally, at least—is virtually impossible without one. Ellen White occasionally wrote of a spiritual passport. At times she defines it as "the blood of Jesus" or His name. She also speaks of a "passport to heaven," gained not by the works-only righteousness of the rabbis; nor by worldly wealth, property, or position; nor through worldly wisdom or zealous busyness. It is given to "those only who bear a likeness to Christ in character." Entering heaven will be impossible without it—and there will be no illegal crossings there.

Not that we earn salvation by developing character—we can't. Character is not the ticket that takes us to heaven, but the passport that identifies our citizenship. It makes clear to all observers that its bearer is a citizen of heaven, just as my U.S. passport clarifies my citizenship.

I cannot *earn* my U.S. passport. It is issued to me, though I must meet certain conditions. 1. I must be a citizen. 2. I must apply for it, submitting proof of my identity, photos, and fee. To develop a heaven-fit character, I must choose to be a citizen of Christ's kingdom and ask Him to bestow His character on me. He knows me, has paid the fee, and will issue the passport.

When my son Robert received a sudden opportunity to go to Poland with the New England Youth Ensemble, a kind clerk in Chicago got him a passport in two hours. This exciting trip eventually included a command performance in Warsaw at the dinner President Gerald Ford hosted for Poland's state officials. God is even more gracious in granting us the passport to heaven, if we but ask.

Getting a passport is not a once-in-a-lifetime experience. Repeated travel abroad requires periodic passport renewal. My relationship to Christ must be renewed daily if my passport to heaven is to be kept current.

When our family went to the mission field, our toddler got in on my passport. When his brother and two sisters were each born, the U.S. Embassy amended my passport to include them. Living in a country technically at war but in a state of truce, we didn't wait long after a birth to get photos taken, obtain a birth certificate, and get to the embassy. We wanted all our children covered.

We cannot develop character for others, but the character we allow Christ to develop in us does exert an influence that may lead them to desire a character passport of their own.

My passport also serves as a log of journeys past. Looking at the various entry and exit stamps affixed to its pages, one can reconstruct the itineraries of our family's missionary years. The pages that build Christian character likewise contain the stepping-stones, detours, scars, and joys that have brought us to our present point. I am reminded of how the Lord has saved and led me.

MADELINE S. JOHNSTON

JULY 17

Lessons From My Passport—2

Not by works, so that no one can boast. Eph. 2:9, NIV.

Certain restrictions are listed in my passport; violations lead to dire consequences. If I take out citizenship in another country or fight in another country's army, I may forfeit my U.S. citizenship. Either action would presume a choice to prefer that country over my own. Likewise, if I willfully join Satan's ranks, I cannot remain a citizen of both this world and heaven.

I am also warned that altering or mutilating my passport may invalidate it. Only authorized officials are to place stamps or notations in it. Likewise, only Christ can give me the stamp of His character.

Two brief but bold warnings appear: "When traveling in disturbed areas, you should keep in touch with the nearest American embassy or consulate" and "If you reside abroad . . . you should register at the nearest American embassy or consulate." My government, like that of heaven, wants to be able to contact me in case of trouble. It is responsible for getting me home safely if the trouble gets too intense.

My passport expressly forbids travel to certain countries. Willful violation will cost me the protection of my government and may result in prosecution. The priorities of Jesus may also forbid trespassing onto certain areas of declared enemy territory, and willful violation of the warning could result in forfeiting heaven's protection.

My passport also contains some general information about regulations affecting my return to the homeland. No immunizations are required; the world's major diseases aren't a threat there. But it is unlawful to bring in foreign agricultural items that might introduce plant or animal pests or diseases. And I am advised that my entry will be easier if I don't bring much money or many foreign goods. God, who has taken care of the sin problem, cannot allow it to be introduced into heaven. We must go there unencumbered by worldly goods. MADELINE S. JOHNSTON

JULY 18

Lessons From My Passport—3

For we are God's workmanship, created in Christ Jesus to do good works, which God prepared in advance for us to do. Eph. 2:10, NIV.

Missionaries are advised to hang on to their passports. In some countries, foreigners are required to carry them at all times, for identification purposes. One could land in a heap of trouble if unable to prove his or her identity.

But in some countries one has to weigh the risks of disobeying this requirement against the risks of having the passport stolen if carried. There are people out there who will go to almost any lengths to steal a passport from certain countries. They are experts at making significant changes that will enable a new bearer to gain entrance to the homeland, perhaps to improve his or her status in life, perhaps to function as a spy. Though the falsification may gain the desired end for the new bearer, it still doesn't make him or her the original, rightful owner.

236

Some people would like to steal a passport to heaven, bypassing the citizenship route, falsifying their identity, and neglecting the development of a godly character. But it will not work.

Even temporarily losing one's passport is a dreadful experience. One summer, my husband spent a few days in the Netherlands after directing a Holy Land tour for pastors. Scheduled to conduct ministerial seminars throughout the Far Eastern Division soon after his return home, he had obtained all the visas necessary for that trip before leaving for Israel. On his last day in Holland, loaded heavily with baggage, he took trains and buses to Amsterdam. Suddenly he realized that the shoulder bag containing all his documents had disappeared. Returning to the last bus stop didn't help.

Flight time was approaching and he had no ticket, no passport, no checkbook. Siesta time prevailed downtown. Finally the airline issued him a new ticket, full price, on a charge card; and the U.S. Embassy gave him a letter that would admit him into New York, where he paid a heavy fine for entering without a passport. During the intervening week before his next departure, he made several trips from Michigan to Chicago to replace his passport and visas.

Shortly after he left for Asia, I received a package from a U.S. Air Force sergeant stationed near Amsterdam. It contained the little bag, contents complete, shoulder strap broken. A man had found it at a bus stop and brought it to the air base. The sergeant had spent $5 postage to send it to us. Our faith in humanity was restored, and I thanked and repaid the sergeant. But how much trouble that weak strap had caused!

Christians who through neglect lose their passport to heaven are in grave danger. They may never get it back. And even if they do, the effort will require time, agony, and personal cost—even as it did for Joseph and Mary to find Jesus once they had negligently lost Him.

A heavenly passport is indispensable. Through God's enabling grace, apply for one, keep it current, do nothing to jeopardize it, and hang on to it.   MADELINE S. JOHNSTON

JULY 19

Pull the Plug on Sin

Do not be conformed to this world, but be transformed by the renewal of your mind, that you may prove what is the will of God, what is good and acceptable and perfect. Rom. 12:2, RSV.

I met her on a sunny afternoon as I searched for a diversion from childish chatter, endless housework, and the monotony of running a home.

Julie Horton Banning Anderson, a fashionable brunette, swirled into my life and regularly paid a visit. I began to know her well. Her troubles fascinated me, and even though she'd been through three marriages, given a baby away for adoption, suffered through the death of one husband and divorced another, she seemed to cope terrifically. Her exciting life seemed vibrant, happy, and never dull.

After attending a 10-day spiritual retreat, I decided to end my visits with Julie. When I took inventory of my life, it disturbed me to admit that inwardly I was beginning to admire this lady and her lifestyle. I loved what she looked like, and I eagerly drank in the sordid details of her licentious life. But the Holy Spirit convicted me that our sterile friendship was definitely contributing to a drastic downward spiral.

And so with regrets I said goodbye. The funny part was that Julie didn't miss me—because this classy lady was the heroine of a daily soap opera that I followed closely for six and a half years.

As Christians we campaign against drunkenness, profanity, sexual immorality, and violent crime. And yet we allow sin to enter our homes every day by television viewing. And without much deliberation we invite the standards of a secular world to capture our imagination and influence our minds—the only channel through which God can communicate with His children.

There's no lack of research to back up the fact that long-term viewing of violence affects the behavior of children. Many secular authorities are sounding the alarm that TV has literally created a society of people who care for nothing except their own self-indulgence. Like alcohol or drugs, TV can be enormously destructive to personal relationships, and our society is saturated with crime—beatings, robberies, and killings. One doesn't need to be a psychologist to realize that TV has played an important role in the increase of sin.

We can't overlook the powerful positive effects of the media. And if we are not constantly vigilant, TV will control us.

Through prayer and complete television blackout for a month, I was able to conquer the horrible habit of indiscriminate television watching. And through the years, I'm happy to say, our family's viewing habits have been carefully planned and monitored.

God has blessed our commitment. And through the daily study of His Word and with much prayer, I've claimed His promise of transformation and renewal.
MADLYN LEWIS HAMBLIN

Shortcuts

Then you will understand righteousness and justice and equity, every good path; for wisdom will come into your heart, and knowledge will be pleasant to your soul. Prov. 2:9, RSV.

If you're caught in heavy traffic and need to travel across town, or if you're in a crowded building and you need to get out fast (to beat the parking lot crush), a few side streets clear of traffic or a quiet corridor that leads to a little-known exit can seem priceless.

Shortcuts do sometimes serve their purpose. They can save a little time and reduce considerable stress, especially when it comes to traffic! But there are other times when they just won't do, when they just don't work.

There are no shortcuts to good health, heavy advertising notwithstanding! All the vitamins or tonics or quick weight-loss plans (which all have their place) still won't substitute for a faithful practice of the Golden Eight, which the word NEWSTART can help us remember: nutrition, exercise, water, sunlight, temperance, air, rest, trust in divine power.

There are no shortcuts to good mental development, either, and last-minute cramming just won't do. There's something Dr. Ben Carson terms "in-depth knowledge," the kind that comes from diligent study. It takes a lot of time and effort. Only then does something happen. The learning process ignites the mind. It becomes more than just an exercise to get a good grade and to earn a diploma. When the mind does grasp a tough accounting problem or business concept, the beauty of a Renaissance sonnet or a new medical procedure, God's handiwork in His Word or in crystals under a microscope, then learning is its own precious reward.

And finally, there are no shortcuts to spiritual growth and maturity—but you knew that already! Once again, there's no improvement, only new variations on an old successful formula. Growing in God takes prayer, Bible study, and witnessing. The process is like opening doors.

First, in prayer, open the door to the deepest part of your heart to God. Let His love flow in. Let your burdens and cares and pain flow out. Talk to Him. Wait. Listen. Let Him lead.

Then open the door to His Word, and read prayerfully, faithfully, systematically. Study the Sabbath school lessons, and find the gems of inspiration that are often below the surface. Open your mind to God.

Then open the last door and share. Share with kindness, with new faces at your church, with familiar ones at home. Pray for the tactful, sweet graciousness that Jesus mastered, and follow His lead.

KYNA HINSON

JULY 21

God Enables in Love

It is God who is at work in you, enabling you both to will and to work for his good pleasure. Phil. 2:13, NRSV.

At the completion of graduate school, I wanted to work as a nurse clinician. And I knew where I wanted to work as well. But God sent someone to beg me to take a job in nursing administration 500 miles from where I had wanted to be. Confused by what I wanted and the pull to do something not appealing to me, I asked God to lead.

For God to enable us to will and to work, we must be willing to allow God to do just that—enable through love. My answer to what God in His love wanted me to do came soon and sure—go 500 miles away and be an administrator. Shortly thereafter, pressure came to me to accept the clinical specialist job in the city of my choice.

During a brief wavering period I almost reneged. I almost prevented God from enabling me in love. The phone rang, and a colleague asked that I just make an appointment to talk about the clinical specialist job. Yielding to her gentle persuasion, I made the appointment. Later I called a friend and told her of my decision to go for the interview. My friend reminded me that I had accepted the other job on the basis of answered prayer. Then she said, "To go to that interview is playing with the devil himself." Her remark caused me to examine my motive, and I canceled the appointment.

I took the job that God in His love had directed me to. Looking back a few years later, realizing what I had learned, what I had accomplished, coupled with where I might have been and how my life might have turned out, I thanked God for His enabling love.

When I opened myself to God, His love became my will and ability. When temporarily I shut Him out, I almost made the mistake of a lifetime. But His love reached me as He met me through a friend, and again I was open to His direction.

His great love works in us. Rejoice!

ELIZABETH STERNDALE

Love in Action

Above all hold unfailing your love for one another, since love covers a multitude of sins. 1 Peter 4:8, RSV.

Love is varied, with many sides to it. Here's the one I want you to think about today.

Find a mirror. Now look yourself straight in the eye and say "I love you!" Now try "God loves you!" You may want to say these six words with different facial expressions. How do they sound with a smile? A frown? Can you put your face in neutral?

I used to be one of those *Christian* wives and mothers who prided themselves on being good examples. That is, until my 6-year-old asked, "Mama, why don't you ever smile?" Instant excuses came to my mind, but they didn't work, and I knew it. In desperation I gave up and put my face in God's hands. And God began changing my face. It wasn't easy—smiles, happiness, laughter. Often I longed to take back my face and let the world know how I was feeling: tired, lonely, or discouraged. But slowly, finally, I began to like my new face.

Ten years later I'm changed. It gets increasingly harder to frown. I've traded frown lines for smile lines. I love them. They give my face character. It's true that "when happiness gets into your system, it's bound to break out on the face."

I've got a story to tell. A story about a God who loves me so much He died for me. I don't want to tell my good news like the man Becky Pippert tells about: "I remember once encountering a zealous Christian. His brow was furrowed, he seemed anxious and impatient, and he sounded angry. Then he told me God loved me. I couldn't help noticing the difference between his message and his style. His message was arresting (me—a sinner?) but ultimately appealing (a just and holy God who loves me deeply). But his style put me off. I recall thinking, *If God is so good and loving, then why is this guy so uptight? Surely the way we communicate a message of good news should be as marvelous as the message itself.*" * Love in action. That's what I want my life to be. Not only for the strangers I meet but for my church and my family.

---

* From Rebecca Manley Pippert, *Out of the Saltshaker and Into the World* (InterVarsity Press).

Sunshine Pie

A pound of patience, you must find
Mixed well with loving words so kind.
Drop in two pounds of helpful deeds
And thought of other people's needs.

A pack of smiles, to make the crust,
Then stir and bake it well you must.
And now, I ask you that you may try
The recipe of this Sunshine Pie.
—*Favorite Amish Family Recipes*
GINGER MOSTERT CHURCH

JULY 23

From My Camp Meeting Window

The Lord looked down from heaven upon the children of men, to see if there were any that did understand, and seek God. Ps. 14:2.

I was at camp meeting, where carefully planned meetings by godly speakers were bringing me great spiritual blessings. But I was about to discover that there were many side effects on the campground—unexpected fringe benefits that result from the over-all atmosphere of at-oneness with God.

Early one morning a movement in a tree outside the window caught my eye. Looking out from my room on the third floor of a school dormitory, I saw a bird glide gracefully from the top of the tree to the ground far below. I gazed down with new interest at the towering trees. Instead of looking up, seeing from the ground as I usually did, I could look right into the hearts of the trees. I had the vantage point of the birds.

Close by a cardinal sang, "Cheer, cheer." When he heard an answering call from his mate, he quickly flew to a perch beside her. His bright red made a splash of color against the green leaves.

Then a handsome blue jay flew by, accompanied by an outcry of smaller birds that seemed to warn that this nest robber was near. On the ground a redbreasted robin satisfied its hunger as it pecked for insects and worms.

The air seemed filled with a stereophonic chorus as the birds broadcast their songs. The glistening dew of the early morning imparted freshness and beauty to the moment.

As I contemplated the scene below, I was suddenly reminded of

God's vantage point in the heavens. "For he hath looked down from the height of his sanctuary; from heaven did the Lord behold the earth" (Ps. 102:19).

I remembered how God promises protection for those who will accept it. "The eyes of the Lord run to and fro throughout the whole earth, to shew himself strong in the behalf of them whose heart is perfect toward him" (2 Chron. 16:9).

And even as the birds of the air are loved and cared for by the Creator, God also surveys the hearts of men and women to discover those who will respond to divine care and direction. "The Lord looked down from heaven upon the children of men, to see if there were any that did understand, and seek God" (Ps. 14:2).

But beyond providing us as created beings with the bare essentials of life, God is eager to discover men and women who are seeking to serve wholeheartedly. God searches for any to whom He may reveal Himself, and who will also be willing to reflect His divine character to the world.

In my early-morning reverie I realized anew that God watches over all those who accept Christ and receive His righteousness as their own, and whose relationship with Jesus is growing day by day.

The Bible portrays God waiting expectantly for all who want to enter a relationship throughout eternity. To these Christ will one day say, "Come, ye blessed of my Father, inherit the kingdom prepared for you from the foundation of the world" (Matt. 25:34).

From my vantage point high above the campground, all these words of Scripture came to mind. Looking at the birds outside my window renewed my heart, and I said yes to God again.

BEATRICE HARRIS

JULY 24

Created for More

The kingdom of heaven is like a treasure hidden in a field. When a man found it, he . . . in his joy went and sold all he had and bought that field. Matt. 13:44, NIV.

Is there a woman anywhere who has not at some desperate moment in her life cried out, "There must be more to life than this!" We want more from life than the drudgeries of day-to-day existence. We want more from relationships than the exchange of porcelain smiles. We want more from our families than the constant tangle of household chores, errands, and fragments of human relationships. We want more from our careers than a

243

paycheck and a chance to compete and prove our worth. We want more from our church than mere tokenism because of the climate of our age. We want more from ourselves than we have left to give.

To desire more is not wrong. We are, after all, creatures created for more. But all too often we spend our lives and our energies in a futile search in the wrong direction. Not knowing how to feed the spirit, we throw ourselves indiscriminately into committees and causes, stuffing the empty space of our lives with continuous activity, chatter, and companions to whom we do not even listen.

But this meaning of life, this personhood, this inner peace for which we yearn, can be found only as we look first for Him, who came that we might have life more abundantly. In His presence we may shed our Martha-like anxiety about many things and attend to our own inner springs.

It is He who invites us to come and who promises rest. Rest from the whirlwind of daily living, rest from hearts that condemn us, rest from the pain of the wrongs of our existence. In Him there is a fountain of grace that can keep us willing to be vulnerable, when silence would be so much easier. Grace that comforts when walls seem impenetrable. Grace that understands when we must retreat in pain. Grace that shields us from bitterness and over time draws the sting from the wounded place so we can serve again. Today His invitation is to spend a few moments of solitude with Him to replenish your soul. He knows that without this stillness, we will have little to give. KAREN FLOWERS

JULY 25

Stray Hearts

Then he said to her, "Daughter, your faith has healed you. Go in peace." Luke 8:48, NIV.

The kitten spent the night on my porch again. He is scrawny and black, and his ribs stick out. His eyes are a brilliant blue, and they are always wide open and watchful. He lives under my house. Occasionally he drinks the milk I leave out for him. Sometimes it sits in the bowl for two or three days at a time, and I worry that he might have been killed by a car or a dog. Then, sooner or later, he comes back.

I'm not a cat lover, but I am touched by his plight. He was born wild. His mother spits and hisses whenever she sees me, but for some reason the kitten never makes a sound. He comes around to watch me do yardwork, yet is always wary and keeps his distance.

Seeing his undernourished form makes me feel guilty as I compare it with my dogs'. Those two have plenty to eat, and they eat it out of little plastic bowls with their names on them. They have a box of toys and they get their coats brushed and their nails trimmed regularly. But the kitten never gives me a chance to be his friend.

A coworker of mine reminds me of that stray cat. He wears a three-piece suit and a bright smile, but inside his heart is hurting, and sometimes there is a haunted look in his eyes. He fills his free time with wild partying "because of business obligations." Most of the other employees see him as a charming, polite man who drinks too much.

For some reason he confides in me, and I see something completely different from a smiling businessman. He is disappointed in himself because his life is so meaningless. He has few real friends and relies on the fantasy world flickering across the screen to provide him with happiness. He is desperately searching for the safety and comfort of a home, an inner life of peace—and doesn't realize that God would like to give him one.

The Scriptures are full of stories of people searching for a home. Zacchaeus, the much-hated tax collector, just wanted a glimpse of the Man everyone was talking about. It would be so nice to talk to the Teacher, to eat with Him and discuss the Scriptures. But that was impossible, of course; no rabbi would want to be seen talking with him.

So Zacchaeus stayed on the edge of the crowd. He hadn't climbed a tree since boyhood, but he found he had lost none of the skill necessary. Up and up he went and perched on a branch looking over the heads of the crowd. From a safe distance he looked straight into the eyes of Jesus. To his amazement, Jesus called out, "Zacchaeus, come down! I'm going to your house." In an instant, contact had been made with a stray heart.

Or think of the woman who had been ill for 12 years. She was sick in body and sick at heart. The doctors could do nothing for her, but she had heard of Jesus, a healer. Surely such a Man would not want to talk to her, she thought. But could she get near enough that some of His goodness would rub off—perhaps without Him even noticing? Fearfully she inched through the crowd, managing to touch the hem of His garment. In an instant she was healed.

When Jesus stopped and asked who touched Him, she was afraid. Was He angry at her for presuming on Him? But for this healing she owed Him the truth, at least. When she told Him all that she had done, instead of being angry He praised her for her faith. Contact! Another stray heart won.

On a cold night I look out my window and see the kitten sitting in the glow of the porch light. How I long to go outside, scoop him up in my arms, and take him into the warm house. But I know that if I open the door he will only scurry away. The kitten has condemned himself to a life of fear just outside my reach. Inside there is warmth, food, and love, but he will never know that, because he is not brave enough to make contact with me.

I thank God that I have found the courage the kitten does not possess and have accepted Someone's offer to be my Master — Someone who was willing to take in one more stray heart.

GINA LEE

JULY 26

Angels on Guard

For he will give his angels charge of you to guard you in all your ways. Ps. 91:11, RSV.

A ngels watching over me, every move I make. . . .' " My sister and I were driving back from skiing at Killington, Vermont. The growing darkness reminded me that the Sabbath had come, so I pushed an Amy Grant gospel tape into the cassette player. "This is a great song," I told Danielle as I reached down to raise the volume on the car stereo. " 'Angels watching over me,' " I sang. I quickly focused my attention back to the narrow, icy road as we approached a particularly sharp curve. "Whoa, this turn is really severe . . . Uh-oh, I think I'm going to lose it," I faltered as I felt my rear wheels spin out to the left. I fought the steering wheel; the car skidded to the right, to the left, to the right. Finally, the Honda CRX crossed the median, crashed into a snowbank, spun around 180 degrees, and hit the snow wall again — this time with the rear of the car.

Silence. The engine had died. I dreaded getting out of the car to see the damage. "I hope the skis didn't break." I looked over at Danielle. "I wonder how we're going to extricate ourselves from here before a car crashes into us. What if the car won't budge?" I voiced the fears of two women broken down on a deserted mountain road. I turned the key, my hand unsteady, and the car started. With a little fancy clutch-work the car slid out of the icy snow, and I did a U turn.

Several miles later, my sister observed, "At least you picked your setting well. If we had spun off the road anywhere else, we would have been seriously injured — a ravine on the right, trees and guardrails on the left . . ." Her voice trailed off. "We really need to thank the Lord that He had His angels watching over us."

I've marveled at it for days now. Little miracles are rare in our

246

mundane lives. It's easy to be complacent or consider ourselves simply lucky. I've often felt "lucky" because I've never been hurt in any accidents in which I've been involved. Two weeks ago, a friend told me that his best friend had been killed in a Honda CRX like mine. He warned me to be careful as I took to the road in Vermont. When we returned, he said we were lucky. But it has nothing to do with luck. We are not pawns on fortune's wheel. At 16, when I fell onto concrete from a second-story window and suffered only a concussion, the doctors told me, "If you believe in miracles, you can believe that you are one."

Often I feel reluctant to think God performs small miracles and sends His angels to look after me—little insignificant me. Yesterday my 13-year-old nephew and I sang in my car as I played and replayed that Amy Grant song. Even this cool kid was impressed as I told him the story. Sure, my bumper should be replaced, but now that I've straightened out the license plate, it really doesn't show. By the way, that particular tape had just showed up in my car one day. I have no idea whose it is or where it came from. But hearing Amy Grant sing "Angels watching over me, every step I take" always makes me see things more clearly.   MICHELE BEACH

JULY 27

My Old Yellow Car

Make me to know thy ways, O Lord; teach me thy paths.
Ps. 25:4, RSV.

It was a 1953 Plymouth convertible. I was 18 years old, with enough money in my savings account to pay the $600 on the price tag plus tax and insurance.

After weeks of searching used-car lots all over Lansing, Michigan, I'd finally found this yellow car that was about to separate me from my life's savings. Every entry in my dog-eared savings passbook represented lawns mowed, dishes washed, letters typed, and nights of baby-sitting. Now I was about to spend all of it at one time in one place.

"It's in mint condition," the salesman said.

"Sure is," I agreed.

"The elderly lady who owned this beauty hardly ever took it out of her garage," he said, polishing a strip of chrome with his shirt sleeve.

"I can tell it's had good care," I said as I opened the door and sat on the thick upholstered seat. I ran my hands over the shiny black steering wheel, thinking how much fun I would have driving this car to Lake Michigan on Sunday afternoons.

My mind was made up. But still, this was simply too big a purchase to make alone. I needed someone else's approval. Someone experienced in buying cars. Someone whose opinion I trusted. My dad. If he looked at it, I knew he'd like it, and then he'd say it was a nice car, and I would feel free to buy it.

Actually, when I finally got him to the car lot, he didn't say much at all. He did a lot of hmphing. (Hmphing is a low muffled sound a father makes in the back of his throat when he's thinking seriously.)

Dad hmphed when he kicked the tires. He hmphed when he sat behind the steering wheel. He hmphed when he looked at the price tag. He really hmphed when I told him about the car's previous owner. I was a little disappointed that he didn't show more enthusiasm, but at least he wasn't saying no, and that was very important.

In the end, I bought the car despite Dad's lack of enthusiasm. I figured that in time, as he saw how well I took care of it and how much I enjoyed it, he'd agree that it had been a good buy.

I quickly learned one thing about car ownership that I hadn't considered: maintenance—oil changes, tune-ups, battery, tires, muffler, and those tiny-as-a-pinhead holes in the canvas top that seemed to grow in size and number every time it rained.

I don't know whether Sears still sells convertible tops by mail order, but in those days they did. So one night after supper, Dad and I sat at the kitchen table with the Sears catalog in front of us. He read the specifications from the catalog, and I filled in the order form.

Dad said he would help me put the new top on my car. He said I'd save a lot of money if we installed it ourselves. In about two weeks the oversized package was delivered to our house, and Dad and I spent a long quiet autumn evening together in the garage putting that giant vinyl accordion top on my yellow car.

Dad didn't talk much. In fact, as I recall, he didn't even hmph. He'd just tell me when to "pull" or "hold." But somehow I clearly sensed what he was thinking. Unlike the day in the car lot several months earlier, on that cool evening as we quietly worked together in the garage, I could hear him more clearly than I'd ever heard him in my life.

He was saying that buying that car had been the stupidest thing I'd ever done. I'm sure he wanted to say, "I hope you've learned something from this experience." He must have struggled to keep from shouting, "Look at all the trouble and money I could have saved you if you'd just listened to me."

But wait, I thought. I had taken him to see the car before I bought it. He definitely had not said, "No. Don't buy it." I recalled distinctly that he had let me make the final decision. I also remember how nervous I felt when I turned to the salesman and said, "I'll take it." Why hadn't Dad stopped me, or at least warned me that I was headed for trouble if I bought that car?

Or had he?

Why is it sometimes so hard to hear what our Father is saying?

JANE ALLEN

JULY 28

The Broken Begonia

He heals the brokenhearted and binds up their wounds. Ps. 147:3, NIV.

A friend entrusted an everyday bloomer begonia to my care while he traveled. The flowering plant was healthy. Everyone who saw it commented on its beauty: its delicate deep-pink, heart-shaped blossoms and variegated green-and-white foliage. I loved the plant and decided I must get a similar one for myself.

When my friend returned for his begonia we carried it outside, setting it down on the driveway next to the car. We chatted some more, forgetting that the flower had not been loaded into his trunk.

He started the engine. Suddenly realizing that he was backing toward the begonia, I yelled, "Stop! Stop!" But the white plastic urn was crushed—and most of the plant. I was embarrassed that my absentmindedness had partially caused such misfortune.

As I sadly began picking up the pieces, I remembered that my aunt had once said that begonias are very prolific. If I put some of the broken parts in water as slips, would the plant grow again? I wondered. "It takes only a small piece," Aunt Clara had said. "A couple of leaves and a bloom or two."

Working quickly, I soon had enough pieces to fill four quart-size canning jars, a 16-ounce tea tumbler, and two small vases. Though my friend regretted the mangling of his flower, he stayed reasonably calm. I optimistically promised him one of the new plants.

Some pieces of the everyday bloomer were so damaged that they died within a few days. But I was able to save and root nearly 50 stems. The first plant went to my friend, and I kept the second. But 47 other people have benefited too! I have given away new little plants to friends, family, office coworkers, some who were sick or shut in, some who had been recently bereaved, and a friend who was burned out of her apartment.

The Bible compares plants to people. Christ tells His followers,

"I am the vine, ye are the branches" (John 15:5). The psalmist says a righteous man "is like a tree planted by streams of water, which yields its fruit in season and whose leaf does not wither" (Ps. 1:3, NIV).

People are also like plants in another way. My friend's begonia was badly injured. People too may be terribly hurt when they are run over by some tragedy such as illness, an accident, fire, flood, or divorce. The begonia had regrowth potential. But it could not pick up its own broken pieces and start over. It needed my help and God's.

When we feel as bruised and broken in spirit as the run-over begonia, we have difficulty understanding the Bible text that says "And we know that all things work together for good to them that love God, to them who are called according to his purpose" (Rom. 8:28). We need help—from God and loyal human sources—so that we can cope.

This experience suggests to me that even if we bear physical and emotional scars, God can heal. He can restore our souls. And those of us who have suffered can, from the depths of our experience, aid others who are reeling from life's hard knocks by giving them "slips" of ourselves in the form of sympathy and understanding.

I have derived much comfort from seeing the broken begonia become a source of joy to everyone with whom I shared it. It reminds me again that God is big enough to bring good out of tragedy.   BONNIE MOYERS

JULY 29

In Praise of Badlands

In all things God works for the good of those who love him. Rom. 8:28, NIV.

Badlands. The word in my mind sounds desolate and haunting. I imagine the barren, the dry, the unlovely. And yet as I stand at this overlook above the South Dakota Badlands on our summer vacation, I am in awe. The breathtaking beauty and majesty of the vacant, the empty, overwhelms me.

There have been other times in my life when I've been overwhelmed, not at the earth's landscape and the paradox of its desolate beauty, but at looking over the landscape of my life.

"O Lord, how is it that You can take the badlands of my life and create a panorama of beauty? Beauty for ashes! How do You

250

make all things work together for my good and for the good of those I love?

"It has been said that hindsight is better than foresight. I marvel at the threads of pain You have woven into a rich tapestry of joy and blessing. In Your skillful hands, even the grief and hurt are somehow entwined together into a pattern vivid with meaning, lovely with beauty.

"I look across the windy, open plains of my life—though torrents blow, and vulnerability threatens to overtake me, still I stand. Even now You are painting sunrises and sunsets, creating subtle colors in the open land, filling in the sky and stoking the plains of my life with Your paint and brush . . . even now all things are working together for my good.

"I wonder at You, Lord. Again the wind blows through my hair as I stand on this rise with You. I overlook the badlands of my life and give You all my praise."

MARLA WEIDELL

JULY 30

I Wasn't There to Wipe His Brow

And we know that in all things God works for the good of those who love him, who have been called according to his purpose. Rom. 8:28, NIV.

Two months ago my youngest son died. He was a lovable young man, and his desire was to make everyone he came in contact with happy.

The last few days we spent together were happy, but I could see a streak of pain on his countenance. For the second time he told me that he was angry with God. "Mom, it's not like the first time," he quietly said. I assured him that his heavenly Father understood all that he was experiencing. He knew his pain, and was very concerned about him. I knew my son loved the Lord, but his burden was heavy and his real feelings were showing.

I was reminded of my own weaknesses, and silently I prayed for both of us, that our heavenly Father would sustain us. I didn't know that a week after that conversation my son would be gone.

He wanted to attend his friend's graduation at Columbia Union College in Washington, D.C., and even though he had started a new job, he asked for time off to go. When he left on his trip I wasn't home. A week later, soon after returning home, he died. He was walking in the heat of the day and collapsed just a few minutes away from home.

My son was born with a blood dyscrasia and wasn't expected to live to be 25 years old. But, thank God, he persevered through life, completing high school and almost five years of college.

I knew he wrote poems, but it wasn't until after his death that I realized the deep love he had for God and others as expressed in his many poems. I wasn't there to wipe his wet brow, and this makes me very sad, but as I wrote his obituary, Jesus, through His Holy Spirit, reminded me that there was no one to wipe His brow, no one to wipe His bloodstained face.

My son did his last kind act for a friend when he attended his graduation, but Jesus did His "act," His death on the cross, for the whole world. His heart is still bleeding for all those who reject Him. He died that we might live the eternal life. I look forward to the time when I will see my son again, and there will be no more parting.

Although we cannot see a moment away, let us remember that God knows the present, the past, and the future, and most of all He knows what's best for all of us, whether the experience is joy or sorrow.

GLORIA C. McLAREN

JULY 31

Gentle Reminder of God's Care

He will send his angel before you. Gen 24:7, NIV.

L ord," I prayed as I bent over the steering wheel, "the road is long, the car is unfamiliar, and the body is tired. Please get me to Massachusetts safely, and send Your angels with me."

I was leaving my home in Maryland to drive a friend's car to my parents' home, where my dad would become its new owner. The car was a larger member of the Chevy family than my own, and I felt uncomfortable in it. At least an eight-hour drive lay ahead of me, and I was both physically and mentally fatigued. I needed the assurance that those angels would be with me.

Midway up the New Jersey Turnpike, when a sign announced a service area in one mile, I prepared to pull off for gas and some exercise. But then, seeing another sign that said "Next service area 22 miles" and noticing that the car still had plenty of gas, I decided to drive on.

Impulsively, as the exit to the first service area approached, I changed my mind again, pulling off the highway and up to the gas pump. When the station attendant asked to check under the hood, I hesitated before assenting. I'd heard more than my share of stories about men who take advantage of women drivers!

"Ma'am, would you please come take a look?" the attendant asked after lifting the hood and poking around for a minute. He pointed to a radiator hose and told me, in language graphic but unprintable, that if I planned to drive much farther, I'd better get it replaced. It would burst and drain all the water out of the radiator, he warned, and leave me stranded on the highway.

Still skeptical, I agreed to the replacement. After seeing the worn-out hose with its large bulge, I knew my 10 minutes and $21.40 had been well spent.

As it turned out, the service area 22 miles up the turnpike was closed. Had it been an angel who whispered in my ear to pull off the highway when I did, knowing the car wouldn't make it to the next service area? To a weary woman whose spirits were lower than usual that Friday morning, the thought that it might have been was a comfort—a gentle reminder of God's care.   JOCELYN FAY

AUGUST 1

A Plan for Daily Living

Let all things be done decently and in order. 1 Cor. 14:40.

A personal daily plan is my term for the patterns we create in our everyday living, how we tackle and complete ordinary, everyday tasks. These tasks can be handled as menial labor and drudgery, or they can be elevated to "enjoyable rituals"—rituals that can be uplifting, special, and even fun. It's all in the attitude we develop toward each task.

Developing a personal daily plan helps us make the most of our time. It actually saves time. Following a personal daily plan puts us in charge of our time rather than letting the tasks of the day control us. Some people make no plans for their time, allowing things to "happen." Then they wonder why others get so much done. In my home organization seminars I suggest that women actually write down a plan. This provides a "picture" or map of how we use our time. Once we see the picture we can improve on our use of time.

On the left side of a piece of paper, jot down the hours of your day. Write the days of the week across the top. Quickly sketch in rising and bedtime, meals, regular weekly appointments, work hours if you work outside the home, etc. Add time for personal activities such as devotions, exercise, hobbies. Now personalize a plan for daily chores. List all major weekly tasks: laundry, bathrooms, dusting, vacuuming, etc. Assign one major task to each workday. Add three to five minitasks (any chores requiring less than five minutes) to each major task. If you organize your work load with one major and several minitasks per day, and do the vacuuming and dusting at the end of the week, it is possible to have your home in an acceptable state of readiness for the Sabbath and weekend.

As you make better use of your time, you will naturally enjoy each day more. As you gain control of your time, you will experience peace and eliminate the feeling of constant pressure. As your days begin to flow, your self-worth will soar and you will have more energy since you can count on doing something you enjoy. This will fuel your zest for living and greatly enhance enjoyment of "present moment" experiences. Now the way is paved for adding touches of beauty, joy, and elegance to your everyday life.

Create your own personal daily plan for today, remembering to schedule personal time for yourself. After following your personal daily plan for a week, you will begin to enjoy the benefits of having your home "decent and in order." NANCY VAN PELT

AUGUST 2

Peace Recaptured

For thou art the God of my strength: why dost thou cast me off? why go I mourning because of the oppression of the enemy? Ps. 43:2.

A warm Caribbean sun danced over the sea as I prepared my snorkel gear. I waded in and let the cool clear water surround me. My eyes fastened hungrily upon the beauties God had gathered together and flung into the reef. I felt great joy as small rainbows with tails and fins floated past. Excitement surged through me when I lifted a rock and found a small smooth shell hiding there.

When I kicked my fins, my body slithered past sea fans and lazy nudibranchs with wild colors painted on their bodies. Then I noticed several indentions into the rock wall to one side of the bay. Piles of shells lay 10 feet below me in the far end of one of these small caves. I determined to dive down and search these mounds for treasure.

I kicked my fins, doubled up, and thrust myself down. At that moment I saw a great curved mouth edged with white pointed teeth. Beyond the mouth stretched a long gray body. *Shark!* my brain screamed. My curiosity fled, along with my intention to explore. Thrashing around, I managed to halt my downward dive, and I fled for shore.

I lay on the sandy beach, my joyful feelings suddenly gone. Even though the sun warmed me, I shivered. "I'm never going back in there!" I said to my diving partner.

But then I realized that clinging to my fear meant I'd never see a rainbow parrot fish again, never discover a shell hiding in the sand, nor thrill to the excitement of watching an octopus slither from its cave and stare at me.

How often we plunge into a new day, anticipating beauty and joy. Then the shadow of an enemy circles us, nibbling at our peace. Suddenly criticism, hurt, disappointment, or worry crash into us. The eyes of our heart cease to focus on life's joy and beauty, and stare openly at the work of the greatest shark of all, Satan. We shriek in dismay and dash for the safety of the shore of uninvolvement.

I lay on the sand, gazing at the shimmering water calling me back to discovery. A wonderful Creator was prepared for the day when my innocent pleasure would become marred by fear. My God-given desire to explore and learn to know Him through "sea adventures" finally overcame my fear. A new and wise dependence upon Him accompanied me.

As we journey through life, the presence of our Saviour enables us to proceed with joy. Though we seek safe harbors for rest and refreshment, we are still able to sail the open sea with confidence. For it is in the open sea, where sharks patrol the water, that others thrash about seeking rescue.

"When trials arise that seem unexplainable, we should not allow our peace to be spoiled. . . . There is by our side a witness, a heavenly messenger, who will lift up for us a standard against the enemy. He will shut us in with the bright beams of the Sun of Righteousness. Beyond this Satan cannot penetrate. He cannot pass this shield of holy light" *(Christ's Object Lessons,* pp. 171, 172).

So, sail your seas, dive down, collect beauty and joy. God will surround you with the most efficient and wonderful shark repellent—His own presence. SALLY STREIB

AUGUST 3

Sharing God

Heal the sick, raise the dead, cleanse lepers, cast out demons. You received without paying, give without pay. Matt. 10:8, RSV.

Every year about this time, boxes of zucchini appear in the lobby of our office building. The newspaper runs articles on the proliferation of zucchini and recipes for using it up. Folks everywhere complain about having too much zucchini and bemoan their naiveness in planting it last spring.

Yet for all this glut of zucchini, I don't believe anyone has ever offered me any zucchini fresh from the garden. Now, please understand, my friends are not selfish. In fact, I'm sure they offer their extra zucchini to so many people and get turned down so many times that it never occurs to them there might be someone who would actually want zucchini.

I wonder how many people in my sphere have never been asked if they want to know Jesus? Do I ever offer to share Jesus and His love with my friends or neighbors or whoever? Do I know someone who wants the peace and joy of God's love but doesn't know how to ask for it? Am I so secure and comfortable in His love for me that I don't remember there are people who don't know Him? Do I just assume everyone is already happy with his or her life just the way it is? Am I afraid of being turned down if I offer to share God's love?

I was sure I didn't care for zucchini until a dear friend prepared a lovely recipe and shared it with me. Do I have a recipe for sharing Jesus? Am I aware of what He's done for me? Can I explain it succinctly, in a loving and humble manner?

"Lord, please help me to be aware of those people in my life who would like to know You. And just as important, give me wisdom and courage to share Your boundless love and peace and joy with them. Thank You. Amen."   SANDY JOHNSON

AUGUST 4

My Sabbath Rock

If anyone serves, he should do it with the strength God provides, so that in all things God may be praised through Jesus Christ. 1 Peter 4:11, NIV.

Why had I agreed so quickly to do a special feature for the earliteen group Sabbath morning? I had already promised weeks ago to sing in a special choir this coming Sabbath. The choir leader had asked us to come to church early that morning for one final practice. To complicate matters even more, the commitments were at separate churches. True, they were close in distance, but it would still take valuable time to get there and back.

I knew why I had agreed. As the youngest daughter in a family of six children, I often had the duty, and sometimes the pleasure, of serving siblings and parents. As I matured, the pleasure of service replaced what had often seemed to be dreary duty. Besides, I cannot resist the leader of a children's Sabbath school when she pleads for help, for I have often been the pleading leader. And yes, there was another reason I had agreed—it is exciting to talk with young people; their enthusiasm is so delightfully contagious.

Friday afternoon I left work early to drive to a place that had a wonderful selection of rocks. I was looking for a geode. These rounded rocks have a cavity inside lined with glittering crystals that are exposed when the rock is split open. During my dialogue I show the rough, hard exterior of the stone, and talk about how often young people see the Sabbath as something rough and hard. Then I turn the stone around and show the shining radiance of the crystals inside, and talk about opening the Sabbath, and discovering the unexpected beauty and promises it holds.

Always before when I had given this particular presentation to young people I had borrowed one of these special stones from a friend, but now I wanted to have one of my own. As I drove up into the hills, surrounded by beautiful fall colors, I talked with God as I would a friend. I told Him what a long difficult week it had been, and how very tired I was. I asked Him: *How am I going to be able to get the cleaning and cooking done for Sabbath? How am I going to have the time and energy to prepare for the earliteen group? How am I going to be able to get from one appointment to the other?*

It was then that I recalled one of my favorite psalms: "I lift up my eyes to the hills—where does my help come from? My help comes from the Lord, the Maker of heaven and earth" (Psalm 121:1, 2, NIV).

Driving through the fall haze of that late afternoon, I asked for and received strength. Strength that would take me through the preparation for Sabbath and my presentation, strength that would help me during choir practice and performance. Strength provided by God so that my story about a unique rock might reach a special group of young people. But most of all, God provided strength so that in all my human efforts, He would be praised.

P. DEIRDRE MAXWELL

Jesus Sets Us Free

Therefore if any man is in Christ, he is a new creature; the
old things passed away; behold, new things have come.
2 Cor. 5:17, NASB.

A ll of us have problems that tend to keep our minds from being at peace. Perhaps we have relatives, friends, or neighbors who upset us. In our prayers we frequently ask God to work a miracle and change them. Then something wonderful happens. As we pray we begin to feel differently, not because they have changed, but because we have changed. We begin to see them through the eyes of Jesus. There is love and compassion in our hearts for them. Perhaps they change too, but if they don't, we are able to cope with the situation because God has helped us change our attitude toward them.

When Jesus dwells in our hearts, our true feelings and attitudes are revealed to us. Jesus gives us a glimpse into the real person we are, and He sets us free—not only from wrong attitudes but from any sin that binds us. While on earth, Jesus said, "If you abide in My word, then you are truly disciples of Mine; and you shall know the truth, and the truth shall make you free." "If therefore the Son shall make you free, you shall be free indeed" (John 8:31, 32, 36, NASB). As we are liberated from our critical and jealous attitudes and other sins, we are transformed into the image of God. "We all, with unveiled face beholding as in a mirror the glory of the Lord, are being transformed into the same image from glory to glory" (2 Cor. 3:18, NASB). This comes about through prayer! We behold the glory of Jesus while communing with Him. His glory in our hearts transforms us into His likeness. "The effective prayer of a righteous man can accomplish much" (James 5:16, NASB)—more for ourselves than for others. Although progress in ourselves may seem so slow, the Spirit of God lets us know that transformation is taking place in our lives.

We do not set out to change ourselves by having an idea or making a plan for ourselves, asking God to help us fulfill our plan. Never! As we commune with Him, we get to know Him. We ask Him to take over the control of our thoughts, motives, and actions. We ask Him to fill our hearts and lives with His glory, and change naturally follows. Change is possible—we don't have to be what we are! What a miracle! And what a wonderful God we serve!

Has prayer become obsolete in your life? If so, start praying today for renewed hope and determination to commune daily with Him. Your life will be transformed into the likeness of Christ, and He will set you free!   Marie Spangler

AUGUST 6

Prayer and Presence

I have set the Lord always before me: because he is at my right hand, I shall not be moved. Ps. 16:8.

Where did I get the idea that prayer had to be spoken? That I had to tie my tongue around my teeth with thees and thous? That I had to remember all the items on my list just in case God forgot something?

Who did I think I was? His personal secretary? I wonder if I grated on God's nerves sometimes. Do this, Lord. Do that, Lord. At the same time, I knew it wasn't wrong to ask God for things.

I began to notice that many of the prayers I'd had answers to never had words at all. Then I read a book about practicing the presence of Christ, and a whole new world opened up to me.

It's not as difficult as it may sound, but those who attempt from the beginning to put themselves in the presence of Christ at all times are heading for a nervous breakdown. It will be achieved only gradually—like a snowball traveling downhill, it will grow. And what a difference it makes to the prayer life!

Now I start each day by saying good morning to Jesus as soon as I wake. Not a formal prayer. Just "Good morning, Lord. Thank you for a good night's rest." When I thank Him for breakfast, I look at it and try to imagine sharing it with Him. As I leave for work, I ask Him to come with me and keep me from harm or from harming others. As I start work, I pray that everything I do will be to His glory—even the thoughts I think. As I change jobs, another invitation for His continued presence. If I find myself walking down a corridor or the street, I sing a snatch of praise to Him. And so on, throughout the day. Not exactly prayers always, but more than just thoughts; not exactly words, but a living in His presence.

There are snags. It makes it very hard to become upset with an inefficient salesperson if you've just spoken to the Lord and can actually feel Him beside you!

It doesn't work all the time—yet. Like all good habits, it will take a long time to become part of me. But I am getting to the point that when I'm not practicing the presence of Christ I miss Him.

259

Then I welcome Him back as I would my husband if he'd been away.

Why is it that the simplest solution is often the best?

ANITA MARSHALL

AUGUST 7

Life as a Prayer

Have no anxiety about anything, but in everything by prayer and supplication with thanksgiving let your requests be made known to God. Phil. 4:6, RSV.

When my children were little, I could not imagine a time when I would not have enough hours in the day. I chose to stay home with them and enjoyed watching them develop and grow. My husband was very busy during those years, and so the days sometimes seemed very long. As my children grew older, started school, and went on to Pathfinders, piano lessons, and other such activities, life was much busier. It was then that I began having difficulty finding time for personal devotions. I was reading three or four different Sabbath school lessons every night and praying with my children, which left little time for my own prayer life.

During this time I read a letter in a magazine from a woman who said that every time she made her bed in the morning, she would spend the time thanking God for her loving husband and for their life together. Then a friend of mine gave me a book to read written by a Catholic priest. It was written especially for women. The book points out that everything that needs to be done in the home can become a ministry. No matter how humble the task or how boring the job is, if it is done to the best of one's ability and to God's honor and glory, it becomes a ministry. There is time for prayer too when your hands are in a sinkful of dirty dishes or when the laundry needs sorting and folding.

This letter and this book started my mind thinking of other ways that I could find time for prayer. Traffic jams are a good possibility, especially if driving alone. Exercising is a big part of life now, and can become a prayer opportunity too. This past year I have been using a stationary bicycle every day and find this a good time to read and pray. "Prayer is the opening of the heart to God as to a friend" *(Steps to Christ,* p. 93), and that can take place anywhere we happen to be.

OLIVE CROUCH

The Lord's Slice

Behold, I stand at the door, and knock: if any man hear my voice, and open the door, I will come in to him, and will sup with him, and he with me. Rev. 3:20.

Just before bedtime I knelt to pray and offer thanks to God. As I did, I remembered how I had knelt that morning, asking God to bless my day. Then I had rushed off, too busy to spend time with Him. Now I was almost too tired to listen for His answer—but answer He did.

In my mind the Lord showed me a loaf of bread that I was sharing with Him. I had been giving Him the two ends—and keeping the rest for myself. He told me that the slices I had been sharing with Him lately had been getting thinner and thinner. He wondered if I might soon be giving Him only crumbs.

The two end slices represented the time I gave the Lord each day—morning and evening. Giving the Lord the first and last part of my day is good. But I found myself wondering if these were really quality times. In the morning I am too groggy to think. In the evening I am too tired to pay attention. The Lord seemed to be asking for a slice out of the middle—out of the good part of my day!

Wasn't that asking a lot? Wasn't it a bit selfish? But then, would I call someone who would give me $10 if I would just give back $1 selfish? I would stand in line for a long time to benefit from such an offer. The promise in Malachi 3:10 now echoed in my mind: "Bring ye all the tithes into the storehouse, that there may be meat in mine house, and prove me now herewith, saith the Lord of hosts, if I will not open you the windows of heaven, and pour you out a blessing, that there shall not be room enough to receive it."

Might the Lord be willing to bless in this same way if I would return slices of time to Him? Why was I holding back? By saving all those slices for myself, I was actually starving spiritually. The time I had once spent in Bible study and prayer had dwindled until those slices were shamefully thin. The quiet hours of thoughtful meditation had crumbled away in the hurry of life.

I felt like answering, "Lord, I don't have many slices." But remembering how Jesus blessed the widow who gave her *last* two mites, I couldn't bring myself to complain. If the Lord could bless her, surely He could bless me; I determined to take another look at how I sliced my loaf.

One reason I had neglected the Lord was that I was not

listening very well. Revelation 3:20 describes this very situation: "Behold, I stand at the door, and knock: if any man *hear* my voice, and open the door, I will come in to him, and will sup with him, and he with me." I prayed, "Lord, help me find ways to share my day with You—and to hear You knocking when You want entrance into my life."

I began opening my thoughts to God during quiet walks at the end of the workday. I soon discovered He was close beside me, waiting to help me understand more about Himself just as He had when He walked with the two travelers on their way to Emmaus.

I also found moments at my workplace to ask for guidance, and to thank God for blessings. I can easily call on the Lord as I walk down the hall on an errand or when I'm put on "hold" on the telephone. At times when I normally would have felt overwhelmed by cares and duties I sensed my attitude beginning to change. Why had I ever thought my relationship with the Lord could survive on crumbs?

I have not found the Lord to be selfish by asking for a slice out of the middle of my day. It has paid to be extravagant in sharing some of the best time with Him. I've found the meaning of Jesus' words: "Freely ye have received, freely give" (Matt. 10:8).

KAREN D. LIFSHAY

AUGUST 9

The Meeting of Hearts

A word fitly spoken is like apples of gold in pictures of silver. Prov. 25:11.

My grandfather was skinny, long-boned, and gentle as autumn sunshine. He lived by himself in a one-room house in his sister's backyard. He had an enamel pitcher and washbasin in his room, and an old-fashioned water closet in a shanty to the side. Papa lived in Fort Worth. We lived in Dallas, a long, hot 35 miles away. Sometimes he took the bus to visit us. More often we made the trip on a Sabbath afternoon or Sunday morning, my parents, my sister, and I sweating the stoplights between the two cities. We must have gone in the winter also, but it's the heat that I remember.

A trunk took up a good part of the floor space in Papa's room, and from the time we were small we searched through the compartments for things he'd hidden there. The gifts rarely varied. We found candy bars and all the pennies he'd collected since our last visit tied snugly in a little cotton tobacco bag.

As my sister and I entered our teens, the treasure hunt lost its mystery, but we kept up the pretense of the search. Only now we'd find black seamed nylon stockings along with the chocolate and pennies. We'd give Papa a hug of thanks, and he'd fold us in his flabby old-man's arms and say, "I don't know what people who don't have grandbabies do."

He was terribly hard of hearing, but hungry for talk. He especially enjoyed debating the Sabbath and the state of the dead with my father. Papa shouted because he couldn't hear himself, and Dad shouted to be heard. Neither ever convinced the other, and Papa once said that his only hope for his son was that he'd stood up at a revival when he was a child, indicating he wanted to be saved. Dad had joined the Adventist Church in his early thirties.

We'd stay three or four hours. Often we brought lunch or took Papa out for a ride. When it was time for us to go, Papa would stand in the weedy, curving driveway, shading his eyes and waving until our car turned into the street. We always left with a mixture of sadness and relief that the visit was over. No doubt Papa was sometimes lonely, but I don't remember thinking a lot about it. He had his friends and a portable TV, and his brother lived a few blocks away. His room was his home, and he was content.

A few weeks ago my husband and I left our third daughter at Southern College. We hauled an incredible amount of stuff out of the car and up the dormitory stairs. By nightfall Bronwen had her little world in order, with everything arranged and put away. She didn't want any help.

We stayed an extra day; for me, not for her. She and a girlfriend were leaving on a walk. They'd been talking and laughing ever since we arrived, making plans for the coming year. I teased them about cute boys on campus. Bronwen insisted she wasn't interested.

Bronwen prefers to ignore goodbyes, but I insisted on a hug. As I clasped her slim form against me I thought of all the goodbyes I'd had in the past. One last squeeze, and she gave a quick smile, then turned and walked back to the dorm. As we drove away into the sun, I thought of my grandfather shading his eyes and waving until he couldn't see us anymore. A 16-year-old has little understanding of an elderly grandfather, nor an eager college student of a mother's tears and fears.

At best, communication is difficult in our sin-shadowed world. Using our fragile tools—a touch, a glance, mere words—we grope toward each other, trying to reach each other's hearts or shying away from the touch. True meeting of hearts is an extraordinary gift.

And yet the wonder of it is that we do communicate. Parent to child, husband to wife, friend to friend. For there is One who specializes in building bridges of understanding across the abyss of years or culture or learning. It is rare, that precious gift of experience, the intuitive knowing what the other meant to say. But it actually happens now and then. Saying goodbye, for example, and knowing that mere space can never separate you from one you love. And when this happens, it is like touching the heart of God.

PENNY ESTES WHEELER

AUGUST 10

Nocturnal Panic

The Lord is my shepherd; I shall not want. He maketh me to lie down in green pastures: he leadeth me beside the still waters. He restoreth my soul: he leadeth me in the paths of righteousness for his name's sake. Ps. 23:1-3.

Panic attacks in the night. My pulse rate elevates. My abdominal muscles clench. My jaw tightens as I begin to grind my teeth. Fear carves a hollow place in my chest. I begin to breathe rapidly. Terror batters my mind. Nameless dread vies with nameful dread, both seeking to gain my full attention.

I fear abandonment. I fear growing older. I fear being unable to pay the bills. I fear I know not what. I fear, and the fear consumes me.

Then in the maelstrom of panic comes a calm voice:

"Fear thou not; for I am with thee: be not dismayed; for I am thy God: I will strengthen thee; yea, I will help thee; yea, I will uphold thee with the right hand of my righteousness" (Isa. 41:10).

How long have I known those words, Lord? Why do I forget?

Panic still beats its heavy black wings against the windows of God's protective love. But now I remember that I am not alone. As I write my prayer—words of anguish mingled with words of hope—God steeps my soul in peace:

"Thou wilt keep [her] in perfect peace, whose mind is stayed on thee . . . Lord, thou wilt ordain peace for us: for thou also hast wrought all our works in us" (Isa. 26:3-12).

O, God, place the peace which passes understanding in my heart today.

KATIE TONN-OLIVER

Forgive

Be kind and compassionate to one another, forgiving each other, just as in Christ God forgave you. Eph. 4:32, NIV.

It was one of those days! I rushed through the morning chores so that I could reach the office on time. My husband had the day off and was indulging in a little more rest in bed. As I was getting ready to leave, my husband and I engaged in a discussion that turned into an argument. He said something that hurt me very much, and I left the room very upset—mad, actually.

Just before I opened the door to leave the house, parts of this scripture came to my mind: "But if any have caused grief, he hath not grieved me, but in part: that I may not overcharge you all. Sufficient to such a man is this punishment, which was inflicted of many. So that contrariwise ye ought rather to forgive him, and comfort him, lest perhaps such a one should be swallowed up with overmuch sorrow. Wherefore I beseech you that ye would confirm your love toward him. For to this end also did I write, that I might know the proof of you, whether ye be obedient in all things. To whom ye forgive any thing, I forgive also: for if I forgave any thing, to whom I forgave it, for your sakes forgave I it in the person of Christ; lest Satan should get an advantage of us: for we are not ignorant of his devices" (2 Cor. 2:5-11).

I had read Evelyn Christensen's book *What Happens When Women Pray*, in which she tells the story of a member in her church who hurt her. Because of the resentment she had in her heart, she was unable to pray. She came across this passage and with great difficulty put it into practice. I wanted to ignore this text, but since I had given talks on prayer and told this story, I felt I would be a phony to preach what I did not practice.

But there was so much resentment and hurt that I did not feel like doing anything nice for my husband. So I asked God to give me a forgiving spirit and for help in following His instructions. I made my husband a cup of his favorite hot drink (probably the smallest thing I could think of), which I really did not feel like doing. I took the drink to him, practically dragging my feet, left it on the night table next to him, and told him I was leaving for the office. There was a look of surprise—almost shock—on his face. He did not say anything.

As I walked out of the room, I felt like a heavy load was lifted from me. I felt as free as a bird in flight. It was as if the black river of resentment and self-pity that was beginning to poison my mind was not only halted in its destructive course, but pushed completely out of my system. What a feeling of exhilaration. I sang all the way to the office. (There was an added bonus to this. When I got home in the evening, the dishes were washed, the kitchen was clean. Even the living and dining rooms were straightened up.)

I had to acknowledge with humility that our Creator has the right prescription for healing hurts that we do not deserve.

HEPHZI OHAL

AUGUST 12

Measure of Faith

Ask, and ye shall receive, that your joy may be full. John 16:24.

After a morning in the strawberry field, I visited an elderly friend. I intended to offer him as many berries as he would take.

"How many can I give you?" I asked somewhat teasingly. "And what shall I put them in?" Purposely I left the choices to him.

He seemed pleased, and brought a medium-sized mixing bowl. I heaped the field-warm fruit into it, happy to share with him.

I was disappointed that he had not asked for more. I would have filled all his mixing bowls, if he would have had the faith to bring them.

Many times we do the same thing with God. While the wealth of heaven can be ours, we hesitate to claim boldly as much as we desire, as much as God would willingly give us.

He demonstrated His love for us with His best gift—His only Son! For the more we ask of God, the more He delights to bestow upon us.

"Ask, and ye shall receive, that your joy may be full." Let us never doubt God's love and readiness to grant greater blessings than we could ever dream of asking.

FANNIE L. HOUCK

The Art of Prayer

I call on the Lord in my distress, and he answers me. Ps. 20:1, NIV.

Iwas born into a Christian home in Tanzania, East Africa. When I grew up, I learned that both my parents had been baptized not long before I was born. When I was a young child my parents prayed often, thanking God for giving them children, and asking God to spare our lives, not to let us die like their other children. I didn't know I had had brothers and sisters who had died. I thought I was the first born. "What happened to your other children?" I asked my mom and dad.

My mother explained that her parents were pagan, and according to local customs they arranged her marriage to a man who had two other wives. Her husband loved her more than the other wives. All her first three children died in infancy, and their death was thought to have been caused by the two jealous wives. My grandparents withdrew my mother from her first marriage. My mother got married once again. I was born in her second marriage. My father told me his story—that his arranged wedding was to a lady who could not stand labor pains. Instead of relaxing her pelvis, spreading her legs apart and pushing the baby, she did the opposite. As a result she lost three children at birth. My father's parents and friends convinced him to divorce her.

Thus father and mother, who shared a common experience of failed first marriages and of losing children, met and married. They soon met a Seventh-day Adventist pastor, Mispeles Rutoryo, who eventually baptized them. My mother, Nyabweke, was baptized as Anastazia; and my father, Magai, became Phares.

In our home we prayed every morning before starting the day's chores. In the evening we sang and prayed to thank the Lord for the day. Praying is a special art that I learned from my parents in childhood and that has worked miracles in my life.

My mother became seriously ill when I was in first grade. Many thought she would not survive. But I applied the art of prayer that my parents had taught me. I prayed wholeheartedly and my mother recovered, quite miraculously. She lived 38 more years.

During my mother's long illness my father lost hope. The devil overcame him, and he became a backslider spiritually. Again I prayed and cried. He repented and was rebaptized. He has served the Lord as church elder and stands firm as a Christian.

I got married in August 1968 but remained childless. Once again I prayed to God. In 1973 God gave me a baby girl and two boys who were born in 1976 and 1979.

In 1990 the doctors discovered I had breast cancer, and thought it was too late to treat it. While the doctors were doing further tests, I prayed. My relatives and friends too prayed. A surgery and chemotherapy treatment ended successfully.

Where did I get the courage to go through such a devastating experience? From the art of prayer that I acquired from my parents as a child. God answers prayers. Let us pray so that our children can acquire the art and grow with it. RACHEL NYIRABU

AUGUST 14

"Ye Are the Salt of the Earth"

You are the salt of the earth. But if the salt loses its saltiness, how can it be made salty again? It is no longer good for anything, except to be thrown out and trampled by men. Matt. 5:13, NIV.

One summer I took a job at a factory, on an assembly line filling boxes. I had worked primarily in an Adventist environment, so I had to readjust the way I perceived others and the way I thought things should be.

One day, Charlotte, a coworker, after discovering from our conversation that I was a minister's wife, went to see the supervisor and requested that she no longer be assigned to work with me. "Christians make you think you are filthy and make you guilty about the way you talk," she said. The supervisor asked whether I had done anything to make her feel that way, and she replied that I had not as yet, but she expected me to soon. I began praying that the Lord would make me a good disciple.

For some reason I was assigned to work with Charlotte for the next three weeks, standing directly next to her. During that time she missed many boxes that I managed to fill in addition to mine. One day two new people were assigned to our team. Charlotte asked me not to change my position because she was less anxious with me beside her. She noticed that I didn't curse and swear at her when I had to fill her boxes, but the other workers would reprimand her when she didn't work efficiently. She wanted to know why I was different, and I told her about the golden rule and what Christianity is all about.

Charlotte is not in the baptismal class today, but she does not think the same way about Christians as she did before I met her. Other workers have also learned to trust me. They tell me about important decisions in their lives and ask for my counsel. People tell me about their fears and aspirations, their disappointments and pain, and I realize how lonely many people are and how many there are who just needing a listening ear. They ask me to pray for them and their family members.

As I reflect on my experience at this job, I realize I have gained a better understanding of what Christ meant when He said that the Christian is the salt of the earth. Salt seasons, preserves, and creates a thirst. I believe that when we as Christians season rightly, we will create a thirst in our acquaintances that will cause them to ask "What makes you different from all the others?" Then we can lead them to the Fountain of Life, where they can drink living water that will give them eternal life.

Mabel Owusu-Antwi

AUGUST 15

Show Us the Way

I will fear no evil, for you are with me. Ps. 23:4, NIV.

Troubles and doubts seem to plague each of us in varying degrees at some time during our life. We try to do the Lord's work His way, but so often we are unsure. We often stumble and fall. Yet God is there to pick us up and heal our wounds, all the while reminding us how much we are loved by Him. Recently He has been doing just that for me.

Our church has been going through a very difficult trial. A member had to be disciplined, and the discipline was not accepted. The church became divided, and some members left, while others were confused. Accusations flew that the church had not dealt fairly and had no authority. The tension was sickening. Many hearts were heavy with doubt and concern. Many hours were spent in prayer and study. We wanted to do the Lord's will in the spirit of love and humility, but were we doing it? Many times I wanted to get far away from the situation. I felt I couldn't take any more, and I cried, "Lord, this is *Your* church—show us the way!"

He did. Not just once, but many times and in many different ways, so that there was no room for doubt in my mind. Letters came from people we didn't even think knew about the situation. We received phone calls from people who had moved from the district, letting us know they were praying for us. Every time we picked up the Spirit of Prophecy we found comfort and answers to our questions. Even the Sabbath school lesson dealt with similar issues. What amazed me most was that my children's favorite Christian radio program presented a program that dealt with a similar situation!

My heart was filled with wonder and love. I had heard about letters from Mrs. White arriving "just in time," but when it happened for me, I was in awe. What love God has for even me! Truly He will see me through every future trial. For this I am thankful beyond words. SUE GLEASON

AUGUST 16

Taught by a Tree

We are afflicted in every way, but not crushed; perplexed, but not driven to despair; persecuted, but not forsaken; struck down, but not destroyed. 2 Cor. 4:8, 9, RSV.

I walked along a narrow path that meandered through the deep woods. Early springtime sunshine sent small golden fingers of sunlight filtering through the green fluttering canopy of leaves above. Jack-in-the-pulpits peaked out from beneath green ferns that stood uncurling themselves in the cool morning air.

Birds flitted from tree to tree singing out their joy at the newness of life, and butterflies hovered over wild azalea blossoms.

A sudden darkness encompassed me, as though a giant hand reached down and snatched the sun from its place. The air became cool, and I shivered. Rain sprinkled me with scattered droplets, then the floodgates opened, and the heavens poured themselves upon my unprotected head.

I scrunched down into my jacket, searching in vain for some scant shelter and hurried down the trail toward home.

Crash! The earth shook as a flash of lightning blazed a searing white trail across the black sky. It reached down and bore itself into a giant elm tree that stood at some distance from me. Every hair on my body stood up and I felt prickles run up and down my spine. As I watched in stark terror, the great tree burst into flame.

Gusts of wind whipped my wet clothes against my legs as I stared at the elm tree sizzling in the increased downpour. I heaved a sigh of relief as the flames were snuffed by the rain, but nature wasn't finished yet.

The elm teetered and swayed in the wind, then began to fall. Its mighty branches flailed helplessly, grasping at everything in its downward path.

Sounds of ripping and tearing filled the whole forest, and I braced myself for the sound of its final agony as it crashed toward the soggy earth.

The parting clouds allowed enough light to pierce through the darkness, and I saw a slender oak directly in the monster's downward path. I winced in pain at the spectacle of the great elm smashing itself onto the back of the young oak. They fell together toward the earth.

An agonizing wrenching sound arose from the stricken oak. I expected at any moment to hear it snap like a toothpick beneath its suffocating load; instead, the oak held. Its roots strained to maintain a grasp on the earth's breast. At last the trees settled together. Leaves wrenched free in the wind, zigzagged to the earth, and silence filled the forest.

I felt amazed that the oak held. It was badly bent, but not broken. Fallen, yes, but not destroyed. It groaned like a living thing as its very fibers ripped and stretched, giving gradually to the weight of the elm that pressed its face to the earth, but it did not break!

The storm ended as suddenly as it had started, and I made my way to the fallen trees. I ran my wet hands on the oak's rough bark and moved my fingers along the muddy surface of several above-ground roots. With great joy I realized that the roots had held. The tree would live.

I knew that in time new shoots of growth would pierce the bark and shoot heavenward. Leaves would unfurl and later turn gold in autumn. New roots could reach down and grasp more firmly the breast of the earth.

For more than a year I watched with great interest the amazing growth of the bent oak tree. It pressed itself against the ground with a mass of great roots and sent branches skyward.

The oak sheltered a chattery squirrel family, held robin's nests in its arms, and shaded the faces of wild violets from the noontide sun. Although no one ever removed the elm that lay like a stricken animal along its bent form, the oak flourished.

Isn't it true that we as women are sometimes like the oak tree? Trials and burdens lay heavy across our shoulders. Grief and pain sometimes threaten to crush our hope and joy, our usefulness in the Lord's army. We long to have all the problems removed from us.

When I feel like this, I visit the spot deep in the woods where the oak tree grows. I remember how I was taught by a tree that, praise God, "we are afflicted in every way, but not crushed; perplexed, but not driven to despair; persecuted, but not forsaken; struck down, but not destroyed!"

SALLY STREIB

271

My Personal God

If I rise on the wings of the dawn, if I settle on the far side of the sea, even there your hand will guide me, your right hand will hold me fast. Ps. 139:9, 10, NIV.

I felt like I had risen on the wings of dawn. Though it was very early, I was already on my way to a speaking appointment. Whenever I commute alone, I spend the first few minutes of my trip talking with God and developing a positive affirmation for the day. This particular morning I began by telling God about my plans for the next few hours, and asked for wisdom and energy to complete the day's activities.

The weather was gray and foggy. As the traffic thickened, it soon seemed as if my car was but another speck on the great expanse of asphalt—just another commuter, lost among so many others lined up on the multiple lanes. I thought of a recent dinner at which I'd been seated next to a rather eminent theologian. During one of the many courses the cleric had declared rather pompously, "We bring God down to our level when we assume that His Majesty is really interested in our everyday minutiae. Our God is a great God, and He has a universe to run!" I had protested, "It is precisely because God has a universe to run that I know He is interested in me personally. I am part of that universe."

Thinking back on that conversation and my present enmeshment in a stop-and-go prison of glass and steel, I could see how a person might subscribe to that perception. At a time like this it wouldn't be too hard to imagine that the Creator and Sustainer of the universe was way too busy to notice where I was located on the planet at this precise moment. Was it too simplistic to think that God truly knew where I was and what I was doing every minute of every day?

A few verses in the tenth chapter of Matthew came to mind. I remembered that Christ said the very hairs of our head are numbered; that God notices even when a little bird flies into a building or a telephone pole and falls to the ground.

Maneuvering my way through traffic, I again thanked God for guiding me, personally; for knowing where I am at all times; and for giving me evidence of loving care in so many ways. Suddenly, even as I was speaking, one small, pure shaft of brilliant sunlight broke through the dim overcast and for just an instant, lighted the world directly in front of my car. It was as if God had taken an extra moment not only to recognize the conversation we were having, but to confirm that my heavenly Parent did indeed know exactly where I was at that precise moment. As the tiny beam of sunlight faded, I felt enveloped with a warm, comfortable sense of confirmed importance. In terms of eternal value, I, as an heir of the Creator of the universe, am much more important than many sparrows. No, the theologian's perception could not be mine.

Today, wherever you are, remember that my God and your God is so powerful and so caring that there is room for all of us on the computer screen of the Omnipotent. Realize that your heavenly Parent always knows exactly where you are on this planet at all times—and sometimes, He even pauses long enough to evidence that. Watch for that confirmation.   ARLENE TAYLOR

AUGUST 18

Fire in the Canyon

The angel of the Lord encamps around those who fear him, and he delivers them. Ps. 34:7, NIV.

It was summertime. There had been no rain for several months, and all land cover and brush was very dry, especially on the vacant hillsides and canyons. Often during the day, and even at night, the radio carried announcements of fires here and there.

I have reason for remembering one particular night. Often, not being able to sleep, I would listen on my little bedside radio. That night I heard, to my surprise, that there was a bad fire in the little canyon right where my home was located. At the time I was living in a retirement home about an hour's drive away from my own home.

So, I immediately offered a little prayer telling God about it—that I was helpless to do anything about it and that He would have to take charge. Then I turned over and fell asleep.

My phone awakened me the next morning. My daughter-in-law, who lives on the canyon's hillside and whose husband was overseas, called to tell me fire fighters had been on her roof and they'd said that the houses on the whole street would soon be in flames. But before that happened, the wind changed, and the many homes were saved, including the conference president's home. I wanted to thank the Lord for taking charge and saving all the homes in that little canyon.

There's another part to this story. One of my sons, who was living in my home at the time, had gotten back late from teaching a night class and was sleeping very soundly. But he suddenly awakened for no reason. He took a drink of water, thinking that might help him go back to sleep. But no. So he opened the window wider for more fresh air, and saw the flames on the hillside. He immediately alerted the neighbors, then quickly drove up the hillside to awaken my daughter-in-law and the minister's wife. A little longer, and they with others could have been overcome with smoke.

The fire fighters did their best, and my son helped them all he could. Apparently an angel awakened my son about the time of my prayer. God understands and cares, and we are so thankful.

"Trust in the Lord with all thine heart; and lean not unto thine own understanding. In all thy ways acknowledge him, and he shall direct thy paths" (Prov. 3:5, 6). MABEL E. RICHARDS

AUGUST 19

Neither Snow nor Heat nor Gloom of Night . . .

Before they call I will answer; while they are still speaking I will hear. Isa. 65:24, NIV.

The U.S. Postal Service claims to deliver the mail despite varied exigencies. The intercampus mail service at Andrews University, where I work, tries too; but quite often something indeed "stays these couriers from the swift completion of their appointed rounds."

Recently, during remodeling, six pieces of mail, dated 1968 and 1969, came to light in the seminary. They had apparently fallen into obscurity during distribution 22 or 23 years ago. Undaunted, the dean's secretary sent them on to their rightful owners.

Thus Hedy Jemison, retired secretary to the dean, received a yellowed ad. A parcel notice for Millie Urbish, now Youngberg and also retired, was sent through intercampus mail to her husband John. At last report it hadn't yet arrived. Maybe in another 23 years.

C. Mervyn Maxwell, retired professor, puzzled over his letter from W. Duncan Eva—until he looked at the date, "5 May, 1969." Eva, now retired from the vice presidency of the General Conference, wrote from England as president of the Northern European Division, thanking Maxwell for his letter "in regard to the sculpture of the three angels mounted on our office here in St. Albans." A number of people had inquired about making copies or using the sculpture in various ways. "Certainly it gives expression to something that no one else has succeeded in expressing anywhere near so well," he added. He then referred Maxwell to the sculptor, Alan Collins. Perhaps Maxwell's question had to wait until Collins joined the Andrews faculty a few years later.

Eva told of his visit the previous Sabbath with Mervyn's aunt and uncle at the little church in Weymouth. "They are greatly appreciated in the church and much loved by the people to whom they minister so unselfishly." Heartwarming even now, it would have been nice to hear while they still lived.

Myrl Manley's letter, and one for his wife, were sent to her in California. She was "very surprised." His was a routine business letter, but hers was from her son's mother-in-law, Lois Fouts (now Johannes), a widow working at the Far Eastern Division office at the time. Mrs. Manley had written her that their children were getting off to a good start in their marriage and work at Hinsdale Hospital. This faraway mother responded, "You can't imagine how good your letter made me feel. . . . Like you, I hope they will develop a character that will warrant further development in the great eternal—if they are striving for this, I am sure their work, wherever they are, will be satisfactory, at least before God."

Since this groom had just been drafted for Vietnam, Lois also suggested that maybe his wife could teach in a Far Eastern nursing school. Mrs. Manley says, "This was the first I knew of this idea. It didn't work out." Surely these messages would have been appreciated 23 years ago.

The mail for Drs. W.G.C. and Ruth Murdoch was sent to her in Loma Linda—a Christmas card from a young couple whose marriage has since dissolved. They never knew that the Murdochs didn't receive their greetings.

The famous motto of the Postal Service came originally from Herodotus, speaking of the Persian postal system in 500 B.C. At the seminary it may take an archaeological dig to complete the task, but messages usually do get delivered. But our God gets all of our messages, and answers them, before we even utter them.

MADELINE S. JOHNSTON

AUGUST 20

Tired of Goodbyes

And we know that in all things God works for the good of those who love him, who have been called according to his purpose. Rom. 8:28, NIV.

Once more a moving van was coming to my door, and I was sick and tired of moving. I wanted to be able to put my roots down—deep! How I dreaded the thought of packing and trying to settle into a new community. Adjusting to new places and circumstances had never been one of my attributes, and I felt so happy and secure right where I was. But when one's husband is in the ministry, moving seems to be inevitable.

Every day for the first week I went into my bedroom and shut the door and let my tears flow. Gradually I came to accept the fact that I must go, as I felt sure that this move was God's leading.

It was hard to leave my grown sons. Now my house would be forever empty of children. Saying goodbye to a much-loved church family was almost as painful.

And then, while reading in the book *Patriarchs and Prophets,* I came to something that spoke directly to me. "Who is ready at the call of Providence to renounce cherished plans and familiar associations?" "He calls them away from human influences and aid, and leads them to feel the need of His help, and to depend upon Him alone, that He may reveal Himself to them" (p. 127). Perhaps this was the reason God had called us so far away from family and friends to serve Him.

The moving van would take us 4,000 miles to a new life, where I would be a "stranger" in the land.

Yes, I learned that here in this new land I would have to depend heavily upon my heavenly Father to see me through the adjustments and loneliness of each new day. And I knew in my heart that I could make it—with God.   ROBERTA SCHAFER

AUGUST 21

The Black Vase

Each one should use whatever gift he has received to serve others, faithfully administering God's grace in its various forms. 1 Peter 4:10, NIV.

The black vase died as it had lived, giving pleasure. Chubby fingers, directed by 10-month-old Alex—who has much to learn about the laws of physics—gave it a spin that sent it over the edge of Grandma's kitchen counter and onto the tile floor, where it splintered into a thousand fragments. Chortling with glee over the marvelous tinkling noise, Alex tried to wriggle his way across the floor to where the shiny pieces lay so invitingly, before my broom swept them into oblivion.

Exactly when the black vase came to live at my childhood home, I do not know. Like Mother, it was always there. On Friday afternoons when fresh flowers or branches were arranged for Sabbath, the black vase was there to do its job: hold flowers.

It was unobtrusive. Practical. Modest. Yet elegant in its simplicity. Its plain velvet finish went well with nearly any arrangement. It never detracted from the natural beauty of its contents.

In my growing-up years the black vase was one of two choices for floral arrangements. The other, a glass swan, was considered delicate and could be used only as a centerpiece on the dining table. Besides, it could never be held by the neck, a rather natural handle, I thought. The black vase had no such restrictions. In fact, in the years Mother was a deaconess, it often went to church. In the summer I remember it filled with multicolored zinnias. In the damp, cool winters of Uruguay it could carry a half-dozen calla lilies nested among heart-shaped leaves. One year I planted gladiolus especially so that their salmon-colored spires could go to church in the black vase.

The black vase went on other errands. It visited homes where people lay sick. It carried color and aroma to elderly shut-ins. And it became part of our family heritage. When my father died, neighbors kept it full of fragrant gifts of love for nearly two months.

After I was married, the black vase came to live at our home in Argentina. Not spectacular by any standard, it continued to carry out its purpose. On my birthday it was sure to contain as many carnations as the years I was celebrating. That is, until three dozen spicy, long-stemmed blossoms were too much—whether for the vase or my husband's budget, I am not sure.

Another move took us and the black vase back to Michigan. Cut flowers were now beyond our means. But with poise the black vase held dried eucalyptus leaves to freshen the air during winter's cold, snowy months.

Then we moved to the Philippines. With our children grown and gone, I was eager to take along some memento of the past. The swan, too fragile to travel, went to our daughter as a family heirloom. *Ah!* I thought. *The black vase is a good traveler.* It would accompany us to our new home.

Soon after our arrival, some students' children brought me a bouquet of bougainvillea (in exchange for green guavas from our backyard tree). The bright blossoms went well in the black vase. Often—even on days other than Friday—the black vase appeared on the table holding a floral offering of some sort.

And once again it went on outings: to church, to welcome a new family on campus, to celebrate a volunteer's eightieth birthday. It was the perfect container for a dozen roses, affordable from the nearby rose farm. But just as often it displayed golden yellow bells or flame-red flamboyant from the trees shading our road.

Whether vases know they have a purpose in life, I doubt. But the black vase fulfilled its purpose, I am sure. Quietly, gently, without fanfare, it carried color, fragrance, and joy wherever it went. Its last trip to church, to hold a floral thanksgiving offering for the family reunion that brought Alex to us, came only a week before its demise.

So the black vase died, just as it had lived, giving pleasure and reiterating the lesson of quiet service it had been teaching me over the decades.   NANCY VYHMEISTER

AUGUST 22

In Six Years

Love one another, as I have loved you. John 15:12.

She's been quite anxious to contact you," the voice on the other end of the line said above the faint, characteristic long-distance hum. "It's very important to her right now. You see, you're the only person she's ever liked."

The words haunted me long after I replaced the receiver on the hook. What was he really saying? Had I been the only one in six years who had responded to her silent pleas for acceptance, taken the good with the bad, learned to love the person shielded behind the sarcasm, the struggling Christian hiding under the thin veneer of flippant living?

In six years how many people have I not only liked but loved? And been loved by in return? My head reels to think of it. Moving outward from the obvious support of husband, son, father, mother, sisters, brother, nieces, nephew, aunt, uncle—the circle widens to include so many who have stepped into the progression of my days with a warm smile, the bright spark of an idea to share, or a reassuring nod of recognition.

The child whose scrawled Hallmark bore the message "We love you. We will miss you." The teenager whose strong arms carried a car seat, a carriage, and a high chair in turn when my arms thought they would break.

The young mother whose thoughts were my own, whose feelings flowed through my very veins. The happy father of an exemplary high school boy who took time to confide to me that even at age 2 his Bobby turned the heads of those three pews ahead. The grandmother whose knotted fingers produced a work of flawless beauty from a skein of yarn.

In six years. Three houses. Five churches. Dozens of neighbors.

278

Scores of students. Numerous coworkers. Women have cried with me, men have challenged me, myriads have agreed and disagreed, spoken and listened, heard and understood.

And she? How could one exist six years with so little friendship? Had I known, when our paths traversed the same geographical terrain, would I have injected something more serious into a friendship I assumed was no different from what she shared with others in her life?

I wonder whether there are others like her around me now. Solitary souls whose outstretched hands I see simply as another pair extending into the secure world in which I live—to be grasped, held, shaken—when they would, had they the courage, be waving flags of warning, fear, distress?

It's an elusive path we walk in this life. Our trails lead us in and out of relationships with others; often, like seasons, they unfold one after another. It seems by happenstance that we find one another on the same winding trek for a time. Often we see each other only through half-open eyes. Only dimly do we sense the struggles, the silent yearnings, the midnight questions of those with whom we traipse, three and four, five and six abreast. And tomorrow we find new faces among our companions, while others are gone forever.

Miles often separate us from those we love dearest, outdistancing the thousand little things that make up a life. It is another who will know when my sister's head aches, my father's orders are not in, my brother has had only four hours of sleep, my niece cannot find her history assignment. It is another who must be partner to the trivialities of life.

And for someone else's sister, I have resolved to do the same. Trekking that winding path with those whom I find walking beside me, I will take the time to listen to the concerns of the moment, and to share with them the insights that only our part of the path, today, will bring. SANDRA DORAN

AUGUST 23

Holy Communion

Be wise in the way you act toward outsiders; make the most of every opportunity. Let your conversation be always full of grace, seasoned with salt, so that you may know how to answer everyone. Col. 4:5, 6, NIV.

When I suddenly found myself in the hospital, I thought I'd better have a word with the Lord! During that urgent little talk it came to me that while I was there, maybe God wanted me to tell someone He cared.

You'd be amazed how easy it is to bring your faith into the conversation in a hospital. Especially when others tell you a horror story about their health, it's easy to ask, "Would you like me to pray for you?"

All sorts of people will tell you how they go to church *occasionally*, or how they *used* to. I was amazed that in a ward of seven women, three wanted to attend Communion with me in the hospital chapel.

Four days later, back in the real world, I was still no wiser as to who the Lord had wanted me to talk to. It could have been the elderly man in the wheelchair by the phone. He knew all the hymns we sang during a short service in our ward on Sunday morning, though he wasn't one of the five at Communion. Maybe it was that fifth communicant, a younger man who sat in a wheelchair? After the service I asked him if he was getting better, and he told me sadly that he'd just come back in. I felt terrible about my unthinking question, but that's one of the drawbacks of having only a few seconds for contact—you can say the wrong thing. Mind you, I believe it's better to say the wrong thing occasionally than to say nothing at all. He was touchingly grateful when I offered to pray for him.

Thinking about my hospital experience, I remembered the following story.

Every day an old man came into church at 12:00 noon, stood before the Communion table for a few minutes, then left. Eventually, the church warden asked him why he did this. The man replied, "I'm not well educated to pray a long prayer, so I just stand here and say, 'Jesus, it's Jim,' and then wait a moment. I'm sure He hears me."

Soon afterward Jim became ill and was taken to the hospital. With Jim there, the often-grumbling patients became happier. They said it was because of old Jim's cheerfulness. But people wondered what made him so cheerful. When a nurse asked him, he said that it was because of his daily visitor. The nurse knew he never had any visitors, and questioned him further. He replied, "Every day at 12:00 noon Jesus comes and stands at the foot of my bed, smiles, and says, 'Jim, it's Jesus.' "

Which is just the sort of thing Jesus would do.

It illustrates nicely that we can talk to the Lord without saying a word, but we can't talk *about* Him that way. The more we talk about Christ among ourselves, the easier and more natural it is to talk about Him with others.   ANITA MARSHALL

Forever

The revelation of Jesus Christ, which God gave him to show his servants what must soon take place. Rev. 1:1, NIV.

With my pen in hand
I'm listening while You speak
within my heart the unyielding prayer
Please, Lord, make me more like Thee.

Let me see the importance
of sincere study every day
so I may have knowledge
of Your plans regarding the human race.

Teach me and make me
what You desire me to be.
Use me in whatever way.
Let me glorify Your name.

Give me the strength to move forward
each and every day
as I reach to grasp the truth
You've so mercifully displayed.

Instill within me that "forever" is not beyond my reach
for eternity with Thee, my Lord,
is a precious gift beyond belief
sealed with Your unselfish love
and handed personally to me . . .

DEBORAH SANDERS

AUGUST 25

Persistent Prayer

May he grant you your heart's desire and fulfill all your plans. Ps. 20:4, TLB.

Many times this verse gave me hope during my 16 years as a single parent of two sons. I learned, by laying the needs and desires for my family before God in persistent prayer, that He does grant our "heart's desire." Let me illustrate.

One afternoon several years ago my sons told me that they were going to be in the upcoming school play. They went on to ask if they could call their dad to tell him about it and to invite him to come watch them perform. "All the moms and dads will be there, and we want both our mom and dad to be there, too!"

But Mom and Dad were divorced, a rarity in 1979 in our family-oriented rural Midwest community, and Dad lived four hours away. The boys were in the first and eighth grades in our country church school. And this would probably be the only year in their lives that they'd be in the same school and in the same school play. This could be a once-in-a-lifetime happening, and the boys' request was definitely a heartfelt one. And so I said, "Sure!"

But Dad reacted by saying that he wished he could be there, but was too busy with work and couldn't get away to come. Well, we decided to make it a matter of prayer. In fact, we prayed three times a day—at breakfast, suppertime, and at bedtime. We prayed that somehow God would work it out so Dad would be able to come. The weeks went by. Finally, a couple weeks before the play, the boys again called their father to tell him that the play was really good, that they were practicing hard, and he should not forget that this was the only time in their lives that they'd be in the same school play together. "Can you come, Dad?" they begged. But the answer was the same. "I would really like to come, but I'm too busy with work." And so our prayers continued, three times a day.

One week before the play, the boys called again, but to no avail. Finally, the night before the play, with dress rehearsal completed, the boys called one final time. The answer was the same.

After that much-repeated bedtime prayer request was said for the last time and the boys were sound asleep, I decided to put in one more long-distance call. I told their father how important his coming was to the boys because they desperately wanted *both* parents to share the event with them. I reminded him that it was a once-in-a-lifetime experience. But I too received the same answer—too busy! That night, alone in my bedroom with tears streaming down my face, I begged God for a miracle. "Please, Lord, work this one for the boys."

The next night before eating supper, two hours before the school play would begin, we made the final prayer request, though we knew full well it was too late for Dad to leave and come all that distance. But as we were eating, a car came purring up our country drive. The boys leaped up, raced out the door, and flew down the stairs, hollering, "We knew you'd come! We knew you'd come!"

After things settled down, I asked Dad what had happened.

"Well, when I got up this morning," he said, "it seemed that something said to me that I should just get in the car and go."

"That something was Someone," I told him, "because we've been praying for weeks."

Not only did this experience teach me the value of persistent prayer, it also gave my sons faith in God, who really hears and answers prayer. JUDITH STETSON CRABB

AUGUST 26

Prophet Despite Her Burdened Life

Those who oppose the Lord will be shattered. 1 Sam. 2:10, NIV.

Hannah was a woman like most of us, desiring to be loved and understood, trying her best to relate to others, but also facing frustrations, misunderstandings, and loneliness. Even among family and friends.

She wished Elkanah had better defended her against Peninnah's provocations. She had expected him to listen attentively. She didn't want endless questioning nor expect ready-made solutions to her pain. Secretly, she had hoped to pray with him in the temple, and not facing by herself Eli's unjust accusations.

Hannah was living like many of us, desiring real dialogues, sensitive understanding, and nurturing relationships. We may wonder if she ever reached that point, because after having brought Samuel to Shiloh with her husband, we read that Elkanah went home to Ramah (verse 11). The dramatic silence over Hannah's name at that point may very well suggest a painful separation. Eventually it did not last (verse 20), but it surely brought its share of stress into her life. What is so remarkable and worthy of notice was Hannah's continual commitment to prayer in any situation. She knew how to pause and set aside time to rejoice in the Lord. Her struggles with Elkanah and Peninnah, her stress caused by the new baby, his weaning and departure, could not prevent her from praising God and acknowledging His special care for the barren, the needy, and the weak. In the midst of power fights (verse 9) and arrogance (verse 3), she could still thank her Rock to keep her anchored and courageous enough to confront the ones hurting her (verse 1). Her strength was renewed through prayer, giving up control and trusting in a God capable of changing impossible situations.

But the biggest surprise comes at the end of Hannah's prayer.

Suddenly her private devotion engenders the most striking prophecy regarding God's judgment through a King and Anointed. Astonishing insights are revealed to Hannah, not only through her words and her availability in prayer, but also through her very life: the renewed strength received by the Lord to accomplish her daily task will be the same as the one promised to sustain the Anointed in His judging ministry.

Hannah did not need special titles or commission to become God's prophet. By just being herself—her prayer and faith in a Holy One—changed impossible situations. In her quiet time before the Lord, she became the first prophet to announce the Anointed King, long before God's appointed messenger to Eli (verse 35) or king David (Ps. 132:17)!

Did you realize that the earnest prayer of an overwhelmed, burdened woman was sufficient that God gave her a glorious glimpse from the end of redemptive history? Have you ever conceived that your own life, like Hannah's, may become a living parable for our returning Anointed?

Stop and pray today! God has unique messages, experiences and perspectives to share with you! They are broader than you can imagine!   VIVIAN HAENNI

AUGUST 27

Words of Thanks in All Circumstances

Rejoice always, pray constantly, give thanks in all circumstances; for this is the will of God in Christ Jesus for you.
1 Thess. 5:16-18, RSV.

At only 4 years of age Joey had not yet learned to be tactful, to subdue the frightful candor of a child. He had been asked to say the blessing for lunch, but before bowing his head, he scrutinized the dinner table. Evidently what he saw was not to his taste, for Joey folded his hands, closed his eyes, and said matter-of-factly, "Dear Jesus, thank You for this food I don't like."

"Give thanks in all circumstances," we're told. Really? *All* circumstances?

Are we supposed to say "Dear Jesus, thank You for this car accident I don't like" or "Dear Jesus, thank You for this disease I don't like" or "Dear Jesus, thank You for my friend's death I don't like"?

"Give thanks in all circumstances," we're admonished. What do these words mean?

Another dinner table, another meal. This time an 18-year-old college student. Don had been invited to lunch, a wholesome, even tasty, but informally served buffet. He picked up his plate and joined the line moving around the table. Since I was the hostess, waiting until every guest had gotten food, I noticed that Don hadn't put one serving of anything on his dish, but he walked slowly around the table, checking all the options. Completing the circle and—obviously—his personal assessment of the menu, he handed me his still-empty plate. Then he turned to a friend, saying loudly, "Hey, let's go to a restaurant and get some good food to eat." And with hardly a goodbye, they left.

I excused his discourteous behavior to his not liking my vegetarian fare. Someone who knew him well wasn't so charitable. "He's been rude for all the years I've known him. You'd understand if you knew his parents. They always gave him anything he wanted. He's an 18-year-old spoiled child who needs to grow up!"

Give thanks in all circumstances? Thank you for this food I don't like? Must we pretend to be thankful even when we aren't? The rude, ungrateful response of the spoiled 18-year-old is not acceptable, either. Just how are we to respond to that admonition?

The answer lies in attitude, an attitude of confidence, not that God desired life's tragedies, but that God will somehow work them ultimately for our good. A key to the text's meaning lies in all three commands: to rejoice always, to pray constantly, and to give thanks in all circumstances. All three suggest an attitude of continuing trust. Besides, it may be significant that the text says to give thanks *in* all circumstances, not *for* all circumstances.

"This command is an assurance that even the things which appear to be against us will work for our good. God would not bid us be thankful for that which would do us harm" (*The Ministry of Healing*, p. 255).

WILMA McCLARTY

AUGUST 28

My Magnificent Friend

Greater love has no one than this, that he lay down his life for his friends. You are my friends if you do what I command. I no longer call you servants, because a servant does not know his master's business. Instead, I have called you friends, for everything that I learned from my Father I have made known to you. John 15:13-15, NIV.

While doing graduate studies at Andrews University, I felt my energy waning because of the hard work and intense thinking. At times I thought I'd never complete my degree. But then I'd think, *How can I give up when I know that Jesus has always come through for me?* I struggled in prayer, notes beside me, hoping to get a high grade in order to keep the required GPA, and Jesus never failed me. "He did it again," I'd say. I left my last class holding my grade and giving Him thanks.

Then came my comprehensive exam. I studied hard, but doubt hung over me like a cloud. I felt literally overwhelmed with fear. Like the disciples who hung on for dear life and cried out to Jesus when the angry storm tossed their boat, so I cried and reached for Him in the dark. He gave me strength to take the exam, and the Holy Spirit brought to my remembrance all the subjects I had studied. But I left that room worrying about the results, and the long wait. I'm so glad that I have a Friend who knows all about me and also understands my inner feelings. I remember praying, loudly telling Him, "I leave it all in Your hands, dear Jesus. You know best."

One afternoon as I knelt praying and crying my heart out, the telephone rang. I picked it up and heard the voice of my dear friend in Jamaica. She called to tell me that she was praying for my success and that Jesus would never fail me. I thanked her through my tears, and as I rose from my knees (you see, I was still kneeling when I reached for the phone), I said aloud, "Thank You, Jesus. You did it again. How foolish I am to doubt Your promises." I thanked Him again and again. I knew in my heart that He would keep His word. The following week I received a letter from the acting assistant of the Department of Education congratulating me for my success on the comprehensive exam. This time I cried for joy and remembered part of a verse from my favorite psalm: "I will lift up mine eyes unto the hills, from whence cometh my help. My help cometh from the Lord, which made heaven and earth" (Ps. 121:1, 2).

When I am tempted to worry and doubt, I remember these circumstances of instant help from Jesus. He is my magnificent Friend. I can understand why the disciple John leaned on His breast, and why Mary poured sweet-smelling perfume on His feet. Her inward feelings of joy were made visible by her tears. *I love Him, too.*   GLORIA C. MCLAREN

Under the Lacquer

Search me, O God, and know my heart: . . . see if there be any wicked way in me. Ps. 139:23, 24.

One of my most startling and painful lessons learned in adult life was that Christians who *say* humble things may not necessarily *be* humble. *Saying* is not the same as *being*. With practice, one can pass self-effacing comments in a soft-spoken manner that will appeal to the deepest spiritual convictions in another. Since pride is the archetypal sin, then the apparent absence of pride is easily perceived as pure sainthood.

How bereaved we feel when we must face that we have been betrayed by a friend's superficial humility!

Not only is it difficult to discern whether a person is acting from pride or humility, but it is difficult also to know in ourselves. To illustrate, I recently had the "privilege" of refinishing the resonators on my marimba. With sandpaper and steel wool I stripped the existing finish down to the bare metal and then sprayed the pipes bright metallic gold. All my work looked beautifully ready for the finishing touch—the lacquer.

But, oh! The touch of the lacquer! Every uneven circle I had made with the steel wool showed right up through the overlapping strokes (also showing) of the spray paint. Every muscle movement I had made during the past 24 hours was now glazed—mirrored back to me by the sun hitting the lacquer.

I leaned back against the house and let the lesson have its way. We work and work on ourselves, scraping off our sins and pride, quite pleased with the golden refinishing we have done on ourselves. Then we come to Jesus in prayer, quite sure that He will find only what is precious, genuine, and humble.

But alas, prayer is like the lacquer. Heaven's light shines on us, and that which was left down under the sandpaper and the new paint is mirrored back to us. Under it all some hateful pride still remains. Only the light from Jesus can show us where it still is.

Under this intense examination by the Holy Spirit, we learn to despise the pride within ourselves as much as we despise it in others, especially when we recognize the outgrowths that come with it: pride and competition, pride and materialism, pride and selfishness, pride and jealousy, pride and dominance. We would wallow in these sins forever were it not for the Holy Spirit to convict us and plant the longing to change.

Our prayer is, "Spirit of the living God, fall afresh on us. Break us, melt us, mold us, and fill us. We will not rest until we find our rest in Thee."

JANET KANGAS

AUGUST 30

That Great Noise

When the trumpets sounded, the people shouted, and at the sound of the trumpet, when the people gave a loud shout, the wall collapsed; so every man charged straight in, and they took the city. Josh. 6:20, NIV.

On a rainy evening, before going to bed, my youngest son and I prayed and invited the Lord to take care of us as we slept. My pastor husband was away from home.

About 1:45 a.m. I woke up and prayed again. It was unusually quiet at that time. While I was dozing back to sleep, I saw a light shining through my window. I jerked awake and listened to voices outside. I then heard a hammering noise. Peering through the side of the window, I saw two men standing and a third man working on the garage door, trying to force it open. I did not know what to do. If I phoned, the police might come too late. If I shouted, they would know my husband wasn't at home, so would continue with their mischief. These thoughts and more tumbled in my mind.

I went to my young son's bedroom and woke him up, and we prayed to God to give us a plan to frighten away the intruders. He was only 9 years old and his voice was not much different from mine, so he wouldn't have been much help. Going to the bathroom, I looked around in the semidarkness and saw a detergent bottle. Suddenly I remembered the story of the fall of Jericho.

Then I said quietly, "Lord, please make this noise sound so loud that it scares these men away." I then banged the bottle on the plastic basin. *Bang! Bang! Bang!* Then I went to look. All was quiet and the men were gone. That simple noise scared them away—at least for that night. I don't know how it sounded in their ears. All I know is that it scared them away. That experience made an impression on me and my son, and I still praise God for it.

"God is our refuge and strength, a very present help in trouble" (Ps. 46:1).

ELIZABETH MABENA

AUGUST 31

Remember Jesus

Then Nebuchadnezzar was furious with Shadrach, Meshach and Abednego. . . . He ordered the furnace heated seven times hotter than usual. . . . The king's command was so urgent and the furnace so hot that the flames of the fire killed the soldiers who took up Shadrach, Meshach and Abednego. Dan. 3:19-22, NIV.

Father was a mission director, and one of his many jobs and responsibilities was to build a school building. It would be fairly large, with six classrooms and four offices. Now, in faraway places, in years gone by, one began building a school, a church, or a house by making the bricks. To make the bricks, one began by finding the clay, usually in a valley. The clay must be dug out. Then many feet stomped it with just the right amount of water. Finally the mixture was poured into brick molds, usually three bricks to a mold, and turned out on straw to dry under cover for a few days. Then came the arduous task of carrying the bricks up the mountain and building the kilns. With much manpower but no machinery, all this was just plain hard work.

Day after day I watched the various procedures, marveling that Father knew so much about building. But it was the brick kilns that fascinated me. Each kiln held an incredible number of bricks, and each brick had to be stacked just right to make the right shape. Care had to be taken that there was just the right amount of space between the bricks so the fire could get all the way to the top. Fire wood was collected in large stacks—enough to burn vigorously day and night for a week.

The burning of the kiln was vitally important to harden the bricks for permanent strength. Fires were started in each fire eye on ground level, and stoked until little flames curled out on top of the eight-foot-high kiln. By then the bricks were glowing white, and I couldn't get very near because of the heat.

"Daddy, is this what the fire was like when Shadrach, Meshach, and Abednego were thrown into the furnace?" I asked him.

"Yes. Perhaps the furnace was even hotter."

"Then they must really have loved Jesus to be willing to be thrown in there."

"If you love Jesus," Father told me, "then you can face the fire. Remember, Jesus was in the fire with them."

Life can cover us in a fire of affliction or despair or worry.

When that happens, remember Jesus. And know that "when thou walkest through the fire, thou shalt not be burned; neither shall the flame kindle upon thee. For I am the Lord thy God" (Isa. 43:2, 3).

CAROL BRADFIELD

SEPTEMBER 1

Best Friendship

But Ruth replied, "Don't urge me to leave you or to turn back from you. Where you go I will go, and where you stay, I will stay. Your people shall be my people and your God my God." Ruth 1:16, NIV.

This portion of Scripture is often used to describe a commitment of love between a man and a woman. In fact, many romantic hearts envision a couple standing at the altar, using these words to pledge unfailing love for each other. Upon closer inspection, however, we see that these were not words spoken between a man and a woman but words spoken woman to woman. This was a promise, a pledge of unfailing, committed, loyal, self-sacrificing, and unwavering love for a mother-in-law, a woman named Naomi. Ruth's proclamation is a formula for "best friendship."

Friendship, "woman to woman," is a precious gift, and females have a unique capacity for initiating, nurturing, and maintaining this wonderful experience of sisterhood. I have always cherished my friends. My earliest concept of friendship was that of my best friend, with whom I could laugh and giggle, play hopscotch and jacks, share secrets, and feel comfortable with in any situation. With maturity I have come to recognize that what is most compelling in these special relationships is the knowledge of "whither thou goest, I will go." These are the friends who call to see how I have survived the latest crises, who remain "connected" even when miles separate, and who continue to be best friends even when I am not.

Ruth's promise meant that she would remain close to Naomi's side and would not leave her in spite of Naomi's rejection, protesting, and seeming aloofness. Ruth's commitment to her mother-in-law friend was not dependent on reciprocation of friendship, but rather was a pledge of unconditional love and support for her friend, her mother-in-law. The test of "best friendship" is unconditional love.

Ruth's love was inclusive, for she said, "Your people shall be my people." Ruth loved Naomi, and therefore without question she embraced Naomi's people. The beauty of friendship blessed of God is that it is inclusive rather than exclusive. The boundaries of Christian "best friendship" are not rigid, but flexible, open, and welcoming.

Finally, Ruth said to Naomi, "Your God [shall be] my God." The final test of "best friendship" is the spiritual direction the relationship leads you. Best friends will share their faith with each other. They will comfort and admonish each other with the Word. Best friends are looking for permanent relationships, the kind that will continue on the earth made new. How does your "best friendship" measure up? BARBARA TOBIAS

SEPTEMBER 2

Are You Fun to Live With?

A cheerful heart is good medicine, but a crushed spirit dries up the bones. Prov. 17:22, NIV.

Have you brought something into your relationship lately that was interesting, challenging, creative, or delightful? "Life is a lively process of becoming," Gen. Douglas MacArthur said. "If you haven't added to your interest during the past year—if you are thinking the same thoughts, relating the same personal experiences, having the same predictable reactions—rigor mortis of the personality has set in."

When was the last time you enjoyed a good laugh? Laughter relieves tension. Most of us don't smile or laugh enough. It's conceded that Richard Nixon lost the 1960 presidential election partly because of his dour facial expressions. During the 1968 presidential campaign he was rarely seen in a photo or on television without smiling, and he was successful. Yes, people respond favorably to smiles and laughter.

A smile sets the tempo for the day. It determines how family members will feel throughout the day. It gives assurance that everything is going well. Frowns and worried facial expressions give the impression that something is wrong.

Laughter is a powerful tranquilizer for problems. When a person learns to laugh and make merry over mistakes, a wonderful transformation takes place. Heaven sends cleanup squads that respond to these signals and sweep away the broken pieces, giving relationships a fresh beginning.

A smile is a way of writing your thoughts on your face. It is a way of telling others that they are appreciated, accepted, and liked. And when you begin smiling, you will find others smiling back.

No other gift gives so much enjoyment as inexpensively as a smile. Make today a happy day for yourself, your mate, your family. Come up with a surprise. Share a funny story. Plan ahead for a special occasion. Laugh a little. Take time to play. Find a way to have fun with your mate. Make your family life as happy and enjoyable as possible. NANCY VAN PELT

SEPTEMBER 3

The Gift That Doesn't Break

At that time Mary got ready and hurried to a town in the hill country of Judah, where she entered Zechariah's home and greeted Elizabeth. Luke 1:39, 40, NIV.

In marriage and in society men and women struggle to understand each other. It's been said that men feel completely relaxed only when with each other and completely away from women. It's also true that there is a circuit of empathy and support between women that men neither suspect nor fathom.

Frankly, when I was younger I preferred the company of men. Not romantically. At dinner parties I found I gravitated naturally to a group of men. I found their conversation and philosophizing far more interesting than the banter of women about their daily relationships. I often felt that many women were shallow and superficial.

The years have taught me my own superficiality. I have come to appreciate the company of women. I've realized that all the philosophizing in the world cannot compare to the superior practicality of hope, faith, and love in human relationships. And many women excel in relationships. They possess a certain intuition found less frequently among men. I find that there is a richness of experience that develops among women because of this great facility in relationships. Men are still fascinating, but I have come to love the wisdom of women.

In the story of the Annunciation, we're not told how Joseph responded to the first angelic message to Mary that she was soon to be the mother of the Lord. It took another visit to reassure him. But we are told that at that time Mary hurried to tell Elizabeth. She knew instinctively that with her cousin she would receive acceptance, joy, belief, and sympathy in the manner that only women can give.

The love of men and women for their children is, as a generalization, different. Though there are, of course, bad mothers, a woman's love is more unconditional. It acts as a cushion and protection from the vicissitudes of life. Whoever else may taunt and tease their offspring, that child can knowingly come home to the harbor of his or her mother's love. Other children may ridicule them. Teachers may be cruel. Still, their mother is there to love, accept, and value them as they are—no matter what.

The world outside is a difficult place. It rarely treats grown or even growing children as a mother would. So a man's love reflects more of the realities of the outside world. It is a tougher love, more demanding, more performance-based, with higher expectations. Children need that masculine discipline in order to face a cruel and competitive world outside. Without it, they may face life naively and with constant trepidation. Protected by a mother's love, they may find themselves, as it were, wrapped in cotton wool, unprepared for the jungle of modern life.

However, let's not underestimate this wonderful gift of unconditional love that God has given women. It is only a reflection, a thread of God's love for humanity. But God has put into a woman's nature the ability to reach out, love, and accept in a way that is rich and beautiful. The world desperately needs women's sympathies. Everywhere one looks, there is corruption and cruelty. Little acts of kindness shine as beads of dazzling light in a midnight world.

O that God might give us a love and empathy for others that will restore a little of His goodness to the earth.　　GILLIAN FORD

SEPTEMBER 4

Stay in the Boat

But with thee will I establish my covenant; and thou shalt come into the ark. Gen. 6:18.

The Week of Prayer speaker in 1953 was giving the adults an illustration that permanently wallpapered itself in my 10-year-old mind. He was relating the critical role of the church in this cataclysmic world in spite of our criticisms of it. He paralleled the saving church with the saving ark built by Noah.

Within that ark were a lot of problems the family could have complained about:

- It was crowded.
- The windows were shut, prohibiting ventilation.
- The people, living in each other's teaspoon, got on each other's nerves.
- The animals were smelly and noisy.
- The sameness of the food was boring.

And then the speaker moved in with his question: "But where would you rather have been: in that crowded, boring ark, with all the nerve-racking people and smelly animals—or out there thrashing in the water?"

And so whenever I become somehow disillusioned with the church, feeling crowded or offended by those bumping into me, my mind has returned to that illustration over the years.

I sometimes wonder what might have happened if Noah had had a committee of career people around a table discussing the plans. One materials expert might have begun, "Now, I'm sure God intended the gopher wood to be only symbolic of the best material available. I think we should wait until aluminum is invented."

And a career theologian might project, "It would be impossible to destroy this world in just 40 days, so surely this must be prophetic time. It would be safe to wait for the better materials."

And a futurologist would add, "In that case, then, let's wait for the submarine and the Navy Seals."

And some anthropologist would be sure to add, "It's ridiculous to put the animals in with the people. Instead of one ocean liner, let's build a fleet of smaller vessels: one for people, one for clean animals, one for the unclean, one for food, one for fowl so we don't have them flying at our heads, and of course we'll need one that's just an aquarium for the sea life."

How wonderful it would be in the church today if we could surpass all the committees and receive verbal directions from God. But in spite of jokes about a camel being a horse put together by a committee, church committees do arrive at decisions and accomplish things. The varied suggestions lead them to prayer, patience, and brotherly-sisterly love.

To one independent individual who was sincerely praying to have his own way Ellen White gave this message: "God designed, in His providence, to place you more directly in connection with His church, that your confidence might be less in yourself and greater in others whom He is leading out to advance His work" (*Testimonies*, vol. 3, p. 416).

She continued, "Angels of God will work with your efforts when you are humble and little in your own eyes. But when you think you know more than those whom God has been leading for years, and whom He has been instructing in the truth and fitting for the extension of His work, you are self-exalted and will fall into temptations" (*ibid*., p. 417).

H.M.S. Richards, Sr., when informed in his latter days about various financial and theological problems within the church, also made a reference to a boat, this time symbolic. He said, "Brethren, sisters, stay in the boat. We're almost to the other side. We've only a little way to go.

"Stay in the boat."   JANET KANGAS

Sonny

And after he became the father of Methuselah, Enoch walked with God. Gen. 5:22, NIV.

Dear little Sonny,
If ever you are able to read this and understand, then there has truly been a miracle in your life. Mommies somehow know when their children are blessed, and you, little Sonny, are a rare gift.

Several months before you were born, while on my knees scrubbing the kitchen floor, I felt in my heart all wasn't quite right; it was then I asked Jesus to guide my life. Soon many tears would flow, because mommies and daddies love their babies so. It's their overwhelming desire to mold and shape a perfect little life; but first there must be a little mind that works right.

What a surprise—it's through you, Sonny, that the Holy Spirit has molded and reshaped our lives. And when it's time and Jesus places that little crown upon your head, please, Lord, let there be three special jewels adorning it: one for Daddy, one for Mommy, and one for sister, too.

Sonny's Mommy   DEBORAH SANDERS

Your Touch

Her children arise up, and call her blessed. Prov. 31:28.

Throughout my life
there have been many times
when your touch
made things right.

In the stillness of the moment
as I lay there in pain
before the precious birth of my children,
it was your touch that gave me strength.

When tears stained my mourning face
and my grief I could barely contain,
it was your touch that held me together
and eased my mental pain.

There's something special in your touch
that I desperately need and desire.
It's God's love flowing pure and free
between my blessed mother and her daughter.

DEBORAH SANDERS

SEPTEMBER 7

On Painting Grass Cloth

Your word is a lamp to my feet and a light to my path. Ps. 119:105, NKJV.

My living and dining rooms were screaming for a face-lift. I had neglected them much too long. For 18 months my priority had been to care for my ailing husband; there was simply no time for domestic cosmetics. And then he was gone.

Instead of moving from my home, I decided to stay on, enjoy my quiet neighborhood, and nurture the landscape we had been developing. Yes, a fresh new look in these two rooms would make me feel better about life in general.

With paint and equipment in hand, I estimated it should take no longer than three hours to paint the two rooms. I began to roll on the new dark paint over the grass cloth wall covering. Up and down, back and forth, diagonally. Press hard. Bear down. The grass cloth sucked up the paint, but worse than that, the underfabric kept showing through. The rebellious flax fiber resisted new color. Press hard. Bear down. Vertically, horizontally, diagonally. Keep going!

Twelve painful hours later I had covered both rooms. I considered myself a good painter, but no job had ever taken me that long to cover. Tense muscles, throbbing shoulders, sore back—I questioned my priorities. Still, at midnight the walls looked splendid. It was worth it.

Day dawned. I hurried downstairs to revel in my latest accomplishment. In bright morning sunlight it looked even lovelier than the night before. Soon I'd have the new furniture in place and life could go on. On close inspection, however, I found scores of spots where the underfabric peeked through, revealing the original color. This would never do. I was grateful for the accusing finger of strong sunlight. Without it I would never have seen those spots.

By the time I finished, the afternoon sun was streaming in through the windows on the other side of the rooms. I stepped back to relish the project, to savor its beauty with light from a different angle. Oh, no! More spots. Would I ever get them all? If strong light was the trick, I'd get an extension light with 150 watts. On and on I worked. The stronger light revealed much more than I cared to admit.

Perturbed by the extending time it took to do this project and humiliated at the quality of my paint job, I heard God speak: "My child, can't you see that I've added darkness to your life? Not that I've replaced your sunlight with darkness; you still have the sunlight of My love and all its attendant blessings. But I have added richer, deeper dimensions of beauty. With this darkness that has enveloped you, you'll see beauty you didn't know existed. You'll experience joys you didn't know were possible. Just trust Me.

"Now about those spots, Lorabel, think of this: The imperfections of life can be seen only as you use My Word as your light. You will always need it."

And God was right. Now that I am alone, but not lonely, I see that the more I allow Him to spotlight my imperfections, the deeper understanding I have of His love for me.   LORABEL MIDKIFF

SEPTEMBER 8

Born to Love

That ye love one another; as I have loved you. John 13:34.

Gloria came from Guatemala with her 2-year-old girl, Claudia, to be treated at Miami Children's Hospital. Claudia, her firstborn, was a very beautiful baby—her skin was as creamy as a china doll; her hair was as smooth and wavy as dark-brown silk. But her brain had been injured at birth, and she had frequent convulsions. Although she was otherwise perfect, she couldn't walk or talk. Claudia was a quiet baby that communicated her needs with little noises, and Gloria was a devoted mother who anticipated and provided for all her needs. You never heard her cry.

After the tests were done, the doctor confirmed what we all had been fearing: Claudia was also losing her eyesight.

One day Gloria left me as Claudia's baby-sitter. I had not taken care of her alone before, but because of her condition I was not surprised that she did not respond to me in any way as I bathed and fed her and talked to her. I felt proud that she didn't cry the whole time her mommy was away. However, when her mother came back and Claudia heard her voice, she began to cry immediately. She expressed her love in the only way she could.

Any mother can testify that one of the biggest rewards from her new baby is that very first toothless smile! When baby smiles, coos, and (in Claudia's case) cries in recognition, a mother's love is rewarded.

When does friendship begin for a brand-new human being? It begins developing from the day we are born. We are born to love.

The person who talks to a baby, who feeds and cuddles that baby, and who communicates with that baby every day—"Mommy," "Daddy," or in today's more modern society, "baby-sitter"—is the one who becomes that baby's very first friend.

In the early months a new baby cannot understand love. Even if that were possible, an infant is not capable of responding in a meaningful way. So far he or she is interested only in feeling good—being dry, well fed, and cuddled. The eyes are not fully developed, so an infant cannot focus on the person who day after day feeds, talks to, and smiles at him or her. However, as a baby grows he or she begins to recognize that face and the sound of that voice, and even though the words have no meaning yet, that baby likes to hear "Mom" or "Dad" or "baby-sitter" talking to him or her. And now, every time this special person comes near, the baby follows all that person's movements with great big eyes. From then on, this person has to be careful not to leave the room without bidding "goodbye," or baby will cry. A bond has developed.

As God's children, we need to develop a bond of friendship with Jesus. Like Mary, Martha, and Lazarus, who chose to be friends with Him and opened their home and their hearts to the One who left heaven to be our Best Friend, we too will enjoy the most tender and beautiful friendship.

Sometimes a friendship can develop to the point where silence is understood, but still words of encouragement and genuine love are necessary. God wants us to talk to Him and to listen to Him. Words are a powerful tool; they will greatly influence the lives of others, especially when spoken in love.

"Christ Himself did not suppress one word of truth, but He spoke it always in love. He exercised the greatest tact, and thoughtful, kind attention in His intercourse with the people. He was never rude, never needlessly spoke a severe word, never gave needless pain to a sensitive soul" (*The Desire of Ages*, p. 353).

He invites us to be the extension of His love to befriend the world and tell them that there is no other friend like Him.

"Jesus Christ the same yesterday, and to day, and for ever" (Heb. 13:8).   RAQUEL HAYLOCK

Longing for Togetherness

How often I have longed to gather your children together, as a hen gathers her chicks under her wings. Matt. 23:37, NIV.

This afternoon I've indulged in the luxury of memories as I've been cleaning and reorganizing our house. Just a few short days ago our four children, their spouses, and our three grandchildren shared family fun times together here with us. Now, although we're widely scattered to the four corners of the earth—Sudan, Guam, Kenya, and Minnesota—we are unremittingly bound together by the bonds of family love.

Around our home many visual reminders of their visit teased my emotions. Much, of course, related to our two granddaughters, Evie and Caroline. There were pictures traced and colored; berets and ponytail rubber bands under the beds; teddy bears stuffed in baskets; a jar with a perforated lid for catching fireflies; a doll with a broken leg, and various collections of doll clothes and dishes. All are picked up now, and our house is in order once again. The dolls and stuffed animals sleep undisturbed in the cradle; the tiny tea set of dishes is stored neatly in the corner cupboard; fingerprints have been removed from the sliding-glass door, and no dust specks cover the furniture.

Now our home will retain a semblance of order again for a time. But our hearts will be partially empty. This afternoon my husband and I walked past duck ponds near our home, and as we passed the swing and slide set we could almost hear our 5-year-old Evie shouting with excitement, "Please push me, Grandpa! Faster . . . faster . . . faster . . . higher . . . higher!" For some strange reason today I didn't even think to take bread along to feed the ducks—in my mind, that seems to be a special ritual for children only!

Our two younger sons and their wives left some weeks ago for their mission posts in Guam and Kenya, and now as our oldest son and his family returned this week to begin their second term of overseas service in Sudan, my thoughts have been ambivalent. Our family numbers on this continent are dwindling. It may be several years until we can all gather together again. I've felt twinges of jealousy for mothers who have their children and grandchildren nearby. My arms often ache to hold the little ones. Instinctively my mind has relived much of former years. I remember when each of my children was a babe in arms, and my mother prayers ascended pleading with God to help these little ones grow in His grace and be workers for Him in whatever vineyard He chose. My prayers were heard and answered. Why should I be sad?

Now I can better understand the words of Jesus when with aching heart He spoke of His beloved Jerusalem: "How often I have longed to gather your children together, as a hen gathers her chicks under her wings." And His heart is still aching, waiting for His children to be gathered home!   YVONNE MINCHIN DYSINGER

SEPTEMBER 10

The Whole World

The earth is the Lord's, and everything in it, the world, and all who live in it. Ps. 24:1, NIV.

I was on my way to speak at an eighth-grade graduation in a small church school in central Pennsylvania. My 4-year-old granddaughter, Tammy, accompanied me because I had forgotten about this appointment when I had agreed to baby-sit for her working parents that same evening.

It was a two-hour drive from home, and I knew Tammy would be restless if we didn't stop along the way. Just as we neared the town, I saw a sign that read "Scenic View Ahead" and decided that would be just the place to stop for a few minutes so the already restless child could move about before being confined to a church pew for another hour.

I pulled off the highway, and we got out of the car. We walked over to the chain-link fence that would keep us safe while we looked down on the Susquehanna River and the little town that cuddled up to its bank. "That's where we're going, Tammy. We'll be there soon," I explained.

Her little face turned up to mine with a wondrous question in her eyes.

"See," I explained, pointing off to the right. "Look over there. That's the church. We'll be there soon."

She said nothing, but turned back to the view—breathtaking by any standard. We stood in silence for several minutes. Finally she turned to me and said in childish awe, "Gramma, it's just like God! You can see the whole world from up here!"

Somehow her little 4-year-old mind had grasped a concept that we had talked about, but had never made sense to her before: God *can* see us, and He watches over us, no matter where we are.

Now a grown young woman in college, Tammy doesn't

300

remember much of that day we spent together. But that's all right, because she *does* remember that God watches over her no matter where in "the whole world" she goes. The experience may be forgotten, but the lesson lives on. What more could a grandmother ask?   PATRICIA A. HABADA

Servanthood

He that is called, being free, is Christ's servant. 1 Cor. 7:22.

As new missionaries, we received much advice about servants. They could steal, talk about us, destroy our privacy.

Then Yun-ssi came to our home for six years. From this little woman who'd never attended school I learned about servanthood.

Yun-ssi apologized for knowing no English. We told her, "It's better that way. You help us learn Korean." Thus, when one of our children requested a drink, Yun-ssi repeated the Korean equivalent in a singsong, refusing to comply until asked in Korean. Outside, she made a game of counting fenceposts. Cooking, she talked as the children helped. When we didn't understand, she rephrased until we did. She explained Korean culture and interceded for us when we'd goofed.

If dishes broke, Yun-ssi simply told me. Never did she take anything of ours, though our home must have seemed vastly wealthy.

Unpleasant and routine tasks became her ministry. When the electricity failed, she laundered in the creek. She scrubbed our vinyl floors daily to remove the soot. Even after days without running water she cleaned out the toilet cheerfully.

Paul's stuffed basset hound, whose tail got stroked during naptime thumbsucking, eventually had more new than original threads in its bare "skin." Yun-ssi thus spared our family an unthinkable crisis.

Yun-ssi was always there, the work always done. If she wasn't sure how something worked, she asked. She didn't put poultry seasoning in the apple pie, or use a whole can of imported wax on the floor at once, as did some.

Her faith was simple, personal, real. She pored over her Bible daily, to read "my Jesus' very words to me," though she'd had only a few childhood reading lessons from a venerable teacher. Her mother had said, "You must learn to read, even though you're a girl."

When our family dragged in late on Saturday nights from missionary socials, hot chocolate awaited us. When we left for furlough during monsoon season with a baby with dysentery, Yun-ssi ironed the diapers dry. When we returned, she couldn't leave her current employer; but every few weeks, after a full day's work, she'd come out by bus—and wash dishes and make cookies as we talked.

Shortly before we left Korea, Yun-ssi saw me and explained, "I won't come to the airport, because I'd cry." As she spoke, tears began—and evolved into racking sobs. As she pulled off a sock to stanch the flow, I handed her a wrinkled handkerchief and assured her I'd understand. But at the airport she tucked the laundered hankie into my hand and followed as far as permitted, tears mingling with hugs.

None of us ever doubted that Yun-ssi would have died for us gladly. Hers was real love, real servanthood, real ministry.

Yun-ssi stood in good company. The New Testament alone lists Paul, Timothy, Titus, Moses, James, Peter, Jude, and John as servants of Christ—who Himself took "the form of a servant" (Phil. 2:7). I hope someday to hear, with Yun-ssi, "Well done, my good and trusty servant" (Matt. 25:21, NEB).

MADELINE S. JOHNSTON

SEPTEMBER 12

The Women Who Stayed at the Cross

The women who had come with Jesus from Galilee followed Joseph and saw the tomb and how His body was laid in it. Luke 23:55, NIV.

There were women who had come with Jesus at this impossibly cruel time in His life. Why had they not deserted Him as so many others had; why had they not saved themselves the horror of watching Him die? I believe there were at least two reasons. Of course they loved Him; they could not bear to let Him go until they had to. But they also came because they wanted to provide comfort for Him. They wanted to nurture Him.

Women are nurturing creatures; it is a God-given trait. Sometimes we call it the mothering instinct. We must cuddle the crying child; we must comfort the hurting; we must pour forth love, even from afar. I can picture them there, huddled together, heads covered modestly as custom demanded, tear-washed faces lifted to Jesus. How terrified they must have been when all nature rebelled at the scene, and even the sun gave no light for three long hours! Perhaps they struggled to steady their voices as they called words of love and comfort to Him. Perhaps they prayed constantly for strength and grace to endure what appeared to be a monumental loss. Perhaps their hearts were torn within them and their agony erupted in soul-wrenching sobs. But they stayed. They loved Him, and they stayed.

Joyce Huggett, in *The Joy of Listening to God*, says, "There seems to be a law which links the awareness of God's presence with surrender to Him." Surely their need to nurture and comfort was forever coupled with their need to see Him, to surrender their lives to Him, perhaps *for* Him if necessary.

"As I open my life in total surrender to God, the limitless power of the Holy Spirit enables me to really live for God in gladness and true success" (Garrie Williams, *How to Be Filled With the Holy Spirit—And Know It*, p. 70).

Jesus said, "Abide with Me." He said, "Follow Me." Those women chose to do just that, to be with Him, knowing that their personal cost was as nothing compared to the privilege of His presence. How do you choose today? Let us, as women, choose to follow Jesus. LEA HARDY

SEPTEMBER 13

The Lady

Then children were brought to him that he might lay his hands on them and pray. The disciples rebuked the people; but Jesus said, "Let the children come to me, and do not hinder them; for to such belongs the kingdom of heaven." Matt. 19:13, 14, RSV.

I saw him out of the corner of my eye as I drove past. He looked to be about 7 years old and wore an oversized T-shirt that hung halfway to his knees. Beside him stood a little girl about 5 years old. They were both waving their arms wildly, as if to get me to stop for something. I watched them in my rearview mirror. As I passed, their faces fell and their arms dropped to their sides as they turned and walked to a small table beside the road. Then I saw it—the telltale sign. A pitcher of juice sat on the table. Through my mind raced memories of when I was a child and how my younger sister and I set up a lemonade stand in front of our house. We sold each cup for

5 cents. Life was simple then, and joy was easy to come by. Failure wasn't even an option. As long as someone bought lemonade, our venture was successful. Our faith was invincible. We had the best lemonade around because "our mother made it." God? He was someone who stayed at the lemonade stand with us as we sold lemonade. The only disappointment was over cars that passed without stopping. My decision was made. I made a U-turn and drove back to the corner where I had seen the kids. The little girl began jumping up and down as she saw me get out of the car and walk toward them. Then she ran to a nearby house.

The boy spoke up. "She's running in to tell her mom that you stopped. You want to buy some lemonade?"

"How much?" I asked.

The boy grinned with confidence. "Twenty-five cents."

I was somewhat amazed by what inflation had done to a cup of juice, but I managed to say, "I'll take a cup."

Eager to fulfill the order, the boy began searching for a clean cup. Finally he found the whole stack rolling around under the table on the sidewalk. "Must have rolled off," he said.

Without any apology for the decreased cleanliness of the cup, he filled it with juice. It was a hot afternoon, so I drank it as soon as he handed it to me. He watched in expectation. Much to my disappointment, it was all I could do to keep it down. Evidently it had been sitting outside for a while and had gotten warm. And someone had forgotten the sugar. I'm sure my face must have revealed these facts, but he took no notice.

"Here," he said, "you might want to buy one of these." He pointed to a basket filled with folded-up yellow pieces of paper. "We made 120 of them, and we still have 120 left. We haven't sold a one, but I bet you would like one." He pulled one out of the basket, took the rubber band off, and unfolded it to look like an accordion. "These are to hang on your ceiling when you have a party."

"How much?" I asked as I tried to imagine them hanging from my ceiling.

He looked shocked. "Oh, um, 10 cents." Then I noticed his face turning red. "I just now came up with that price," he said, and then hesitated. "It's not a real bargain. They're only worth a penny." He smiled sheepishly, his brown eyes staring into mine.

I liked his honesty.

"I'll take two at the original price," I said in a businesslike manner.

"Two?" He seemed dumbfounded.

I paid for the two little yellow accordion papers and walked to my car. I noticed the boy running toward the house to meet the little girl coming out. "The lady just bought two of our yellow accordions!" he shouted.

My hand tightened around the folded-up pieces of paper in my hand. The lady. He had called me "the lady." He was too young to understand that "the lady" was also a child and that no matter how old she might become, she would always make room in her life for a cup of lemonade from a roadside stand and all that it represented.

CARLA GOBER

SEPTEMBER 14

Choosing Contentment

I have learned, in whatsoever state I am, therewith to be content. Phil. 4:11.

I've struggled with the message of this text for many years, especially this past year. I've wanted to be content in my circumstances just as Paul says he felt content in his particular circumstances, but I must admit I'm still working on it. I haven't arrived as yet!

My husband does a lot of traveling, and I spend much time alone. I've moved frequently from country to country and city to city. I've had to make new friends, say goodbye to old ones, redecorate innumerable houses of all sizes and shapes, and try to find my way around new communities and neighborhoods.

I've wrestled with moving vans, boxes, barrels, crates, scratched furniture, and broken dishes, and adjusted to different congregations, schools, doctors, and well-meaning individuals who "just want to fill me in" on our new church or responsibilities. It's a real struggle to find contentment deep inside amid these changing circumstances. Contentment isn't always easy to achieve. There is a list of "if onlies" I rehearse from time to time. You know what I mean: "I would be content if only I could live somewhere else." Or "I would be content if only I could lose 10 pounds." And the list goes on.

However, when I read Philippians 4:11, I realize Paul is right. He learned that contentment is not dependent upon circumstances, that circumstances do not have to control us. He knew contentment is a state of mind, a gift of God, a *choice*. It comes with a deep, constant, and growing relationship with my Lord Jesus Christ. I can truly be content only by resting in Jesus, fully trusting Him to do what is best for me.

That's the kind of contentment I want, because I realize that contentment is not an option for the Christian. It is a must. It is only

305

by having contentment and peace in my life that I can reflect His love and goodness to others.

God created a lovely, white, delicately sculptured shell to illustrate this idea to me. This shell has the lovely name of angel wing because opened and laid flat, the two sides of this shell look like the wings of an angel. Where do you suppose this lovely shell lives? In the pure white sands of some tropical heaven? No! Does it move through the sea with speed and freedom, amazing all who gaze upon it? No! It lives elbow-deep in gray, gooey mud flats in Florida. In a lifetime it never sees the sky or the sun. It never leaves the hole that encases it. Only the determined shell enthusiast discovers and sees its delicate beauty.

To live, the angel wing must send a long, soft, flexible, soda straw-like siphon up through the mud into the water above. The tip of the siphon draws in food, and thus the angel wing thrives and builds its remarkable beauty. It doesn't complain or try to change its circumstances, but lives quietly and peaceably in the unusual place where the Creator placed it.

By God's grace I choose to be content in whatever location and circumstances my Creator places me. I want to be like the old Puritan who sat down to a scanty meal of bread and water. His contented heart cried out, "What? All this and Jesus Christ, too!"

ANITA FOLKENBERG

SEPTEMBER 15

Tainted Lady

Wherefore I say unto thee, Her sins, which are many, are forgiven; for she loved much: but to whom little is forgiven, the same loveth little. Luke 7:47.

I spent last evening with a modern "woman at the well." She is as soiled, fallen, and, to casual eyes, as unworthy as the Samaritan woman—four failed marriages, four ex-husbands, an assortment of children, a focus of gossip and rejection.

But when a tired, thirsty Jesus stopped at the well in Samaria, He saw something else—a priceless human soul. He gave her His full attention. Her warm heart and sprouting faith gave Him the refreshment He needed. Her spontaneous enthusiasm and joy drew her whole village to the One who could supply Living Water. Jesus saw her potential and helped her connect with it. From that moment her life mattered, and has continued to matter for nearly 2,000 years.

My "tainted lady" radiates a degree of caring and sensitivity rarely encountered in today's world. When no one else thought of it, she included my ill and depressed son and my widowed self at her Christmas dinner table. When my son died, she ministered to me with a depth of compassion and insight I had never before experienced.

We pray often together. She talks to God as to a cherished father, with intimate loving expressions that help me feel His presence beside me and His arms around me.

I am not surprised. My friend's closeness to her heavenly Father, and her level of confidence and trust in Him have been refined over long years in the furnace fires of suffering and affliction. She is forgiven. She is reborn. She and Jesus walk together every day. That relationship shines on me—makes me a better person.

I know why certain "tainted ladies" were special to Jesus. They understood love. AILEEN LUDINGTON

SEPTEMBER 16

Slow the Pace

Have no anxiety about anything, but in everything by prayer and supplication with thanksgiving let your requests be made known to God. Phil. 4:6, RSV.

I made no pretense about knowing all there is to know about parenting. But I have learned from my years of working with families that happy family members must basically enjoy one another. I thank God for the fun times Harry and I have enjoyed with our children.

Birthday celebrations, camping trips, family worship, and picnics in the mountains were all repeated until they became traditions. Such traditions evoke a sense of belonging and closeness. A family does not consist of loners who share only a roof. Family members must intimately share activities that build a fond heritage of memories. Each family needs characteristics, values, and activities that mark it as unique and different.

It's time to slow the pace. Forget the carpeting, or the furniture for your redecorating project. Put into second place the materialistic things you want to give your child. Your child doesn't need things as much as he or she needs you. Your children need that personal investment of precious time that only you can provide.

This spirit of fun and creativity must have rubbed off on our children, because on one anniversary they surprised us with an unannounced party. The house was packed with guests whom our children had chosen and invited. We participated in a delightful evening of games, food, and music. Even a recording of our wedding was played for guests. The climax of the evening occurred when our three youngsters presented us with a letter along with some money they had collected among themselves to send us on a second honeymoon! What precious memories of fun times we now cherish as we look back upon the days when our family was all together!

Take time for a hand-in-hand nature walk, and answer your child's questions about God's creation. Take time to observe the delight on your child's face as you fly kites, watching them race and dance on the wings of the wind. Take time to listen to your child now, for tomorrow he or she may not wish to talk. Take time today, for tomorrow carries no guarantees.   NANCY VAN PELT

SEPTEMBER 17

Double Delight

In thy presence is fulness of joy; at thy right hand there are pleasures for evermore. Ps. 16:11.

Are you acquainted with the lovely rose called Double Delight? It is so named because of its unusual beauty and exotic fragrance. We have enjoyed such a bush of that variety in our home garden. Often when I pick a fresh blossom to grace our table, I breathe a little prayer that I might bring double joy to someone that day. Then I am reminded of our text for today. Only as I abide in the presence of my Creator can I be blessed with joy and inner pleasure. I must be filled before I can overflow.

Other double delights come to us in small or large surprises. When you need a friend, the telephone rings or the mail comes bearing good news. It is then a happy time to stop and praise God for these special joys and answers to our prayers. I want to share with Him these double delights.

In the hospital where I once worked I observed a new nurse serving the patients. At first you couldn't help noticing her rather disfigured face, but before long she became a double delight to know. Her smile was contagious, her words full of cheer. She had learned the true beauty of unselfish service and the secret of abiding in Christ. Refreshed in her presence, I was always pleased to see her, and was sad when she moved to another hospital in a faraway state.

Psalm 37:4 seems an appropriate way to close this reading: "Delight thyself also in the Lord; and he shall give thee the desires of thine heart." EVELYN DELAFIELD

People in the Book of Life

I urge Euodia and I urge Syntyche to live in harmony in the Lord. Indeed, true comrade, I ask you also to help these women who have shared my struggle in the cause of the gospel, together with Clement also, and the rest of my fellow workers, whose names are in the book of life. Phil. 4:2, 3, NASB.

Euodia and Syntyche were two energetic Christian women living in Philippi whom Paul urged to live together in harmony. Evidently there was some difference of opinion between them. Then he requested help for these women who shared his struggle in the great cause of preaching the gospel. After naming Clement and referring to the rest of his fellow workers, he tenderly spoke of their names being in the book of life.

Our text constitutes a personal insight into the struggles of the people associated with Paul in their pioneer work of establishing the early church. They had their problems and trials even as we do today.

Women were prominent in the formative years of the Macedonian church. It was at Philippi on the Sabbath day beside the river in the countryside where Luke records that they sat down and began speaking to the women who had assembled (Acts 16:13, NASB). In Thessalonica many "leading women" were persuaded to join Paul and Silas. In Berea among the believers were a number of prominent Greek women (Acts 17:4, 12, NASB).

Our own church owes much to faithful women believers. In fact, the majority of our members around the world are women. Their faithfulness and service in our church is a major reason for its growth in various avenues.

Anna Knight learned to read and write by listening to neighbor children and practicing writing by scratching on the earth with a sharp stick. She became one of the denomination's leading Black educators.

In 1874 Mrs. Henry Gardner invited eight women to come to her home in Battle Creek for a prayer band that eventually burst into action with the organization of the first Dorcas and Benevolent

Association. Under the leadership of Martha Byington Amadon, its first president, the Dorcas Society flourished. From this small beginning it evolved into Community Services centers and finally helped to establish the Adventist Development and Relief Agency.

Kate Lindsay graduated at the head of her class with the first group of women to receive medical degrees from the University of Michigan Medical College. She founded our church's first Adventist school of nursing in 1883.

As in Paul's day, so in modern times, women along with men have played a prominent role in the work of our church. We have so much to be thankful for as we study the lives of those who have given their all in the building of God's church on earth.

MARIE SPANGLER

SEPTEMBER 19

Love

Beloved, if God so loved us, we also ought to love one another. 1 John 4:11, RSV.

Morning comes
I rise
Hair asnarl
Eyes puffed
Mind slow
Not for
What I look like
He loves *me*.

Noon comes
I run
Hair wrenched
By baby fingers
Eyes roving
For hidden problems
Mind busy—
Too many trifles
Not for
What I look like
He loves *me*.

Evening comes
I rest

Hair—what hair?
Eyes blank
Mind ditto
Spirit—touched
By knowing
Not for
What I look like
He loves *me*.

CHERI SCHROEDER

Inspiring Hope

And I will give her . . . a door of hope. Hosea 2:15.

After 18 years of marriage Lana and Bud were going through a divorce. The most painful part of the ordeal for Lana was dealing with her eighth-grade son. In trying to sort out his own adjusting feelings, Michael voiced his greatest resistance to not becoming the "man of the house" in place of his father. In other words, not doing *any* chores.

Michael had begun spending more and more of his time in the home of a friend, and his anxieties always seemed reduced after these visits. Lana was grateful that he was welcomed into this family situation, although she worried what Michael was telling about his perceptions of her, the divorce, etc. Consequently, she somewhat avoided contact with this other family.

And then one day Michael went away to boarding academy, where he was somewhat removed from the reminders of his home situation. After a bit the other mother, Rose, phoned Lana just to see when he might be coming home so that they could see him again.

A friendly conversation ensued, and soon the two mothers met for lunch. Tactfully Rose ventured, "I don't know what ever went wrong between you and Bud, but something surely must have gone right for a long time before that, because you have produced such a lovely boy."

Lana could hardly believe her ears. Underneath this rebellious adolescent, someone else also perceived his *loveliness*? Well, yes, of course Lana had banked many cherished memories, but here was someone perceiving that he was *still* that boy!

"You really have done a good job on him," Rose continued. "In some ways he sounds very mature and balanced, and we can tell that someone has spent a lot of time caring for Michael."

At that moment something happened inside of Lana: down in her toes she felt a speck of hope. Of course Michael always had been in Sabbath school, junior camp, Pathfinders, church school, and family worship—where he had witnessed many answers to family prayer. Once when the family of six had all been singing junior camp songs on the way home from a holiday at Grandma's, Michael had abruptly commented, "I don't know how anybody could trade these songs to do things like drink beer and stuff like that!"

Perhaps she and Bud had not been a complete failure after all. Perhaps the two of them *had* done *some* things right! The reason she could believe Rose's encouragement was that it had a ring of truth that she could substantiate evidence for deep in her heart.

People often wonder what to say to divorcing couples. This incident and the following Ellen White passage may help: "[Christ] took the little children in His arms and blessed them and spoke words of hope and comfort to the weary mothers. . . . It was His meat and drink to bring hope and strength to *all* with whom He came in contact" (*Gospel Workers*, p. 188; italics supplied).

JANET KANGAS

SEPTEMBER 21

"We Are Fearfully and Wonderfully Made!"

When I consider thy heavens, the work of thy fingers, the moon and the stars, which thou hast ordained; What is man, that thou art mindful of him? and the son of man, that thou visitest him? Ps. 8:3, 4.

What sobering and yet uplifting words! I am currently majoring in biology. The many functions and processes that occur in nature that we study about are fascinating. The human body is wonderfully made. Every cell, every organ, major or minor, is part of a system that plays a vital role in keeping us alive. All the functions of our bodies, down to the most minute details, have been well thought out and planned in advance by our loving Creator so that there is harmony and coordination within us. Our brains are so complex that the most advanced computers cannot fully measure up in capacity.

Many times during the course of our daily lives we complain and grumble about our uphill climb. Rather than dwelling on the negative, we as women ought to rejoice in our special role as the nurturers of this world, a role entrusted to us by our God. We should feel honored by the way the Lord has so specially created us to fulfill that role of nurturing, as the mothers of Jerusalem. We ought to rejoice for the trust God has placed in us. We must not let Him down. We have been fearfully and wonderfully made to bear His trust!

MYRNA SUELE NORTEY

SEPTEMBER 22

Pilots of Our Conversations

Look at the ships also; though they are so great and are driven by strong winds, they are guided by a very small rudder wherever the will of the pilot directs. So the tongue is a little member and boasts of great things. James 3:4, 5, RSV.

Usually if two men talk together, it is about ideas, whereas two ladies talk about persons. And besides, whenever a lady phones a friend for some information, doesn't she often ask the latest news about the children, the husband, or the grandmother's health? She'll talk for a half hour about many other things before coming to the real purpose of the call. But after all, wouldn't the world be sad and dry if we were interested only in ideas and would never take time to be concerned about individuals?

It is true that women, as wives and mothers, are induced to attend to people. They watch over the comfort of those they live with, and therefore are naturally concerned about them. This particular care for people leads women to be concerned about their doings and behavior and by all those little things that compose life. But, as in all things, a quality may turn into a default. When the doings of others are focused on, it doesn't take long until those others are the main topic of the conversations.

James says that we should tame our tongue. He warns us against a bad use of the tongue. And his advice is aimed at men as well as at women.

At the center of his negative description he uses a positive picture that held my attention. He compares the tongue to a rudder, which, though very small, guides huge boats, and he underlines: "wherever the will of the pilot directs." So are we promoted to be pilots of our conversations.

I know a lady who is a missionary in Africa. She is lively, merry, devoted, and attentive. She has felt an interest in others all her life, taking care of everybody, concerned by the needs of each one,

313

seeing to the comfort of those she receives at home, advising some, and looking after the others. Her house is a real rest center where one is never bored, because she always has some experience to tell and some good counsels to give to new missionaries. I noticed that whenever someone was gossiping or criticizing, she pretended not to hear, finally changing the conversation or finding some good excuse in favor of the criticized person.

The radiance, the faith, and the unchanging joy of this lady made me understand how right the wise man was when he said: "He who guards his mouth preserves his life" (Prov. 13:3, RSV).

TANIA LEHMANN

SEPTEMBER 23

One Day at a Time

Make me to know thy ways, O Lord; teach me thy paths.
Ps. 25:4, RSV.

L ord, use me today," I prayed at my typewriter one morning. Within the hour the back door banged open. "The house across the valley is on fire!" my husband shouted. Then off he sped.

Grabbing a camera, I hurried to my car. I too could now see the thick column of black smoke that billowed above the evergreen trees a half mile to the east.

At the fire scene the searing heat of the fire held me at bay as flames hungrily destroyed my neighbor's possessions. Soon only ashes and memories would remain.

A handful of volunteer fire fighters stood by, watching helplessly. Nearby a portable pump drew a thin stream of water from a tiny creek that ran by a barn. A fireman alternately hosed the flaming house and the endangered barn.

"Got here about four minutes after the call," the fire fighter said. "Windows were already blowing out." The fire had started in the basement soon after the owner and her two teenage daughters had left for the day. They were safe.

I skirted the building, searching for interesting camera angles and words to describe the fire. *The weekly newspaper will want this story*, I thought. Deadline: 4:00 p.m.

My stomach in a knot, I frantically wrote and edited. At last I rolled the finished story out of my typewriter, grabbed some lunch, shot more pictures, and hurried into town. Knotted nerves began to loosen as I drove.

"Poor woman!" the sympathetic editor exclaimed. "She's lost it all—antiques and her business, too! I know her. She's had her share of troubles!"

I left the news office, wondering *Now what? They've lost almost everything. What do they need tonight?*

Bedding. And sleepwear. Food and toothbrushes and—

At the church's clothing bank I hastily chose a few garments, praying for help on sizes and colors. Then a phone call to obtain a cash gift.

That evening I found the burned-out family at a local motel.

"People have been so good," said the misty-eyed woman who came to the door. Gratefully she accepted the check and the sacks of clothes.

At home I sank wearily onto the couch. One day of doing the Lord's work had worn me out.

As I lay there relaxing, Mark 14:8 came to mind: "She hath done what she could."

I could sleep on that.

FANNIE L. HOUCK

SEPTEMBER 24

Precious Opportunities

Teach me your way, O Lord. Ps. 27:11, NIV.

How often we interact with others without realizing that they are hurting deep inside! Even when we do feel that all is not well with them, do we spare a few moments to comfort and encourage them?

Our Lord Jesus Christ, while He was on this earth, showed a tender love and compassion for humanity. We are admonished to seize every opportunity that comes our way to seek out the downhearted and speak words of hope and encouragement to them. Our Lord Himself always made the most of such precious opportunities.

We can ask the Lord to open our eyes that we may see the needs of people around us. We can also pray to Him to give us discernment so we will know how to respond when opportunity beckons us to assist a suffering soul. We can follow the example of the priest Eli at Shiloh. When he saw Hannah praying in the temple, he at first took her for a drunken woman, for her lips were moving but he could hear no sound. He was ready to rebuke her. However, when Hannah explained her condition to him (1 Sam. 1:15, 16), the priest was deeply touched. Eli blessed Hannah, saying, "Go in

315

peace: and the God of Israel grant thee thy petition that thou hast asked him" (verse 17).

Showing genuine interest in those around us fosters an atmosphere of mutual trust in which we can effectively reach out to them and let them know that we care. What joy we feel in our heart when we have helped to lighten others' burdens!

Today you may not be able to find solutions to all the problems brought before you, but you can at least point those discouraged souls to the Saviour, for He alone can take care of all our needs and give us peace in our daily walk with Him.

"Blessed be the God and Father of our Lord Jesus Christ, the Father of mercies and God of all comfort, who comforts us in all our affliction, so that we may be able to comfort those who are in any affliction, with the comfort with which we ourselves are comforted by God" (2 Cor. 1:3, 4, RSV).   LILY DOWUONA

SEPTEMBER 25

Difficult Marriages

Let marriage be held in honor among all, and let the marriage bed be undefiled; for God will judge the immoral and adulterous. Heb. 13:4, RSV.

A 29-year-old woman sat across from me saying that if I could not drastically change her husband, she would have to divorce him. (I was supposed to accomplish this in spite of his refusal to accept counseling.) I listed for her the alternatives, which are the same for all unhappily married partners. Whether the problems are trivial or severe, each spouse has only three choices.

The first alternative is divorce—the great American cop-out. Many determine they have real provocation for divorce and obtain one. Too often, however, divorce is an escape mechanism and is thus the most immature of the three choices.

The second alternative is to endure a standoff relationship—tough it out, grin and bear it, mask the problems. All this goes on without working to improve the unfortunate situation. The world will never know how terrible things are unless told, so game-playing proceeds while a rotten relationship is silently endured. Millions have chosen this alternative because it is easier than facing personal deficiencies and doing something about them—another immature decision.

The third alternative involves facing personal problems and making an intelligent choice to build a happy marriage out of the existing one. Even those with "incompatible personalities" can learn to work out personal deficiencies. The word "incompatible" is frequently used by those too lazy to work out their own hang-ups.

"There are no unhappy marriages, only marriage partners who are immature," says the late Dr. David Mace, renowned marriage counselor. If partners could develop more mature attitudes, all areas of their relationship would improve.

Difficult marriage problems have no instant cures. Even the best of counselors can basically offer only support and compassion. But surely the Lord smiles on those who search for new and creative ways to improve family relationships, because the Christian life involves continual growth and improvement in all aspects.

The journey toward a "compleat" marriage is the journey from childishness to personal maturity. Why not begin that journey today? NANCY VAN PELT

SEPTEMBER 26

The Watered-down Soup God Blessed

Contribute to the needs of the saints, practice hospitality. Rom. 12:13, RSV.

My husband was away for the weekend, and when I asked my two small boys what they would like for lunch on Sabbath, they said, "Nuttolene." It was rare for us not to have guests on Sabbath, and so I treated Friday as a holiday, did the minimum preparation for Sabbath, and spent time having fun with the boys.

As I fetched the children from Sabbath school and got them settled in church, I noticed a very striking couple sitting at the back. When the church service was over, I had duties in the vestry and was just about to leave when a deaconess came in, saying that some visitors from Europe were in need of hospitality. Somehow no one else was able to take them, so I offered to. As we left the vestry, the deaconess said, "Oh, by the way, they aren't Adventists." *Great*, I thought. *They're just going to love Nuttolene!*

I must admit feeling dismayed when I was introduced to a tall and handsome man and his very beautiful wife. Feeling the absence of my husband to entertain them, I thought they would not feel too comfortable with just a woman and two boisterous lads. However, I took them home and settled them with a drink in the living room, and left the boys to entertain them. Between watering down Friday evening's soup, defrosting a savory pie from the freezer, and setting

317

two extra places at the table, I popped in and out of the living room trying to make them feel welcome and at home. Why, oh why, did my husband have to be away this weekend?

Eventually we sat down to our meal, and I apologized that we were vegetarians, only to be told by our guests that they were as well! Over lunch we chatted and found out a little about each other, and it became apparent that they knew something of Adventists. After lunch, the boys clamored for a Bible game, and as soon as I realized that the wife was out of her depth, I made her the question master. Some friends arrived later, and while I was out making drinks, they questioned them more closely than I had.

After our guests left, my friends told me that the husband was a former Adventist and today was the first time he had been in an Adventist church in about 20 years! As the boys and I prayed that night, I thanked God fervently that I had taken them home.

The husband, who traveled between England and Europe, turned up at church again a few weeks later and again came home with us. (My husband was at home this time!) We learned that he had left the church many years ago and that he and his wife lived a very high life. Recently, though, with events in the world, he began to remember the teachings of his youth about the end of the world, and he and his wife had given up drinking and smoking, become vegetarians, and were searching the Scriptures.

Over the next few months we became firm friends and visited with them in their home in Belgium. We gave prayerful thanks, when they were baptized, that I had not passed up the opportunity God had presented to me. AUDREY BALDERSTONE

SEPTEMBER 27

The Words of Self-abasement

Let no one disqualify you, insisting on self-abasement. . . .
These have indeed an appearance of wisdom in promoting
rigor of devotion and self-abasement. Col. 2:18-23, RSV.

He played French horn better than anyone on campus. He held down first chair in band all through college. He often soloed, playing for chapel, Sabbath school, or an SA function. All of these he did expertly, as outstanding a musician as any student could be. What he did not do expertly was receive compliments.

"You played so well today, Robert. I always enjoy hearing you perform," some pleased listener would comment.

"Oh, I did horribly. Never can get the rhythm right. I messed up several times." Robert would cut the compliment short, always managing to degrade himself. Is this true humility, or rather the undesirable self-abasement that Paul's words warn against?

Robert's type of humility reflects low self-esteem, an attempt to be meek and mild that ironically results in a put-down of the one complimenting.

True humility involves more than modestly denying praise. "Oh, that old dress. I'm surprised you like it. I've had it for ages." True humility involves more than meekly negating a compliment: "Oh, I did nothing, really. Anyone would have rushed into the burning building."

Another form of self-abasement involves dress. I was shopping one scorching July day when I noticed the two of them, a young mother and her elementary-aged daughter. Both were covered like mummies, long pants under wool skirts, high-top shoes, unmatching long-sleeved shirts, and a bonnet. Their dress, an unfashionable attempt at modesty, attracted more attention than any other outfit in the store.

Ironic, isn't it, that their striving to cover their bodies on that blistering summer afternoon made them the most conspicuous patrons in the store. But then Paul knew that self-abasement has its problems, which is why he warned against it in the first place.

The kitchen of the small restaurant was always too hot, unbearably so in the summer. The short-order cook would not permit the room to be air-conditioned since the hot foods would get cold before served. One noon a waitress, a short, stout lady who often doubled as second cook, was unusually warm as she helped out during rush hour.

"The *humility* is so high in here," she said, mopping her brow. And too many Christians have humilities that are "too high" also, being almost proud of their self-abasements. To those, Paul's words still apply: "These have indeed an appearance of wisdom in promoting rigor of devotion and self-abasement."

WILMA McCLARTY

SEPTEMBER 28

Willing Anonymity

And Joanna the wife of Chuza Herod's steward, and Susanna, and many others, which ministered unto him of their substance. Luke 8:3.

The Bible mentions other anonymous women. In chapter 8 of Luke's Gospel we read, for instance, of "many women," besides Mary Magdalene and Joanna and Susanna, who "ministered unto him of their substance."

If only I knew *their* names, and what they actually did in ministering unto Him.

"Did you," I would ask them, "care for His garments? Did you shake the dust of the Palestine roads from His outer robe when He sat down for rare relief? Did you wash the undergarment while He slept? Did you watch from afar while He prayed, and pray with Him and for Him?

Did you sometimes long to sit at His feet and listen as He taught, as the men were allowed to do, as Mary Magdalene did? I know how it is to cook and wash the dishes while the men talk. I understand Martha's feelings as she worked alone in the kitchen. Did you sometimes wish He would send *you* out two by two to preach the kingdom of heaven for Him, if not to perform signs and wonders and miracles?

As He had no place of permanent abode, where did you reside while He and the disciples were itinerating? Were you aware of smirks and innuendos about your accompanying Him? Did you hear whispered behind your backs the Aramaic words that meant "camp followers"?

Did you, women of Galilee, purchase loaves and fishes at the market and prepare food for the Master and His twelve? The "substance" with which you ministered to Him, where did it come from? Did you open your purses and pour your means into the Lord's small store, or even hand them over to Judas to husband— and sometimes squander?

Who were you, unsung heroines of substance, so willing to follow the Lord and supply His needs anonymously?

Lord, give me the grace to serve behind the scenes, as they did, at my small tasks, "unhonored and unsung," willing to be Your hands, Your feet, Your voice in my little sphere of influence.

JEANNE JORDAN

SEPTEMBER 29

Our Boys and Girls

There is neither Jew nor Greek, slave nor free, male nor female, for you are all one in Christ Jesus. Gal. 3:28, NIV.

The year 1990 was declared to be the Year of the "Girl Child" in India. There were good reasons for it. A large portion of the Indian population finds it economically difficult to educate girls. In lower strata families in which both husband and wife are working, the older girls are called upon to look after their younger siblings and care for various other household duties. Because of the illiteracy of parents and some age-old customs and traditions, there are those who feel that there is little to be gained by educating daughters. They are to be given in marriage and there is not much point in wasting money on daughters' education.

Little Shanta, whom we know, is just 9 years old. She does not go to school, because she has to look after her younger sister. But her brother, Balu, who is 7 years old, goes to school. The difference is that Shanta is a girl and Balu is a boy.

In recent years the government and some voluntary organizations such as the Christian Children's Fund have come to the aid of children. Yet there is much to be done. There is much that Christians and Christian organizations can do in this sphere.

In God's plan we are to love our boys and girls and train them the way they should go. They are to be educated to take up responsibilities of life. They are to be brought up in the fear of the Lord. Both boys and girls are to be given the best we can give. We believe that children are the "heritage of the Lord" (Ps. 127:3). Parents have the sacred responsibility of bringing up their children in the fear and nurture of the Lord. They are precious in the sight of God. The psalmist says, "That our daughters may be as corner stones, polished after the similitude of a palace" (Ps. 144:12). Peter writes, "I will pour out my Spirit upon all flesh: and your sons and daughters shall prophesy" (Acts 2:17), making no difference on a sex basis. God is not partial, and the Holy Spirit recognizes as equal both boys and girls.

All of us have the privilege of creating a better world around us for the children of our community and of our church. Let us make the following prayer a reality:

"My life must touch a million lives in some way ere I go
From this dear world of struggle to the land I do not know.
So this wish I always wish, the prayer I ever pray,
Let my life help the little lives it touches by the way."

PREMILA CHERIAN

A Model in Service

For I am not seeking my own good but the good of many,
so that they may be saved. 1 Cor. 10:33, NIV.

When the terrible accident was over and they uncovered his mangled body, so little life was left in it that they thought he was dead. And when the surgeons had finished their work, there remained but the physical wreck of a man.

Both legs were gone; the left arm was missing and had taken with it the greater part of the collarbone. Of the right hand, only a finger and the thumb remained. Of the man that had been, there was only enough left to suffer and remember.

But he still possessed a brilliant mind, stored with the rich fruitage of a college training, and enriched by travel in every part of the world. And it was all wasted, wasted.

A sudden thought came to him. To receive letters would be little comfort to him, but why should he not write them? But to whom? Could there be any persons so shut in as he who could be cheered by his letters? Possibly the men in prison were a little more to be pitied; yet even they had hope of release, and he had none. But it was worth trying.

So he wrote to the secretary of the organization for the names of some prisoners. He was informed that his letters could not be answered. But he undertook the one-sided correspondence.

Twice a week he wrote, and each letter taxed his strength to its limit. But into those letters he put his whole soul, all his experience, all his faith, all his bright wit, all his Christian optimism.

It is hard to continue writing when writing costs labor and pain, and especially hard when there is no reply. There were times when he grew discouraged, and was tempted to give it up. But it was his one remaining talent, and he resolved to use it as long as it lasted.

At length he got a letter. It was very short, and written on the stationery of the prison by the officer whose duty it was to read the letters of the convicts. All it said was this:

"Please write on the best paper you can afford, for your letters are passed from cell to cell till they literally drop to pieces."

ANONYMOUS

This article appeared in the *Wisconsin Shepherdess Newsletter.*

The Treasure Box

Come, O sons, listen to me, I will teach you the fear of the Lord. Ps. 34:11, RSV.

O ne morning I was driving to school, my mind occupied with students and activities and lesson plans, when the flashing red light in my rearview mirror snapped me back to reality. Had I been speeding? It certainly was possible. I had been eager to get to school.

A tall, muscular Los Angeles police officer approached the window. He stood for a moment, looking at me with an impassive expression on his face that suddenly gave way to an odd, boyish curiosity.

"You're Mrs. Richards, aren't you?"

I nodded.

"I was one of your kindergarten students."

I looked at his name tag and then at the face.

"Do you remember me?" he asked.

"Of course," I said. "You're Tommy."

"Everyone calls me Thomas now."

Tommy had become Thomas, and patched jeans had been replaced by a carefully pressed uniform. But I remembered the look in his face. The eagerness of his eyes.

"But how did you remember me?" I asked. "You were just a little boy."

"I got to pick from the Treasure Box," he said simply.

The Treasure Box was a large brown box secured with a padlock. If a child had been especially good—quick to do his or her work or courteous or quiet when it was time for quiet, the reward was a chance to choose from the Treasure Box. In it was a trove of colorful balloons, little heart-shaped erasers, bright new pencils, plastic farm animals, and funny little stickers.

The trip to the Treasure Box always involved much pomp and circumstance. For some children, it may have been their first tangible reward for doing something right. In any case, it was always marked with considerable joy.

"Thomas, do you remember what you did to earn a trip to the Treasure Box?" I asked.

"No ma'am, I don't remember that," he said. "But I remember what I got. I got a bright-red pencil. I kept it a long time, too. It was

323

the first time anyone had given me anything just for trying. I never forgot that."

He had been encouraged and rewarded early in his life, and his character had been formed accordingly. A simple lesson had been learned. A set of values nurtured.

Eventually we got around to the reason he stopped me in the first place. I had been speeding, but he let me off with a brief but official warning. It didn't matter that his letting me off the hook for my crime was the opposite lesson that the Treasure Box was intended to teach. I didn't argue. Maybe it was my turn to learn about grace.

I resumed my drive to school, and in between watching the road and the speedometer, I found myself wondering out loud, "Maybe this day another child will earn a trip to the Treasure Box and, in the process of grasping a prize, learn a simple lesson in character building." What could be more rewarding than that?

MARY MARGARET RICHARDS

OCTOBER 2

I've Never Been Out of His Care

The Lord will keep your going out and your coming in from this time forth and for evermore. Ps. 121:8, RSV.

There are three lines in a song by Joni Eareckson Tada, the quadriplegic artist and singer, that bring me a lot of comfort when I've not been quite the good servant of the Lord that I'd like to be.

> "And although many times
>   I've stepped out of His will,
>   I've never been out of His care."

It was a great comfort the other day after I had read the following statement: "When we disobey God, He withdraws His protection and we suffer."

Now, I don't know about you, but I think that's a terrible thing to say about God. (And it was written by someone who ought to know better!)

To be quite frank, my mind has been reeling with that statement ever since I read it. Not that I believe for a minute we can sin without suffering the consequences, but when we do, God doesn't just wash His hands of us!

If good earthly parents don't withdraw their protection from their naughty children, what on earth makes anyone think God does? And who was looking after my family long before any of us even thought of obeying Him? I know that He loved and protected us. I personally wouldn't have survived if He hadn't!

When I was a child, I got into trouble just as much as any other (well, maybe not quite as much!), and when it was a case of flagrant disobedience I suffered a "laying on of hands" from my mom. But it never occurred to me for one instant that she would actually stop loving me or withdraw her protection. (I know there *are* children in the world who don't have that assurance, but remember I'm talking about a good parent/child relationship.)

What kind of assurance would there be in life if we lost the protection, and presumably the love, of the person we rely on just because we didn't do what he or she asked? And when it's the love of God you're considering, to think that way makes mockery of such statements as "Come unto me, all ye that labour and are heavy laden, and I will give you rest" (Matt. 11:28). What rest could there be if we might find ourselves suddenly unprotected and unloved?

> "And although many times
> I stepped out of His will,
> I've never been out of His care."

No wonder Joni can enjoy life despite her awful handicap. She has the assurance of God's love—always—and just can't help singing about it.

Can you relate to words like that? If you can't, you really ought to try to get to know God better than that fellow who wrote such utter rubbish about his heavenly Father. The fact is that not one of us could survive for a moment without God's protection!

ANITA MARSHALL

OCTOBER 3

Old-fashioned Principles

Train up a child in the way he should go: and when he is old, he will not depart from it. Prov. 22:6.

"Now I lay me down to sleep; I pray, dear Lord, my soul to keep. If I should die before I wake, then save me, Lord, for Jesus' sake."

Sound familiar? I'm sure that for many of us this was one of the first prayers taught to us by our mothers. Of course, at the age of 2 or 3 years it was simply a matter of memorization rather than an application of principle.

As I, a mother of three, reflect back on this and many of the other teachings I learned at my mother's lap, I can understand the values and principles she was trying to instill in me and my 11 siblings.

Mom worked from 5:00 a.m. to 3:30 p.m. as a cook in a restaurant seven days a week. Although she was off only on special Sundays in the month, she would always rise early to be certain that our clothes were laid out for Sunday school. Although she could not go with us each week, it was an unwritten rule that we all were to go—and go we did.

There were many unwritten rules in our home, such as (1) you must show respect to any adult you come in contact with; (2) you must not take anything that does not belong to you; (3) you must be willing to share with those who are hungry; (4) you must do as you are told; (5) you must get your bath each evening; and (6) you must never go to bed without giving thanks to God for the day's blessings and asking for His watchcare over you as you sleep.

My mom has been dead for almost four years. In my last conversations with her, she told me always to remember what she had tried to teach me from early on. She said, "Never forget, now that you have your own family, what I have taught you about dependence upon Christ. Even though I won't be with you, He can and will always be with you if you just let Him."

As a child I hated all of the "old-fashioned" ways of my mother. Now I smile when I think about those days. I must admit that I truly am my mother's child, because I am raising my children on these same "old-fashioned" biblical principles.

NETTIE ANDERSON

OCTOBER 4

Among the Eight

But I will establish my covenant with you, and you will enter the ark—you and your sons and your wife and your sons' wives with you. Gen. 6:18, NIV.

I sometimes wonder about the anonymous women of the Bible. They played their roles unnamed, a "chorus" in the background of an all-male cast. Noah's wife and daughters-in-law, for example. I certainly have some questions for them.

"While your husband preached the end of the world, what did you, wife of Noah, do during those 120 years? You didn't have that many children to look after—only three sons. Later, when they grew up and you were in the female ascendancy, you had their wives to help with the cooking and washing, the spinning and weaving.

Did you take part at all in the building of the ark, in the preaching of the "last-day message"? Was "your place" in the home that was about to be swept away by the Flood? Or did the four of you go among the women, at least, and explain to them the phenomenon of rain? (I realize the men would not have accepted the word of mere women about the impending Flood!) Did you warn them to get ready, or did you cower before their ridicule and shrink from "witnessing," as I sometimes do when people sneer?

Tell me, you who were among the exclusive eight, as the years went by and the ark grew apace and nothing happened, did you sometimes even have *doubts*? I confess that I too sometimes have doubts. Time goes on and on, and more than 120 years have passed since my church proclaimed a last-day message, and the Lord hasn't yet come. A half-century ago when I was baptized, I thought I would never get married, have children, and grow old before He came. And now I am threescore and ten, and still I wait. And reread the chapter in *Steps to Christ* "What to Do With Doubt." And search the Scriptures, for in them I *know* I have eternal life.

If any of you had doubts, you didn't let them prevail. Even before a drop of rain fell, you went into the ark. Let it be said of me, in the end: She went into the ark and was saved.   JEANNE JORDAN

OCTOBER 5

Mothers and Daughters

Bring your children up in the training and instruction of the Lord. Eph. 6:4, NIV.

My daughter Margaret, at 2, would announce to anybody who crossed her, "You are not my fwiend." One day, after being teased about it, she felt sheepish. All day, periodically, she said to me, "You my fwiend." She mastered her *r*'s later, and we remained friends.

Recently, on Mother's Day, Margaret got married. The next New Year's Day her sister Beth got married. We've had adjustments to make, but we still remain good friends. Those friendships are highly valued treasures I hope to enjoy throughout eternity.

Responses to my question-answer column in *Guide* magazine suggest that four *r*'s are often missing in mother-daughter "fwiendships."

Reasonableness. One wrote, "I'm 17. . . . My parents won't let me go out on dates." Another, wearing long dresses and forbidden to attend church school or even visit grandparents, wrote, "It's like living all caged up. . . . I don't think I can wait till I'm 18 to leave. . . . I just want to die!"

Expectations—we should examine each requirement, preferably before stating it, to see if it is extreme or reasonable and fair. We can be conservative, but we need to share our convictions lovingly, with reasons, and be willing to listen.

Reproof. Though positive discipline is preferable to negative, to neglect needed reproof indicates false love. To build true friendship with a daughter, one sets limits and reacts to infractions consistently. Often a simple word suffices. Sometimes it takes more persistence, or even a spank.

Proper reproof and relationship-building take time and energy. Kids write me about working parents who don't have time for them. As one 10-year-old put it, "I feel that I don't know my mom."

Respect. Any friendship requires respect, best learned through modeling. A sassy, demanding, temper-tantrum child often has a mother who attempts to discipline by yelling, cuffing, or putting down.

Daughters need us to respect their opinions, friends, privacy. One wrote, "I try to please my mom . . . but . . . she always seems to find something wrong. . . . Sometimes I feel worthless."

Disrespect can take many forms, from teasing to physical or sexual abuse. Kids need more strokes than knocks to gain self-respect. I once felt a mite of success when a visiting couple mentioned wanting a family, and Beth, 4, promptly told them, "My mommy is very lucky to have her little Beth."

Religion. To build a lasting mother-daughter friendship, it's crucial to transmit spiritual values, principles, doctrines, and lifestyle. A few mothers actually oppose their daughters' religion. A girl, 12, wrote me of her mother's refusal to allow her baptism because of bitterness from her divorce, adding, "I know God loves us all, and He will help me!"

Don't just assume they'll absorb religion from home or school. Introduce each child personally to Jesus. Family worship helps. More important is example. What answer can I give to the girl who writes, "My mom has a new boyfriend. . . . He's recently moved in. I want him out. What should I do?"

Children learn Scripture and hymns easily, and these last a lifetime. One day Beth repeated her memory verse throughout the house all day, "God is a lovely cheerful giver." I decided there's a lot of truth in that version. One of His best gifts to me is the friendship of two daughters.　　　　　　MADELINE S. JOHNSTON

Assets = Liabilities

I am debtor both to the Greeks, and to the Barbarians; both to the wise, and to the unwise. Rom. 1:14.

The basic accounting principle on which all bookkeeping practice is based is: assets = liabilities + capital.

In other words: All in my possession (assets) consists of what I am holding that you have a claim against (liabilities), plus what is actually mine (capital).

Ellen White, however, has a different idea for the Christian: "By *all* that has given us advantage over another—be it education and refinement, nobility of character, Christian training, religious experience—we are *in debt to those less favored*; and so far as lies in our power, we are to minister unto them. If we are strong, we are to stay up the hands of the weak" (*The Desire of Ages*, p. 440; italics supplied).

If we take the liberty of translating her word "advantage" to mean assets, and her word "debt" to mean liability, we find that the formula she pronounces for the Christian is: assets = liabilities. No capital.

She, along with some other early Adventist Church pioneers, practiced this formula. For our example I present these vignettes of their sacrificial spirit:

Ellen White: "We have passed over the road to and from California twelve times, and have not expended one dollar for meals at the restaurants or in the attached dining car" (*Testimonies*, vol. 4, p. 299).

Edward and *Victor Thomann*, colporteurs, missionaries, and leaders in Chile, endured such close times for a while that the two brothers were reduced to a single pair of shoes between them, which they took turns wearing. One went out canvassing, while the other stayed home to pray (*The SDA Encyclopedia*, p. 1482).

The *Loughboroughs* and the *Whites* in 1867 asked public forgiveness for selfishly spending money on photographs of themselves (R. W. Schwarz, *Light Bearers to the Remnant*, p. 178).

Part of *Mrs. Hiram Edson's* wedding silver was sold to finance the publication of the new sanctuary views as understood by her husband and O.R.L. Crosier following the 1844 disappointment (*ibid.*, p. 62).

Lacking proper tools, *Uriah Smith* spent many hours trimming the rough edges of the *Review* tracts with a penknife, frequently resulting in blistered hands (*ibid.*, p. 81).

The dozen *employees* who helped James White with the Review press in Rochester, New York, often received nothing more than mush and beans, meal after meal (Eugene Durand, *Yours in the Blessed Hope*, Uriah Smith, p. 24).

But to me, the most touching example is reported about *W. A. Spicer*, one of the most trusted men who ever walked the halls of the General Conference: Rather than pay for a berth to sleep on the trains, W. A. Spicer, who held four General Conference posts, including the presidency, would sit up night after night to save the Lord's money. He did his own laundry in his cheap hotel rooms when traveling. Frequently a bag of peanuts lasted him all day, keeping food expenses to a minimum. On several occasions he refused to draw his salary for weeks so that the amount saved would be available for pressing calls from mission stations when needed (*Light Bearers*, pp. 377, 355).

On my first overseas mission trip, I threw in several packs of peanuts and sentimentally laughed, "Now you're a real tried-and-true missionary, Janet, just like W. A. Spicer!" I reasoned that Spicer had made a good choice in packing peanuts—for preservation, nutrition, and satisfaction.

Later, while absorbing the initial shock of a Third World country, the value of those peanuts was no longer survival, or sentimental, or economical. I picked up one of those peanut packs and fingered it. "O God, help me be the same kind of missionary W. A. Spicer was—not just the same fed."   JANET KANGAS

OCTOBER 7

The Day the Easter Bunnies Disappeared

If you turn back your foot from the sabbath, from doing your pleasure on my holy day, and call the sabbath a delight and the holy day of the Lord honorable; if you honor it, not going your own ways, or seeking your own pleasure, or talking idly; then you shall take delight in the Lord, and I will make you ride upon the heights of the earth; and I will feed you with the heritage of Jacob your father, for the mouth of the Lord has spoken. Isa. 58:13, 14, RSV.

It was the chairman of our local flower club on the telephone. "I know you don't like doing competition work," she said, "but we are in real trouble and you are the only one who can help us." It turned out that the two ladies who were to do the club entry in the area show were both ill and there was no one else who was used to doing pedestal work. Knowing that I do pedestals at church, they thought I was the one!

"I know it's your Sabbath," she went on. I interrupted her: "Margaret, you know if it is on the Sabbath there is no way I can do it."

"The staging is from 2:00 p.m. until 9:30 p.m., and your Sabbath is out at 7:00 p.m.," she said, "and we really are desperate." Because of Sabbath I am often not able to help with functions at the flower club, and so, although very reluctant, I felt I had to help out.

The title of the class was "Easter Parade." Now, to many that title brings to mind Easter bonnets and bunnies, but Easter to me means only one thing—the Crucifixion. And so I planned my exhibit to be a towering pedestal in beautiful white flowers—lilies, lilac, guelder rose, stocks, freesia, and carnations, with, at the foot, three large rocks, a wooden cross up which climbed a branch of thorns with a delicate spray of lilies and freesias at its base, and a sign that read "Then they led Him out to a place called Golgotha."

By 7:30 p.m. Saturday evening I was ready to start. All the other ladies were packing up to go home! Without exception the exhibits were of bonnets and bunnies and Easter eggs. I trembled, because I knew that if the judges felt that my exhibit did not interpret the title, our club would be disqualified—a terrible disgrace. I trembled too because I had never done such a big display in such a short space of time. With a prayer on my lips I set to work, and it was with very shaking hands that I placed the last flower and fled from the room at the very last minute, not even having time to top up with water or see that all was well.

Imagine the delight next day when our club won for the first time in 17 years! My non-Adventist friends felt we owed our success to the fact that I had kept the Sabbath. I only know that never before or since, no matter how hard I have tried, have I been able to do a large pedestal in under two hours!

AUDREY BALDERSTONE

We Wait—God Works

Wait on the Lord; be of good courage, and He shall strengthen your heart; wait, I say, on the Lord. Ps. 27:14, NKJV.

As a very young Christian I had to make some far-reaching decisions. It seemed that I faced a blank wall with no way over, under, or through. It was then that Psalm 27:14 became a precious text to me. I repeated it daily, thought about its meaning, and claimed its promise. While I waited, God opened doors and closed other avenues and showed me the way through. Behind the scenes He was silently working, not only for me, but for the loved ones I had been praying for. I learned that sometimes it takes time, but in His own time and in His own way, if we leave our lives in His keeping with faith and trust, He will work out every situation for our good.

Of course, life has its disappointments. God does not always say yes and give us our heart's desires. We may pray and ask Him to spare a loved one's life. He may answer: "No, my child, it is best that your dear one go to sleep." You may pray for years for the conversion of someone dear to you, and you know that it is God's will for all to be saved, but years pass and your prayers are unanswered. We must not grow discouraged, for God continues to work. I prayed for 51 years for my brother and his wife; then one day a letter came with the wonderful news they had given their hearts to the Lord and been baptized. No earnest, sincere prayer is ever forgotten by our heavenly Father; it remains on record, and the Holy Spirit and angels seek to answer our prayers.

Our world may seem to be on the brink of disaster, but our Lord knows how to make everything right for the child of God. We can trust our little problems to Him who guides the universe and, like Isaiah of old, say, "I will wait on the Lord . . . and I will hope in Him" (Isa. 8:17, NKJV). A Hebrew translation of Zephaniah 3:17 gives us the beautiful promise that while we are waiting we can be assured: "He is silently planning for thee in love, for it mattereth to Him about thee."   DOLLIS PIERSON

Mother and Daddy's Prayers

And it shall come to pass, that before they call, I will answer; and while they are yet speaking, I will hear. Isa. 65:24.

"Precious memories, how they linger, how they ever flood my soul." In the quiet times of our hurried lives how sweet it is to remember the joys of being brought up in a Christian home.

The memory of how Mother and Daddy would call us all together at the beginning and closing of God's Sabbath to hear a story, perhaps read a Bible text, sing a song, or mention something for which we were thankful. To close worship, Daddy would pray to his heavenly Daddy, calling God's attention to his Sandy, Linda, David, and Donna, to guide and protect them. That part was never left out.

Time has passed. I'm not only a mother of four children, but also a grandmother. Even now, without fail, each time I go home my parents still call us all together to open and close Sabbath. How precious that is to me. Always at the close of each day, if you listen very carefully, you can hear a small voice praying to her heavenly Father to remember Sandy, Linda, David, and Donna, calling us by name as she kneels by the side of her bed. What a comfort to know Mother never forgets to pray.

Without fail, when it is time to separate and we need to return to our own homes, we all join hands together in a family circle and once again Daddy prays for guidance for his children and for God's protection on them. Many times the tears trickle from the corner of his eyes and drip down his cheeks as he prays.

God is very real to my parents, and that heritage has been passed down to me. For that legacy I will ever be grateful. Today, I thank my heavenly Father for a Christian mother and daddy and for God's Spirit being present in our home. SANDY DANCEK

A Woman of Wisdom

Wake up, wake up, Deborah! Wake up, wake up, break out in song! Judges 5:12, NIV.

I had heard stories about the Statue of Liberty for years. I had seen pictures of her standing majestically on Liberty Island in the New York Harbor. I had read about her being a gift to the people of the United States in 1886 from the people of France. I knew that Edouard de Laboulaye, a French author, had suggested the erection of a memorial to commemorate the alliance of 1778 between France and the United States. I knew that August Bartholdi had been assigned to create the memorial. I knew that his creation represented a woman who had just won her freedom, and I wanted to see her in person. Finally, when I was about 10 years old, my parents arranged to take the family on a vacation that would include a visit to the Statue of Liberty. I could hardly wait!

As we drove across the border separating Canada from the United States, I was already tingling with suppressed excitement. When the Statue of Liberty finally came into view, nothing I had studied about her had prepared me for her immense and commanding presence. She *was* liberty! I could almost feel the way some of the early immigrants must have felt as they first glimpsed this symbol of freedom. The fact that a woman had been chosen to represent liberty and freedom made an indelible impression on my heart and mind. Over time, I have seen her several more times: from the air, from the land, from the sea, from her feet, and from deep inside her. The thrill is always there, and my heart still responds whenever I think of the words by Emma Lazarus:

> "Give me your tired, your poor,
>   Your huddled masses yearning to breathe free,
>   The wretched refuse of your teeming shore.
>   Send these, the homeless, tempest-tost to me,
>   I lift my lamp beside the golden door!"

The story of Deborah, judge of Israel, made a similar impression on me when I first heard the story. The judges were both civil and religious authorities. They really represented Christ—our Leader, our Judge, and our Saviour. Othniel was the first, Samson was the last, and in between was Deborah, the fifth judge of Israel. The name Deborah means "a bee." The bee ranks among the highest in intelligence of all the animal kingdom; Deborah ranks among the wisest of all the Old Testament women.

The book of Judges, chapters 4 and 5, lists some of the roles that Deborah fulfilled: prophetess, wife, judge, leader, rescuer, poetess, warrior.

Although as far as we know, Deborah never bore any natural children, yet she was a mother to all in Israel.

Most of us are familiar with Deborah's participation with Barak in battle. We sometimes lose sight of the 40 years of peace she helped to create for Israel; we forget how she energized men and women alike to throw off the oppression that had blanketed the nation for two decades; we gloss over the fact that she was a female "role model" in many capacities; and we miss the way in which she exemplified the ability to integrate multiple roles—successfully.

Today, wake up. Allow the Lord to use you in whatever role you can best fulfill. Wake up, and break out in song!

ARLENE TAYLOR

OCTOBER 11

The Ultimate Lifestyle

The thief cometh not, but for to steal, and to kill, and to destroy: I am come that they might have life, and that they might have it more abundantly. John 10:10.

In today's fast-paced life people often feel so pressured and stressed, so full of pain and disappointment, and so hopeless that they become increasingly willing to gamble their health, and even their lives, on almost anything that promises relief, no matter how temporary. "Follow your feelings," they are urged. "If it feels good, do it." "Hurry, life is passing you by."

For every skid-row bum there are scores of closet alcoholics. And for every street punk looking for a "hit," there are many so-called respectable people numbing their pain with prescription pills.

But people are becoming increasingly disillusioned. Lasting joy doesn't come in snorts, and they can't shoot up peace of mind. Bottles and pills don't erase guilt, and well-being cannot be purchased with a prescription. Even many medical breakthroughs are only temporary patch-up jobs.

Alcoholism is a conspicuous example. The medical miracles and the technological advances of the past half century have hardly touched this disease. Alcoholics Anonymous still offers the most consistently effective treatment with the best long-term results. AA uses a 12-step program that involves a recognition of human helplessness and the acceptance of a Higher Power. Similar 12-step programs based on the philosophy of AA are proliferating in almost every area of human need. They are bringing healing to thousands for whom medical care, drugs, counseling, and other human solutions have failed.

Health and fitness are not enough. Neither are wealth, fame, good looks, or power. The ultimate lifestyle must include spiritual growth and development. We didn't arrive in this world, as some evolutionists claim, with only the minimal equipment needed for survival. We are born with a conscience to keep us on track; a full range of feelings and emotions to enrich our lives; and a brain that we can never use up or wear out.

In every human heart there are deep, inexplicable longings for something better, longings planted by our Creator to lead us to the One who can fill our lives with meaning now and for eternity.

AILEEN LUDINGTON

OCTOBER 12

A Chance at the Role

Rejoice in the Lord, O you righteous! Praise befits the upright. Ps. 33:1, RSV.

It has been my great good fortune, as a speaker, to attend Adventist women's retreats all over the country. When 200 or 300 women sing together, it's a very special sound. In Minnesota, song leader Barbara Eno broke us into units according to the parts that we sang best (some of us weren't sure we belonged anywhere, but were carried along on the superb musical skills of others). She drilled each group fiercely, then brought us back together, and we sang like angels, the harmony so beautiful that Barbara, standing on a chair to lead her big choir, had to brush away tears.

I have heard retreat women testify shyly and eloquently, but always with an openness that I rarely hear in churches. It's as though, shut away together for a brief time, we are freed to express our deepest loyalties to God in a way uniquely feminine. Are we afraid that husbands, our own or someone else's, will be amused at our spiritual ardor? I guess sometimes I feel that way.

Don't misunderstand me. Husbands and children are an integral part of our lives. We worry when we go off for a weekend and leave them, and we babble excitedly when we return, attempting to share some of the blessings. So seldom do women lay aside the role of nurturer. Often we arrive tinged with guilt. But when the singing begins, or when a soloist stands up and opens the doors of heaven, we know it's OK—more than OK—to be there. It happened for me so poignantly at Glacier View Ranch when Rene Pollard picked up the mike, her lovely voice settling and calming us, lifting us into celestial places. I knew every woman in the room would go home a better wife and mother. Ysis Espana did the same for us in Texas. I wonder if musicians realize what power they have to transport us from the mundane into God's very presence?

During the social moments at retreats women talk and laugh and share. I watch them sitting about on Saturday night, munching popcorn and discussing their kids or their jobs or the quilt they're making. Sometimes I see two or three sitting apart and tears are flowing. Women tend to share at deeper levels than men do.

But this isn't really about retreats or gender differences. I simply wanted to say I've had the most wonderful time being a woman all my life, and I praise God that He imagined a being whose purpose was to gentle husbands, band-aid small knees, bake blueberry pies, teach children to pray, wear perfume, enjoy pretty clothes, stretch budgets, and demonstrate aspects of His character that bring comfort and healing in our scary, out-of-kilter world.

"Thank You, Lord, for what You did with Adam's rib, and for giving me a chance at the role. It is my prayer that You will lead me closer daily to what You meant me to be."　　　　　JUNE STRONG

OCTOBER 13

Tell Me, Mary

"I am the Lord's servant," Mary answered. "May it be to me as you have said." Luke 1:38, NIV.

Sometimes during my personal devotions I wish I could bridge the gulf of time that separates me from the characters in biblical drama, especially the women who played such key roles in some of its cosmic scenes. Mary, for instance. If only I could talk to her, question her, what insights she could provide to my understanding of how it was to be a woman in her time.

Where did you find the courage, Mary, I would ask her, to accept the challenge of becoming the mother of a member of the Trinity? You must have known, when you acceded to the plan announced by the angel, that you would be the focus of village gossip, of speculation and innuendo. Though honored above all women and innocent of the whispered accusations, you must have felt the weight of guilt imposed on you as you carried the divine burden in your womb.

How did you feel about your engagement to a man so much older than you, this widower, who, unless the Lord had intervened, would have put you aside? Had you been given any voice in the decision that espoused you to Joseph? Didn't the prospect of taking care of him and his home seem more than should be expected of someone of your tender age, scarcely yet a woman? Then before you were even used to the idea of mothering Joseph's children, were you not overwhelmed by the stupendous task of mothering *God's* child?

Whatever your fears, whatever feelings of inadequacy you may have had, you did not utter them. You only said, "Be it unto me," and magnified the Lord.

What an example you left me, left all of us women, Mary. When I am overwhelmed by a task the Lord has assigned me, I shall try to remember your submission.

I know the burdens of motherhood, of being teacher at school and teacher at home. I wonder how you found time to spend with that special Son, laying the groundwork for His unique mission of saving humankind and vindicating God's name. I wonder how you, who had no special training in behavioral sciences, were able to mediate between Him and His taunting stepbrothers. I see you at work—making the daily bread, *from scratch*; picking the stones out of the dry pottage-lentils; bargaining over the price of a jar of oil at the market; doing the washing at the village well; carrying the water jugs; spinning and weaving the family wardrobe; yes, even sweeping up the curls of planed wood and the sawdust in Joseph's shop because that was "woman's work."

I have known some pain in raising my family, have suffered for my children's pain. I still do. But you, Mary, knew the greatest pain of all—giving Him up, in your widowhood, to an unpaid, itinerant ministry and, ultimately, to the cross.

Tell me, Mary, the things you pondered in your heart, especially when that heart was pierced by the sword. Tell me how to bear up, Mary. I too would be a handmaid of the Lord.

JEANNE JORDAN

Unprecedented New Realities
for Women

*And there was a prophetess Anna. . . . She did not depart
from the temple, worshiping with fasting and prayer night
and day. And coming up at that very hour she gave thanks
to God, and spoke of him to all who were looking for the
redemption of Jerusalem. Luke 2:36-38, RSV.*

In the first two chapters of the Gospel of Luke, Jesus' birth is
narrated through unexpected happenings, upside-down values,
and astonishing surprises.

Men, priests, and governors are not the only focus, but women
and especially couples like Zechariah and Elizabeth, Mary and
Joseph, Anna and Simeon! Amazingly, the one who should speak,
Zechariah the priest, remains silent, and the one who should be
silent, young Mary, speaks like Jesus, Paul, Peter, Jude, and James.
Bethlehem, a small village, is chosen as Jesus' nest over the
appointed City of David. Shepherds around a manger, not Temple
priests in their grand decor, welcome the Lord. Finally, Anna, day
and night, is in the Temple fasting and praying. Her experience
must be noticed. It had precedent neither in the Jewish world nor in
the biblical accounts. Women were not allowed to stay in the
Temple courtyard at night!

What is Luke trying to unveil in this short narrative about
Anna? Why does he take so much care to present her identification
so precisely?

In all of Scripture few characters are so well identified. Anna's
name is given in connection with family and tribal backgrounds,
marital and professional status. Luke's point cannot be missed:
With Christ's birth, unprecedented realities are dawning for
women. Anna not only is prophesying like Deborah and Huldah,
but also is now in the Temple, day and night, praying and fasting,
as if to underline that now with the Messianic era, women are going
to be on holy ground, involved in the most demanding spiritual
exercises. With Anna the prophetic function merges with the
priestly, opening henceforth the priesthood of all women and all
believers.

Are we open today to unveil our traditions and conformity to
risk living as Christians with upside-down values, allowing God to
change our routines, agenda, and fallen worlds?

Are we today submitted enough to our Lord to let Him shape

us and the Messianic era through astonishing surprises and unprecedented realities?   VIVIANE HAENNI

OCTOBER 15

An Unbelievable Gift

*If you then, who are evil, know how to give good gifts to
your children, how much more will the heavenly Father
give the Holy Spirit to those who ask him? Luke 11:13,
RSV.*

What woman doesn't like a gift—a dozen roses, a bottle of
perfume, a box of stationery? The gift might also be pears
from a friend's tree, a loaf of fresh bread, or tomatoes from my
neighbor's garden. Women love receiving gifts. They also thrive on
giving them.

One birthday my daughter sent me a lovely cotton dress in a
color and style she knew I particularly liked and could not find in
the stores. She had used spare minutes after working nights on her
first job to sew it for me. The belt was made of narrow ribbons in
the colors of the material, hand-stitched together in a most artistic
fashion. As a final touch she embroidered a tag for it: "Made at
home by Heidi." I wore it 10 years before I sadly decided it must go.
Even so, I cut out the tag and put it among my treasures. The ribbon
belt is now part of a decorative wreath in my bathroom.

Women crochet, sew, quilt, knit, and embroider gifts for those
they love. You may also find them sawing, varnishing, and
papering—making gifts. Some spend hours cooking, baking, and
freezing delicacies to share with others. Some creative ladies write
poems or paint pictures to give away. Creating and working to
provide a happy surprise seems to be part of the feminine mystique.

All of this does not suggest that men do not enjoy giving gifts.
Long after I finished playing with it, I treasured a doll bed my father
made for me when I was 6. And I remember with gratitude how my
husband of two months came home a day early from his business
trip, surprising me in the middle of the night—just to be home on
my birthday!

My heavenly Father is a lover of gifts. Today as we drove home
from church we admired the bright autumn colors against a blue
sky. At sundown the cardinals came to the feeder by the kitchen
window. A starlit sky is another gift of love to my senses.

Jesus told the multitudes sitting on the mountainside that the heavenly Father is more willing to give good gifts than any earthly parent. If we ask, we receive.

One gift, above all else, He wants to give me: the Holy Spirit. The Helper or Advocate will assist me in becoming like Christ. He will remind me what I have already learned and teach me new truths. He will stay with me and comfort me. The Spirit will set me free—from sin and self. Since I am a daughter of God, He is appointed to lead and guide me. Even more, He will be the source of the "love, joy, peace, patience, kindness, goodness, faithfulness, gentleness, [and] self-control" in my life (Gal. 5:22, 23, RSV). In His power I can be strong—mentally, emotionally, and physically—to go about my daily tasks.

Mine for the asking! Mine if I am willing to receive the Guest from heaven! How could I dream of not wanting such a gift.

Lord, I'm asking for the gift You have promised. I open my heart and home. May the sweet presence of the heavenly Guest be felt in my life today! NANCY VYHMEISTER

God's Formula for Homes

Thus says the Lord: "Learn not the way of the nations, nor be dismayed at the signs of the heavens because the nations are dismayed at them, for the customs of the peoples are false. A tree from the forest is cut down, and worked with an axe by the hands of a craftsman." Jer. 10:2, 3, RSV.

Recently a newspaper report told the tragic story of a young wife by the name of Kamala who committed suicide by pouring kerosene on her clothes and setting fire to herself. She was 18 years old, her husband was 21, and they had been married for just four months. While lying on her deathbed, Kamala pleaded to her parents, "Please take me home. I will not go back to my husband's house." She died the next day. At the time of Kamala's marriage, a dowry was agreed upon, the amount her parents were to pay to the parents of the husband. This amount was far above the means of her parents to pay, and therefore only a part of it was paid at the time of marriage. Failure on the part of Kamala's parents to bring the rest of the dowry led to severe ill-treatment of her by her husband and his family. There was no way she could escape this, as her husband was a part of a joint-family system. She was made to work like a slave, denied adequate rest and food, constantly shouted at, and even physically abused. Unable to bear the treat-

341

ment any further, she finally decided to put an end to her miserable existence.

An Indian bride who is taught to view her husband as a god rarely complains to her parents about the pressure. Even if the parents come to know about the ill-treatment their daughter is facing, they advise her to stay with her husband and in-laws for fear of social disapproval. This is one of the reasons a dowry-hungry husband has the upper hand in the social system.

Despite the efforts of the government and many voluntary organizations and increasing public opinion against it, deaths because of ill-treatment arising out of the dowry system occur in India. In many cases these families are respected members of the society.

In a joint-family system (which is observed by about 75 percent of the population), even if the husband desires to treat the wife better, he is pressured to give in to the demands of the other members of the family.

How grateful we are for Adventism, which teaches a different way of life and calls for a better relationship between husband and wife and their families. Thank God that the dowry system is not a part of Adventist culture. Let us rejoice that our philosophy of life calls for greater respect for individuals. In Adventism, marriage is a sacred union of two individuals in which mutual love and respect provide the basis for the partnership, enriching family life and ensuring an opportunity for service of men and God. Let us cherish and preserve this heritage.

Relationship between husband and wife is to be governed by the biblical principles. The apostle Paul tells us, "Husbands, love your wives and be not bitter against them" (Col. 3:19). Peter advises, "Ye husbands, dwell with them according to knowledge, giving honour unto the wife . . . and as being heirs together of the grace of life" (1 Peter 3:7). And Paul says to the wives, "Submit yourselves unto your own husbands, as it is fit in the Lord" (Col. 3:18). PREMILA CHERIAN

OCTOBER 17

Joining the Family

For as many of you as were baptized into Christ have put on Christ. There is neither Jew nor Greek, there is neither slave nor free, there is neither male nor female; for you are all one in Christ Jesus. Gal. 3:27, 28, RSV.

The line was long—longer than any I'd ever seen in my life—and the people waiting were there to welcome me into the family and wish me well. I was so happy! In fact, I cannot remember a day in my life since when my facial muscles have ached from smiling so broadly.

Moments before, I had stood before the pastor and all the witnesses and pledged my life and love with fervent devotion. It was all so meaningful. At 12 years of age I was sure I understood the importance of baptism. As I look back on that day now, my memories focus on the preparation that went into my baptismal classes, during which we studied the fundamental beliefs. I know that I didn't really understand all that was presented to us in the preparation classes, but I knew God loved me and in return I loved Him. I was able to love because God first loved me (1 John 4:19). How exciting it was (and is) to be in the family of God!

With spiritual growth I have come to realize that the love I felt that day was the beginning. There have since been times in my life when I have questioned whether I was loved or not by different individuals. It has been a great comfort to me at those times, and all the time, to know that I never have to wonder about, verify, or question the love of God. It is constant, always with me, and always with you.

Every now and then, when I smile and feel the muscles in my face stretch to the limit, I recall my baptismal day experience. I remember that the power of sin is dead. It died when I was 12 years old. Praise the Lord, I am alive for God in Jesus Christ. I was buried in baptism (which symbolizes death) so that (even as Christ was raised from the dead) I can live a new life (Rom. 6:3, 4).

Do you remember a day in your life when you smiled till your face muscles ached? STARR PINER

OCTOBER 18

Tablets of the Heart

For I was hungry and you gave me food, I was thirsty and you gave me drink, I was a stranger and you welcomed me, I was naked and you clothed me, I was sick and you visited me, I was in prison and you came to me. . . . Truly, I say to you, as you did it to one of the least of these my brethren, you did it to me. Matt. 25:35-40, RSV.

I hadn't expected to spend the week of my birthday in the hospital. I'd expected to be at work—the same as every other week.

Not this one. I would never forget this birthday.

The eight days in the hospital were filled with phone calls, cards, visits from friends (one of them told the nurses she was my mother so she could get in to see me!), prayers from the pastor, and late-night visits by my concerned young husband.

On the second day of my stay, a woman whom I'd never seen before came into my room. She introduced herself, but I don't remember her name. I can vaguely visualize her face. But I remember her.

She was a member of the church we attended, although we had never met. It was a large church, and we were new there. She said she was a volunteer, going to the hospitals to visit members who were there. She visited a few minutes. I remember she was kind, motherly.

I didn't see her again until the first time we returned to church, several weeks later. We sat down, and there she was, next to me in the pew. She recognized me; we said hello, and sat quietly for several minutes before she turned to me.

Her eyes glanced quickly over my body before she whispered the dreaded question: "You didn't lose the baby, did you?"

I nodded and quietly said, "Yes, I did."

"I'm sorry." I believe she was.

I don't recall ever seeing her again, but I remember her. Every year, the day before my birthday, I think about the little tiny baby boy who lived and died the same day. And many times over the years I've thought about the woman who took a few minutes out of her day to visit a young woman she didn't even know.

I wonder if she has any idea that someone she has forgotten from long ago remembers her.   MARY JOHNSON

OCTOBER 19

Right-sized Day

Give ear to my words, O Lord, consider my sighing. Listen to my cry for help, my King and my God, for to you I pray. Morning by morning, O Lord, you hear my voice; in the morning I lay my requests before you and wait in expectation. Ps. 5:1-3, NIV.

et's see. I've got to get the wash done today. The ironing is piling up. Tucker has a doctor's appointment. I need to learn the music for Vacation Bible School. I'll need to stop by the grocery store and get some milk—oh, and a birthday card for my sister-in-law." I lay in bed first thing in the morning mentally ticking off the day's activities. The longer I thought about things, the longer my list grew, until I was feeling pushed and frantic before the day even began.

"Mommy, I eat 'affles." Jace, my oldest child, was headed for the kitchen. Why did he have to choose waffles on this busy day? I thought about giving him cereal despite his request, but decided that it would take less time to make the waffles than to convince his independent 2-year-old will that something else might taste as good.

Those waffles surely smelled good. I got them buttered and syruped and placed them on a "bear" plate for Jace and a "dinosaur" plate for Tucker, my 10-month-old. While I affixed bibs onto each of the boys, Jace kept saying, "Mommy, cut up 'affle. It too big."

All of a sudden, it clicked. My day was too big. It needed to be cut up. But just as my son did not have the skills to cut up his waffle, I did not have the perspective to cut up my day. I needed Someone to give me that perspective. I needed God to slow me down. I needed to ask for His help in prayer.

"Give ear to my words, O Lord, consider my sighing. Listen to my cry for help, my King and my God, for to You I pray. Morning by morning, O Lord, You hear my voice; in the morning I lay my requests before You and wait in expectation."

When I cut Jace's waffle, the sweet syrup seeped down, and the food was much easier for Jace's stubby little fingers to handle.

When I allowed the sweetness of prayer into my day, it seeped down through my busy activities and made the duties seem more manageable. My outlook improved. And the things I didn't accomplish seemed less important.   CYNTHIA R. COSTON

OCTOBER 20

Training Your Child

Train a child in the way he should go, and when he is old he will not turn from it. Prov. 22:6, NIV.

It's the third time I've caught 10-year-old Rick kicking the dog. Why does he insist on being so cruel to an animal that not only never fights back, but keeps coming back for more? Where have I gone wrong in raising my son? What is this horrible glitch in his character that makes him want to hurt animals? Please, God, help me know the right words to say and the proper punishment so he will realize how much he is hurting the animal, me, and You.

All these thoughts and more went through my mind—several times. I was sure that I was a total failure as a mother and that I was raising a horrible monster.

Now my son is 20 years old. Let me tell you what happened last week.

Rick was home from college for the summer and agreed to go with us early Sunday morning to collect our winter's supply of firewood. Rick and Dad found a tree just the right size, dead, and without an orange mark. Dad started the chain saw, and Rick and I backed away. Suddenly we heard a screech, and a bird flew from the tree. Then another bird flew away. Rick and I looked at each other with question marks in our eyes.

The tree fell in just the right direction, and we scrambled up to it. Little tiny squeaks were coming from a huge branch. We had cut down a tree with a bird's nest in it. Rick lifted the branch, and we noticed movement on the ground. A featherless, ugly, tiny baby bird had fallen out of the tree.

We would never deliberately hurt God's defenseless creatures, but Dad and I didn't have any idea how to help the birds. But that didn't stop Rick. He stood the branch up and held it while his dad braced it so it wouldn't fall over. He very carefully shoved his gloved hand under the bird on the ground and gently placed it in the hole with the other babies.

Then we went back to work. But Rick wasn't through. He kept looking over at the nest, watching for the parent birds. He went back to the branch at least three times to make sure it was solidly braced. Finally we saw one of the parent birds land on the branch and go into the hole of the nest. Rick let out a deep sigh and relaxed.

Maybe my efforts and prayers had not been in vain after all.

If there is ever a time to pray without ceasing, surely it is when we are trying to raise our children in the fear of the Lord. There will be times when it seems like your best is not nearly good enough and you are positive nothing you do or say is making any difference with your children. But never give up. Keep working with those precious lives; do the best you know how for them. Most of all, keep praying. Cling to God's promise and trust Him.

SANDY JOHNSON

The Ultimate Connection

Pray without ceasing. 1 Thess. 5:17.

Do your prayers lead you heavenward? Have you ever experienced the presence of God in prayer? How often? Or seen a bit of His unlimited power through an answered prayer? How often?

Nyla is a hardworking woman with a very demanding, often hectic schedule. In an effort to organize her time more efficiently, she sets out her clothing for the following day before going to bed the night before. However, last night she was so tired that she opted to forgo the ritual, rationalizing that she could pull something together easily enough in the morning. Unexpectedly, she overslept, and all was a big rush to get ready. Not wanting to be late and not wanting to rouse her husband, who worked a different schedule than she did, she didn't turn on the lights as she hurriedly felt about for what she needed. Rushing into her office just a few minutes past 8:00, she closed the door and stepped to the mirror to be assured that all was in place. To be sure, all was not in place! One shoe was black, the other blue. The hose she wore were twisted and even another hue. The jacket and skirt were somewhat the same, but the blouse and tie surely put her to shame. If she played it low, perhaps no one would object, but the outfit indeed was one that didn't connect!

Do we ever walk out disconnected, unprepared to meet the world because we dressed in darkness by failing to turn on the lights through prayer? As Christians we owe it to the world to let every aspect of our lives reflect Christ's character. A challenge? Certainly! And even more, a precious endowment—perfecting our oneness in Him.

We are told that "no man or woman is safe for a day or an hour without prayer" (*The Great Controversy*, p. 530). Imagine your prayer life as a tank of gas. Are you close to empty, at a point marked "Maybe"? *Maybe God hears my prayers, maybe He'll answer, maybe I won't ask Him, maybe I'll have to do this myself.* Perhaps your needle is at the half-full point called "Sometimes." *Sometimes I hear You, Lord. Sometimes I'm going strong, and I know it's only through You. Sometimes I look away and seem to lose my speed.* Or do you stay close to the fountain so your needle is on "Full"? *Full of the Holy Spirit. Full with joy and gladness. Full with compassion and tenderness, rejoicing evermore!*

Only the "Full" tank will get us up these rocky hills, through storms and slides to the glories that wait above. Let's turn on the lights and fortify ourselves *now* in Christ through prayer. Prayer is our spiritual umbilical cord. Here is our fresh air that keeps us from suffocating in the earthly smog of sin. Prayer is the tool by which each of us can claim God's promises as ours. It is the broom that sweeps the webs of hopelessness out of our way. It is the inner garment that protects us from the deceiver's sway.

CHERRYL A. GALLEY

OCTOBER 22

Transitions

I am not saying this because I am in need, for I have learned to be content whatever the circumstances. I know what it is to be in need, and I know what it is to have plenty. I have learned the secret of being content in any and every situation, whether well fed or hungry, whether living in plenty or in want. I can do everything through him who gives me strength. Phil. 4:11-13, NIV.

I write these words following a visit from our children, who are now married but have been "home" with their children. Our house was full of children, love, and laughter. Our family was "compleat" again. Yesterday the house was hustling and bustling with activities, meals, babies, and wonder. Today it is very quiet. Everyone is gone.

I wander through the house. It isn't as clean as it usually is. There are fingerprints covering the sliding-glass door, Cheerios on the kitchen floor, and a small teddy bear that got left behind. I smile. This is good for me—to have my extremely neat home messed up a little. I walk to the sofa and straighten the pillows.

How much I love our children, their partners, and our grandchildren. I'm proud of them. I am concerned about them. Have their father and I set a good example? Are they prepared to meet the complexities and crises that a lifetime of living together will bring?

Someone has said we must learn to remarry a different and changing person several times during our married life. During these transitional changes we can choose divorce and seek a new partner who matches our current changes, or we can adapt ourselves to the changes. Experiencing and surviving change in a relationship can be as interesting as it is difficult, but it is much easier and less painful than the change associated with divorce.

If you are in transition now, the tendency is to behave as if you can fix things later. But transitions call for communication. There never will be a better time than *now* to talk about how you want your relationship to work. Don't wait. Talk *now*.

Some couples get so busy pursuing life that their marriages are forgotten. Such couples live together but don't love together. They forget to touch each other, listen to each other, or share intimacies with each other.

Don't let this happen to you.   NANCY VAN PELT

OCTOBER 23

The Powerful Influence of Example

How from infancy you have known the holy Scriptures, which are able to make you wise for salvation through faith in Christ Jesus. 2 Tim. 3:15, NIV.

In our text Paul, writing an affectionate, fatherly, pastoral letter to Timothy, reminds him how the Scriptures have influenced his life. Just how did Timothy gain an understanding of God's plan and learn about Christian virtues and graces that should characterize our conduct? The answer is in 2 Timothy 1:5: "I have been reminded of your sincere faith, which first lived in your grandmother Lois and in your mother Eunice and, I am persuaded, now lives in you also. For this reason I remind you to fan into flame the gift of God" (NIV).

Timothy's father was a Greek and probably was not a Christian. Clearly, then, it was the moral influence of his grandmother, Lois, and his mother, Eunice, that created an atmosphere of consistent and constant piety in the home. The apostle makes it clear in 1 Timothy 5:4 that piety is putting religion into practice at home. We are told that the piety he saw in his home and in his homelife was sound and sensible. How important! True piety is practical godliness whereby through the grace of Christ we become living epistles, clearly seen and read of all persons. Most people agree with the verse "I would rather see a sermon than hear one any day."

Timothy's life story helps us understand the powerful influence of a mother's and grandmother's faith and exemplary life.

"Next to God, the mother's power for good is the strongest known on earth. . . . Her influence will reach on through time into eternity" (*The Adventist Home*, p. 240).

My dear mother was a major influence in my life. I grew up on the north side of Chicago, and my father was not a practicing

Christian. For this reason it was difficult for my godly mother to influence her family in the way she knew was God's design. Even though she died at an early age, when I was only 18 years old, her kind, loving, consistent life made an impact on me that will always stand the test of time.

When I accompanied my husband to Rio de Janeiro to attend the large international meeting in 1986, I had no idea that I would end up spending eight days in the Silvestre Adventist Hospital with a critical bleeding ulcer. When it became evident that I would need blood, Ted, our son, insisted that he be the first to donate two units. It is an emotional memory when I recall the extreme kindness of physicians and nurses and when I realize how many church leaders offered and actually gave blood to see me through this emergency.

Our son confided his feelings to his father in this way: "Mother has always been an example of unselfishness by putting her family and others ahead of her own desires. Her sweet, selfless influence led me to love Jesus and to be thankful that He freely gave His blood on Calvary to ensure my salvation. I was convinced that if I needed blood, she would give every drop she had and even her life itself for me. I wanted to do everything possible to save her life."

Until this experience in Rio de Janeiro, little did I know the extent to which my unconscious example had influenced our son as he grew up in our home. Never underestimate the powerful influence of your example on others and especially those in your own home.

"Throw a pebble into the lake, and a wave is formed, and another; and as they increase, the circle widens until it reaches the very shore. So with our influence. Beyond our knowledge or control, it tells upon others in blessing or in cursing" (*Christ's Object Lessons*, p. 340).

ELINOR WILSON

OCTOBER 24

Remembering Emily

And let us not grow weary in well-doing, for in due season we shall reap, if we do not lose heart. Gal. 6:9, RSV.

Etched into early memory is the aroma of freshly baked bread, a broom, and Emily. She first impressed my 8-year-old mind that day she walked into our old farmhouse. I was sweeping the kitchen floor. Mother slept in her room, recovering from what I later learned was a mastectomy. Emily, who barely knew us, came bearing gifts. Christianity in a loaf of bread. That day marked the beginning of a long and meaningful friendship.

As a youngster, I believed she loved me and cared about how I felt. While a teen, I may have confided that I wanted to be like her. Now I would say she recognized and responded to an inner, unidentified need—my search for Jesus. Now I understand she discipled me. Emily became my mentor.

For more than 10 years, I considered Emily a best friend. Though years my senior, she talked to me as a peer sharing what the Lord taught her as she struggled with raising her family and caring for needs at home and church.

I can still see the special smile saved just for me (at least I always thought so) that came from the back row of the church while I sat in the choir loft. And as we prayed together when she led our youth prayer group, I heard the depth of feeling and the intimate way she spoke to God. Though her personal life was laced with sadness, I read joy in her eyes, peace on her brow, love in her voice.

Time and change press inevitably into life. Distance and commitments keep me from seeing Emily, though I think of her often. The last time our paths crossed, Mother was losing the battle that began one long-ago summer when Emily brought her bread while I swept the kitchen floor.

Her husband occupied the hospital room down the hall from Mom, and I visited them occasionally during my pacing. She asked about my spiritual life, and we shared what we had learned over the years. Although our beliefs now varied, she remained the sincere, supportive friend I had known many years before.

When Emily stepped into Mother's room two nights before her long miserable struggle ended, another indelible impression was mine. Emily and my mother had never been close, yet that night, when our family was there, Emily asked if she could pray with us. Joined in a circle around Mom's bed, Emily spoke to the Lord for our hurting family. I will never forget her caring, her ministry, her model.

In my mind's eye, Emily still ponders the pages of her worn Bible in her favorite chair, learning. To emulate her remains a goal. And though she may not have known at the time and probably wouldn't admit it today, I know that if she had not been part of my life, I would not be quite who I am.

I'm thankful the Lord prepared Emily for her roles of friend and teacher. "By beholding we become changed" (*Christ's Object Lessons*, p. 355). I know that's true, because for all those years, you see, I watched while Emily wrote Jesus on my heart.

MARY JOHNSON

Lessons Children Teach

My sheep hear my voice, and I know them, and they follow me; and I give them eternal life, and they shall never perish, and no one shall snatch them out of my hand. John 10:27, 28, RSV.

One of my favorite pastimes is baby-sitting. I have had opportunities to watch children and admire them, and I have come to know that they are very important treasures. Taking care of children is not an easy job. One gets to do messy things, like changing diapers and cleaning up, and much of the time there is little opportunity to observe the child.

Children have lessons to teach, if only we stop and watch! A child has a way of getting attention—sometimes by screaming. Mothers know how to interpret each cry, each scream. It could be the baby is hungry, sick, or wet. Sometimes the child just needs to be carried. So mothers and baby-sitters get to know that their babies scream or cry when they need them.

But apart from these, children teach us some spiritual lessons, also. Children learn to trust those they identify with—their parents, siblings, and baby-sitters. They know their voices, and once they are around them to carry them and talk to them, they feel relaxed and comfortable. As children grow, they learn to depend more and more on their parents. They do not fear a fall when Mom or Dad is around; they feel confident that all is well with Mom near. When they are hungry, they trust that Mom will provide the food.

We can unmistakably liken the relationship between a child and his or her parents to that between us and Christ. Jesus gave all in order to save us, and He still sustains us. He tells us we are His sheep. His sheep know His voice, and He knows His sheep, and they follow Him (John 10:27). Jesus promises eternal life to all those who follow Him, and He says, "They shall never perish, and no one shall snatch them out of my hand."

In our Christian experience in the world today, we need childlike faith that trusts completely and depends totally on the Lord Jesus Christ, for without Him we are nothing, and can do nothing. We must let the children teach us total dependence on our Source of life, because "to the death of Christ we owe even this earthly life. The bread we eat is the purchase of His broken body. The water we drink is bought by His spilled blood. Never one, saint or sinner, eats his daily food, but he is nourished by the body and blood of Christ. The cross of Calvary is stamped on every loaf. It is reflected in every water spring" (*The Desire of Ages*, p. 660).

CONSTANCE C. NWOSU

OCTOBER 26

Is It Over?

Even so it is not the will of your Father which is in heaven, that one of these little ones should perish. Matt. 18:14.

My favorite weekends include a visit from our two grandchildren. While Heather still prefers to stay close to home, her 3-year-old brother, Ryan, is always eager to spend the night at our house.

He has a bedroom at our house that he calls his own, but lately he's become conveniently convinced that there are wolves in our upstairs. According to him, he's heard them growl, and he's even seen their *big* eyes! No amount of convincing has erased his fear of a night visit from the wolves. So we came up with the idea of using the mattress from the guest room crib to make him a bed on the floor beside Grandpa and Grandma's bed. Need I say that this was a very popular decision?

My husband and I had made up the "floor bed," and the three of us had knelt to pray that the wolves would be kept at bay through the night. We had showered Ryan with hugs and kisses and I had just tucked in his covers when I felt a little hand reach out for mine. "Let's hold hands, Grammie," he said. So we did.

It seemed that only a short time had passed when the next thing I knew there was some movement from the floor bed. I opened my eyes. Through streams of morning light creeping in around the shades, I saw Ryan watching me. He was kneeling on his bed, and his big blue eyes just cleared the top of our mattress. He asked me a simple question: "Is it over?" Now, in his mind that meant "Is the dull night over? That period of time when play ceases, and Grandpa lies still in his bed instead of playing hide-and-seek?" To a 3-year-old, nighttime is a dreadful waste of time, and when it's over—that's incredibly wonderful news! As for me, I can't remember a night that felt too long! But I couldn't help smiling at my grandson. "Yes, Ryan," I said. "It's over!"

Time is relative, isn't it? It all depends on our situation. For instance, our degree of tiredness or our age may determine whether or not we're ready for the night to be over. This same idea applies to our spiritual life as well. Sometimes I feel like crying, "Lord, is it over?" Because I'm tired of the pain I see, and the separation, and the painful situations people get caught in in this world. But then there are other times when I want to plead just as urgently, "Lord, wait just a little longer!" That's when someone I love isn't walking with the Lord, or when I sense my own need to come closer to Him. There's only one Person we can trust to know when it's time for the "night" to be over, and that's our heavenly Father. Because when the timing seems just right for me, it may seem all wrong for you. He and He alone will know when there's been enough night. But for now, He's given us today to get ready for the glorious morning of His soon coming—when there will be no more night! Praise Him for His loving-kindness!   ROSE OTIS

OCTOBER 27

The Rod or the Child?

For the Lord reproves him whom he loves, as a father the son in whom he delights. Prov. 3:12, RSV.

In one of the classes I teach I had to put my foot down and insist that two of my students who refused to take the class seriously repeat it before registering for the next level. It was not an easy task. I was called names by other students who did not know the details of the story. To some, I was unnecessarily strict and wicked, and enjoyed overworking students in all my classes.

During the quarter that these students repeated this class, there was always tension in the class. As hard as I tried to make them feel at home, they maintained their distance and refused to reason. Sometimes I had to force them to respond to questions in the class. I was overburdened. I did not know what else to do to prove to them that I had good intentions and that my actions were for their own benefit. I left the situation in the hands of the Lord and kept praying about it. Toward the end of the quarter there was a remarkable improvement in their performances, and when the final examination was taken, the two of them emerged successfully. Right now, one of them is ahead of the other students in one of my other classes and has become very serious with his studies.

The Bible said it well in Proverbs 13:24: "He who spares the rod hates his son, but he who loves him is diligent to discipline him" (RSV). In many homes today, it has been the case that some parents choose to spoil the child and spare the rod. They are not diligent to discipline their children and bring them up in the fear of the Lord. The result of this is that the children become spoiled at home and carry that "spoiledness" wherever they go. They become irresponsible when they are supposed to exhibit mature characters. This has led to regret and ruin on the part of many of our young people.

Our God loves us greatly and so gave His only Son to die on our behalf. Yet He does not spare the rod to our ruin. In our text today, He "reproves him whom he loves." There are many instances in the Scriptures and in our world today when God showed His love for His children by "reproving" them. Many times the Lord allowed the Israelites to be taken captive by heathen nations in order to call them back to Him. And most of the time it worked; they realized their sins and asked for pardon. Even King Nebuchadnezzar, after spending seven years with the wild animals and eating grass like them, acknowledged that there is no other God except the God of heaven (Dan. 4:28-37).

A story is told of a man who said he would not give his life to Christ until he was 58 years old. God waited patiently for him and revealed Himself to him in many instances, yet he would not heed the call before his target age; he wanted to enjoy life in his youth before acknowledging God as his Lord. In love, God allowed him to face trials. He lost all his wealth and got involved in many accidents. When finally he accepted Christ and gave a testimony to the goodness of the Lord, he was all bruised and had only one good leg and hand; the others were either deformed or artificial.

The Lord has a thousand ways to call us back to Him. Therefore, when we are faced with trials and temptations, let us stop and ask God what message He has for us.

"Count it all joy, my brethren, when you meet various trials, for you know that the testing of your faith produces steadfastness" (James 1:2, RSV).   CONSTANCE C. NWOSU

OCTOBER 28

My Father Listens . . . and Hears

This is the confidence we have in approaching God: that if we ask anything according to his will, he hears us. And if we know that he hears us—whatever we ask—we know that we have what we asked of him. 1 John 5:14, 15, NIV.

I couldn't get my father's attention . . . unless I was performing. He listened if I was perfecting a temperance oration for a speech contest. He listened if he wanted me to learn a new song at the piano. He listened if I would accompany my talented singing, trumpet-playing brother. A speech, a tune, an accompaniment . . . then he listened.

But he didn't hear my thoughts, my needs, my feelings—me. He didn't listen. I couldn't get his attention. He didn't hear me.

Today my father lives in silence in my life . . . mute testimony of a father's lack of presence; the living absence of father. He is there, but not here. He lives in a corner of the earth, but doesn't make himself real in my life. And yet, paradoxically, he does. Somehow as a ghost of my past—not living and vibrant and nurturing and fathering me, but hauntingly reminding me of his very absence and what might have been, what could yet be. So I reach out to You, my heavenly Father. I enter this morning into Your presence, knowing that You are already present. I climb into Your lap and snuggle close, needing to be enveloped by Your warm embrace. Then I marvel that before I sought Your presence, Your embrace, You had already found me, held me close, and I heard Your fatherly voice in my listening ears: "I will never leave you nor forsake you." Praise You, Father! I am Your daughter . . . even a child in Your arms. You hear. I do have Your attention.

"But while she was still a long way off, her father saw her and was filled with compassion for her; he ran to his daughter, threw his arms around her and kissed her."—Jesus, in His "Parable of the Lost Daughter," Luke 15:20, NIV. (Gender respectfully supplied.)

ANONYMOUS

OCTOBER 29

Changes

If you, then, though you are evil, know how to give good gifts to your children, how much more will your Father in heaven give good gifts to those who ask him! Matt. 7:11, NIV.

Before my husband and I had children, well-meaning individuals told us that we would never understand how much babies change your life until we had some of our own. I really hated that. I was a smart person—I was sure that I could understand what they were speaking of.

Well, then we had two sons. What a change—good and otherwise. Just last week we got all dressed for church in our Sabbath best. I had been in cradle roll for 10 minutes busily watching over my 2-year-old, Jace, and vainly attempting to restrain my 10-month-old, Tucker. I glanced down to get our offering out of the diaper bag and realized to my chagrin that three of the buttons on my dress were unbuttoned and my once perfectly tied scarf was encircling not only my neck but also the neck of my 10-month-old.

Yes, having children has meant changes. My once-organized, neatly ordered life has been plunged into utter chaos. But there have been good changes, too. Watching Tucker's face light up when we play peekaboo, singing songs with Jace at worship, kissing them good night and hearing one say "I love you, Mommy" and the other say "da-da-da."

I realize now that the changes children bring to a family have to be experienced to be believed. And the intense love I feel for them can't be understood on an intellectual level. I love those little boys with all of my heart—because they are part of me. They even look like me. I would do anything to keep them safe; I would protect them at any cost.

And when I think about my intense love for them, it is incredible to remember that God compares His relationship to me as that of a parent to a child. He loves me with His whole heart—because I am part of Him. I even look like Him. I'm made in His own image. He will do anything to keep me safe; He will protect me at any cost—even unto death.

"If you, then, though you are evil, know how to give good gifts to your children, how much more will your Father in heaven give good gifts to those who ask Him!"

As the song says: "He may be the ruler of everything, but I know Him better than that. He is Father to me. I call Him, Father."

CYNTHIA R. COSTON

OCTOBER 30

Beloved Saint, Blessed Hope

O death, where is thy sting? O grave, where is thy victory? 1 Cor. 15:55.

The sad punctuation of a funeral service marked the end of a long, fruitful Christian walk. This believer had lived her life as a "saint," with a calm, steady faith in God. It showed in her life. She couldn't help it.

She loved children, all children, and made teaching them her life's work. She married, then had children and grandchildren and great-grandchildren. Her family did indeed call her blessed.

In her later years, after teaching children in church school, she gave their younger siblings and friends a good foundation by directing a day-care center. Then she caught up with her former students by starting a Pathfinder club, and took them camping!

Noticing the natural love children have for music, she started a band—and campaigned for instruments. Today many young adults in her home church glance at dusty instrument cases and old sheet music, then think fondly of her.

In her golden years retirement did not mean seclusion. She moved close to a college campus, welcoming a steady stream of grandchildren, new friends and old. Instead of simply resting in a favorite chair, she used it as a place to teach. She learned to make charming crafts, and shared the art to spark new relationships. She made delicious meals that satisfied the heart. She loved those around her, exercising a solid wisdom sprinkled with lots of good humor.

Letting go was hard. The day of her funeral was gray and chilled. The quiet form belied her vibrant Christian example and influence. They will go on through eternity.

Still, death brings pain. It breaks hearts and crushes spirits. And sometimes, when it's our turn to stand beside an open grave or open sea and bid a last farewell, the pain may be too much to bear. It is. God knows it is. This separation was never what He intended.

It would be too much, too cruel, if the story of life ended at an open grave. But it doesn't. God promises life eternal, and His promises are sure. So incredibly, in the eternal sense of things, death is only sad punctuation. It is not the end. This is a precious promise to have. We hold it as we turn away from the grave and turn our hearts and minds toward the glad reunions. KYNA HINSON

OCTOBER 31

What Is God Like?

Now this is eternal life: that they may know you, the only true God, and Jesus Christ, whom you have sent. John 17:3, NIV.

My understanding of this text is that the key to eternal life is to know God. From that premise it would seem that the greatest need of the world is the need to *know* God. The world will be convinced, not by what the pulpit teaches, but by "what the church lives" (*Testimonies*, vol. 9, p. 21). It challenges me with the responsibility of helping the world understand what God is like.

"You're the only Jesus some will ever know" also indicates my responsibility.

So what is God really like? This is an inexhaustible subject, but there are several attributes that are important to me. First, He is love. He loves unconditionally. "Love" is a word that is often misunderstood and overworked. Someone said to me recently, "Love, love, love—that's all 'they' talk about." But it is only because "God is love" that the plan of salvation is available to me.

Too often our love for people is dependent on their performance. Unconditional love is based on what we can give rather than on what we can get. Most of us parents understand this from experience. Several years ago I had a conversation with one of my sons that showed me how important it is for me to love him, as my son, in spite of what he may be doing that does not meet my approval. If he cannot understand that I, whom he can see and touch, can love him just as he is, how can he possibly understand that God loves him?

Another important attribute to me is that God is forgiving and accepts each of us regardless of experience. That is difficult to comprehend because it is so difficult to forgive and accept ourselves. And because of our inability to forgive ourselves, we find it difficult to forgive others.

Jerry Cook, in *Love, Acceptance, and Forgiveness*, helped me understand this concept. "Never labor under the misconception that . . . acceptance breeds license. To the contrary, your very acceptance of a brother will make him strong. It will never confuse him in questions of right and wrong if your teaching and personal lifestyle establish clear standards. . . . But if you communicate personal rejection . . . he will never be around long enough to be touched by God through you" (p. 19).

My prayer is that my experience may be so close to my God that others will see Him through me and desire to know Him personally.

BETSY MATTHEWS

NOVEMBER 1

Contentment

For I have learned to be content in whatever circumstances I am. Phil. 4:13, NASB.

A dairy farmer was showing a visitor around a barn that housed 100 thoroughbred cows.

"Notice that well-dressed man over there," the dairyman said.

"He comes here often and stays for a long while. Let's see what he's doing."

They walked over, and the farmer asked, "Excuse me, sir, but I see you here often. Is there anything special I could show you?"

"No, thank you," the man replied with a chuckle. "You see, I'm a psychiatrist, and when I've had a really tiring day I like to come here among the cows. How refreshing it is to spend a quiet hour with 100 happy, contented females!"

Stop for a moment and rate your level of contentment. From the doctor's viewpoint, would you fit in more with his patients or the cows? On a scale of 1 to 10, with 10 being perfectly contented, where would you rate yourself?

On one particular occasion when my life seemed to be falling apart, I could have rated myself about a 3. I wasn't depressed, but then I was far from happy and content. Nothing seemed to be going right, so I decided to tell God just how bad it was. On that day I decided to list all my trials so that God could see how bad things really were!

I started out with trial 1. How good it felt to tell God about how bad that one was! Trial 2 was just as bad. But then it seemed I heard God whispering to my heart, "Dorothy, haven't I done anything good for you?"

"All right, God," I answered. "For every trial I'll try to think of a blessing."

So I wrote "Blessing 1, trial 3, blessing 2, blessing 3, trial 4, blessing 4, blessing 5, blessing 6 . . ." By the time I finished I had 14 blessings and only 4 trials. And my contentment level had shot up to an 8.

Today I would rate myself as a 9. I have never been surer that I am just where God wants me, doing just what He wants me to do for this stage of my life. I am content, not because everything is going well, but because I know that God is in control of all the circumstances of my life.

A few moments ago I sat curled up in my easy chair looking out over the lacy landscape of an Alaskan winter. A flock of pine grosbeaks were at my feeding station, a fire crackled in my stove, and my adoring golden retriever, Matt, lay at my feet. Tonight Ron will call from some far-off motel room and we will talk. Friday he's coming home. I lay my cheek against the soft brown velvet of the chair and smiled. What more could a woman want?

DOROTHY EATON WATTS

Meditation on a Falling Leaf

I will sing to the Lord all my life; I will sing praise to my God as long as I live. May my meditation be pleasing to him, as I rejoice in the Lord. Ps. 104:33, 34, NIV.

Here, in my part of the world, fall is arriving. It's a season I look forward to. The crisp nights make for good sleep, days are bright and sunny, and the trees seem to compete with each other to see who can show the most stunning attire.

I love to take long leisurely walks, shuffling my feet through the falling leaves that have silently fallen to earth after shading us from the hot sun all summer long. Their cooling color of green has turned to warmer colors to suit the season.

One of my favorite walking places follows a winding, babbling brook. It seems to be laughing as it dances over rocks and carries along brightly colored leaf boats. It makes me feel like laughing with it for the joy I feel to be alive on this fall day. I lift my thoughts above in praise and thanksgiving, and I see a story unfold about a leaf.

God placed that leaf on that particular tree for a special purpose. The leaf fulfilled that purpose by spreading its fresh green self out to make shade, thus making the beings comfortable that came by on a hot summer day. It joined together with many other leaves in a concerted effort to shield and protect.

When fall comes and it's time for the leaf to leave the tree, it goes without a word of protest, swirling quietly to the earth, knowing it has served its purpose. As the leaf nourishes the earth it enables others to serve another season. "Their works do follow them" (Rev. 14:13).

Lord, please make me like that leaf.

ELLEN BRESEE

NOVEMBER 3

A Meal for Jesus

Now as they went on their way, he entered a village; and a woman named Martha received him into her house. And she had a sister called Mary, who sat at the Lord's feet and listened to his teaching. Luke 10:38, 39, RSV.

I really do think this story is the most delightfully personal story we have of Jesus, and I love to "see" it happening over and over again. Two women wanting to do their best for an honored guest and deeply loved friend. Despite all His selflessness and modesty, Jesus must have felt very special whenever He entered the haven that was their home.

I would give anything to have the experience of those women. To prepare a meal for Jesus Christ! To have Him come into my home, all hot and tired. To give Him a welcoming hug, a cool drink, water to wash His feet. In fact, I'd gladly get down on my knees and wash His beautiful feet myself!

Of course, I can't. But God in His great love sent me someone special to care for. Because my husband is a minister, he has very much the same sorts of needs that Jesus had.

I—and I alone—can make my home a haven for a tired hubby. What I would do for the Lord if He were to visit, I can do for that special man the Lord has given me. The man He has set aside to do His work on earth. There is no one else so uniquely placed to bring joy and peace into his busy, self-giving life. Because no matter how much I do my bit to help and lighten it, the burden falls squarely on his shoulders. His is the final responsibility.

David, who hates the buildup he sometimes has to submit to as a platform "personality," was once described (to his utter delight) as "least but not last." So, bearing in mind that little phrase, you could say that in caring for his needs (when my own cry out for attention), listening sympathetically when he needs to unburden his soul (and never repeating what he says in anguish or anger), serving him healthy meals (and not getting cross if he arrives late for them), putting his need for peace and quiet first (when I'd like him to deal with my problems), and always being there when he needs a friend (one he can really rely on), I am directly serving the Lord as few women will have the privilege of doing.

The rewards are out of this world. Maybe, when He returns, as a special favor the Lord will come to my home in the earth made new and allow me to give Him a welcoming hug, serve Him a cool drink, sit at His beautiful feet . . . Till then I'll do it for His servant, my husband, and rejoice in having so vital a part in the service of my Lord and Saviour Jesus Christ.

ANITA MARSHALL

The Lord Is at Hand

Let your moderation be known unto all men. The Lord is at hand. Phil. 4:5.

In the trying days we live in, often it is easy to be filled with anxieties, worries, and frustrations. Sometimes we might feel as though we should never get out of bed!

However, there is a way of escape from these emotions and negative feelings. There is that act of communicating with God—that puts us in touch with Him and makes everything all right!

Prayer isn't something we *have* to do. It is something we *get* to do. *We* get to bring to God every daily concern and burden of our hearts. Through prayer we discover that when trials, troubles, and fear knock on the doors of our lives, no one is there to react! God's cure for doubts and worry and lack of faith is prayer. He offers a way of action—not inactivity.

We get to pray in faith, because as today's text tells us, the Lord is at hand. He is near (NIV). Because He is near, at hand, we need not feel anxious about anything. His nearness brings peace—a deep abiding peace within.

Because the Lord is at hand, living waters from a wellspring of joy flow into our lives, refreshing every phase. Our mind and hearts are renewed and restored in Jesus Christ. When we are thus restored, we become fully alive, fresh, and vibrant Christians.

Now we can understand the necessity of taking our eyes off our weak, human natures and beholding instead whatever is pure, honest, true, noble, and lovely.

Let us take comfort in this thought as we face another day in Jesus' name.   CAROLYN T. HINSON

Love Is the Source

The fruit of the Spirit is love, joy, peace. Gal. 5:22.

It was a hot Sabbath afternoon. We sought refuge from the heat in the cool woods of the nearby forest preserve. As we entered the shaded paths, we felt the cooling breezes as the leafy tree branches gently swayed as natural fans. I felt a sense of peace—the heat-induced irritability replaced by relief and renewal. How cheering were the anemones and lady's slippers nodding by the way. The bright-yellow faces of black-eyed Susans brought a smile of delight. Bluebells and trillium feasted our senses with their perfect forms and colors.

Almost imperceptibly I became aware of the gurgling sound of water. We were close to the little rushing stream that watered this small earthly paradise. Leaving the well-worn path, I decided to follow the water to its source. Carefully stepping through the undergrowth, I followed the stream upward. It wasn't long until I found what I was searching for—a bubbling spring splashing life generously to its surroundings.

This little spring reminded me of God's love in our lives. Love is the source of life that seeks to be released outward in our relationships. The more open we are to the Source, the more love we are able to give. As love flows outward, joy blooms, just as the small flowers and majestic trees flourish from continuous watering. Then the forest refreshes us with peace. Thus from love, joy results and peace is released. For "the fruit of the Spirit is love, joy, peace."

SELMA CHAIJ MASTRAPA

Delicious Expectation

I rejoiced with those who said to me, "Let us go to the house of the Lord." Ps. 122:1, NIV.

She was 2 years old, with tousled blonde hair and blue-gray eyes that sparkled all day and often long into the night. Her parents were away but would be coming back in a few days with a very special baby brother. In the meantime my little niece and I were getting better acquainted. She was a happy girl, full of insightful questions, which often she answered with great assurance.

Each morning when I went into her bedroom she greeted me and the morning with a sunshine smile. And each morning the first words she excitedly spoke were "Is today Sabbath school day?" There was such disappointment in her little face and voice when I had to tell her that, no, today wasn't the day for Sabbath school. Later, at breakfast, she would relate wonderful stories about the activities in her tiny tot division, and was sure that tomorrow when she woke up it would be Sabbath school day.

Now, whenever I hear or read this verse from Psalm 122 I remember that precious little child, so full of joyous anticipation, eagerly wanting to go to the house of the Lord. I sometimes wonder how often we older "children" rejoice at the thought of Sabbath school day. When did we lose that excitement, that delicious expectation?

Sometimes I like to bring out my mind's-eye tapestry and see eventful Sabbath school days of years long ago. I see the little chairs that were just my size, the sandbox tables with their colorful tableaus made of mirror lakes and moss trees, little camels and little sheep, with stick figures draped in fanciful fabrics. I see the storytellers who made the Bible characters become almost real and so very familiar year after year. I see the Picture Rolls and little children, myself included, repeating memory verses, though many times we may not have been quite sure what they meant. And how comforting it is that no matter how many years have come and gone since then, we still remember many of those precious promises, but now with greater understanding.

I see the Sabbath school days of the college years. How stimulating it was for us to hear such learned men and women discuss to such depths the simple truths of our childhood. Our expanding intelligence and increasing sophistication seemed infinite.

I see the vivid colors of early motherhood in my tapestry and remember taking my little ones to sit in just-their-size chairs. Sand tables have been replaced by felt boards, but yes, I do see Picture Rolls with little children eager to repeat their verses. I see a new generation of tellers of Bible stories. How deeply grateful I am for all the faces I see, faces of caring, dedicated men and women who love children and love God, and make Sabbath a happy day for my children.

Gently I fold my tapestry and put it away in a secure corner of my mind.

In case you are wondering, yes, many years later Tousled Blonde now rejoices with her children and says, " 'Let us go to the house of the Lord' for Sabbath school day!"   P. DEIDRE MAXWELL

Therefore With Joy

The water that I shall give him shall be in him a well of water springing up into everlasting life. John 4:14.

A young woman of Samaria was involved in a relationship that was not in her best interest. It was her pattern: she always picked the wrong kind of men. Her reputation was legendary.

On this particular day something extraordinary happened to her. She went to draw water at a familiar place and instead obtained much more than she could have ever imagined. She received pardon, freedom, and acceptance. She met Jesus at the well.

A mother of a 21-year-old lupus patient recognized that her daughter was dying. Her prayers for healing had been answered in the past, but now her child continued to weaken. As I talked with this mother, I could feel her fear and her pain. At that point "Thy will be done" was not her prayer.

Several weeks after the death of the young woman, I made a follow-up call. This mother expressed to me her praise to God for giving her a special gift of peace and strength at the moment she needed it most. Anticipating only grief and pain, she found peace, hope, and comfort.

Paul wrote that "God is able to do exceeding abundantly above all that we ask or think" (Eph. 3:20). I especially like the "exceeding abundantly" part of that scripture. *The Living Bible* interprets it "far more than we would ever dare to ask or even dream of—infinitely beyond your highest prayers, desires, thoughts, or hopes." All this is to say that in all our experiences we can hope for—yes, even expect—His best gifts to sustain and encourage us.

We can find Jesus at the "wells" of our lives. At our "wells" of difficulties, confusion, our anxious and fearful times, He awaits us to enlighten, forgive, refresh, and direct. We can expect His abundant grace to strengthen and guide our steps. "Therefore with joy shall ye draw water out of the wells of salvation" (Isa. 12:3).

WANDA DAVIS

When God "Jumps for Joy"

Fear not, O Zion; let not your hands fall slack. The Lord your God is in your midst, like a warrior, to keep you safe; he will rejoice over you and be glad; he will show you his love once more; he will exult over you with a shout of joy. Zeph. 3:16, 17, NEB.

Several times already I have discovered Bible texts that have triggered in me great joy and surprise. When I read today's text consciously for the first time, I was going through a very hard time in my life. There was big trouble in the little church we were then attending. My heart was filled with deep sadness on that Sabbath morning. Then I found this text, which at the end states, in my German translation: "I jump with joy when I see you."

The Father jumps from His throne! He runs toward me with open arms. As I visualized in my mind the divine joy, so full of life, expressions of cheerfulness and laughter came to my face. The worries were gone. Peace and hope filled my heart. I delighted in the Lord! All around me there was, humanly speaking, no reason for joy. But at that moment, in my heart, I looked away from the earth toward God and saw His joy, His impulsive movement, and how He jumped up and ran toward me and my church. This picture both moved me and filled me with happiness. Nothing leaves Him unaffected, and He expresses His feeling openly and spontaneously. As I reflected on all this and saw the liveliness of God before me, it was one of those moments when I loved Him also emotionally. Most of the time we love Him by faith and out of gratefulness. But this text brought God near to me, as though I could see Him. And I wished to make Him always happy and to give Him no reason to be sad.

This text also helped me to bring the Father closer to other people: "Do you know that God leaps with joy when He sees you? You are a deeply loved person. God is longing for you!"

Sometimes I have demonstrated how it looks when God runs toward us. This has been helpful especially to people who were spiritually down by worries or guilt feelings. I ran up to them and took them into my arms. And then I showed them how it can be if they themselves turn to God. This will be discussed in tomorrow's text. RENATE NOACK

Skipping Toward God

Let us therefore come boldly unto the throne of grace, that we may obtain mercy, and find grace to help in time of need. Heb. 4:16.

I have known this verse since my youth. But recently, in a book, I found the exact meaning of the Greek word *parrhesia*, which the German Bibles translate "openness, confidence, joyfulness." In English Bibles the believer is encouraged to come boldly, with boldness, or with confidence to the throne of God. These translations, however, render but a faint gleam of *parrhesia*'s rich variety of meanings. *Parrhesia* is the attitude of joyful confidence, full of trust, almost of freedom without worries, found in someone who knows that he or she is loved and accepted, and who feels totally at home, like a child who runs from one room to another in a big house in the countryside, where he or she has always spent vacations (Frere John, *The Way of the Lord*).

If I want to illustrate this graphically, I see myself "skipping lightheartedly" toward the Father. More than once have I demonstrated it to participants in Bible circles, ladies' meetings, or seminars by skipping buoyantly and merrily toward a person. This has always produced cheerfulness and a deeper understanding of the certainty of faith. Skipping expresses unburdened joy. I come to my Father without worries and sorrows and snuggle up to Him. Jesus calls Him "Abba" and wants to encourage us to develop the same trusting love for our God.

Would you try once and go skipping to God? When I was a child I used to like to skip down the street swinging rhythmically. And if nobody is looking, I sometimes still do it today. Dare to do it once when you are alone, and you will see how joy wells up in you. For your Father comes to meet you! He jumps up with jubilation when He sees you!

If you want to demonstrate the gospel to others, that they may "taste and see" the goodness of God and thus perceive with their senses (Heb. 6:5), then use the two texts from Zephaniah 3 and Hebrews 4. Read the original text of these verses to them and show them the happy movement not only on God's part but also on man's. And if you have enough courage, skip and run so that they can see. When we will be at home with the Father, we will "go out and leap like calves released from the stall" (Mal. 4:2, NIV)!

RENATE NOACK

Jesus, the Welcoming Servant

It will be good for those servants whose master finds them watching when he comes. I tell you the truth, he will dress himself to serve, will have them recline at the table and will come and wait on them. Luke 12:37, NIV.

What is the first thing Jesus will do when He welcomes us to heaven? Ask this question in your family, among your friends, during a Bible study. You will receive many different answers, but what Jesus Himself has said about it will in all likelihood not be included. As I read for the first time this word in Luke 12:37, I had to read it twice, since I could not believe it.

Jesus bids us welcome, dresses Himself, and serves us. That is beyond us! We may be able to understand His action at the foot washing. But now, in His kingdom, in the midst of the angels, the Son of God puts on an apron and serves us. I become very quiet; I find no words.

On the earth Jesus went around doing good (Acts 10:38), and in heaven He still goes around doing good to men and serving them. That is His holiness! He does not want to be served; He is the one who serves. In heaven, too. This is incomprehensible for our conception of God. In the gospel God meets us in ways completely different from the religions of people. We do not come to God; God comes to us. We do not sacrifice something for God; God sacrifices Himself for us. We do not serve God; He serves us. That is our giving God!

I am stirred by amazement and adoration, but also by strong bonds of solidarity. I want to follow Him, I want to be a friend He can fully trust. Of utmost importance in the last days, says Ellen White, is the true representation of the character of God (see *Testimonies*, vol. 5, p. 746).

Can a human heart remain closed if we present God as the one whom we have learned to know in these texts? This message can transform hearts of stone into living hearts. The gospel thus demonstrated is like the creative word of God in the beginning of the world, when He said, "Let there be light!" The dead come to life! And they put on an apron like their Redeemer and serve one another. RENATE NOACK

The Happy Hormones

But the fruit of the Spirit is love, joy, peace, longsuffering, gentleness, goodness, faith, meekness, temperance. Gal. 5:22, 23.

Feel-good drugs are almost irresistible. From cocaine to caffeine, Americans are reaching more and more for something that can help ease the numbing stress and paralyzing pressures that make up so much of modern life. But evidence is mounting that these drugs are destructive, and scientists are discovering that a healthy body can make its own feel-good substances that are both protective and health-promoting.

Years ago Dr. Hans Selye found that fear or anger could trigger a blast of adrenaline in the body. The extra adrenaline produced a surge of energy that enabled the person either to fight or flee the source of danger.

Research later demonstrated that fear and anger can harm the body if continued over long periods of time. Other negative emotions such as grief, hatred, bitterness, and resentment, if prolonged, can also exhaust emergency mechanisms and weaken the body's defenses against disease.

Norman Cousins opened the door to the new field of psycho-neuroimmunology when he healed himself of a fatal, hopeless disease by using such positive emotions as joy, laughter, love, gratitude, and faith—along with sensible health practices. Since then, scientists have isolated many of the substances these emotions produce in the brain. They are endorphins, morphine-like substances that produce wonderful feelings of well-being. They also promote healing and strengthen the immune system.

These ideas aren't new. The Bible warns us of the consequences of "works of the flesh": "adultery, . . . hatred, strife, . . . murders, drunkenness, revellings, and such like" (Gal. 5:19-21). We are pointed to better things—"love, joy, peace, . . . gentleness, temperance." God's "medicines" are not only health-giving—there is an eternal payoff!   AILEEN LUDINGTON

The Diet

*Oh, how I love your law! I meditate on it all day long.
. . . How sweet are your words to my taste, sweeter than
honey to my mouth! Ps. 119:97-103, NIV.*

I would very much like to have a model figure. And although I've
come to realize there is very little I can do about my height, I have
tried many times to make some change in my width.

There was the grapefruit and cottage cheese diet, the "only fruit
for supper" regime, the liquid diet, the no-fat program, and more.
I lost weight on all of them for a while. The problem was that none
of these diets was a lifestyle that was workable for very long.

Why am I telling you all this? It has to do with another diet, a
spiritual diet. You see, I really want to be a beautiful, model
Christian with faith, wisdom, and kindness showing in all I do. In
my mind's eye the robe of Christ's righteousness fits me perfectly.
But when I go to the mirror of God's love as shown in the
Scriptures, I am appalled to find bulges and rolls in all the wrong
places.

Now, I have tried many religious diets to take care of the
problem. There was the diet of early-morning Bible study, the
liquid course of fictional religious stories, and the self-denial
method of fasting and praying. I was blessed by all these diets, but
each method alone was too narrow to meet all my needs. At times
I even tried the religious stress diet of letting my Bible fall open and
reading everything I saw. The problem was that I couldn't hold out
until the Lord came. He was taking too long for me to stick to one
rigid plan. I'd begin to slip.

The answer I found is the same for my spiritual life as for my
physical life. I don't need a quick-fix diet just to remove some
bulges here and there. I need a complete lifestyle change that
recognizes what it is my body and spirit need to be healthy and
strong. I need a variety of foods all through the day to sustain
me—hearty, healthy foods that taste wonderful and that I can chew
on. I need exercise to keep my muscles and faith strong.

Now, knowing this doesn't mean always achieving the ideal.
But I have finally been freed from the restless and unsuccessful
search for a quick diet to get me into that perfect robe and hold me
until the Lord comes. I now have a way of life that I can live with
if the Lord comes today, tomorrow, or not until sometime long in
the future.

And when I look in God's mirror, He says to me, "O taste and see that the Lord is good" (Ps. 34:8). And I say to Him, "Oh, how I love your law! I meditate on it all day long. . . . How sweet are Your words to my taste, sweeter than honey to my mouth!" This is a way of life that beats any diet I ever tried.   RACHEL I. PATTERSON

The Birthing Process

And God saw all that he had made, and it was very good. Gen. 1:31, NIV.

The birth of a child is a very powerful experience. A tremendous amount of energy is generated, and most people feel profound excitement when witnessing this event. The experience is intensified when the mother is someone you know, whether it is a friend, daughter, or sister. Many people feel deeply moved by the birth experience and say they have never seen anything like it. But for me the most beautiful thing I have ever seen was my daughter just minutes after she was born. Although I was tired from labor, my delight at her tiny face and body was unbelievable. My husband and I still look at each other and remark, "Isn't she cute?"

As a child, I enjoyed immensely hearing my mother tell the story of the first time she saw me after I was born. She would say, "What a little red wrinkled prune you were, but I loved you from the first minute I saw you!"

God beheld the perfect world that He had created. It pleased Him very much. After everything He made He saw that "it was good." Our world is no longer perfect. All we see here is marred by sin. However, there are still many things that are beautiful.

God created us with the ability to see and to appreciate beauty in a variety of things. Each one of us interprets what we see differently. Our idea of beauty is unique, although it is influenced by society and culture.

When we behold Jesus, we are changed into His image. "And all of us, as with unveiled face, because we continued to behold in the Word of God as in a mirror the glory of the Lord, are constantly being transfigured into His very own image in ever increasing splendor and from one degree of glory to another; for this comes from the Lord Who is the Spirit" (2 Cor. 3:18, Amplified).

Consider what you have chosen to see in your mind's eye today. Matthew reminds us, "The lamp of the body is the eye; if therefore your eye is clear, your whole body will be full of light" (Matt.

6:22). Let Jesus be the focus for your eyes, and light will fill your life.   Carel Sanders Clay and Sheila Birkenstock Sanders

NOVEMBER 14

I'd Pick More Daisies (and Share Them With Others)

Remember, O Lord, what the measure of life is, for what vanity thou hast created all the sons of men! Ps. 89:47, RSV.

Tomorrow! That's it, I'll smile more tomorrow. Yes, and I'll also have more time just to sit and listen. Or at least I'll look at you once in a while as I wash the dishes, vacuum, and dust. Right now I want everyone to remember those wonderful meals I cook. You do understand, don't you, Dennis, Doug, and Dony?"

I don't think I ever said the words out loud. But I wonder how many times I thought them or acted them out. And I can't take those yesterdays back. Or can I?

No matter how I figure it, those years are done. The impressions I gave my two boys and my husband, of their importance or unimportance to me, have been made. My friends know where my interests lie and what means the most to me.

Today I thought of Psalm 89:47. It says, "Remember how short my time is; for what uselessness have you created all the children of men!" The Bible writers too expressed how short life is and wondered about their lives.

Some of us need to read the following letter written late in his life by an anonymous friar in a monastery in Nebraska. We probably need not only to read it, but to allow it to seep down into the marrow of our tired and serious bones. You may not agree with everything, but think it over:

If I had my life to live over again,
I'd try to make more mistakes next time.
I would relax, I would limber up,
I would be sillier than I have been this trip.
I know of very few things I would take seriously.
I would take more trips; I would be crazier.
I would climb more mountains, swim more rivers, and watch more sunsets.
I would do more walking and looking.
I would eat more ice cream and less beans.

I would have more actual troubles, and fewer imaginary ones.

You see, I'm one of those people who lives life carefully and sensibly hour after hour, day after day.

Oh, I've had my moments; and if I had to do it over again, I'd have more of them.

In fact, I'd try to have nothing else, just moments, one after another, instead of living so many years ahead each day. I've been one of those people who never went anywhere without a thermometer, a hot-water bottle, a gargle, a raincoat, aspirin, and a parachute.

If I had to do it over again, I would go places, do things, and travel lighter than I have.

If I had my life to live over, I would start barefooted earlier in the spring and stay that way later in the fall.

I would play hooky more.

I wouldn't make such good grades, except by accident.

I would ride on more merry-go-rounds.

I'd pick more daisies.

It's not too late to start today!   GINGER MOSTERT CHURCH

NOVEMBER 15

God Gives

Jesus said to him, "I am the way, and the truth, and the life; no one comes to the Father, but by me." John 14:6, RSV.

Have you ever walked into an empty church and sat down just to listen to the stillness of God's presence? My family lived beside a church, and as a teenager I went into it many times alone. Sometimes I'd just sit and pray; other times I'd play the piano. The church doors were always open then. Anybody could go in to pray at any time. How things have changed!

Raymond Holmes was standing in his church alone looking at the pulpit. In two days he would have to stand there and preach the Word of God. He was filled with dread and with joy.

In order to preach, a person must know why and on whose authority before daring to speak the Word of God. Yet it is a joyful thing, because a person having the courage and faith to do so must be in fellowship with the living Saviour, who prepares that person for the message and who is the authority.

I remember when I first preached, a question came to me: Would I be mocked? The answer came: "Say something to help the people grow more like Jesus. He is the way and the truth."

As we start to prepare, the Saviour steps in and helps us to prepare. And the Holy Spirit leads us to the subject God wants us to speak on. God gives us faith to believe that what we are doing is important. He gives us the words to say that will meet the needs of the people who will hear us preach. God assures us that when we preach His Word, He is always with us. God gives us experience, knowledge, and wisdom, and calls us to the greatest privilege, challenge, and responsibility any human being can possibly have.

The message comes from God. He is the author, and it is given to those selected to be God's messengers. First they must accept the message for themselves before they can give it to others.

Ellen White said, "The minister is not infallible, but God has honored him by making him His messenger" (*Testimonies*, vol. 5, p. 298).

Romans 12:1, 2 says, "I beseech you therefore, brethren and sisters, by the mercies of God, that ye present your bodies a living sacrifice, holy, acceptable unto God, which is your reasonable service. And be not conformed to this world: but be ye transformed by the renewing of your mind, that ye may prove what is that good, and acceptable, and perfect, will of God."   NELLIE CARTER

NOVEMBER 16

Bread, Not Stone

Or what man of you, if his son asks him for a loaf, will give him a stone? Or if he asks for a fish, will give him a serpent? Matt. 7:9, 10, RSV.

Jesus had a way of taking human nature at its best, then pointing out the incomparably greater character of God. He plugged into our understanding of what we wish to be good in us—such as parenting. Who of us would give a child a stone when that child is hungry and asks for bread? What adult would give another person a stone when bread is needed? Who of us would give ourselves stones when we are hungry?

We give stones to our children when we criticize, or when we are dishonest, violent, or impatient. We give stones when we ignore them, or don't try to understand their plea for help, or when we represent God as a severe disciplinarian instead of a loving and compassionate friend.

We give stones to each other when we ignore, fight, criticize, or encourage guilt; when we don't reach out in friendship; when we don't live God's love by loving others.

We give stones to ourselves when we put ourselves down, when we don't accept our growth, when we don't forgive ourselves, or when we deny our soul's longing for God and human friendship.

I am a pastor specializing in family life and counseling, and I dream of a caring church family in which families of all structures are supported and accepted; in which ethnic, racial, economical, or sexual discrimination does not exist; in which fatherhood is just as important as motherhood; in which marriages share equal responsibilities and joys; in which single persons find joy in being loved by a church family. I dream of a church filled with children who experience godly self-worth because they are treated with kindness; a church in which God is represented as a loving Saviour, not a harsh disciplinarian; a church in which we take each other's needs seriously, bear each other's pain, and trust each other with our feelings. I dream of a caring church family in which self-esteem will be the result of relational fulfillment, not achievement. I dream of a church family that will be strong because all family units are strong; of a church family that will be instruments of healing to wounded people.

I believe that when we care for ourselves and others, God heals. I pray that I will be such an instrument.   HALCYON WILSON

NOVEMBER 17

The Journey

And lo, I am with you always, to the close of the age. Matt. 28:20, RSV.

Prepare me, my Lord, for the journey ahead,
with my hand in Thine onward we'll tread

I know not what tomorrow will bring,
or what my Lord may ask of me

Love and joy and happiness we'll share,
together the pain and sorrow we'll bare

Encourage me, my Lord, when the way seems dark and bleak,
from devastating storms head-on we meet

Give my trembling hand a gentle squeeze,
then Thy comfort and mercy I shall receive

I pray afraid I will not be,
by that which I don't understand or see

The tears that fall will strengthen our grasp,
and by faith over bridges we'll safely pass

Long ago this road was made,
with tears and blood and redeeming grace

Though very narrow and steep the grade,
within my Lord's heart every step is engraved

Lost and alone I'll never be,
for to my Lord's loving hand tightly I'll cling

When we reach the narrow gate,
and just beyond Heaven awaits

If I be weary now I'll rest,
my Lord Jesus will know what's best

With my trusting hand still in Thine,
the journey will end and so does time . . . DEBORAH SANDERS

NOVEMBER 18

You Are Free Indeed

There is therefore now no condemnation for those who are in Christ Jesus. For the law of the Spirit of life in Christ Jesus has set you free from the law of sin and death. Rom. 8:1, 2, NASB.

It was a beautiful Sabbath morning. As I drove toward my destination, bolts of light from the sparkling sun streamed out of the heavens, dancing like drops of mercury on the dew-drenched streets. I was so involved in praising the Lord that I did not notice that I was being followed by a police car until the blaring sirens jolted me back to reality. I was pulled over and given a speeding ticket. Even though I tried to tell the officer that he was mistaken—and he was on this occasion—I still received the dreaded citation, accompanied by a challenge to take it up before the judge on the date assigned. Since I knew that I was innocent, I decided to see him in court!

The day seemed uneventful as I slipped into the packed courtroom. The first two cases were both traffic tickets from the same officer who had cited me. They passed quickly and routinely. The next case did not! A young man was charged with operating a vehicle without registration and state-required road tests. He explained that he was simply moving the car from one location to another to prepare it properly for inspection/registration. The judge accepted his explanation and, being in a generous mood, told the young man that although his was a criminal misdemeanor that demanded a harsh sentence or heavy fine, he was letting him go free of charge. The judge also warned him not to repeat such a foolhardy act as he waved at the young man, instructing him to step down from the witness box. But the young man refused to move. The judge repeated in a kindly manner, "Young man, you are free to leave." But again the young man deliberately ignored him.

"I have something to say in my defense!" he said in a very belligerent voice.

"This is a traffic court. I've decided on your case. You're free to go," the judge said, his voice a little testy but still generous.

"You talking to me, bro?" asked the young man disrespectfully. "For I ain't leavin' till I get to say what I have to say!"

"You must address the bench as 'Your Honor'!" the judge added quickly as he banged the desk with his gavel to bring some order into his courtroom, which had erupted with laughter, heckling, and mimicking of the young man.

"Bro, you listen to me," said the young man, leaning menacingly toward the judge. "I have something to say, and I have a legal right to say it, and you ain't gonna send me outa here till I say it!"

As he jumped to his feet, two officers pounced on him, dragging him out of the witness box to wrestle him to the floor while the audience screamed, mingling protest with profane words. The judge angrily banged his gavel, shouting: "Order! Order! Order! Or I'll clear this room immediately!"

By then the young man was thrashing about violently, writhing and swearing as he struggled to free himself from the grip of the officers who tried to restrain him. Eventually he was handcuffed and his legs locked in iron shackles as he was dragged out by marshals to be transported to jail.

My case was next. Like a timid child I sat in the witness box, afraid of the judge's wrath that had been stirred by my predecessor.

"What's a nice woman like you doing in a place like this?" he asked, attempting to regain his composure.

"Guilty, Your Honor," I answered quickly, staring at my fingers.

"Pay the fine and don't let me see you here again," said the judge. I couldn't believe it; I was free—free to leave. As I stepped down, the judge's words to the clerk, "Remove all evidence of this incident from her record," rang in my ears. Since that day I've often thought of the object lesson that was played out in that court drama. It's like a parable of a future judgment scene that is being scripted by the choices we make today.

We all have sinned and come short of the expectation of our loving Lord, and the enemy is only too quick to write out a citation and accuse us before the judge of all. But because of the work of our personal Advocate and our faith in Him, there's no condemnation, and we are free indeed! Yet like the young man, we insist on defending ourselves. We try so hard to prove by our works that we are worthy of the Judge's generosity. We seek vindication where none can be found. We try to exercise our rights with God when we ought to submit—a word that in a spiritual context defines the act of giving up one's rights even when one has the right to exercise them.

All we can do is admit our guilt, accept the gift of forgiveness and freedom, then arise and go by faith into the promised fullness of life. For when the Son sets you free, you are free indeed!

HYVETH WILLIAMS

NOVEMBER 19

Working Smart

Whatever your hand finds to do, do it with all your might, for in the grave where you are going, there is neither working nor planning nor knowledge nor wisdom. Eccl. 9:10, NIV.

I found her in the lunchroom, sobbing over her sandwich as if her heart would break. She had recently transferred to a new department, and in addition to the chaos of changing offices and supervisors, the manager had just informed her of several new tasks that would now be her responsibility. "I am working as hard and as fast as I know how to work; I just can't do any better. I really shouldn't even be taking five minutes to eat," she wailed.

Sitting down beside her, I suggested that she lean back, put her feet up, and listen to an old story about two men who earned their living by cutting trees in the forest. One day they both ended up being assigned to a new crew. The first man's modus operandi was to attack the trees relentlessly. The minute one tree began to fall, he would rush over to the next one and begin to chop on it furiously.

379

He had so much work to accomplish that he never took any breaks and gulped down his lunch on the run.

Some of the other men marveled that he could keep up such a fast pace. At the end of the day, however, they were somewhat surprised to see that the second man had actually cut down more trees. This was very puzzling to them. The second woodsman had not chopped quite as hard as the first one. In addition, he took regular breaks all day long and sat down while he ate his lunch. How in the world could he have cut down more trees?

The men stood around discussing this seeming contradiction. Then someone recalled that every time the second woodsman took a break, he also sharpened his ax. Of course! He could chop more wood—with less effort—because his ax was sharp. The crew reckoned that the second woodsman was "working smarter," and would outlast the first man in the long term.

When I had finished telling the story, she mused, "I think that is what I have been doing—working hard, but maybe not with 'all my might.' I've not stopped long enough to 'sharpen my ax.'" Perhaps that is what the text in Ecclesiastes really means. Working with all our might should include brains as well as brawn. It means using knowledge and wisdom to achieve better results in the long term. Sharpening our axes means taking the time to keep ourselves fit: mentally, physically, emotionally, and spiritually.

We all need to be reminded from time to time that the Lord said, "Not by might nor by power, but by my Spirit" (Zech. 4:6, NIV). It takes wisdom to "work smarter." Fortunately, God offers that to us also, saying, "If any of you lacks wisdom, he should ask God, who gives generously to all without finding fault, and it will be given to him" (James 1:5, NIV).

I watched her leave the lunchroom and return to work. There was a lift to her step and a light in her eye. She was repeating to herself, "Not by might nor by power; ask God for wisdom to work smarter." God's "letter" to each one of us had changed the atmosphere of her world from bleak to better.

SHARLET BRIGGS WATERS

Joy in the Lord

The joy of the Lord is your strength. Neh. 8:10.

I fell in love and got married in 1967 while the war in Vietnam was in full swing. My husband was a private in the U.S. Army, which meant moving far away from the support of my family. I had never lived in a military town, and had no idea what to expect.

The rent for our little cottage alone took 70 percent of my husband's monthly pay! The utilities, tithe, and enough groceries for *one week* took the rest! That left no money for gas, food for the other three weeks, clothing, entertainment, or anything else! Very few jobs were available for wives, and there were hundreds looking for those few jobs!

I had never lived in such poor conditions. It had been many, many years since those worn-out hardwood floors in our little cottage had seen any varnish or wax! The walls were dirty, so we bargained with the owner for some paint, which he agreed to purchase if we would do the painting ourselves. Of course, we first had to fashion scrapers to remove the old paint, which was so bad it was peeling and curled in some of the rooms. We shampooed the living room furniture in an effort to improve the appearance.

I had been raised in a good home in which my parents provided me with everything I needed and wanted. I had been pampered and spoiled. The reality of life was a shock, and needless to say, I was bored. I didn't have any friends, and our savings were evaporating quickly. I sat home alone day after day feeling sorry for myself, and I became more and more depressed as I took my eyes off Jesus and looked at myself.

My only comfort was my loving husband and the Lord. As my depression grew deeper, I became more and more angry with myself. I didn't like myself that way. I realized that my only help out of the depression was God.

I reached out to Him in prayer, confessed my sin, asked forgiveness, and pleaded for help in overcoming my self-pity and depression. I studied the Bible and read *The Desire of Ages*. I found today's scripture and this promise: "A merry heart doeth good like a medicine: but a broken spirit drieth the bones" (Prov. 17:22). I daily claimed these promises as my own. I began singing all the songs I could remember from Sabbath school, and borrowed a songbook from church and wrote down the words to more songs that I knew the tunes to.

I made a list of all my blessings and daily added to the list, although sometimes I had a hard time finding a blessing. As I focused my thoughts on God and His goodness to me, praised His name, and recognized and thanked Him for all the blessings I had, I gained the victory over self, and my whole outlook on life began to change. I learned through many repeated experiences to be happy wherever God put me.

Now, 25 years later, I can look back and thank God for the way He has led in my life. My husband became a minister, and we have had 18 wonderful years learning to depend daily on God, to be creative on a minister's income, ministering to others in crisis, and helping them to learn to be joyful and trust in God.

In retrospect I see that every experience He allowed me to go through was to teach me not to count this earth as my home and to prepare me to help others.

God's promises to us are sure. We need only to claim them as our own, determine to be happy regardless of our circumstances, and accept His grace to gain the victory.　　　　CELIA CRUZ

NOVEMBER 21

The View From My Quarters

I will be glad in the Lord. Ps. 104:34.

A visitor to a small town asked an old resident, "What kind of town is this?" The visitor had a desire to move to the town. The old man replied by asking a question: "Well, what kind of town did you come from?"

The visitor proceeded to tell about the terrible town he had just left. The people did not act friendly, they felt that the churches contained hypocrites, and unemployment existed everywhere.

"You have just described this town, too," exclaimed the old man. "This town is just as bad."

Not long after, another visitor, thinking of moving to the same town, inquired about the town from the same old gentleman. The old man responded with the same question. "What kind of town did you come from?" The young visiting man described his last town as friendly. The people felt concerned for others, the churches acted caring and exhibited strong spirituality. Plenty of jobs existed.

"That is wonderful!" exclaimed the old man. "And you will find this town is just like that. It is a wonderful place to live."

When I heard this story, I thought of how well it fits some

people I have met. Believe it or not, when we lived in Hawaii, we met many people who were very unhappy there who found many things wrong with "paradise," while others were putting in for extensions. The same is true here, and it was in Missouri, and New York City, and everywhere we have been. Some love the weather, some hate it. Some love the church, and some stop attending. Some can't get the Sabbath off from their hospital unit, and the next Seventh-day Adventist in the same unit has no trouble. What is the difference? Attitude!

Most people keep the same attitude no matter where they live or work or worship. The location isn't nearly as large a determinant as is attitude.

What can you do if you find yourself in a location, church, or job that you don't like? First, decide to like it anyway. Then begin to find all the positive things you can about it. Make positive things happen. Don't wait for everything to happen to you. Determine to make the workplace more pleasant for those around you. Begin to look for things to do to improve the church—volunteer a little, and you will soon find plenty of things to do and wonderful people to work with. Try to make your community a better place just because you have been there. Be a good neighbor and reach out to the community as time allows.

There isn't much one can do about those endless miles that separate you from home, or the weather, or that inhuman boss, or even the pastor, but by taking a positive attitude and doing what you can do in a situation, you will soon find that you live in a great place with nice people and the best church around. Try it—you just might like it.

Maranatha!

ARDIS STENBAKKEN

NOVEMBER 22

In the Sunlight

For the Lord God is a sun and shield. Ps. 84:11, NIV.

For a time our family lived in New Mexico, and we were able to visit Carlsbad Caverns, one of the largest series of caves in the world. Their full extent is not known, but levels as deep as 1,100 feet below the surface have been explored. The three-mile walking tour ends in a main chamber called the Big Room, which is more than a mile in circumference and nearly 300 feet in height. I felt very small and insignificant. That far down below the surface of the earth, without artificial illumination, the darkness would be oppressively intense. I knew that if the lights ever went out, on our own we would be helpless in terms of finding our way. When we emerged at the surface and saw the sun shining in all of its glory, it made me appreciate light in a new way.

The sun, spoken into existence by God on the fourth day of Creation, brings life, warmth, and growth to the earth and to each one of its inhabitants. The Bible compares God to the Sun. Christ was and is the true light of the world (John 1:9). That metaphor helps me to understand the life, warmth, and growth that He so lovingly provides for us. Without the sun, plants wither away and die; without the Son, human beings cannot realize their full potential.

We have all experienced times of discouragement, pain, and even disillusionment, when everything looked oppressively dark. How many times, in my experience at least, one shining ray of sunlight has pierced that gloom and made a difference in my life. Sometimes it was a literal ray from the sun; sometimes it was a ray from the Sun of righteousness; and sometimes it was a ray of warmth sent to me by another caring individual. The following words were written shortly after I realized that God had sent such a person to me:

It was not so long ago that sunshine came—
Displacing shadows . . .
Filtering into places once so dark and cold.

Illuminating rays of love burst upon my heart—
Wrapping blankets of warmth and caring
Around frostbitten feelings.

Icy edges penetrated . . . thawing . . .
Can these be icicles of fear
Melting down my cheeks?

Drops of hope—
Nourishing the tender growth
Of new self-worth.

Rain—and sun . . .
Bringing bright prism rainbows
Shining through my tears.

Thank you, friend,
For it was not so long ago
That sunshine came.

God can bring light into our lives directly through the Bible.

"Your word is a lamp to my feet and a light for my path" (Ps. 119:105, NIV). However, sometimes it is in God's plan to use other human beings to illuminate our thinking and to show us a new way to look at ourselves. Their input can help us to see who we really are and what we can be with the help of God.

DEBBY GRAY WILMOT

NOVEMBER 23

Preparing for Winter

Thy word have I hid in mine heart, that I might not sin against thee. Ps. 119:11.

Spring in Washington, D.C., is a changing time. There are warm days that send the impatient gardener to digging in the yard or garden plot. Then winter suddenly reappears. Once more winter coats are donned against the chill. Only the crocus bravely pushing its way through the sod proves spring has really arrived.

Change. Isn't that a good descriptive word for life? One day a person gives you a word of appreciation. You soak it up as you would a warm early-spring day. Then, without warning, a critical word sends you hiding from the stinging sleet of winter. You desperately look for something warm to keep out the chill.

Change. From good health one day to a devastating illness the next. From vibrant life to cold, still death. Change will come to each and every one of us. Eventually you will be wrestling with or trembling from some sorrow in your life.

So how do we cope with change? Like the squirrel. By instinct the squirrel knows the cold and snow are coming, so it "squirrels" acorns away while the weather is warm. It can hardly hope to dig up more in the winter than it put away in the summer.

Be at least as wise as the squirrel and remember on the warm days that the cold will follow. When love is warm and all is well, squirrel away precious memories and Bible nuggets to feed on when the cold comes.

ELLEN BRESEE

God's Unfailing Love

Even though I walk through the valley of the shadow of death, I fear no evil; for thou art with me; thy rod and thy staff, they comfort me. Ps. 23:4, RSV.

When I awoke from surgery in the fall of 1988 and was told I had cancer, two thoughts went through my mind. How long do I have to live, and how much suffering will I have to endure?

How comforting to know at a time like this that God does care. "I will trust, and will not be afraid; for the Lord God is my strength and my song, and he has become my salvation" (Isa. 12:2, RSV).

Early each morning my husband would come by the hospital, read Scripture to me, tell me, "You're going to get well—God told me you're going to live," and would thank God every day for healing me. He has continued to do that to this day. He never fails to call when he's away, and assures me of God's care and that I still have a work to do.

I claim the beautiful promises in the Bible, "Bless the Lord, O my soul, and forget not all his benefits, who forgives all your iniquity, who heals all your diseases" (Ps. 103:2, 3, RSV). "O Lord my God, I cried to thee for help, and thou hast healed me" (Ps. 30:2, RSV).

When we walk through the valley and it is dark and foreboding, remember that as you start climbing, on the opposite side things start looking up. You can once again see the sunlight, and as you climb higher you begin to see the flowers, hear the birds singing, see squirrels playing in the grass and trees. You realize you are still alive, and the beautiful things in this world take on new meaning. God gives songs in the night.

The most beautiful thought of all is that at Christ's second coming all will be made right. We will then mount up with wings like eagles, we will run and not be weary, walk and not faint, live without sickness, and shall be with the Lord our Maker forever.

MARIAN MILLER

I'm Thankful for . . .

*Have no anxiety about anything, but in everything by
prayer and supplication with thanksgiving let your requests
be made known to God. Phil. 4:6, RSV.*

You've probably had years when you took a few minutes at
Thanksgiving time and made a list of the things you were
thankful for. Things like family, food, house, and warm clothing
likely made the top of the list.

But I read about a young man who decided to add a column to
his "thankful" list entitled "things to be thankful for." Years later
he came across the list, and what an eye-opener it turned out to be!

Events of the intervening years made him want to revise the list
almost completely. In many instances it turned out he should have
given thanks for that which was listed on the opposite side. This
experience helped explain an often-quoted but hard-to-understand
Bible passage: "In every thing give thanks" (1 Thess. 5:18).

An old man whose manner of looking at life was entirely
different from that of others in the village had only one horse, and
one day it ran away. His neighbors came to sympathize with him,
telling him how sorry they were for the misfortune that had befallen
him.

His answer surprised them.

"But how do you know it's bad?" he asked.

A few days later his horse came back, and with it were two wild
horses. Now the old man had three horses. This time the neighbors
congratulated him upon his good fortune.

"But how do you know it's good?" he replied.

The next day, while attempting to break one of the wild horses,
his son fell off and broke his leg.

Once again the neighbors came, this time to console the old
man for the bad luck that had befallen his son.

"But how do you know it's bad?" he questioned.

By this time the neighbors decided his mind was addled, and
they didn't want to have any more to do with him.

However, the next day a warlord came through the village and
took all the able-bodied men off to war. But not the old man's son,
because he was not able-bodied.

Is there something in your life you don't understand? Some sad
experiences that have left scars of pain and understanding? Give
them to your Creator. Ask Him to heal your brokenness and

replace anger, bitterness, or resentment with the joy of living the full Christian life.

During this Thanksgiving season, find some time to give thanks to God for all things. Maybe you can't be with a loved one—find a lonely person and make his or her holiday special. Maybe you or someone you love is suffering from sickness—on the other side of the valley is our heavenly home. Joy, gladness, and renewal will then replace suffering.

"Lord, thank You for my problems"? Yes, it seems impossible. But I can promise you that if you make it a habit to thank God for everything, your life will never again be the same.

GINGER MOSTERT CHURCH

NOVEMBER 26

Suddenly . . .

The day of the Lord will come like a thief in the night.
1 Thess. 5:2, NIV.

A cold wind blew as we arrived in the Athens airport. After taking our turn in the long line waiting for a taxi, we finally reached our small hotel in the city. It was 10:00 p.m. and we were tired. We decided not to unpack our cases, and gave way to the urgent need for rest.

Bang! Suddenly we were jolted awake by a terrifying explosion. It was past midnight. "It must be thunder," said Ron. "It's a bomb!" I shouted.

People were running up and down the corridors. Someone pounded on our door, yelling instructions. Sirens screamed in the night. Children cried and adults shouted. From our balcony I stared in disbelief at clouds of black smoke. Windows of surrounding buildings reflected fierce flames.

"Out!" said my husband, bringing me back to reality. We grabbed our still-packed cases and fled down two flights of stairs, pushed through the hotel foyer, and burst out onto the street. Fire fighters and their equipment, police officers, and photographers were everywhere.

Eventually we learned that a car bomb had exploded in an adjoining building. It had turned one car into molten metal. Pieces of it were embedded in the wall of our hotel. And a second car was now a gutted, burned-out shell.

When it was determined that our side of the hotel was safe, we returned cautiously. Little by little an uneasy peace settled over us.

Although we were fatigued, sleep did not come easily.

I remembered that the apostle Paul, while in this same city of Athens, had written to new Christians in Thessalonica in northern Greece. He had said, "While people are saying, 'Peace and safety,' destruction will come on them suddenly, as labor pains on a pregnant woman, and they will not escape" (1 Thess. 5:3, NIV).

Paul was not talking about bombings, of course. He was explaining the suddenness of Jesus' second coming: "The day of the Lord will come like a thief in the night." In using this figure of speech, Paul was repeating Jesus' own words in Matthew 24: "If the owner of the house had known at what time of night the thief was coming, he would have kept watch. . . . So you also must be ready, because the Son of Man will come at an hour when you do not expect him" (verses 43, 44, NIV).

Inadvertently, we'd had our cases packed for immediate departure when the bomb went off in Athens. In a way, we were prepared. But how about being prepared for Jesus' coming? Fortunately, our Lord has given us ample instruction about the need to live close to Him day by day, moment by moment. He may return suddenly. And we learned the meaning of *suddenly* at midnight in an Athens hotel.   SYLVIA TAYLOR

NOVEMBER 27

Give Until It Aches

Cast your bread upon the waters, for you will find it after many days. Eccl. 11:1, RSV.

In the late seventies, when my husband was working in a check clearing bureau, an Adventist friend related a wonderful experience. Recently, he said, he was having financial problems, and was down to his last $100, with which he intended to pay his rent. So he went to the administrative offices to pay. On his way he met this poor, shabby-looking lady with a little child. She greeted him, then she cried and said, "My child and I are very hungry. We've been without food for several days."

He was stunned. He didn't know how to respond. He said to himself, "If I give this lady this money, my family and I are going to be thrown out of the house, because that's what the administration normally does when one cannot pay the rent. And if I don't give, the poor lady will go hungry again, and what will God say?" He then decided to give the whole $100 to the lady, who thanked him profusely.

When he got home his knees were wobbling. He did not tell his wife, he was so afraid. He kept on praying that he would not receive a letter from the administration until the end of the month. Such a letter never came. Immediately when he got his salary, he thanked God and went to pay his debt for the two months.

But the administrative clerk insisted that he had already paid his rent for the past month, this month, and the following month. They argued, but the clerk showed him copies of the receipts. He kept on saying, "There's a mistake somewhere," but the clerk was adamant. So he went home and praised the Lord.

Who do you think paid that rent? It is said that if you open your hand to give, the Lord puts back something in return. But if you close it and don't give, He has nowhere to put your blessings, because your hands are closed. So give to the poor; the Lord will refund you!   LINDENI XABA

NOVEMBER 28

Unlimited Divinity

The Lord helps them and delivers them; he delivers them from the wicked, and saves them, because they take refuge in him. Ps. 37:40, RSV.

What? *Trevor** *is drinking?*
Waves of shock crashed on the beaches of my mind as I tried to comprehend that Trevor, someone I had gotten to know through a drug and alcohol use prevention program, was drinking.

Trevor, of all people, should know better. His dad is an alcoholic. He knows what alcohol does to a person and a family! What is he going to do to himself?

I prayed a lot about the situation. I talked to a mutual friend. I talked to our school guidance counselor. I did not want Trevor to feel like I was meddling; I wanted to talk to him because I cared about him.

After many conversations with God, I decided to talk to Trevor. Nervously and with a lot of apprehension I confronted him, telling him what I had heard. He told me he was absolutely and positively not drinking. "I wish there was something I could do to convince you that I am not," he added.

I still am not sure whether Trevor was telling the truth or whether Sharon, the girl who told me about Trevor's sporadic

---

*All names are changed.

drinking habits, had gotten her information mixed up. I do not know whether Trevor thinks that I believe every bit of gossip that goes around, or if he realizes that the reason I talked to him is that I care. One thing I do know: I am human; God is not.

What is that supposed to mean? First of all, I am human. I do not need to know everything; in fact, I cannot know everything. It is God's job to know everything. He knows whether or not Trevor is drinking.

Because I am human, I cannot solve all the world's problems. But God is not human. God is all-powerful. If Trevor is drinking, God can change him. I can pray for him, but God is the only one who can change Trevor.

It is nice to know that when I am limited by my humanity, God is not. His limitless divinity encompasses every situation.

There is tremendous freedom in allowing God to be God. We are only instruments He uses. We do not have to know what is going on in every case. God does. And He is capable of handling any situation. He certainly has had more practice at it than I.

O Lord, make me less dependent on my limited humanity and more dependent on Your unlimited divinity. Thank You that You are my God. MINDY RODENBERG

NOVEMBER 29

When Relationships Fester . . . Sweet Release

If we confess our sins, he is faithful and just, and will forgive our sins and cleanse us from all unrighteousness. 1 John 1:9, RSV.

The sliver was deeply embedded in my finger, causing an infection to form. The resulting swelling and tenderness was uncomfortable and a constant nuisance as I tried to work.

I remembered well when I had gotten the sliver. I was working on one of my wood projects, sanding an especially rough piece of lumber, and accidentally rubbed the wood vigorously with my unprotected finger. Ouch! It hurt at the moment, but I quickly forgot it and went on with my work.

Now a couple days later, I was feeling the results of my unguarded moment. As I squeezed the area, a tiny little piece of wood emerged, along with infectious matter, and I felt sweet release.

My spiritual life sometimes receives slivers when I let down my guard. When this happens, the festering and pain are constant until I find sweet release.

Sometime ago while interacting with an individual we hit a rough spot in the lumber of life, and both said words that should not have been said. I know this was not God's plan for our lives; I needed to apologize and ask to be forgiven, which I did. We prayed together, and I felt I had done all I could to make it right between us and God.

I knew God had forgiven me, but for some reason I never felt the other individual was able to forgive me. I prayed for God to give me an answer as to why I did not feel the needed forgiveness from the other person.

While reading an article dealing with a similar situation, I was again impressed that I had done everything I could to make the matter right between the other person, me, and God. It was as though the Lord was speaking to me through the words of the author, and I now knew that the inability to forgive was that person's problem. Knowing I could not change another's thoughts or feelings, and accepting this fact, I thought all would be right within my own heart at this time. Yet within my mind I did not feel completely at peace.

I was attending a women's retreat in Minnesota, and as our speaker was addressing us, she talked of our need to trust God for release from our guilt. Trust God for release—what a wonderful thought! I bowed my head at that very moment and thanked Him for that release. The burden lifted, and I felt that wonderful sweet release. I felt the sliver leave my heart, and along with it the infectious matter of guilt, planted by Satan in my mind, the guilt that made me feel I was not truly forgiven.

I had discovered the final step to complete forgiveness. This step was needed to be able to forget along with forgive.

"Thank You, Lord, for showing me the way to peace and to feeling sweet release." May each reader of these words find that sweet release from guilt also, and accept the forgiveness God so willingly has offered to us, guilt-free.   EVELYN GLASS

NOVEMBER 30

Accepted in the Beloved

For God so loved the world that he gave his one and only Son, that whoever believes in him shall not perish but have eternal life. John 3:16, NIV.

So often when we speak of Christ's atoning sacrifice, we pass quickly on to other topics, as if the abundant salvation secured at the cross is a given, fully grasped and understood by all. Sometimes I just need to bask awhile in the good news.

The other night I was preparing a script for an agape feast at my office. I fingered through my Bible, reading passages from Genesis to Revelation about Christ's atonement. Wanting to share the blessing I received, I placed 12 of my favorite passages underneath the plates at each table, giving time in the program for my colleagues to share these passages together around the symbols of His death. I could not have fully anticipated their impact, read one after the other around the circle.

So today I invite you to sit awhile and ponder. Turn your eyes upon Jesus in Genesis 22:7, 8; Isaiah 53:5, 6; John 3:16; John 12:31, 32; Romans 5:8-13, 18, 19; Romans 8:1; 2 Corinthians 5:21; Galatians 3:13, 14; Ephesians 1:7; 1 Peter 2:24; 1 John 4:10, 11; Revelation 5:9, 10.

It's good news worth shouting from the housetop! The cross forever secured the good news that when we are in Christ, we are "accepted in the beloved" (Eph. 1:6), once again God's children in whom He is "well pleased" (Matt. 3:17). It is an objective, unchangeable fact that must be allowed to minister to our feelings when Satan urges our sin upon us and causes us to despair. Even in the darkest moments of self-condemnation, we can rejoice, "for if our heart condemn us, God is greater than our heart" (1 John 3:20).   KAREN FLOWERS

DECEMBER 1

Sorting Through the Clutter

For everything there is a season, and a time for every matter under heaven: . . . a time to keep, and a time to cast away. Eccl. 3:1-6, RSV.

The single biggest cleaning problem is clutter. Clutter here . . . Clutter there . . . Clutter everywhere! Housecleaning or maintaining an orderly home is next to impossible around clutter.

This may be a new thought, but the piles, mess, jumble, and disorder that clutter your counters, drawers, closets, and cupboards is affecting your life today, even if it is stashed away or not seen. It takes mental energy to stash, hide, and pile things.

It has been estimated that the average household has about 3,500 items, but that one third of it is little more than clutter! Think about what you are storing in your home. How much of it is useless? But once you have it, you feel obligated to keep it. How much of your valuable time is spent polishing, dusting, washing, storing, rearranging, or thinking about it?

We really can't afford to waste our time on clutter or "junk."

A house full of clutter also affects our relationships with family members. Some families are so buried in hodgepodge litter and disarray that they can't find each other. Women tearfully complain to me that their husbands aren't attentive or romantic anymore. But a man can't be attentive or romantic until he can find you! Many families desire more closeness. But we simply can't draw close until we get rid of the clutter that separates us from one another.

Decide to make your home more functional and manageable. Begin today by weeding out nonessentials. Fact: If you haven't used it in two years, you likely never will.

To lead the life you really want to lead, you must eliminate clutter and excess baggage from your mind, home, and habits. Doing so makes it possible to be "born again" into a new standard of living.

Today you can be free of clutter and junk. Today you can be more free to love others, and more available for affection from your family. Life begins not at 40, but when you discover life without bondage to clutter.   NANCY VAN PELT

DECEMBER 2

Yesterday's Dreams

For the Lord gives wisdom: from his mouth come knowledge and understanding; he stores up sound wisdom for the upright; he is a shield to those who walk in integrity. Prov. 2:6, 7, RSV.

We've just moved to Wyoming! I love it here! Mountains on all sides, lots of wildlife, the big sky with its huge suspended cloud formations, beautiful horses, and the honest openness of the people make the West a favorite place to me.

With moving comes unpacking. It is always fun to try to make every house an attractive home. Hanging plants and choosing picture places, creating beauty out of chaos, has been a challenge to my creativity, and after all the hard work there is a satisfaction that is rewarding.

One evening, in the midst of all the setting up of housekeeping, I took time out to take a walk. I chose the lane to the right and over the bridge to a deserted log cabin that lured me into rustic bygone days.

I entered its hospitable open door. There was an old stove in the kitchen and the remains of a baby crib. The living room had at one time been painted a pretty pink, and bits of pink-flowered linoleum lay scattered across the floor. We have a lot of "open range" here in Wyoming, and as the doors were ajar, much evidence of cattle traipsing through was left on the floors. Birds had made three or four nests on the walls also, giving a very desolate and lonely feeling of emptiness.

Maybe because I was currently hanging pictures in our house, I noticed the nail holes in the cabin's walls. Ah! Long ago, some other mother had no doubt lovingly hung pictures for her family here. She had probably chosen the pink-flowered linoleum with care and maybe sewed some pretty curtains to match.

But now all that was gone. All her creativity in making the cabin attractive seemed in vain as I viewed the run-down remains. The only thing of any permanent value this mother left was another generation that might be alive today. Her pictures and curtains, wallpaper and rugs were gone. Only her children and her children's children remained. Were they a godly generation?

I thought of my greatest desire as a mother: to "raise up the foundations of many generations" that will "repair the breach and restore paths" for God (see Isa. 58:12).

Then I thought of Proverbs 24:3 and 4: "Through wisdom is an house builded; and by understanding it is established: and by knowledge shall the chambers be filled with all precious and pleasant riches." I more thoughtfully returned to my job of interior decorating.

"Lord, give me Your wisdom, understanding, and knowledge as I make this house a home, and may it only be a tool for raising up a godly generation."

GERITA LIEBELT

DECEMBER 3

The Freedom to Leap

Fear thou not; for I am with thee: be not dismayed; for I am thy God: I will strengthen thee; yea, I will help thee; yea, I will uphold thee with the right hand of my righteousness. Isa. 41:10.

I watched a squirrel running in the trees outside my dining room window. Although I made no scientific inspection, I decided that squirrel was a female because of the way she hesitated when faced with a risk. Have you ever noticed that women are often the cautious ones of the human species, holding back, afraid to take a leap into the dark?

She did fine going from branch to branch along the birches, until she came to the end of a limb on the last birch tree. She stopped short and looked around.

"Now what am I supposed to do?" I could imagine she was thinking. "I want to jump, but the risk is too great. What if I don't succeed?"

She ran back along the limb and tried one higher up. Again she stopped short at the end of the branch. She was still too frightened to make the leap.

Up and up she went, trying out several limbs, but still going higher. At last she let go and sailed through the air, landing on the wide spruce branch she had eyed from the lower branches. Quickly she went about her chore of finding seeds for breakfast.

What a lesson in life Mrs. Squirrel gave me that day! We come to the end of our limb. We want a new experience. We see the opportunity, but the risk seems too great. What if we fail? What happens if we fall flat? Who will be there to pick up the pieces?

Take a lesson from the squirrel and look up. Climb a little higher spiritually. God will give the courage to leap when we are closer to Him. What cannot be done from the horizontal position becomes possible from a vertical position.

What a picture that squirrel made as she glided through the air from birch to spruce. I can see her yet, her graceful body silhouetted against the golden brightness of the rising sun.

In that moment an inner voice spoke to me, saying, "You can be like that! You can know the freedom to leap! Come up a little higher. The closer you come to Me, the more courage you will have."

I've thought of that squirrel often when I've been faced with a terrifying risk—the opportunities of a new job, the challenge of a move, the possibilities in a new relationship, a change in careers, or any of a thousand small risks that face a woman trying to be all that God has gifted her to become—and I simply look up, and go a little higher. In my relationship with Christ I have found the freedom to leap.

DOROTHY EATON WATTS

The University of Citizenship

I have loved thee with an everlasting love: therefore with lovingkindness have I drawn thee. Jer. 31:3.

Every face-to-face encounter Christ had with women as recorded in the four Gospels is a cameo of acceptance, love, and affirmation.

While He would label the Pharisees and rulers of the synagogues as hypocrites, vipers, and whited sepulchers, there is not recorded any such ringing indictment against women. Amazingly, Christ uttered no comment regarding Herodias' daughter who danced before Herod for John's head. Could it be that Jesus knew it was not the dance, but Herod's power and authority, that cost the Baptist his life?

A society that valued women little more than chattel must have been amazed, then angered, as Jesus, by example, individualized and sanctioned women.

A woman caught "in the very act" of adultery, humiliated and shamed, is brought before Jesus. Fully expecting to be stoned according to the Mosaic law, she sees Jesus bend down and write in the sand. She witnesses the melting away of her accusers and hears instead, "Neither do I condemn thee: go, and sin no more."

In Matthew 15:22, seeking to instruct His disciples, Jesus challenges the Canaanite woman's right to gospel power, and then rewards her perseverance: "O woman, great is thy faith; be it unto thee even as thou wilt" (verse 28).

The woman at the well, while boldly and aggressively challenging Jesus to a theological debate, encounters His Messiahship, is converted, becomes a missionary, and turns a city upside down (John 4:6-42).

The shy and self-effacing woman, shrinking from a face-to-face encounter with Christ, touches the hem of His garment. Not only is she healed of her chronic illness, but Jesus halts the large procession and gives public acknowledgment of her faith and affirms her worthiness (Luke 8:43-48).

It was to the women following Him, with sorrow and weeping, up the hill to Golgotha that Jesus gave prophetic guidance regarding last-day events. Women were first at the tomb on Resurrection morning; and a woman, Mary Magdalene, was commissioned by an angel to go tell Peter and the others that He had risen (Mark 16:5-7).

One of Jesus' last acts as He hung dying on the cross was to provide for the future welfare of His mother. Indicating John, He said to His mother, "Woman, behold thy son!" and to John, "Behold thy mother!" (John 19:26, 27). And also, lest we forget, it was a woman who was called as a prophet to a church that is to give the last warning message to the world.

To those who believe, trust, and wait upon the Lord, there is no such thing as second-class citizenship. — CHRISTENE PERKINS

DECEMBER 5

The Beauty of Praise

Sing joyfully to the Lord, you righteous; it is fitting for the upright to praise him. Ps. 33:1, NIV.

So often in today's fashion-conscious world, we want to make sure that we are dressed to look our best. We also want our homes to look their best. We work to coordinate styles of furniture and textures of carpet, along with attractive window and wall treatments, to bring good housekeeping and good design into a well-focused balance.

In making personal choices, we realize that correct color and style combinations enhance natural beauty. A dress or suit that is well made and that fits "just right" will highlight our best features.

However, we are never more beautiful than when we offer sincere praise to God. He designed us as creatures for His glory. Whenever we praise Him and offer homage to Him, we magnify natural beauty welling up from within.

Now picture a beautifully sculptured fountain, water gushing in full cascade, sprayed by a rainbow of light. The fountain fulfills its purpose—to appeal to the eyes and heart. But should that fountain go dry, or if dirty water sprays out, the beauty is diminished, even tarnished.

So it is with us as God's sons and daughters. We are designed to pour forth praise, to fulfill the purpose for which we were created. The enhancement of beauty is simply a wonderful aftereffect. As water is to the fountain, so praise is to the faithful.

Praise is becoming to the child of God, like a mantle (Isa. 61:3, NIV).

May we wear the garment of highest praise to God today, and remember that we are truly His children. — CAROLYN T. HINSON

Prayer: First, Last, and Best

Whatever you ask for in prayer, believe that you have received it, and it will be yours. Mark 11:24, NIV.

As I was leaving the church after a recent Sabbath service, I couldn't help overhearing part of a conversation between two women. I realized from their faces that they were discussing something very sad and very serious. As she summed up the conversation, one woman said to the other, in the most hopeless and doleful tone imaginable, "Well, there's nothing left to do now but pray." Both shook their heads in despair.

The incident saddened me, for it revealed that these women considered prayer as only a kind of "last resort" when all else fails. I've since wished that I had stopped and, polite or not, intruded myself into the conversation. For isn't prayer the first, best, and ultimate solution to nearly, if not all, our problems? Without prayer, many rich blessings are lost.

As I understand it, prayer is communicating with our Saviour; and proper communication depends on a number of points. First, think of *attitude*. In this world, our communications with one another vary a great deal because of our differing attitudes. My friend and partner for 53 years is my favorite "communicant," and at times during the day I often call his office just to hear the sound of his voice. If we can cultivate that attitude toward God, that's the first step.

Communicating is not a one-way street, as we have all discovered, in more or less painful ways. And prayer cannot be just a hurried, dutiful, formal exercise. We should tell the Lord that we *do* love Him best of all—and then wait for His response, which never fails to come, if we are properly "tuned in." Conversations (communications) with old and dear friends are so rewarding, so satisfying. The years of shared experiences have forged a strong bond. And we must form the same bond with Jesus so that He is a familiar and well-loved friend to whom we are confiding joys and sorrows, wishes and dreams. You see, unless we are comfortable with God, we cannot visit together as friends.

I find it rewarding at night, after I am in bed, to have a "visit" with Jesus. I tell Him things that He already knows, of course, but I am sure of His interest. And sometimes I must apologize to Him when I have not represented Him as I should. Sometimes it has seemed to me, while lying there in the dark, with no distractions, that I can almost hear His reassuring answers, and sometimes His gentle reproof.

In the beautiful book *Christ's Object Lessons* Ellen White says: "Our prayers will take the form of a conversation with God as we would talk with a friend. . . . Often our hearts will burn within us as He draws nigh to commune with us as He did with Enoch. When this is in truth the experience of the Christian, there is seen in his life a simplicity, a humility, meekness, and lowliness of heart, that show to all with whom he associates that he has been with Jesus and learned of Him" (p. 129).

We cannot afford to overlook the importance of knowing the *nature* of God if we are going to have beautiful communication. God is high and holy and lifted up, so far above even the most consecrated of women and men that it is only Jesus' death on the cross that makes it possible for us even to be able to approach the Godhead. We should always be aware that it is possible to cut off communication with the Deity if our prayers are disrespectful and irreverent.

And think of obedience in relation to prayer. In current thinking and teaching we are bombarded with such reminders as "He will always say, 'I forgive.' " This is overly simplistic. The universe is not structured this way, and women can lead out in making it plain that there are conditions to forgiveness. Obedience gives us the right to feel secure and comfortable with our Saviour.

In this often sad, often unfair, and too-often tragic world, I wonder how people who do not really know Jesus survive. But some of those who know Him or have been introduced to Him need to know Him better through earnest prayer. Then we will never say or think, "Well, there's nothing left to do but pray."

MIRIAM WOOD

DECEMBER 7

Company for Dinner

Behold, I stand at the door and knock. If anyone hears My voice and opens the door, I will come in . . . and dine with him. Rev. 3:20, NKJV.

Whenever we have company coming for dinner we have some feelings of anticipation. There are times we are very excited and tell everyone who is coming and what we are fixing to make things extra-nice. Other times we feel unprepared, tired, incapable, or uninterested. Some of us think we don't have the right dishes or tableware; some feel self-conscious about cooking the best food (what if it doesn't turn out perfectly?). Others like to shine at what is a special talent and enjoy all the preparation and putting it all on the table for others' pleasure. In this day and age of gourmet dining it can be intimidating to try to live up to others' expectations or to our own. However, with this particular guest who is coming, our feelings of personal love and warmth will make the difference. Naturally we want to be prepared and have our best dishes ready; our mental and emotional thoughts will turn to when we last dined together and what we will want to talk about now. Does Jesus come often and feel welcome, or are we too tired for company? Some live such busy lives that there is little time to think beyond the heavy demands; others have interests in holidays, shopping, or finding time to relax, and find TV is lulling many into nowhere.

In the days of Jesus we find the wonderful story of two women looking at the situation of having company. Mary was intensely interested in spending time with the much-loved guest; Martha was putting her energy into making the nicest meal and having everything prepared. Jesus loved both of these women and recognized their interests and abilities, and He helped them put the priorities in order (Luke 10:38-41). It is not difficult to see that the essential matters are the guest and the time spent together. Rarely are we pleased to have spent two days preparing for company and having only a few minutes to share the concerns of our hearts. How many times have we taken hours to prepare a meal and considerable time cleaning up and had minimal time for heart-to-heart conversation?

Every day is our opportunity to get ready for a guest who will knock on the door and come and dine with us. Anytime we know and love a guest who is coming, we think of little else and keep looking out the window or waiting to hear the knock on the door. It depends on how well we know the guest and how much we love the one who is coming to see how often we look out the window and how tuned our ear is for the knock at the door. Only now do we have the possibility of knowing and preparing for our Guest, who already waits at the door. JULIA L. PEARCE

DECEMBER 8

How Important Is Prayer?

From new moon to new moon, and from sabbath to sabbath, all flesh shall come to worship before me, says the Lord. Isa. 66:23, RSV.

On our way to a church meeting, my husband and I spent a whole day at Singapore Airport, voted by air travelers as the most beautiful airport in the world. While waiting for our connecting flight to Perth, we wandered around the duty-free shops and the science center, admired the gorgeous flower arrangements, and took the free city tour. During one of our rounds I saw a woman dressed in ankle-length apparel, her head covered with a scarf, pull out a mat from her bag. Spreading the little mat on the floor, and facing toward Mecca, she prostrated herself on it, oblivious of curious spectators and unaware of what was going on around her.

The picture of this praying woman made a lasting impression on my mind. I asked myself if I would ever kneel in a public place to pray. What gave her the courage to do so? Was it fear, love, or just a duty? Was it only a ritual that had to be performed, or was it a sense of loyalty and respect to Allah? What would prompt me to do the same?

Our God is the Creator of the universe. He sits on His majestic throne, and His kingdom lives forever. We were created in His image. We are redeemed and granted eternal life through His death and resurrected life. He leads, guides, and sustains us throughout life's journey. His love demands a response of worship. After all He has done for us, do we not have every reason to kneel and worship Him in private as well as in public, and that more often than we do? Our worship will continue throughout eternity. The angels count it a privilege to worship Him.

True worship is not only talking to God but listening to Him through the reading of His Word. Worship must not be hurried or just a form to soothe the conscience, but a pouring out of our innermost thoughts, sorrows, and joys to the One who loves us.

BIROL C. CHRISTO

DECEMBER 9

The Roast Duck Theory

I am the Lord your God, who brought you up out of the land of Egypt. Open your mouth wide, and I will fill it. Ps. 81:10, RSV.

My father raised six children. Not an unusual thing during his time, but what stands out is the way in which he accomplished the task. In spite of a modest income, he fed, clothed, educated, and provided many extras for this family of eight.

Born and raised Jewish, Daddy emphasized two important rules for living: (1) always leave a little for the other guy (based on Leviticus 19:9, 10) and (2) open your mouth and a roast duck will fly in. This second rule of life provided a way for God to fill every need, not just with the necessities but with the finest gifts one could ever desire.

He often enjoyed expounding on his "duck theory," stating "When you need something, you simply open your mouth and a roast duck will fly in. But remember, you *must* open your mouth!" My father believed that first you expressed your need to God, then you waited for Him to send you something absolutely delicious. Although we never ate duck ourselves, we recognized it as a delicacy. When God fed the children of Israel, He gave them manna (Ex. 16:35). He could have sent them corn cakes, but He didn't just meet their need for food. He gave them the finest, tastiest morsels— "bread of the angels," the psalmist calls it (Ps. 78:24, 25, RSV).

The roast duck theory breaks down into three easy steps: (1) tell God what you need or desire; (2) expect, believe, and wait for something to happen; and (3) accept your "roast duck"—knowing that God will give you the best of things, not just the ordinary.

For many years I heard my father claim that his theory was written in the Bible. One day, while I was in my teens, my mother challenged him regarding its origin. Out came the Bibles and concordances as we furiously searched to exonerate the beloved theory. When my mother read the words from Psalm 81:10, we unanimously concurred. In my Bible the notation still stands: "Roast Duck Theory: Psalm 81:10!"

Not long after locating this text in the Bible, my father had ample opportunity to put his theory into practice. Both my older sister and I would be attending Pacific Union College at the same time. This meant substantial tuition bills. Because of our large family, setting money aside for college had not been a possibility. Once again my father opened his mouth and waited for roast duck. As usual, God did not disappoint him. Each time tuition came due, my father had enough. My sister and I graduated from college without any student loans. During my second year of college my father sent us on a wonderful trip to South Africa and Europe. God provided for our tuition, but He didn't forget the "sauce."

Matthew says the following about gifts: "If you then, who are evil, know how to give good gifts to your children, how much more will your Father in heaven give good gifts to those who ask him?" (Matt. 7:11, RSV).

Our loving heavenly Father longs to shower us with every good thing. Throughout His Word He promises to take care of us. Not just the necessities, but the pleasures as well. All we must do is ask.

Just think, God has "roast duck" waiting for you. "Open your mouth wide" and He "will fill it." CAREL SANDERS CLAY
AND SHEILA BIRKENSTOCK SANDERS

A Time to . . .

A time to weep, and a time to laugh; a time to mourn, and a time to dance. Eccl. 3:4, RSV.

I always thought real loss involved the death of a cherished one. I lost my best friend when I was 18, but we were attending colleges on continents separated by the Atlantic. I still get teary-eyed when I think of my dear grandfather who died several years ago. But recently I realized that other kinds of losses, ones for which you have to take some responsibility, need a grieving period too. My Siamese cat Chaucer disappeared one day: the one who was always going to be with me. Sure, when feeling rational, I realize that cats don't really have nine lives, but I knew that Siamese cats live longer than most, and mine was my constant companion. Unlike some furless friends, *he* was dependable.

In that same month, I closed the book on a long-term relationship. Even though we had broken up several months prior to this, I knew I needed to go through a grieving period before getting involved again. The loss felt tremendous. But now was the time to open the first chapter in a new relationship.

Then just as I began to anticipate a new commitment, the friend disappeared without a trace. I progressed through the various stages: anxiety (Was he hurt somewhere?), bewilderment (Where could he possibly be that he couldn't call?), anger (How could he do this when we were on the verge of a promising relationship?), and finally, grief at the loss of a rewarding friendship.

That same month my best friend moved across the continent to New Mexico, and my $450 car stereo was stolen *twice*.

That month my life did not come to a halt, despite six different losses. In fact, I remained quite happy and cheerful, much to the amazement of my friends. I acknowledged rather than submerged my feelings, examined the parts I possibly was responsible for, took an active role in my own life, and did a lot of praying. Playing "amateur detective" to look for the missing friend and to try to find who stole my stereo at 1:00 p.m. from my alarm-armed car in front of an unsuspecting audience at work exercised my problem-solving skills and also involved my creative thinking.

A grieving period is necessary so that you accept instead of repress the undesired loss. My first instinct was to replace Chaucer—and even the missing friend—as soon as possible. Then I realized that they too deserved a period of healthy mourning.

Loss is relative. That thought keeps me cheerful. Mourners can claim the promise in the Beatitudes: comfort (Matt. 5:4). The Lord can turn "mourning into dancing: . . . put off my sackcloth, and [gird] me with gladness" (Ps. 30:11). There is indeed "a time to weep, and a time to laugh; a time to mourn, and a time to dance."

MICHELE BEACH

DECEMBER 11

My Consolation

Surely goodness and mercy shall follow me all the days of my life; and I shall dwell in the house of the Lord for ever. Ps. 23:6, RSV.

God is closer
 Than we can see
And nearer than
 We can feel.

When we trust Him
 With our pleas,
  His loving presence
   Is very real.

I cried to Him
 From the depths
  Of my soul,
   O God,
    Where have You been?

His voice spoke softly,
 "Be not afraid.
  Though death bells toll,
   I am with you;
    I have control!"

Praise God
 Today I live,
  I love, I laugh.

Now my soul
 In Him I rest
  Because I know

God only gives
  That which is best!

And I will
  Always live
    In His land
      Of the blest!

MARIAN MILLER

DECEMBER 12

A Spot of Sunshine

In him and through faith in him we may approach God with freedom and confidence. Eph. 3:12, NIV.

The cozy sunlit corner of our dog's bed caught the cat's eye as he balanced on its edge. His dilemma was visibly revealed in the quick flips of his bushy tail.

Could he curl into that corner and absorb the warmth without disturbing the large dog whose bed he hoped to share? Would he be accepted, or suffer the consequences of trespassing? They were usually on friendly terms, but what *were* the limits of their rapport?

With his eyes fixed on the sleeping dog, one front paw, in deliberate slow motion, stepped down into the padded box. Hesitating, immobile, he watched, waiting. No reaction.

The other front foot cautiously inched down. Tense, alert to the slightest indication that this coveted sun-covered napping place was inaccessible, he waited. The dog did not move. He was encouraged.

One back foot descended guardedly, now more vulnerable should the dog awaken and not be willing to grant him admission. Vigilant, he paused again. Then with a sharp twitch of the long tail, all four feet were committed, yet ready to leap away should the bed suddenly become too perilous. Still, the dog appeared unaware of her companion.

Perhaps it was safe now. Ever so carefully, the large cat gracefully lowered his weight into the niche he sought. With eyes still wide, he curled his tail around his feet and touched his nose with its very tip. Still no sign of rejection.

For several seconds the watch continued. Then, with a deep, relaxing sigh, the cat closed his eyes, snuggled into the sunlight, and purred himself to sleep, content, comfortable, and secure.

I contemplated, albeit with a grin, the universal experience I had just witnessed. How many times have I needed, or at least desired, a safe, warm place to rest in my relationships? a place where I felt comfortable and accepted and unafraid?

Maybe you have felt like the cat did as you've tried to enter into relationships with people around you. Doubting acceptance, we dare go only so far, measuring our every move, waiting for signs that will encourage more commitment, dreading reactions that drive us away. Recalling past exposure to rejection and failure, we are on guard, setting up defenses to keep pain from disturbing what could be a mutually satisfying friendship.

And we play games. Pretending we are not lonely, acting as if we have no need, we don't ask for what we crave. "Will you share with me?"

The lesson I learned from our family pets that day as I watched trust be tested spoke loudly. Can my friends trust me? Am I a safe place for them to come when they need warmth and a spot of sunshine in their day? Do they come with apprehension or concern that my own needs will make them feel as if they have intruded, and cause them to step away feeling less than important, unwanted?

The text from Hebrews 4:16 came to mind. "Come boldly unto the throne of grace . . ." Isn't it wonderful and aren't you glad we can approach our Saviour Friend without having to pussyfoot our way into His presence? Isn't it encouraging to know He won't chase us away simply because we are in His territory? "Come unto Me and rest," the invitation reads. No conditions to meet. Room for all.

"Lord, I don't want to be too tired or too busy to share my life with those around me. Help me rest and be ready to give when someone has a need to be met. Thank You for giving us peace and warmth that we can share, like sunshine in the corner of a safe place."

MARY JOHNSON

DECEMBER 13

Through the Fire

But my God shall supply all your need according to his riches in glory by Christ Jesus. Phil. 4:19.

The sun shone warm and gentle on our garden that Sunday as we gathered a crop of string beans and tomatoes for the freezer. The bees hummed in the scented air as we took our bounty to the house.

My husband was church pastor, and our four children were healthy and intelligent. Our oldest daughter had just returned to academy for her second year. I should have been happy, but depression hung over me like a cloud. For months the struggle to make our small salary cover the needs of our growing family had distressed me. I had denied myself the option of employment outside the home, choosing rather to stay at home to nurture our preschool children. Did God understand? Could He supply our needs?

Suddenly there was a piercing scream from the basement! "Ron, quick—it's Kerry!" My mind raced as I thought of our 13-year-old son filling his tractor mower with gasoline in preparation for his day of mowing.

With heart pounding wildly I leapt down the basement steps to be confronted by a veritable wall of fire. Flames filled the entire garage area. I could see Kerry grab the fire extinguisher just as his father ran up behind him through the open garage door. At least he's moving! Was he hurt otherwise? Dashing back upstairs where smoke was already coming through the floor, I punched the operator button on the phone and yelled, "Fire! Fire!" and ran from the house with the only treasure saved—a telephone book!

Where were the younger children who had been playing in the back part of the house? Shelly, 7, hearing the commotion, followed me out of the house. Panic seized us as we saw, amid the swirling smoke, 4-year-old Robbie framed in the picture window. Hysterically I darted back for him just as he ran out the door. Smoke billowed from doors and windows as they popped in a series of quick explosions. Minutes seemed like hours till we heard the sirens of fire trucks. A crowd gathered quickly and someone asked, "Is there anyone in the house?"

"No," I answered. "We are all here."

"You have all that's important" was the reply.

We found that Kerry was unhurt, only his hair singed and his hands superficially reddened. We knew this to be a miracle after we learned that a five-gallon can of gas had exploded in his hands.

Months later, as I thought of the experience—the almost total loss of our household possessions—I could see God's hand. I remembered the miracle of the $50 bill that had been anonymously given my husband several weeks before and that was found still intact though scorched around the edges amid the ashes on my husband's desk. This was used as a deposit to obtain temporary housing. God also preserved the food inside the severely damaged freezer. Things were restored in time, but the greatest restoration was my faith in God to supply our needs, and the realization that temporal things can vanish in an instant. The only important thing is life itself. Our lives had been spared, and in walking "through the fire" we had "not been burned" (Isa. 43:2).   JOAN M. NEALL

A Pivotal Experience

*I tell you the truth, whatever you did for one of the least of
these brothers of mine, you did for me. Matt. 25:40, NIV.*

The old man in rags lay moaning on a cot, his sunken eyes
staring ahead. The closer I came to him, the less human he
seemed to be.

I had seen Antonio before, walking the long dusty road to the
Mexican village where I volunteered as a lay missionary. He lived
alone in a tiny mud shack near the river, and his only friends
seemed to be his burro and his garden. Sometimes I would see him
slowly walking the long rough road home from the village, his back
bent with the weight of his provisions.

Now Antonio lay in the filthy abandoned government clinic. A
stroke had taken everything from him but his bones and the thin
flesh stretching over their sharp angles. Gone was his speech, his
mobility, and his manhood. Flies swarmed on his decaying flesh in
the hot airless room, pressing for a chance to continue their own life
cycles.

Efrain, an Adventist brother who offered to come each day to
care for Antonio, had brought me to see him. A neighbor had found
him lying helpless in his shack.

I stood looking forlornly at Antonio, not knowing what to do.
I wanted to comfort his dying body with a kind touch, but I could
not. Repulsion coiled in my stomach. I could not seem to force my
hands to bring comfort to his purpling flesh.

Psychologists speak of "pivotal" or "nodal" experiences. These
are experiences that permanently alter the course of our lives. For
me this moment was one.

As I walked away from Antonio, I recognized the loathing I felt
for his body as a "normal" human feeling, yet I felt deep shame.
Why? Clearly and slowly came the truth that it was my Jesus who
lay on that cot while I cowered in selfish misery. Wasn't it I who
had asked to go to the mission field to meet Him? And now He had
come to me in the form of "the least of these," and I had turned
away.

I was new to the mission field, and it was becoming clear God
had many things to teach me. He seemed to be saying to me,
"Karen, your religion has been easy. Following rules and tradition
are not the lessons you need. Love, My daughter, is the lesson you
must now learn. Let Me teach you uncomplicated, nonrational,

unqualified love; love for the unlovely, the difficult, the repulsive, the arrogant. Then let Me show you your own ugliness, which I will heal. My lessons will take a lifetime, but come now, My child, and follow Me."

Prayer: "O my Lord, I stand naked and poor before You. My nakedness and poverty are not material but of the Spirit. Character and discipline cover my inner poverty, but these thin rags are not enough. You know the truth. I need Your love to fill me and Your righteousness to cover me. Open my ears to listen for You in all who call my name. Help me not to turn away."   KAREN KOTOSKE

DECEMBER 15

Plans for Good

For we are his workmanship, created in Christ Jesus for good works, which God prepared beforehand, that we should walk in them. Eph. 2:10, RSV.

Are there times that you wonder what you are here for? Does your work or job seem useless? Is everything trivial and meaningless? Whether at home or in the marketplace, we run into those moments when we feel that our work is insignificant, if not a complete waste. Even those who work in such places as intensive care units can have frustration and feelings of uselessness.

As a young nurse on a surgical unit I cared for a lady that I had known as a child in another place. She had cancer, heart trouble, and other quite serious physical problems, but she always cheered me up! She must have been 85-plus; she knew that her illnesses were life-threatening, yet she always looked at me with a smile and said, "If now is my time to die, that is OK, and if now is not that time, that is OK too." I was amazed at her calmness at a time when most are filled with anxiety. She taught me lessons more than once, as I would occasionally visit her in a retirement home near the hospital. She had oxygen by the bed, her room was small, but her sense of contentment and peace was real. As a person she was wonderful to be near. She probably did not feel that she was accomplishing a great deal by living in the small room, surviving with oxygen when she needed it. But her gift to me was great. Associating with her, whether in the hospital or in her little room, was a rare privilege.

How much we can look at our associations as well as our little chores can have meaning beyond our immediate awareness. Sometimes God puts someone in our path who needs our encouragement or help, perhaps in a way that seems minor to us. We don't have to be thanked over and over to feel that what we did had some benefit. It certainly is nice to have someone say thank you, and we need to show our appreciation when we receive help from others, but more than that, we need to know that God has good plans for us. He will put that work in front of us and direct us in the way (Ps. 32:8).

Our society places inordinate worth on executive jobs with big titles, but minimizes the work and pays far too little for jobs that actually are worth the most. Where would we be without the cooks, housekeepers, and nurse's aides in hospitals and nursing homes? Have you had a loved one whom you are unable to provide for who needed to be placed in a long-term care facility? Don't you want that person to have good food and be clean and well cared for? When I see workers who get minimum wage give not only good care but special personal attention, I say "BRAVO" and know in my heart that they have God's blessing in their work. I must also show my appreciation now while I can and while they are helping.

In my own life I need to appreciate God's leading and watch each day for the person who crosses my path and needs special encouragement or care. If my job seems useless and I don't think I am doing God's bidding, then I can pray daily for direction, ready to move on to the work that will be indeed His own and in which I can reflect the character of Christ (Ps. 119:168; see also Eph. 2:10, TEV).

JULIA L. PEARCE

DECEMBER 16

The More Excellent Way

But earnestly desire the higher gifts. 1 Cor. 12:31, RSV.

If God considered a chapter in the Bible so vital to our Christian experience that He instructs us to read it every day, isn't it important that we do so?

"The Lord desires me to call the attention of His people to the thirteenth chapter of First Corinthians. Read this chapter every day, and from it obtain comfort and strength. Learn from it the value that God places on sanctified, heaven-born love. . . . Learn that Christlike love is of heavenly birth, and that without it all other qualifications are worthless" (*The SDA Bible Commentary*, Ellen G. White Comments, vol. 6, p. 1091).

Catherine found herself feeling dislike, even contempt, for another woman who worked at her office; in fact, she didn't want to be with her or speak to her. When she analyzed her feelings, it disturbed her. How could she, a Christian, harbor such feelings in her heart? Turning to her Bible for help, she prayerfully read 1 Corinthians 13 each morning before she went to work. Imperceptibly, as the days passed, when she came in contact with this individual her feelings for her began to change from dislike to acceptance, then to a better understanding of her personality and character.

Finally there was born in her heart real agape love for the one she had hated. Catherine's experience could be related by many others who have won the victory over an un-Christlike attitude because of 1 Corinthians 13, and what Paul calls a more excellent way.

As the apostle explains: Love goes far beyond all natural gifts of knowledge, faith, healing, miracles, prophecy, tongues, and zeal to labor for God. Without love these gifts are powerless to change the heart of the most zealous worker for God.

Love inspires us to see the best in those with whom we come in contact. Love draws us close to God and makes us Christlike children of our heavenly Father. There is one great binding force that removes barriers, smooths misunderstandings, and draws us together: it is love—the love of Christ.   DOLLIS PIERSON

DECEMBER 17

Paradigm Shift

But he who looks into the perfect law, the law of liberty, and perseveres, being no hearer that forgets but a doer that acts, he shall be blessed in his doing. James 1:25, RSV.

Change. At the mere thought we experience anxiety or excitement, are threatened or challenged. Some individuals thrive on change; others resist it with passion. It's been expressed in words similar to these: "For some people to experience paradigm shift, they feel they have to admit failure. Others say, 'This isn't working . . . let's do something different.' "

What is paradigm shift? A major change in a pattern of thinking or working or behaving that gives people groups or individuals a new beginning is labeled "paradigm shift." Consider women's ministries as related to paradigm shift. By developing new patterns of thinking about ways we can minister to one another, women can have a significant influence on families, churches, and communities. If every woman went through personal paradigm shift and began accomplishing new goals for ministry, developing unused talents, daring to reach out to people who hurt or have special needs, what would be the result?

Are you willing to allow a paradigm shift in your life? Is there room for change, growth, new experiences?

Consider the opportunities for helping or encouraging those around you. Your personal ministry could also cause a positive paradigm shift to happen in the life of someone you know.

Jesus Christ is the ultimate giver of paradigm shift. "Therefore, if anyone is in Christ, he is a new creation; old things have passed away; behold, all things have become new" (2 Cor. 5:17, NKJV). As the Holy Spirit works in the hearts of women, He can make a difference in the lives of people we touch. I believe the Lord desires women to be catalysts for change . . . healthy, positive, creative growth.

We need expanded vision, fresh ideas, courage to dare, a personal paradigm shift. Won't you join me in asking the Lord for a new heart, a heart for service, a heart for women? Change. It's an exciting challenge. MARY JOHNSON

DECEMBER 18

Morning Musings

Commit your way to the Lord; trust in him and he will do this: He will make your righteousness shine like the dawn. Ps. 37:5, 6, NIV.

Good morning, Lord. Did You wake me, or did my natural internal clock just kick into action? It seemed like a short night, and my eyelids haven't seemed to have gotten their wake-up call yet. But it's still nice to talk with You just as the morning dawns. Thank You for the night's rest and Your angels who stood by my bed through the night. I wish I could see them and tell them "Thank you" myself, but for now I'll just send them a message through Your communication network. And thank You for Your love—Your marvelous, incomprehensible love.

Sometimes I wonder, *Lord, why do You love me?* I lost my temper yesterday when everything seemed to go out of control, and I had bad feelings toward that person who always takes advantage of me. And some things I said I know weren't the most Christian. It's not that I don't try to be like You. I really want to be. But it's so hard. If I didn't know that You would always be there for me, I'd have given up a long time ago. But Your love just won't give up on me. And I guess that's the secret element that keeps me going.

413

There are some other things that help to keep me going that I must thank You for—my husband and children. Thank You for the husband You've given me. He's one of the greatest things that could have happened to me. Please bless his life and his ministry to others. And the wonderful daughters that you've given me—bless each one of them. Help them to discover the beautiful plan that You have for each of their lives and then help them to follow that plan. And You know the young men that each of them will one day marry. Give them a special blessing too. And may they turn out to be as terrific as the husband You've given me.

I have so much to be thankful for. I live in a free country where I can worship freely. I have a job that helps pay the bills. And I'm healthy. Even though my body may not be as young and elastic as it used to be, everything still works.

Uh-oh! There goes the alarm. Excuse me, Lord. I must turn it off before it wakes the rest of the family. But I'll be back in a few minutes for our "morning date." Then *You* can talk to *me* and let me know what "our" plans are for today.　　　NANCY VASQUEZ

DECEMBER 19

Peaceful Sleep

Jesus was in the stern, sleeping on a cushion. Mark 4:38, NIV.

Sleep takes up the largest single block of time in our lives. It is necessary, mysterious, misunderstood at times, and has been a topic of poets and philosophers for centuries. Shakespeare called sleep "Nature's soft nurse," and Keats wrote:

> O magic sleep! O comfortable bird,
> That broodest o'er the troubled sea of the mind
> Till it is hushed and smooth!

Our culture even describes people based on their sleep patterns. The morning person naturally awakens early, prefers to go to bed early, does not need an alarm to wake up in the morning, is usually alert very soon after awakening, would rather take tests and exercise in the morning, and rarely sleeps during daylight. The evening person naturally awakens late, prefers to go to bed late, often needs an alarm clock to wake up, has difficulty getting out of bed in the morning, is not very alert first thing in the day, prefers to take tests and to exercise in the evening, and sleeps quite well during daylight.

Sleep needs do vary and have sparked endless discussions about how much is enough. There have even been articles written outlining the steps people can take to train themselves to get by on less sleep. Perhaps the key phrase here is "getting by," something very different from optimal functioning—that state of being in which people feel vigorous, refreshed, creative, and mentally competent. Sleep behavior experts believe that many Americans are not getting enough sleep. The effects of sleep loss are cumulative, too. If you lose a few minutes of sleep every night during the week, you can feel far worse on Friday than you did on Tuesday.

One of my favorite Bible stories is about Christ falling asleep on the Sea of Galilee. It had been a busy day, and when evening came, Christ suggested that they get into a boat and go over to the other side of the lake. One of the disciples noticed that Christ was very tired. Kindly, he put a large cushion up in the stern of the boat so Christ could lie down—and almost immediately Jesus fell fast asleep.

You know the rest of the story (Mark 4:35-41). A furious squall came up and the waves broke over the boat so that it was nearly swamped, but Christ slept on until the disciples became so frightened that they woke Him and said, "Teacher, don't you care if we drown?" (verse 38, NIV). Christ obligingly got up, rebuked the wind, and said to the waves, "Quiet! Be still!" (verse 39, NIV). Then the wind died down, the waves smoothed out, and the lake was completely calm.

You see, the disciples panicked in the storm. They saw themselves at the bottom of the sea. Christ, on the other hand, had entrusted Himself to God's care every moment, and so He could relax. His was not a fearful, anxious, sleepless journey in the boat—even in the midst of the storm.

On the sea of life there are often sudden and unexpected storms. How well do you sleep amid those storms? We do not need to panic and see ourselves at the bottom of the sea; we do not need to bale water frantically, lose sleep, and become exhausted. We can accept the storm as a gift during which we can exercise our trust—and sleep in peace. We can invite God into the boat with us; or, better yet, get into the boat with God.   ARLENE TAYLOR

Winter in Its Splendor

A time to gain, and a time to lose; . . . a time to tear, and a time to sew; a time to keep silence, and a time to speak; a time to love, and a time to hate; a time of war, and a time of peace. Eccl. 3:6-8, NKJV.

Falling snow outside my window signals the arrival of my favorite season of the year. Winter winds may blow and the storm may lash in all its fury, but I am secure and snug in my warm home. Winter is, for me, a time of renewal. This is the time when I am rejuvenated and have the time to prepare for the busier seasons of life.

When I was growing up on a farm, I looked forward to and longed for the arrival of winter. This was a time when I would no longer have to endure the heat and humidity of the summer and a time when life was lived at a slower pace with fewer stresses. My greatest delight was to curl up with a favorite book and listen to the storm blowing outside, knowing that my family was all home and safe with me. It spelled security and comfort to me. Through the years this feeling has stayed with me, even though today the pace of life is not very slow.

At times we have had to endure snow-drifted roads, cold temperatures, and zero visibility in order to be able to get home. Somehow this makes home seem all the more precious and the security and comfort more beautiful.

Winter is the season to bake and cook, to share our home with family and friends. The sweet smells and the comfort of familiar and traditional dishes bring to mind other happy times and family gatherings. The excitement of the holiday season for the children gives every member of the family a lift. Thinking of others and planning gifts for their enjoyment brings a glow of contentment to our lives.

Creating items for our homes and those of friends and family is great fun. A time to tear and a time to sew. As a child, I remember Mother giving us old clothing to tear into strips, and from these strips she taught us all, boys and girls, to crochet beautiful rugs for our home. Making something beautiful from that which is old and worn is a challenge to enjoy.

Though I enjoy winter, I know that its silence can be heavy and oppressive for many. Christ has promised to be with us through these times of oppression and will bring the sun to shine upon the white snow, making our lives brilliant with His love. Winter is a time to be silent and study His plan for our lives.

Solomon reminds us that there is a time of war and a time of peace. In the winter of our lives we go through times of war, when we are struggling with problems and difficulties in our lives. But there is sweet peace when we invite Him in to take control and handle all the situations that seem beyond us.

The seasons of our lives will go on, though not always in the sequence of spring, summer, autumn, and winter. In each day of our lives we may encounter some of each season. For there is the newborn to attend, the growing child to nurture, and the care of the aging. So it is in our spiritual walk. We may feel the cold storm of winter in the midst of the summer of our life, and the rains of spring when the autumn season is in progress.

Women who have put their trust and faith in God will grow and develop and bloom for Him through every life season! As we do this, we will feel compelled to help one another through the snow-drifted roads, cold temperatures, and zero visibility so that all may reach home safely.

As daughters of God, may we always treasure the memories life has given us. Remembering those special times when we accepted and shared His love with family, friends, neighbors, and strangers. Celebrate the seasons of your life!   EVELYN GLASS

DECEMBER 21

Cherishing God's Gifts

In my Father's house are many rooms; if it were not so, I would have told you. I am going there to prepare a place for you. . . . I will come back and take you to be with me that you also may be where I am. John 14:2, 3, NIV.

My husband works swing shift, so three to four evenings a week he doesn't get home until 1:00 a.m.! Conversely, I work mornings two to three times a week. Because of this, our schedule is sometimes rather backward. On mornings we have together, we get up and linger over a bountiful breakfast. Or we take a morning walk with our dogs before we even shower. When home together, we try to make the most of our time.

This schedule often leaves me cleaning house late in the afternoon and finishing my final chores even later after our toddler has gone to sleep for the night.

I like nothing better than to leave the house "polished" for his return from work. My ingredients for a pleasant homecoming include a warm house (which for us depends on a merry blaze in our woodburning stove), a cup of herbal tea with honey in the microwave, and a loving note of welcome with tidbits of information and instructions for the morning. Sometimes I leave the mail laid out along with the local newspaper on our dining room table and his pajamas folded on the bathroom counter. I know these small things make coming home a real joy for him, and I take pleasure in the preparation as well as the final outcome. Somehow, by doing these loving chores he doesn't seem so far away.

Our loving Jesus is also preparing a place for us; a heavenly home far beyond anything we can imagine.

Although He resides in heaven, He left us some reminders of His love. Our biggest reminder is found all around us, every day. Ever notice how calming a walk in the woods or a trip to the ocean can be? Even our pets help us to feel at peace. God created nature to be a constant reminder of Himself and His gifts to us.

He left us a special day of the week so that we may rest and reflect on all that He has done for us.

In the Bible He left us a "loving note" filled with instruction and information from which we can draw inspiration and knowledge.

However, the biggest gift He gave us was that of Himself. "This is how we know what love is: Jesus Christ laid down his life for us" (1 John 3:16).

He continually reaches out to us. We need only to accept His love.

Jesus, thank You for the heavenly home You are preparing and even more for the gift of Yourself, that we may feel closer to You until we are united in Paradise.   CAREL SANDERS CLAY

DECEMBER 22

The Gift

Salt is good: but if the salt have lost his saltness, wherewith will ye season it? Have salt in yourselves, and have peace one with another. Mark 9:50.

The annual Christmas program, one that everyone looked forward to, was only a couple weeks away. Once a year the 11:00 service was devoted to music and meditation honoring the God who gave to the world the greatest gift of all. This year the theme revolved around "gifts from the manger." Not only would the gift of the Christ Child be recognized, but some of the other priceless gifts that His coming brought would be highlighted as well—gifts such as joy and love, family and grace, light and peace.

A friend of mine, who had been asked to sing, wanted to find a selection that expressed the need we have in our lives for peace. But as the days went by, she could not find any songs that appealed to her. The topic of peace intrigued me also, and as we talked together I stated my interest in composing a song on that theme. I wanted to express a modern style word picture. Something that contrasted what normally happens around the holiday season (e.g., the hustle and bustle, the buying of gifts, the frantic pace) with what *should* happen. The focus of this time of year should bring us more peace—not less.

As I went about my daily routines, I thought about the meaning of peace. It is generally a scarce commodity throughout the world, and yet it is one of God's wishes for us (1 Tim. 1:2; 2 Thess. 1:2). *Webster's Dictionary*, that universal source of collective wisdom, defines peace in several different ways:

"Freedom from war, civil strife, disorder, disagreement or quarrels."

"Harmony, calm, quiet, tranquillity; an undisturbed state of mind; absence of mental conflict; serenity."

The mind is a wonderful incubator. As the days went by, gradually my thoughts distilled into poetry:

> Sitting quietly by the fire, I look around and see,
> Packages wrapped with love beneath the Christmas tree,
> Seems it took a lot of time to choose the gift that's right,
> I want to find some peace of mind before I sleep tonight,
>
> And I need Your gift of peace,
> Sent with love
> From above
> Into my heart,
> The most precious Son of God, You are my gift of peace.
>
> Christmas morn the paper's torn and boxes scattered 'round,
> I wonder if the best gift is still waiting to be found,
> For when I think I have it all—perhaps, could it be?
> What is missing in my life comes from You to me.
>
> For You are my gift of peace
> Sent with love
> From above
> Into my heart,
> The most precious Son of God, You are my gift of peace.

You came that we might see
How our lives could be,
Filled with joy and rest
Calm amid the stress,

And You are our gift of peace,
Sent with love
From above
Into our hearts,

The most precious Son of God, You are our gift of peace.

God wants us to experience serenity during the Christmas season and throughout the year. Christ freely bestows peace: "Peace I leave with you, my peace I give unto you" (John 14:27). We can go about our activities of daily living in a calm state of mind, with an absence of mental conflict.

Peace is one of the marvelous gifts "from the manger."

DEBBY GRAY WILMOT

DECEMBER 23

Enjoying the Wait

Wait for the Lord; be strong and take heart and wait for the Lord. Ps. 27:14, NIV.

The Christmas tree dwarfed her as she sat cross-legged and motionless on the floor in her Minnie Mouse pajamas. She was staring at the colorful packages that were piled on top of one another, jostling a bit to peek out at the world. Melissa was staying with me for a few days while her parents were away on an unexpected business trip. I watched her for a few moments and then went over and sat down beside her. (I couldn't manage the cross-legged routine.)

"I bet you wish you could open one of those presents right now," I said softly. "Nope," came the terse reply, followed by silence. "Are you thinking about anything special?" I finally asked. Turning, she fixed her expressive blue eyes on me, said calmly, "Not particularly; I'm enjoying the wait," and turned back to look at the presents. Another long pause. "Do you want to tell me what you mean by 'enjoying the wait'?" I asked. Once again she looked at me, took a deep breath, and in her precocious 7-year-old way (which I was enjoying immensely), began her story.

"Ever since I was a teeny girl I wanted to open presents as soon as I saw them. I hated to wait for Christmas Eve. I begged my mommy and daddy to let me open them early.

"One day my daddy told me I needed to learn about anticipation. [She lisped delightfully over that word.] He said if they let me open the presents early I would miss the anticipation. I didn't know that word, so he said it meant learning to enjoy the wait. So I practice doing that now, every year, while I look at the presents. I am enjoying the wait."

We sat by the tree in companionable silence, and I thought about her explanation. Enjoying the wait really was all about patience. I had always struggled with that quality and jokingly blamed it on the fact that I had to wait for a couple hours even to enter this world. It was 56 degrees below zero on the day I was born, and by the time my father started the coal oil heater in the garage and got the car warmed up, he and my mother arrived at the hospital none too soon. I was ready to arrive! The problem was that the doctor was having car trouble too. The nurses dutifully tied a sheet around my mother's legs, and we all waited, and waited, and waited . . . It wasn't a pleasant experience for either one of us, and once I did make it to the light of day it took a long time for the hematoma on my head to disappear.

"Are you enjoying the wait too?" Melissa asked me. She was thinking about Christmas and presents; I was thinking about life in general. This was a new way to look at patience. Instead of telling myself not to be impatient, I could simply begin enjoying the wait. It reminded me of Paul's statement that "if we hope for what we do not yet have, we wait for it patiently" (Rom. 8:25, NIV) and Christ's promise to come again soon (John 14:1-3). Melissa had already found the secret of patience—enjoying the wait. "Yes, Melissa," I replied. "I think I am. I am enjoying the wait too."

ARLENE TAYLOR

DECEMBER 24

An Empty Baby Book

He was in the world . . . and the world knew him not. John 1:10.

In honor of Jesus' birthday, let's look into His "baby book"—which is pretty bare. There is no footprint, for no nurse was present to impress it. Father: unknown. Attending physician: Joseph. Hospital: barn. The visitors page contains just one entry—

"shepherds." (It would be some time before the Wise Men would show.)

Those shepherds! Don't you love them? Without them there would have been no welcoming committee at all for our Jesus, and we don't even know their names. Years later only one person— John—would remain with Jesus at the judgment hall. His entrance to earth, like His exit, was marked by just one loving entry.

There is no photograph in the book. And so we try to invent our own, by publishing pretty little Christmas cards that romanticize the birth scene. The animals look so lovable—as if they came right from the Garden of Eden. The hens are up in the rafters, winking down at the Baby. The little lambs are kneeling before Him, wide-eyed. The straw looks clean and sweet and soft. *The Great Controversy*, however, calls the place a wretched hovel.

How the angels themselves would have loved to ring the bells of Bethlehem that night. Not then only were angels watching to see who was ready to receive the Christ: "Holy angels are watching with intense interest, to see if the individual members of the church will honor their Redeemer, to see if they will place themselves in connection with heaven" (*Testimonies*, vol. 5, p. 116).

And not angels only. "Christ walks in the midst of His churches throughout the length and breadth of the earth. He looks with intense interest to see whether His people are in such a condition spiritually that they can advance His kingdom. Christ is present in every assembly of the church. He knows those whose hearts He can fill with the holy oil, that they may impart it to others" (*The SDA Bible Commentary*, Ellen G. White Comments, vol. 7, p. 956).

Referring to the original search for prepared hearts at His first coming, we are thrust forward to the same search for prepared hearts at His second coming: "Oh, what a lesson is this wonderful story of Bethlehem! How it rebukes our unbelief, our pride and self-sufficiency. How it warns us to beware, lest by our criminal indifference we also fail to discern the signs of the times, and therefore know not the day of our visitation" (*The Great Controversy*, p. 315).

And so, in addition to remembering the first occasion by singing "Away in a Manger," we are jerked forward to His next coming with another song warning us not to be found in a sleepy Bethlehem:

> Watch, ye saints, with eyelids waking;
> Lo! the powers of heaven are shaking;
> Keep your lamps all trimmed and burning,
> Ready for your Lord's returning.
>
> Lo! He comes, lo! Jesus comes;
> Lo! He comes, He comes all-glorious!

Jesus comes to reign victorious,
Lo! He comes, yes, Jesus comes.

There is one more page to glimpse at in the baby book of Jesus: "Gifts." Have you written "my heart" there? If so, the other empty pages won't matter to Him. JANET KANGAS

DECEMBER 25

If Only I Could Be a Bird!

And the Word became flesh and dwelt among us, full of grace and truth; we have beheld his glory, glory as of the only Son from the Father. John 1:14, RSV.

Once upon a time there was a man who looked upon Christmas as a lot of humbug.

He wasn't a Scrooge. He was a very kind and decent person, generous to his family, upright in all his dealings with other men.

But he didn't believe all that stuff about an Incarnation that churches proclaim at Christmas. And he was too honest to pretend that he did.

"I am truly sorry to distress you," he told his wife, who was a faithful churchgoer, "but I simply cannot understand this claim that God became a man. It doesn't make any sense to me."

On Christmas Eve his wife and children went to church for the midnight service. He declined to accompany them.

"I'd feel like a hypocrite," he explained. "I'd much rather stay at home. But I'll wait up for you."

Shortly after his family drove away in the car, snow began to fall. He went to the window and watched the flurries getting heavier and heavier.

"If we must have Christmas," he reflected, "it's nice to have a white one."

He went back to his chair by the fireside and began to read his newspaper.

A few minutes later he was startled by a thudding sound. It was quickly followed by another, then another. He thought that someone must be throwing snowballs at his living room window.

When he went to the front door to investigate, he found a flock of birds huddled miserably in the snow. They had been caught in the storm, and in a desperate search for shelter had tried to fly through his window.

I can't let these poor creatures lie there and freeze, he thought. *But how can I help them?*

Then he remembered the barn where the children's pony was stabled. It would provide a warm shelter.

He quickly put on his coat and boots and tramped through the deepening snow to the barn. He opened the doors wide and turned on the light.

But the birds didn't come in.

Food will bring them in, he thought. So he hurried back to the house for bread crumbs, which he sprinkled on the snow to make a trail to the barn.

To his dismay, the birds ignored the bread crumbs and continued to flop around helplessly in the snow.

He tried shooing them into the barn by walking around and waving his arms. They scattered in every direction—except into the warm, lighted barn.

"They find me a strange and terrifying creature," he said to himself, "and I can't seem to think of any way to let them know they can trust me."

"If only I could be a bird myself for a few minutes, perhaps I could lead them to safety."

Just at that moment the church bells began to ring.

He stood silently for a while, listening to the bells pealing the glad tidings of Christmas.

Then he sank to his knees in the snow.

"Now I understand," he whispered. "Now I see why You had to do it."

L. CASSELS

DECEMBER 26

Hugs in the Mailbox

Let us not become weary in doing good, for at the proper time we will reap a harvest if we do not give up. Gal. 6:9, NIV.

Write her a letter."

"Her? I hardly know her!"

"Write her a letter."

"But Lord, what should I say?"

"Write her a letter."

"I'm not sure I even have her address . . ."

"Write her a letter."

"Why would she need a letter from me?"

"Write her a letter."

"But I've spoken with her only twice!"

"Write her a letter."

The letter was sent the next day, then forgotten.

Three weeks later the phone rang. "I've been wanting to thank you for your letter. I was so down and discouraged, and your letter really helped. It came just when I needed some encouragement."

A week after that, she came up to me. "Thanks again for your letter." Her hug emphasized that she meant it. An hour later as we parted: "Thanks again for your note." I felt embarrassed to know how I had tried to talk myself out of writing it.

Just a few words: "I'm thinking about you . . . God loves you . . . He can take care of you . . . I'll pray for you today." Ten minutes, a piece of paper, a 29-cent stamp, a prayer.

How many times have we missed opportunities to share a few words, a hug, a smile, a few minutes to make a phone call or write a note that might help turn someone's day from "gloom" to "bloom"!

Someone who is very special to me lives on the West Coast. After she moved there, a couple letters went between, but I sensed that distance was threatening to destroy what had become important to both of us . . . sharing deep thoughts and trivial nothings. She had a wonderful idea. A cassette tape arrived in my mail one day. I put it into my tape player, and there she was! It was so much fun to hear her voice, her laughter. The things she told about were sometimes the everyday events in a household of two preschoolers with a pastor daddy, but what fun! When time permitted, she shared her deep spiritual concerns, her frustrations, just as if we were curled up on my sofa with a cup of hot cider and an afghan.

But the most precious part of that very first cassette message was this: "I'm committed to staying in touch with you. Will you talk back to me on this tape?" Would I? I could hardly wait! What a blessing, how special it has been to share our long-distance lives—to hear her voice, the laughter, the sadness, the concerns and joys.

On one occasion, when I returned the tape to her I had shared something that was very painful and troubling to me. A few days later a note was in my mailbox. "I'm heading across the country and didn't have time to sit down and talk to you on the tape and share with you all that is in my heart and on my mind . . . but I just couldn't go without sending you this hug."

It "held me" until she "talked back to me."

It's happened that way more than once. On a day when nothing seemed right, a friend looked at me and said, "Are you OK?" My "Yeah" was answered with her raised eyebrow. And the next day's mail brought the message on a card: "If I could give you only one thing for Christmas, I would give you a hug that would last forever."

It probably will.

Have you ever felt that you can't "minister" to anyone? Look at the first four letters in the word "minister": mini—little thing. The little things you do and say, the little personal touches, a hug, a "thinking of you" card or a note of encouragement, a prayer for a healed body, a healed relationship, a healed hurt, may seem "mini," but to the receiver of your sent or personal hug it can make the day, turn it from discouragement, loneliness, pain, fear.

Maybe there is that friend that somehow resists your urge to hug or to share that special something that women call "friendship." Be patient. After five years of storing up hugs inside, someone I've hugged a thousand times in my mind is sharing hers with me. It was worth the wait.

Try it. Mail that letter. Send that card. Give that hug. Make that phone call. Take time for a visit. Help with the dishes. Play with her children. Tell her you love her and value her friendship. It might seem like a "mini" thing, but it will minister to her.

I know. It does to me.   MARY JOHNSON

DECEMBER 27

Time-out

There is a time for everything, and a season for every activity under heaven. Eccl. 3:1, NIV.

I looked at my watch and wondered how I could possibly fit in everything that had to be accomplished before bedtime. There were deadlines at the hospital where I worked full-time, deadlines at home to get the children registered in school, deadlines to make plans with my husband for the weekend, deadlines for arranging vacation, deadlines for . . . and the list went on and on. The college catalog stared up at me from the desk. How could I possibly find time to take classes? There was even an enrollment deadline!

It was definitely "time" for a time-out. Pondering the seemingly impossible, I thought about time and realized what a great tendency we all have to run our lives by clocks and calendars—measurements of time. Clocks help us measure time, but they don't define it. I looked up the word "time" in the dictionary; there was nearly a whole page of definitions, and yet those didn't give me a clue about what time is.

Our safety is often all wrapped up with "timing." Many

accidents occur because a person's timing is off or because someone is at the wrong place at the wrong time. On the other hand, many wonderful things happen because a person is at the right place at the right time.

Writers and poets have talked about time in every way imaginable:

"The time which we have at our disposal every day is elastic; the passions that we feel expand it, those that we inspire contract it; and habit fills up what remains" (Marcel Proust).

"Lost, yesterday, somewhere between sunrise and sunset, two golden hours, each set with sixty diamond minutes. No reward is offered, for they are gone forever" (Horace Mann).

Thoreau was convinced that if you kill time, you injure eternity. Manley's seventeenth-century philosophy was that there's no time like the present. And according to Rabelais, "nothing is so dear and precious as time."

Perhaps time is simply God's way of keeping everything from happening all at once—a perpetual gift to each one of us. It is offered to us every day without favoritism. There are 168 hours in every week. Most people sleep about eight hours each night, which leaves about 112 waking hours. Take out 40 hours for the average workweek, along with commuting and meal times, and that still leaves about 60 hours. In the final analysis, we are given free choice about what to do with time.

Not only does the book of Ecclesiastes remind us that to everything there is a season, and a time to every purpose under the heaven; it tells us that God has made everything beautiful in its time (Eccl. 3:11, NIV). Beautiful? Deadlines? Perspective is everything. Someone said that coincidence is God's method of remaining anonymous while creating a masterpiece of timing. God's timing is impeccable; it's just that we don't always recognize what is happening at the time.

I returned to my work with renewed energy and insight. With a different perspective, I could begin to prioritize all the "deadlines." I would *manage* God's gift of time rather than allow it to *control* me. There would be time for everything—everything of importance, that is—and each would be beautiful in its own time. Once again God had reached down and provided grace and insight for my "time of need" (Heb. 4:16, NIV). SHARLET BRIGGS WATERS

"Wilt Thou Be Made Whole?"

Do not be anxious about anything, but in everything, by prayer and petition, with thanksgiving, present your requests to God. And the peace of God, which transcends all understanding, will guard your hearts and your minds in Christ Jesus. Phil. 4:6, 7, NIV.

Lord, my body is deformed by the ravages of cancer and the surgeon's knife. When You were here on earth, You loved to restore the sick, the lame, and the blind. You thrilled to see and feel their excitement when they were made whole, and I know that it is Your eternal purpose to restore once again all these sin-ravaged bodies to "the image of their Maker" (*Education*, p. 15). In answer to the question asked of the man at the Pool of Bethesda, "Wilt thou be made whole?" (John 5:6), I would shout a resounding "Yes, Lord, and not just my physical body, but my entire being also!"

How I wish, Lord, that You were still walking earth's paths and that I could feel Your healing touch on my body. But I'm planning on major surgery. It's a new technique of using my own body tissue for the reconstruction. It won't be a quick change from deformity to wholeness, and I'll have several weeks of recuperation. Sometimes I question my decision. I've lived now for more than a decade with an external prosthesis, and very few people know. However, I'm tired of trying to conceal my "secret" of lopsidedness when I'm swimming, camping, trying on clothes in department stores, etc. And Lord, insurance money will cover the major expenses. It's human to desire "normality" in this life, isn't it, Lord? Sometimes, though, I feel "self-seeking" when I remember former friends like Lois, Doreen, and Ellen, who following mastectomies some years ago are now not living. Another memory fills my consciousness. Many years ago when I was about to deliver my first child in a Southeast Asian country, the 11-year-old daughter of missionaries who was afflicted with severe cerebral palsy showed a particular interest in the impending event. One day in her own painfully halting speech she queried, "What . . . do . . . you . . . want? A . . . boy . . . or . . . a . . . girl?" I answered that I really didn't mind since this was my first child. Again very haltingly, but with a deep feeling born of the mental anguish of a brilliant mind entrapped in a deformed physical frame, she responded, "Just . . . so . . . long . . . as . . . it's . . . normal!"

O Lord, forgive me for complaining and seeking more for myself! I truly am grateful for life itself, and wonder about my decision for surgery. However, the time clock is relentlessly ticking away, bringing me inevitably closer to my commitment. "If it is not Your will, even now, Lord, You can stop it." Sometimes I secretly hope there will be a bona fide reprieve, and yet I have claimed Your promises to be with me, and mostly feel a genuine "peace" that I am within Your will for my life and that You want me to experience a certain wholeness here. Your will be done . . .

Lord, it's all over now, and I praise Your name. I have experienced a sneak preview of the exciting, glorious scene depicted in 1 Corinthians 15 at the second coming of Christ: "We shall all be changed . . . in the twinkling of an eye" (verses 51, 52). Thank You, Lord, for this little foretaste of what it means to be "whole." Come, Lord Jesus, come!   LYNNE MARIE MARTIN

DECEMBER 29

Women Friends, in God's Own Time

At that time Mary got ready and hurried to a town in the hill country of Judea, where she entered Zechariah's home and greeted Elizabeth. . . . Mary stayed with Elizabeth for about three months and then returned home. Luke 1:39-56, NIV.

How natural it seems to find Mary going to another woman, a relative and friend, to share her experience and to talk things over. And here we have a younger woman, about 13, going to an older woman who is past childbearing years but is also pregnant. An interesting combination, but one that is both warm and full of shared concerns of intense spiritual meaning coming from such unreal experiences. Having angels come and tell them or their husbands what is going to happen to them! This is not your usual announcement of an expected birth. Mary wasn't married and hadn't slept with Joseph; Elizabeth was past her time and was for years unable to have children. Circumstances were certainly unusual. But how warm a bond there must have been in sharing this experience of being with God, being on the threshold of birthing boy babies destined to change the world. How would you feel about such a thought? Most of us can hardly imagine it.

But what a wonderful gift to have a woman friend who loves you, who will support you through unusual times, one who really and truly understands! Some women have such friends; others find it is hard to share feelings with another person, and have not had such a friend.

When I was working as nurse in home health, I helped to care for both a man and wife who had illnesses at different times. He was a typical businessman who saw things with a bottom line and in rather concrete terms. She, on the other hand, had a Christian Science background and viewed matters on a broader scale. We became good friends, and though she was 75-plus and I was 45, we shared wonderful thoughts. One day she said to me, "You are my little sister, and we live in eternity. It doesn't matter how old we are here and now; we will always be friends." As an artist she saw little details of wonder and beauty all around and loved to share the beautiful. Beautiful thoughts are gifts she gives to both family and friends, young and old. Though she had to move closer to family and is not near enough for us to share time together now, I will always treasure her friendship and the gifts of beautiful thoughts. Through the idea of having a special friend, whether of different age or in different geographical areas, we can feel that we are living in eternity now. We can feel that love and warmth and understanding that will go on until we do have the opportunity to share forever. How often have you thought of the special gift of friendship and bonding in the beautiful story of Ruth and Naomi in Ruth 1:16? Perhaps we can look around for opportunities that are less dramatic but real possibilities for special friendship here and now, and likely to be forever. Sharing time, being with God, beautiful thoughts—all gifts in God's own time. JULIA L. PEARCE

DECEMBER 30

Prayer Is the Answer

The Spirit helps us in our weakness. We do not know what we ought to pray for, but the Spirit himself intercedes for us with groans that words cannot express. Rom. 8:26, NIV.

I closed my office door and sat down to finish the devotional that I would share with a group of women in San Antonio the following Sabbath. In a folder that I had received at a women's retreat in Florida, I found just the precious, reassuring thought that I'd been looking for. It read:

Prayer Is the Answer
"Prayer is the answer to every problem in life. It puts us in tune

with the divine wisdom, which knows how to adjust everything perfectly. So often we do not pray in certain situations, because, from our standpoint, the outlook is hopeless. But nothing is impossible with God! Nothing is so entangled that it cannot be made right by the loving Spirit of God. No mistake is so serious that it cannot be remedied. No human relationship is too strained for God to bring about reconciliation and understanding. No habit is so deep-rooted that it cannot be overcome. No one is so weak that he or she cannot be strong. No one is so ill that he or she cannot be healed. No mind is so dull that it cannot be made brilliant. Whatever we need or desire, if we trust God, He will supply it. If anything is causing worry or anxiety, let us stop rehearsing the difficulty and trust God for healing, love, and power."

Again and again I read those encouraging words. They brought courage to my own heart as few others had. Surely they had come from the inspired pen of Ellen White. The language was so powerful! I called the Ellen G. White Estate and asked the source of "Prayer Is the Answer." I was told that while Ellen White has often gotten credit for these beautiful thoughts, they had actually been written by another unidentified writer. In an October 7, 1965, *Adventist Review* article on the subject of prayer, R. A. Rentfro quoted this passage and introduced it simply by saying, "Someone has said . . ."

In heaven I hope to meet the author and tell that person how much those words have meant to me!   ROSE OTIS

DECEMBER 31

My Prize

One thing I do, forgetting those things which are behind and reaching forward to those things which are ahead, I press toward the goal for the prize of the upward call of God in Christ Jesus. Phil. 3:13, 14, NKJV.

God is calling me for "today" and for "tomorrow." I don't know what's ahead of me, but I know His voice calls to an "upward call." He calls me to the present and the future, not to the past.

I am familiar with my past, and I can learn from it. But getting caught in it, trapped by it, bogged down in it, will stop my ears and prevent me from hearing His constant voice, ever calling me to the new. There are joys to be shared, risks to be dared, lessons to be learned, loves to be treasured, sorrows to grow through in the seasons of today and tomorrow.

And so for me, today and tomorrow are times to "clean up" my yesterdays and then to let them go. Jesus Christ has promised to be my "Wonderful Counselor," my "mighty God," my "Everlasting Father," my "Prince of Peace" (Isa. 9:6, NIV).

Today I pray for all He offers me as the Divine Healer of my past and the One who with persistent love patiently directs me toward the "upward call" that awaits me by His grace.

MARLA WEIDELL